Francesca Ervas, Elisabetta Gola, Maria Grazia Rossi (Eds.)
Metaphor in Communication, Science and Education

Applications of Cognitive Linguistics

Editors
Gitte Kristiansen
Francisco J. Ruiz de Mendoza Ibáñez

Honorary editor
René Dirven

Volume 36

Metaphor in Communication, Science and Education

Edited by
Francesca Ervas
Elisabetta Gola
Maria Grazia Rossi

ISBN 978-3-11-065188-1
e-ISBN (PDF) 978-3-11-054992-8
e-ISBN (EPUB) 978-3-11-054812-9
ISSN 1861-4078

Library of Congress Cataloging-in-Publication Data
A CIP catalog record for this book has been applied for at the Library of Congress.

Bibliographic information published by the Deutsche Nationalbibliothek
The Deutsche Nationalbibliothek lists this publication in the Deutsche Nationalbibliografie; detailed bibliographic data are available on the Internet at http://dnb.dnb.de.

© 2019 Walter de Gruyter GmbH, Berlin/Boston
This volume is text- and page-identical with the hardback published in 2017.
Typesetting: PTP-Berlin, Protago-T$_E$X-Production GmbH, Berlin
Printing and binding: CPI books GmbH, Leck
♾ Printed on acid-free paper
Printed in Germany

www.degruyter.com

Table of contents

Francesca Ervas, Elisabetta Gola and Maria Grazia Rossi
How embodied cognition still matters to metaphor studies —— 1

Part I: Theoretical perspectives

Zoltán Kövecses
Metaphor and metonymy in folk and expert theories of emotion —— 29

Tony Veale
Metaphor and Metamorphosis —— 43

Amitash Ojha, Bipin Indurkhya and Minho Lee
Is language necessary to interpret visual metaphors? —— 61

Valentina Cuccio and Sabina Fontana
Embodied Simulation and metaphorical gestures —— 77

Part II: Communication

Kathrin Fahlenbrach
Audiovisual metaphors and metonymies of emotions and depression in moving images —— 95

Elena Negrea-Busuioc
Leading the war at home and winning the race abroad: Metaphors used by President Obama to frame the fight against climate change —— 119

Larisa Iljinska, Marina Platonova and Tatjana Smirnova
Secret codes of metaphor: Anatomy of architecture —— 135

Micaela Rossi
Some observations about metaphors in specialised languages —— 151

Part III: Science

Silvano Tagliagambe and Luca Guzzardi
Classical physics as a metaphorical tool for evoking quantum world —— 171

Carmela Morabito
Integration and differentiation at the basis of metaphor: Dexterity in behaviour and degeneracy in the nervous system —— 189

Giulia Frezza and Elena Gagliasso
Building metaphors: Constitutive narratives in science —— 199

Clara Inés López-Rodríguez and Maribel Tercedor-Sánchez
Identification and understanding of medical metaphors by non-experts —— 217

Part IV: Education

Graham Low
Eliciting metaphor in education research: Is it really worth the effort? —— 249

Susanne Niemeier
Teaching (in) metaphors —— 267

Susan Nacey and Bård Uri Jensen
Metaphoricity in English L2 learners' prepositions —— 283

John C. Wade
Metaphor and the shaping of educational thinking —— 305

Index —— 321

Francesca Ervas, Elisabetta Gola and Maria Grazia Rossi
How embodied cognition still matters to metaphor studies

1 Embodiment and metaphor theory

In recent decades, the ideas developed within the framework of embodied cognition have strongly influenced the understanding of the nature of reasoning and communication (Lakoff and Johnson 1999; Gibbs 2006). The idea of language and reasoning as logic-formal systems that process abstract symbols has received strong criticism from cognitive linguistics and psychology of reasoning (Evans and Frankish 2009; Kahnemann 2003). There seems to be no real point of return to Cartesian dualistic models of reasoning. The importance of metaphor in the process of knowledge construction is widely recognised in the field of cognitive science, as metaphors contribute to model our way of thinking and in building bridges between abstraction and perception (Lakoff and Johnson 1980, 1999). There indeed exists a strong relationship between metaphor and communication processes, including comprehension and learning. In metaphor studies, the pivotal work of George Lakoff and Mark Johnson (1980) has drawn fully from the ideas of embodied cognition model demonstrating how language is rooted in the way we structure our bodily experience and hence conceptualise life.

Since Lakoff and Johnson, different meanings have been evinced to the concept of "embodied". An ever growing literature on embodiment has proposed different views, from the physiological to the cultural, the neural to the social (Lakoff and Johnson 1999; Kövecses 2005; Svensson and Ziemke 2004). As pointed out by Manuela Romano and Maria Dolores Porto (2016: 4), after a "first generation" of scholars focus "on the bodily, material basis of cognition and language", a "second generation" of scholars extended the notion of embodiment to include the social and cultural basis of our conceptual and linguistic structures (Rohrer 2006, 2007). Given the various dimensions (linguistic, neural, intercultural, sociological, etc.) of embodiment, the need for an interdisciplinary approach to the problem of embodied cognition has been emphasized. The object of this research field focused, therefore, on embodiment with a pluridimensional approach. This was open to comparison with theoretical proposals and results reached by every discipline that studies the meaning of "embodied".

Francesca Ervas, University of Cagliari
Elisabetta Gola, University of Cagliari
Maria Grazia Rossi, Catholic University of the Sacred Heart

DOI 10.1515/9783110549928-001

Nonetheless, this intrinsic polysemy of embodiment and the consequent interdisciplinarity of approaches has often constituted the main reason for difficulty. For instance, Margaret Wilson (2002), by reviewing six views of embodiment, points out that the diversity of claims in the field is quite problematic. With the same intention of disentangling different claims and concepts in the field, Tom Ziemke (2003) presents six different notions of embodiment: 1) structural coupling between agent and environment, 2) historical embodiment as a result of a history of agent-environment interaction, 3) physical embodiment, 4) organismoid embodiment, i.e. organism like bodies (e.g. humanoid robots), 5) organismic embodiment of autopoietic, living systems, and 6) social embodiment. Therefore, by trying to define embodiment, and by analysing the concepts involved in its definition, various approaches have produced a misleading multitude of terminologies (e.g. also "situatedness", cf. Zlatev 1997; Linblom and Ziemke 2002, or "sociocultural cognition", cf. Sharifian 2011, 2015; Frank et al. 2008). As a result the greatest difficulty seems to be the definition of the object itself: understanding what "embodiment" is and what "embodied" means (Zlatev 1997; Rohrer 2006, 2007; Ziemke and Frank 2007; Ziemke et al. 2007; Frank et al. 2008).

As pointed out by Zouheir Maalej and Ning Yu (2011) a good starting point is the definition of embodiment by Tom Ziemke and Roslyn Frank (2007: 1) as "the bodily and sensorimotor basis of phenomena such as *meaning*, *mind*, *cognition* and *language*". Lakoff and Johnson (1980, 1999) present a notion of embodiment that puts together the four phenomena (meaning, mind, cognition and language), by focusing on metaphor and its role in people's understanding of language. Lakoff and Johnson's conception of embodiment deeply influenced the landscape of metaphor studies and prevailed over other trends, which especially aimed at analysing and explaining the role of metaphor in communication, more than in language and cognition. However, despite according great importance to the communicative dimension of metaphor, Lakoff and Johnson's theory conflated communication with both language and cognition, maintaining that it could be fully explained by the linguistic and (even more) by the embodied roots of metaphor.

However, in the meantime, an alternative view to Lakoff and Johnson (1980) has been proposed by a number of studies on metaphor from the field of applied linguistics (Cameron and Low 1999; Low and Cameron 2002; Cameron 2003; Deignan 2005, 2010; Charteris-Black 2004; Caballero Rodriguez 2006; Koller 2004), cognitive linguistics (Cienki, Luka, and Smith 2001; Cienki and Müller 2008; Müller 2008; Grady 2000; Kövecses 2005), conversation and discourse analysis (Musolff 2004; Semino 2008; Steen et al. 2010), interactional sociolinguistics (Drew and Holt 1998), artificial intelligence (Barnden 2008), psycholinguistics (Katz et al. 1998; Giora 2003; Glucksberg 2001, 2008; Gibbs 1994, 1999, 2006), and psychology of discourse (Kintsch 1998; Steen 2004, 2006; Van Dijk 2008; Macnamara and Magliano 2009; Graesser and Millis 2011). These perspectives have showed that the peculiar communicative dimension of metaphor cannot be conflated or reduced to the linguistic and conceptual aspects of metaphor (Steen 2008, 2011; Gola and Ervas 2016).

The aim of this book is to present an overview of some recent trends in metaphor studies which – departing from the standard embodied cognition framework – propose new directions of research or further developments/improvements of the embodied cognition perspective, which could give an explanation of the specific traits of the communicative aspects of metaphor. The theme of the volume is thus at the crossroads of the wide range of ways metaphor is theorised and used in the communicative contexts of the real world. The volume devotes particular attention to the fields of science and education. The book consists of a selection of papers presented at the Conference *Metaphor in Communication, Science and Education*, the 10th International Conference of the Association for Researching and Applying Metaphor (RaAM), held at the University of Cagliari (Italy) in June 2014.

The collection is divided into four sections. The first section, "Theoretical Perspectives", introduces new trends in the embodied cognition perspective applied to metaphor studies. The chapters present different theoretical perspectives, ranging from computational to neuroscientific approaches, on how the embodied cognition model should be defended or improved in order to better fit an adequate and comprehensive explanation of both visual and verbal metaphors. The second section, "Communication", specifically focuses on the communicative aspects of metaphor in different fields, such as cinema, politics, and architecture. Even though embracing the standard embodied cognition paradigm presupposed by the conceptual theory of metaphor, the chapters included in this section suggest that the communicative dimension of metaphor has specific features and functions that disallow complete reduction to its linguistic and cognitive dimensions.

The third section, "Science", investigates the role of metaphors in proposing a structure and categorisation of scientific knowledge as well as in exploring new meanings and models. Indeed, as metaphors are possibly useful, and sometimes indispensable, to describe things in everyday communicative situations, they prove to be also powerful devices in generating insights and promoting understanding in scientific enquiry. The chapters included in the section show why metaphors play such an essential role in theory-making, both suggesting interesting questions and fruitful ideas and using specific communicative devices to allow non-experts' comprehension. The fourth section, "Education", considers the large use of metaphor in teaching almost every type of knowledge in both human and natural sciences. The chapters included in the section aim to explore the role metaphors play in education, for instance, reaching a better understanding of a concept or generating new ideas, by anchoring abstract concepts to students' bodily experience. In order to do this – the authors argue – metaphors need to have specific communicative traits which emerge in teacher/learner or in peer to peer communication in educational contexts.

2 Theoretical perspectives

Recent theoretical research in metaphor studies has proposed new ways to criticise and/or rehabilitate the embodied roots of metaphor. Starting from different methodological approaches and traditions, the chapters included in this section focus attention on specific theoretical areas of metaphor studies to draw, at least in part, some conclusions on the embodied aspects of metaphor.

In the chapter *Metaphor and metonymy in folk and expert theory of emotions*, Zoltan Kövecses defends Lakoff and Johnson's theory of conceptual metaphors against criticism of groundlessness by discourse-oriented metaphor scholars (see, e.g., Cameron and Maslen 2010). In particular, the author aims to show that not only folk theories but also expert theories are grounded on conceptual metaphor based on our bodily experience of emotions. Both folk and expert theories extensively make use of metaphors to better understand emotions' nature and functioning. More specifically, folk theories can be described with reference to conceptual metaphors (e.g. PRIDE IS A FLUID IN A CONTAINER, TO BE PROUD IS TO BE BIG/UP/HIGH) based on underlying metonymies (e.g. ERECT POSTURE/HEAD HELD HIGH FOR PRIDE, CHEST (THRUST) OUT FOR PRIDE). The author shows various examples supporting the view that many metaphorical source domains are common to both folk and expert theories of emotions. In this respect, the case of emotions as fluids inside a container is a prime example: for instance, Kövecses supports the thesis that Davitz's (1969) technical notion of "enhancement" (i.e. the phenomenon of reporting experiences related to pride such as "I feel taller/stronger/bigger/strong inside") is based upon the FLUID IN A CONTAINER metaphor.

Kövecses examines some implications of this thesis for the applied linguistic view of metaphors by discussing the role of conceptual metaphor in human thought. In support of this claim, the author argues that conceptual metaphors are creative instruments of thought: the way in which experts modify and develop folk theories of emotions is brought as an evidence of the cognitive role played by conceptual metaphors within the emotional domain. However, in claiming that both folk and expert theories of emotion share certain conceptual metaphors, Kövecses adopts an account of metaphors somewhat different from the "standard" Lakoff and Johnson's account (Lakoff and Johnson 1999), where primary metaphors are embodied. In this chapter, the author argues that first there must be a metonymic stage in the development of metaphors (Kövecses 2013), because only conceptual metonymies reflect real or assumed responses associated with emotions, which can be generalised into concepts as appropriate source domains for both layman and expert theories.

In the chapter *Metaphor and Metamorphosis*, Tony Veale adopts a computational approach to metaphor. Veale shows that even an automatic non-human and non-embodied system (*Flux Capacitor*) can generate stories in which metaphors are used in creative ways, but the inputs of the system are human knowledge. Indeed, in order to generate stories, *Flux Capacitor* needs a corpus of texts that represents a rich knowledge base of our stereotypical perspectives on humans: for instance, the most prominent qualities exhibited by teachers, criminals, nuns, etc. and their most natural direction of change. For example, the system finds it more likely for a prostitute to become a nun rather than the case of a nun who *breaks bad* in the reverse direction. In order to transform this information into a story and to understand the emergent qualities that may arise along the way, the system adopts the model of conceptual blending (Fauconnier and Turner 1998, 2002), translated into a robust and scalable computational model (*conceptual mash-up*) by Veale (2012).

The stories generated by the *Flux Capacitor* are based on a set of purposeful actions shaped in the schema *Source-Path-Goal* (*SPG*), which is one of the central conceptual patterns acting as source domain in primary metaphors (Johnson 1987; Lakoff and Johnson 1980). For instance, when we say that "We are moving forward in our research", we are imagining research as a path in which moving forward is making some progress. Storytelling is an activity that responds to the same SPG schema, i.e. a purposeful activity with a beginning (*Source*), middle (*Path*), and an end (*Goal*). An example proposed by Veale is the sequence: "The *general* who became a *slave*. The *slave* who became a *gladiator*. The *gladiator* who defied an *emperor*".

The effectiveness of the generated story has been tested through a *twitterbot* (*@MetaphorMagnet*), which employs the *Flux Capacitor* to generate mini-narrative (story, metaphors, or story based on metaphors) of 140 characters in 5 steps. The start and the end of the story are represented with hashtags, as in the following example:

#Knight=#Madman
1. *Go on a crusade*
2. *Become a knight*
3. *Launch irrational crusades*
4. *Become an irrational knight*
5. *Get called a "madman"*

There is a notable benefit of implementing the system as a Twitterbot, because you can evaluate the degree to which typical users find system's outputs to be meaningful depending on the number of likes, shares, comments, etc. Veale also submitted the short stories to "official" evaluators and paid volunteers. They were asked to rate the stories on the basis of *comprehensibility, novelty*, and *retweetability*. The results from such evaluation can be considered very satisfactory: even though *Flux Capacitor* is not able to write a new masterwork like *Metamorphosis*, the metaphors and blending mechanisms produce stories that turn out to be plausible without being either obvious or deterministic. As the author notes, "This, after all, is the real power of metaphor: to entice the imagination, to create sparks from the collision of superficially ill-matched ideas, and to lure us toward a satisfying resolution" (Veale in this volume, p. 58).

Amitash Ojha, Bipin Indurkhya and Minho Lee indicate precisely the imaginative route as an alternative way to revise the standard embodied cognition presupposed by Lakoff and Johnson's theory of conceptual metaphor. In the chapter, *Is language necessary to interpret visual metaphors?*, they argue that Lakoff and Johnson (1980) consider metaphor as a conceptual phenomenon, whilst other theories of metaphor comprehension (Gibbs and Bogdanovich 1999; Walsh 1990; Neisser 1976) suggest that various cognitive processes, which are not conceptual in nature, are in place in metaphor comprehension. An interaction between different verbal and non-verbal, conceptual and non-conceptual modalities are indeed required to understand metaphors. The chapter considers visual metaphors, which are normally held to require perception processes rather than verbal processes. Even the interpretation of some verbal metaphors requires mental images that can produce perception-like experiences. Brain-imaging studies have shown that the right-hemisphere brain areas, associated with perception, imagery, and motor planning, are activated by verbal metaphor comprehension, and that the right hemisphere plays an important role in the integration of various modalities during verbal metaphor comprehension (Anaki, Faust, and Kravetz 1998; Faust and Mashal 2007; Arzouan, Goldstein, and Faust 2007; Rapp et al. 2004; Ahrens et al. 2007; Shibata et al. 2007).

Ojha, Indurkhya, and Lee explore the case of visual metaphors, which Lakoff and Johnson (1980) considered visual manifestations of conceptual metaphors, to understand whether they evoke verbal and language areas to be interpreted. In order to do this, the authors adopt an experimental approach and present an fMRI study, which allows to display the active brain areas during visual metaphor comprehension without any interference with verbal responses. They aim to clarify to what extent the right hemisphere, which specialises in holistic, imagistic, and spatial processing (Bryden 1982; Ellis, Young, and Anderson 1988; Jonides et al. 1993; McCarthy et al. 1994), plays a role in visual metaphor comprehension. In the experimental study four different kinds of stimuli were presented to participants: (1) literal sentences, (2) metaphorical sentences, (3) literal images and (4) metaphorical images. The objective was to understand whether language areas are activated during visual metaphor comprehension, and to identify the neural differences and similarities in both verbal and visual metaphor processing.

The results show that, in the interpretation of metaphorical images, a significant activation of language comprehension areas, such as Broca's and Wernicke's areas, has been observed. On the contrary, no significant activity in these areas has been observed in the literal-image comprehension task. These findings confirm that the comprehension process of visual metaphors requires the activation of areas traditionally regarded as responsible for auditory perception, speech, and language comprehension. Moreover, comparing the brain activation patterns for visual and verbal metaphors, no exclusive right-hemisphere (RH) deployment in the processing of visual metaphors has been observed. On the contrary, some common activation areas for both verbal and visual metaphors conditions show that visuo-spatial imagery is required for both visual and verbal metaphors. The authors conclude that the role of other modalities than verbal and conceptual, such as visual, aural, and gestural, need to be further investigated, in order to develop a more comprehensive cognitive model of both verbal and visual metaphor comprehension.

The chapter by Valentina Cuccio and Sabina Fontana, *Embodied Simulation and metaphorical gestures*, specifically focuses on gestural modalities and adopts the *Embodied Simulation* approach to defend the idea that the processing of bodily metaphors, such as "to see an idea" or "to grasp a concept", based on bodily experiences, determines the activation of the sensory and motor systems. *Embodied Simulation* has been defined as the activation of neural circuits in the absence of a corresponding action, perception, or emotion (Gallese and Sinigaglia 2011). For instance, in the case of emotional literal descriptions, the processing of verbs describing facial expressions, e.g. "to smile", determines the activation of the muscles involved in the real occurrence of those facial expressions (Foroni and Semin 2009). In the case of metaphorical descriptions, the processing of a metaphorical expression, e.g. "John grasps the idea", determines the activation of hand-related areas of the motor cortex. In this regard, recent neuroscientific findings support the claim that our bodily experience directly contributes to metaphor comprehension by means of the Embodied Simulation mechanism (Gibbs 2003, 2006; Matlock, Ramscar and Boroditsky 2005; Gibbs and Matlock 2008; Gibbs and Perlman 2010; Ritchie 2010; Semino 2010).

It is worth questioning whether Embodied Simulation is also triggered by the observation of representational actions, which though do not have a direct effect on the physical environment but shape our abstract experiences and concepts and affect our communicative exchanges. Recent studies have shown that the observation of people's gestures results in the activation of the observer's motor system (Ping, Goldin-Meadow and Beilock 2014; Cartmill, Beilock and Goldin-Meadow 2012). In this perspective, Cuccio and Fontana develop a new definition of simulation mechanism to analyse the role of Embodied Simulation in the understanding of metaphorical gestures. In their view, the bodily-centred mechanism of Embodied Simulation and the gesture system are not two different dimensions of embodiment, suggesting that Embodied Simulation and co-speech gestures are a unitary system (Cuccio 2015a, 2015b). Following McNeill (1992, 2005), Cuccio and Fontana intend gestures as a support for both thought and speech, as their internal structure is composed of different units: conceptual and neuromuscular. In the case of metaphorical gestures, gestures support the mapping of abstract concepts into concrete domains. In this regard, gestures are the visible expression of the inner mechanism of embodied simulation that shapes our representations.

Finally, the first section – specifically dedicated to theoretical perspectives on embodied cognition in metaphor studies – displays a range of different but interconnected theoretical positions. The chapters, in this volume, show the need for defending the classical view of conceptual metaphor theory (see Kövecses), extending it (see Veale), integrating it by exploring the imaginative route to metaphor understanding (see Ojha, Indurkhya and Lee) or revising it, following recent studies in the Embodied Simulation mechanism involved in metaphor processing (see Cuccio and Fontana). The following sections specifically focus on communication and the communicative functions of metaphor in different fields where the embodied cognition framework has been applied: science and education.

3 Communication

The section on "Communication" considers the effects of the embodied cognition framework on the study of the communicative aspects of metaphors. Exploring the use of metaphors in different communicative fields, such as cinema, politics, and architecture, and going back to the origins and development of specialised terminologies, the section aims to question whether the standard embodied cognition framework adopted by the conceptual theory of metaphor can effectively explain the specific traits of the communicative aspects of metaphors.

The chapter by Kathrin Fahlenbrach, *Audiovisual metaphors and metonymies of depression*, analyses how conceptual transfer works in different kinds of audiovisual products. The author describes and explains the audiovisual language and the nature of specific audiovisual metaphors generated by these media. In particular, she compares two very different kinds of audiovisual genres: the informative and the fictional. In both cases creators of audiovisual media products draw on conceptual metaphors to communicate complex networks of conceptual metaphors, gestalt patterns, sounds, images, and movements, which contribute to create perceptive, cognitive, and affective meanings. The chapter outlines the way in which this happens, by examining ten videos in three steps: analysis of the communicative framing, identification of metaphorical and metonymic mappings, implementation in audiovisual motifs and compositions. Adopting Kövecses' (2002, 2005) approach to emotions and conceptual metaphors, the author analyses videos that specifically focus on depression. The results show that similar audiovisual metaphors of depression are generated in both informative and fictional videos, but informative videos use a clear-cut metaphoric scenario in order to be quickly understood by the general public, while fictional videos perform a much more complex metaphoric display of depression, which is also different depending on specific cultural and cinematic knowledge of the viewers.

In the chapter *Leading the war at home and winning the race abroad: Metaphors used by President Obama to frame the fight against climate change*, Elena Negrea-Busuioc examines some aspects of the debate on climate change, that has become pressing in the last decades. In particular, the author analyses metaphors in a political speech by President Obama, focusing on two metaphorical scenarios used to address the emergency of fighting climate change: the WAR (at home) and the RACE (abroad). The analysis, which follows the Pragglejaz group procedure (Pragglejaz Group 2007) for metaphor identification, aims, on one hand, to examine the way in which responsibility in fighting climate change is metaphorically assigned to America and, on the other, to exploit the underlying persuasive potential of metaphors politicians rely on.

Two metaphorical scenarios (WAR and RACE) are used to conceptualise the fight against climate change, but, also, at the same time, to exploit the communicative functions of these scenarios. In discourses on the climate change, for example, Barack Obama uses the WAR metaphor, while addressing Americans, but switches to a "race abroad" that America must win while considering the global audience. In this way he on one hand legitimises actions on climate change and on the other hand consolidates the position of the U.S. as a world leader. The use of RACE metaphors, in addition to WAR, seems to be "required" to account for multiple audience (Ritchie and Cameron 2014). The author concludes that such metaphors, thanks to their communicative features, play a crucial role in mapping climate change onto more familiar and tangible aspects of human everyday life.

Larisa Iljinska, Marina Platonova, Tatjana Smirnova, in the chapter *Secret codes of metaphor: Anatomy of architecture*, focus their attention on the mechanism of metaphorical meaning extension in working language. They present a study, part of an ongoing research on contemporary theories on professional language and knowledge representation in scientific and technical communication. In order to examine how meaning can be extended and how much it depends on the linguistic level, the authors analyse terms based on a definite conceptual metaphor – BUILDING IS A BODY – in three working languages: English, Latvian, and Russian. Following Lakoff (1993), conceptual metaphors here are considered the basis for both novel, creative metaphorical expression, and conventional patterns of expression. More "alive" (novel and creative) metaphors are also more dependent on imagination. Starting from these premises, the authors show that the role of metaphorisation is significant in professional communication, in which metaphoric terms expand the scope of information, widening the meaning of the existing lexical units. This is a process, particularly evident in English, in which there is a proliferation of polysemic words in scientific and technical texts, but is also more or less evident in other contemporary languages (Iljinska, Platonova, and Smirnova 2015).

The authors maintain that polysemy is based on metaphors, allowed by the similarity between two concepts belonging to different conceptual domains, semantic or thematic fields. Metaphorical polysemy influences and guides the taxonomy of terms: they are used, indeed, as the basis of nomination of many metaphorical terms in civil engineering and architecture. For example, the human body is represented schematically and mapped onto the structure of the building (the BUILDING IS A BODY metaphor). This is the reason why we find a superordinate concept related to BODY which conditions the mapping of the hyponymic concepts that are members of the same taxonomy (e.g. *leg* denotes support, *eye* window, *face* the façade, *head* the upper part of a structure). The human body is thus represented schematically and mapped onto the structure of the building. Iljinska, Platonova, and Smirnova analyse these kinds of relationships at a semantic, pragmatic, and semiotic level, showing that the majority of metaphoric terms based on the hyponyms of the concept BODY rely on the similarity of shape, so their relationship with the source is primarily of iconic nature.

Empirical study demonstrates that at present users of texts on civil engineering and architecture should rely upon corresponding background knowledge, which includes linguistic competence, knowledge of a special subject field, metaphorical competence and awareness of situational,cultural, and social contexts, as well as an understanding of the pragmatic and semiotic aspects of the contemporary technical text. The more ancient the cognitive concept, the more frequently and extensively it is used as a source in the process of meaning extension and, hence, term creation. This is a never-ending cognitive process, which promotes creative thinking and stimulates the emergence of new ideas described in the categories of other conceptual systems, thus resulting in a constant evolution of meaning. In particular, BUILDING IS A BODY is one of the primary conceptual metaphors that has significantly influenced the development of professional vocabulary in such fields as civil engineering and architecture. The linguistic manifestations of this conceptual metaphor may take different forms contributing to the emergence of new terms in various semiotic systems, triggering various associations framed within a cognitive model.

In the chapter *Some observations about metaphors in specialised languages*, Micaela Rossi offers a survey of the approaches on the use of metaphors in languages for special purposes (LSP). The author argues that, in the first period of studies on terminological metaphors, metaphorical terms were traditionally considered as isolated and episodic *catachresis*, that – in line with the general theory of terminology – represented labels for universally shared concepts. Nevertheless, during the same period, epistemologists focused on the potentiality of the metaphorical projective mechanism for creating, modelling, and promoting new scientific theories. For instance, Stengers and Schlanger (1991) and Schlanger (1995) put particular emphasis on the heuristic function of metaphor. Metaphor, indeed can have a role of a trigger for establishing new analogies and forms of understanding. An example is the concept of the Dutch irrigation canals which in the Seventeenth century allowed William Harvey to formulate his scientific discovery about the cardiovascular system (Oliveira 2009). Or, to consider a more recent case, on the basis of Lakoff and Johnson's theory (1980), Temmerman (2007) identifies the specific transfer from English to French of the metaphorical isotopy of the genetic code as a photographic film.

Starting from the 2000s, though, these different research fields opened to the achievements of conceptual metaphor in LSP. Metaphors in terminology became then a specific and autonomous topic in the last decade. Semiotic and functional analysis of terminological metaphors shows that, far from designating a single concept, they present a variety, that includes different types of conceptual projection, from catachresis to new paradigms. Micaela Rossi examines these different cases, going through various examples, and by also considering the relations between figures of analogy and the influence of language/culture. The problems of comparison or inter-linguistic translation of metaphors in specialised terminology shows the link of terminological metaphors with their culture of origin and other crucial factors like economic, socio-political, and geo-political aspects that deeply influence the communicative dimension of metaphors.

Finally, the first section of the volume specifically dedicated to the communicative aspects of metaphor, shows that the embodied cognition framework, presupposed by the conceptual theory of metaphor (Lakoff and Johnson 1980), helps to systematically seize both multi-modal and verbal embodied expressions in different media discourses and genres: cinema (see Fahlenbrach), politics (see Busuioc), and architecture/civil engineering (see Iljinska, Platonova and Smirnova), specialised terminologies in science (see Rossi). This is further developed in the following section. The chapters included in this section show the need to integrate the embodied cognition framework within cultural and emotional meanings, as well as the specific communicative goals and functions, in order to provide a comprehensive explanation of metaphors.

4 Science

The section dedicated to science aims to explore why and under what conditions metaphors can contribute to knowledge acquisition. The previous section proved that metaphors are ubiquitous in both ordinary speech as well as scientific discourse. History of science is replete with examples in this regard (Hesse 1974; Goodman 1976; Searle 1979; Kuhn 1979). However, metaphors are valuable resources not only for communication purposes but also have specific epistemic and heuristic functions, especially in the field of science (Ervas and Sangoi 2014). The chapters included in this section investigate the role and the heuristic effectiveness of metaphors in specific patterns of scientific reasoning, from classical physics and quantum mechanics to neuroscience, biology to medicine.

The chapter *Classical physics as a metaphorical tool for evoking quantum world*, by Silvano Tagliagambe and Luca Guzzardi, adopts the "boundary epistemology" as a reference framework to understand the differences between classical physics and quantum mechanics. In this view, boundaries have a twofold function: they act as both a demarcation line and an interface. Regarding the first function, a boundary allows to differentiate and separate entities. For example it allows to distinguish between living organisms and their environments. As for the second function, a boundary interface allows to connect two dimensions (living organisms/environments; classical physics/quantum world), pointing out similarities as well as differences. This last characterisation of boundary is analysed to underlie that living beings are active participants within the process of evolution. However, authors use the boundary epistemology framework also to analyse the epistemological exchanges among dimensions or domains (the case in point is the domains of classical physics and quantum physics).

Based on the second meaning of boundary, the authors describe quantum phenomena as *interphenomena* (Reichenbach 1944), that is "something in the middle between the real and the purely possible" (Tagliagambe and Guzzardi, in this volume, p. 173). In particular, Tagliagambe and Guzzardi discuss an experiment by Richard Feynman to demonstrate the possibility of using tools from classical physics to describe quantum contexts. They illustrate how certain metaphorical pieces from the vocabulary of classical physics can be efficient tools for quantum theoretical descriptions. Moving from Donald Davidson's idea of metaphor (Davidson 1978), the authors insist that search for complex analogies is a proper physical method to offer a description, that is – in Feyman's words (1970: 1–10) – a "deeper representation of the situation".

The chapter *Integration and differentiation at the basis of metaphor: Dexterity in behaviour and degeneracy in the nervous system*, by Carmela Morabito, considers evolutionary and neurocognitive concepts relevant to build a plausible model of mind. The chapter is an attempt to describe the concept of metaphor by examining the neuroanatomical functioning of the human mind. The chapter argues that integration and differentiation are fundamental neural mechanisms underlying conscious experience, intelligent actions, and metaphors. More specifically, by adopting a functional point of view, the chapter shows that, as every conscious state is an integrated or unified mental component, not further broken down, in the same way, also adaptive and intelligent actions cannot be decomposed into different and smaller motor acts. But simultaneously, as every conscious state is also differentiated or informative because of its capacity to lead to different behavioural goals, in the same way, also intelligent actions are differentially adapted to the variability of situations and conditions.

The author reconstructs the historical and theoretical relevance of integration and differentiation mechanisms in order to propose a neurologically plausible model of mind. More specifically, she examines Nikolaj Bernstein's ecological action-based theory of development, a theory that explains intelligent behaviours by stressing the deep plasticity, adaptability, and flexibility of organisms with respect to their response to varied and unexpected situations, and environmental contexts. Within this framework, the production of adaptive actions are analysed with respect to Bernstein's notion of dexterity, as "the ability to find a motor solution to any external situation" (Bernstein [1946] 1996: 228). By intertwining three different levels of analysis – functioning of the nervous system, functioning of the mind, and functioning of behaviour in the environment – Morabito discusses the importance of Bernstein's theory for contemporary cognitive neurosciences. In particular, she underlines the evolutionary role of degeneracy, i.e. "the ability of structurally different elements of a system to perform the same function or the same output" (Edelman and Gally 2001: 13763). Degeneracy, as a key property of the neuroanatomical functional organisation of the human brain, is then interpreted as the metaphorical capacity to operate by means of a pattern recognition process. Finally, the dynamic and associative nature of this process is also used to interpret the neurobiological nature of metaphors and metaphorical thinking.

Giulia Frezza and Elena Gagliasso's chapter *Building metaphors: Constitutive narratives in science* also insists on the heuristic relevance of metaphor in science. Here, the question of the role of metaphors in science is the object of inquiry: why are metaphors so spread and still so invisible within the domain of science? To answer this question the authors distinguish three different conceptual levels by considering the opposition of scientific-metaphorical thought: the epistemological level "rational vs. irrational", the methodological level "axiomatic vs. ambiguous", and the cognitive level "counter-intuitive vs. intuitive". Underlying the connections among these levels, the authors aim to support the idea that opposition or dialogue between science and metaphor depends on their respective historical conceptions. For instance, the combination of the rational character of science (epistemological level) and the axiomatic method (methodological level), at the beginning of the XXth century, led to a strong opposition; metaphor was viewed as an irrational way of thought based on an ambiguous lexicon. However, – claim Frezza and Gagliasso – in recent years the notion of rationality has undergone change. This has led to a reassessment of relationship between metaphor and science. Irrationality vs. rationality opposition has been replaced by the unconscious (automatic, fast, and intuitive) cognition vs. conscious (controlled, slow, and reasoned) cognition opposition. In this new context, science is opposed to metaphor because of its counterintuitive (so intentional, conscious, reasoned) purpose in the progress of knowledge. In their contribution, the authors challenge this negative view of the relationship between metaphor and science and use the field of life sciences to show the linguistic, cognitive, and contextual role of metaphors in the production of new concepts, theories and, finally, in the opening of new research domains.

The chapter *Identification and understanding of medical metaphors by nonexperts*, by Clara Inés Lòpez-Rodrìguez and Maribel Tercedor-Sánchez, presents evidence on metaphor identification and comprehension collected from the field of medical language. Their reflection faces an important paradox about the role of metaphors in the field of medical communication: on the one hand, exact information is the strongest requirement in medical discourse, but, on the other, correct information without patients' understanding is useless. In this sense, while metaphors can be used to effectively inform the patient, it runs the risk of a loss in terms of accuracy and exactness of the communicated information.

In order to meet this challenge, the authors investigate whether metaphor can be considered a facilitator in doctor-patient communication within cardiology and cardiovascular diseases. Towards this end, they used a corpus methodology (CombiMed corpus) to obtain a preliminary classification of metaphors. Based on this classification, they proposed to 58 translation students two experimental tasks (a task of spontaneous production and identification of metaphorical terms, and a spontaneous translation task from English to Spanish). Analysing the results, Lòpez-Rodrìguez and Tercedor-Sánchez underline students' recognition and use of the prevalent image schemas (e.g. part-whole, containment, in-out, force, linking) and their overlapping or co-occurrence.

The chapters included in the section of the volume highlight the epistemological function of metaphor and its power in the processes of categorisation and structure organisation in different scientific fields: classical physics and quantum mechanics (see Tagliagambe and Guzzardi), neuroscience (see Morabito), biology (see Frezza and Gagliasso), medicine (see Lòpez-Rodrìguez and Tercedor-Sánchez). From a communicative point of view, the section finally points out the crucial role of the heuristic function of metaphor especially where the audience needs to understand specific scientific contents, as in case of patient-doctor communication (see Lòpez-Rodrìguez and Tercedor-Sánchez).

5 Education

The section on education proposes the concept of knowledge building to replace the traditional idea of learning process as mere transmission of information. Whilst learning is an individual and isolated process, knowledge building is unavoidably social. In this perspective, communication plays an essential role especially when it is designed for knowledge building purposes (Cameron 2003; Low 2008). The aim of the chapters included in this section is to highlight the role metaphors play in learning environments, where they help to fulfil the cognitive, communicative, and affective needs of learning. Establishing meaningful analogies among abstract domains and everyday bodily experience, metaphors may deeply affect conceptual reorganisation and thus knowledge enhancement.

The chapter *Eliciting metaphor in education research: Is it really worth the effort?*, by Graham Low, specifically considers elicited metaphor in education, or, in other words, metaphors which are directly presented to (or solicited for) students in educative contexts. Previous literature has shown that, when a particular underlying conceptual metaphor is presented to participants, it influences them by orienting their opinions or beliefs (see Geary 2010; Gibbs and Colston 2012; Thibodeau et al. 2016). Psycholinguistic experiments rarely deal with educational scenarios and the present chapter aims to bridge this gap in metaphor research, to understand whether and under what conditions elicited metaphor "works" in education.

The author preliminarily wonders whether metaphors are really necessary in educational research and argues that we do need metaphors in education because they provide access to thoughts hard to describe literally; they allow to easily resort to images and are a common device to express emotion or affect. The students, who participated in the experimental study on elicited metaphors, reported activities of interplaying their own individual thoughts and group discussion as being helpful. They also critiqued the appropriateness of metaphors, focusing on concrete rather than abstract tasks, and focusing on the difficulties of defining and labelling metaphors. Finally, students' construction of a new metaphor, with a new rationale, has been taken as a strong evidence of change in their own beliefs, more than the appropriation of someone else's metaphor.

In the chapter *Teaching (in) metaphors*, Susanne Niemeier points out that metaphors, because of their embodied and conceptual nature, have been considered as a strong cognitive and linguistic strategy to facilitate comprehension of abstract concepts, at least by native speakers. However, when it comes to L2 (second/foreign language) learners, the communicative situation presents specific features that makes this standard picture complicated (Littlemore and Low 2006; Littlemore 2011). Foreign speakers normally do not share a native speaker's culture and usually rely on their own conceptual background to grasp the conceptual metaphors of the target language. However, as the author argues, making learners aware of metaphors means equipping them with tools for producing and understanding the target language in a successful way. The chapter explains how this can be achieved by focusing on figurative colour expressions in German learners of English.

Interestingly, in the German curricula for English as a second language, neither the textbooks nor the L2 teachers know the role metaphor plays in language and thought. Therefore L2 learners are not aware of its importance for the target language production and comprehension. On the contrary, from a cognitive linguistic perspective, raising the awareness of metaphor in L2 learners is beneficial for both an increase in their vocabulary and an enhanced intercultural communicative competence. When L2 learners know a conceptual metaphor, they are able to guess the meaning of its linguistic instantiations better, even though they have never encountered it before. Additionally they are also able to "creatively" invent metaphors on the basis of the known conceptual metaphor understandable to native speakers (Juchem-Grundmann 2009; Boers 2004). Moreover, knowing a conceptual metaphor helps L2 learners in deducing meanings from bodily actions, due to their experiential, embodied nature, and thus in retaining vocabulary more easily. This is so because they can extend the use of already known words in other senses and in more ways than just the basic ones. In this way, their communicative competence can be enhanced and a more critical view of the foreign language use can be transmitted (Holme 2004). Finally, L2 teaching through metaphors may make L2 learners think about language and use it in a lively manner which helps them to develop a greater language awareness.

The chapter *Metaphoricity in English L2 learners' prepositions*, by Susan Nacey and Bård Uri Jensen, specifically focuses on L2 learning English prepositions, which are traditionally considered to be the "*bête noire*" for foreign language learners (Gilquin and Granger 2011), because of difficulty in interpreting them due to their high polysemic nature. Interestingly enough, textbooks frequently treat preposition choice as arbitrary and unpredictable, suggesting memorisation or use of dictionaries as solutions. The authors challenge this shared view by analysing metaphorical prepositions in Norwegian L2 learners of English, to explore whether their degree of metaphoricity plays a role in divergent contextual choices by L2 learners, i.e. choices not explicitly listed in dictionaries. In order to do so, the authors propose a corpus-linguistic study based on two corpora: the Norwegian components of the International Corpus of Learner English (NICLE) and the Louvain International Database of Spoken English Interlanguage (LINDSEI-NO).

To identify the metaphorical status of prepositions, the authors applied the Metaphor Identification Procedure Vrije Universiteit (MIPVU; Steen et al. 2010), a procedure specifically developed to allow for reliable and valid identification of metaphorical words in discourse. They categorised prepositions in the corpora according to their degree of "divergence", based on whether their contextual senses were lexicalised in contemporary dictionaries of English. They found that there are relatively few divergent metaphorical prepositions in the two corpora: the majority of prepositions chosen by L2 learners, in both spoken and written forms, follows the standard English codified in dictionaries. However, when it comes to metaphorical use of prepositions in L2 learners, more metaphorical prepositions in the written data have been found, whilst a greater use was expected in the oral data, as metaphorical use is online and necessarily context-dependent. This might mean that prepositions are not as tricky to learn as is traditionally thought.

In the chapter *Metaphor and the shaping of educational thinking*, John Wade investigates how educational thinking has been presented through metaphors in the history of educational theories. In particular, the author shows how the focus has moved from general educational principles towards a greater attention to the needs of individuals. The chapter explores how metaphor is used in the process of changing educational thought and how it shapes different conceptions of learner/teacher interaction. Ranging from the more creative metaphors to the conceptual metaphors underpinning the conception of education, the author investigates the perspectives of both educational policy and the central role-players, i.e. teachers and learners, to understand how the communicative aspects of metaphor in education have changed.

The author concludes that it is possible to outline a trend in the description of educational theories: they are constructed from a combination of conceptual metaphors, which range from learning as a product-oriented activity (the top-down approach of AUTHORITY) to learning as a process-oriented activity (the bottom-up approach of SELF-REALISATION). In the latter perspective, the learner is an active participant in the educational process and needs to be guided towards an independent and critical view of the world. The author argues that, in this educational process, the educational thinking itself changes radically, in that it is no longer seen as a linear series of episodes of "providing knowledge", but as a cyclical process of "generating knowledge" according to the EDUCATION AS CYCLE conceptual metaphor which places the learner at the centre of the process. In this model, the authors identifies three essential elements: "the ability to plan, the ability to make informed decisions and the ability to analyse the outcome of that action in order to feed into a new cycle" (Wade, in this volume, p. 316).

The chapters in this section of the volume aim to understand why and under what conditions metaphors (and elicited metaphors in particular) have a pedagogical function (see Low) and, more specifically, when they are useful in L2 learning, by focusing on figurative colour expressions (see Niemeier) or on metaphorical prepositions (see Nacey and Jensen). They moreover explore how metaphors have shaped the educational thinking itself (see Wade), showing that specific communicative traits of metaphors influence not only education practice but also the role and identity of both teachers and learners.

6 Conclusion

The overall volume aims to be a guide for the reader on the new research in the embodied cognition perspective and, in particular, on the communicative side of metaphors by focusing on two main processes: comprehension processes in science and learning processes in education. In particular, the volume aims to answer two questions. The first concerns the ways embodied cognition paradigm still matters to metaphor studies. The chapters in this volume show the ways the standard embodied cognition approach presupposed by the conceptual theory of metaphor might be defended, extended, and/or integrated. The second question concerns the possibility of integrating the conceptual theory of metaphor to explain the communicative aspects of metaphor. The chapters in this volume show that communication adds specific functions, structures, situated meanings, cultural, and social cues to metaphor.

The volume specifically focuses on two cognitive processes: comprehension and learning respectively in the fields of science and education. In particular, the chapters included in the sections specifically dedicated to science and education suggest why and under what conditions metaphor can contribute to knowledge acquisition, with a heuristic function in scientific discovery and a pedagogical function in educational contexts. Each author provides an answer to both the problem of the influence of embodied cognition in the present research on metaphor and the problem of identifying the specific communicative aspects of metaphor. Finally, the main purpose of this volume is to bring the authors in a dialogue, and to suggest a research approach which requires both theoretical as well as experimental multidisciplinary research.

Acknowledgements: The order of the authors is merely alphabetical: Francesca Ervas wrote sections 1 and 2, Elisabetta Gola wrote sections 3 and 5, Maria Grazia Rossi wrote sections 4 and 6, and the overall edited work has been done together. We would like to thank the authors of the papers collected in this volume and all the participants at the X RaAM Conference "Metaphor in Communication, Science, and Education", the RaAM Association, the Organizing Committee (Valentina Favrin, Antonio Ledda, Giuseppe Sergioli, Filippo Spanu, Pietro Storari), and the graduate students of the School of Communication Science of the University of Cagliari. We are grateful to the Department of Education, Psychology, Philosophy and the Faculty of Humanistic Studies of the University of Cagliari for having hosted the conference. We are grateful to the Scientific Committee of the conference on "Metaphor in Communication, Science, and Education" (Cristina Cacciari, Robyn Carston, Jonathan Charteris-Black, Alan Cienki, Seana Coulson, Alice Deignan, Vincenzo Fano, Charles Forceville, Rachel Giora, Bipin Indurkhya, Beatrice Ligorio, Jeannette Littlemore, Maria Teresa Musacchio, Andreas Musolff, Francesco Paoli, Elena Semino, Daniele Santoro, Vera Tripodi) for a first selection of the papers presented at the conference.

We profoundly appreciate the efforts of the referees (Cristina Amoretti, Grazia Basile, Carla Bazzanella, Marianna Bolognesi, Olga Capirci, Claudia Casadio, Hernan Casakin, Jane Demmen, Olga Denti, Stefano Di Pietro, Valentina Favrin, Luisa Fodde, Charles Forceville, Francesco Paolo Gentile, Seth Lindstromberg,

Jeannette Littlemore, Fiona MacArthur, Sara Matera, Federica Pau, Mihaela Popa, Giuseppe Sergioli, Pietro Storari, Rachel Sutton-Spence) in reviewing the full papers and for all the support given to the publication of this volume.

References

Ahrens, Kathleen, Ho L. Liu, Chia Y. Lee, Shu Gong, Shin Fang & Yuan-Yu Hsu. 2007. Functional MRI of conventional and anomalous metaphors in mandarin Chinese. *Brain and Language* 100. 163–171.
Anaki, David, Miriam Faust & Shlomo Kravetz. 1998. Cerebral hemispheric asymmetries in processing lexical metaphors. *Neuropsychologia* 36. 353–362.
Arzouan, Yossi, Abraham Goldstein & Miriam Faust. 2007. Dynamics of hemispheric activity during metaphor comprehension: Electrophysiological measures. *Neuroimage* 36(1). 222.
Barnden, John. 2008. Metaphor and artificial intelligence: why they matter to each other. In Raymond W. Gibbs (ed.), *The Cambridge Handbook of Metaphor and Thought*, 311–338. Cambridge: Cambridge University Press.
Bernstein, Nikolaj A. 1996 [1946], On dexterity and its development. In Mark L. Latash & Michael T. Turvey (eds.), *Dexterity and its development*, 1–244. Mahwah, NJ: Erlbaum.
Boers, Frank. 2004. Expanding learners' vocabulary through metaphor awareness: what expansion, what learners, what vocabulary? In Michel Achard & Susanne Niemeier (eds.), *Cognitive Linguistics, Second Language Acquisition, and Foreign Language Teaching*, 211–232. Berlin: Mouton de Gruyter.
Bryden, Mark. P. 1982. *Laterality: Functional asymmetry in the intact brain*. New York: Academic Press.
Cameron, Lynne. 2003. *Metaphor in educational discourse*. London: Continuum.
Cameron, Lynne & Graham Low (eds.). 1999. *Researching and Applying Metaphor*. Cambridge: Cambridge University Press.
Cameron, Lynne & Robert Maslen (eds.). 2010. *Metaphor analysis: Research practice in applied linguistics, social sciences and the humanities*. London: Equinox.
Cartmill, Erica A., Sian Beilock & Susan Goldin-Meadow. 2012. A word in the hand: Action, gesture, and metal representation in human evolutions. *Philosophical Transaction of the Royal Society, Series B* 367. 129–143.
Charteris-Black, Jonathan. 2004. *Corpus approaches to critical metaphor analysis*. Basingstoke: Palgrave MacMillan.
Cienki, Alan, Luka Barbara & Michael Smith (eds.) 2001. *Conceptual and discourse factors in linguistic structure*. Stanford, CA: Center for the Study of Language and Information (CSLI).
Cienki, Alan & Cornelia Muller (eds.). 2008. *Metaphor and gesture*. Amsterdam: John Benjamins.
Cuccio, Valtentina. 2015a. The notion of representation and the brain. *Phenomenology and Mind* 7. 247–258.
Cuccio, Valentina. 2015b. Embodied simulation and metaphors. On the role of the body in the interpretation of bodily-based metaphors. *Epistemologia* 1. 99–113.
Davidson, Donald. 1984 [1978]. What metaphors mean. In Donald Davidson, *Inquiries into Truth and Interpretation*, 245–264. Oxford: Clarendon Press.

Davitz, Joel R. 1969. *The language of emotion*. New York: Academic Press.
Deignan, Alice. 2005. *Metaphor and corpus linguistics*. Amsterdam: John Benjamins.
Deignan, Alice. 2010. *Researching and applying metaphor in the real world*. Amsterdam: John Benjamins.
Drew, Paul & Elizabeth Holt. 1998. Figures of speech: Figurative expressions and the management of topic transition in conversation. *Language in Society* 27. 495–522.
Edelman, Gerald M. & Joseph A. Gally. 2001. Degeneracy and complexity in biological systems. *Proceedings of the National Academy of Sciences* 98. 13763–13768.
Ellis, Andrew W., Andrew W. Young & Christine Anderson. 1988. Modes of word recognition in the left and right cerebral hemispheres. *Brain and Language* 35. 254–273.
Ervas, Francesca & Massimo Sangoi (eds.). 2014. *Metaphor and argumentation*. Isonomia, Epistemologica, 5. Urbino: University of Urbino.
Evans, Jonathan & Keith Frankish. 2009. *In two minds. Dual processes and beyond*. Oxford: Oxford University Press.
Fauconnier, Gilles & Mark Turner. 1998. Conceptual integration networks. *Cognitive Science* 22(2). 133–187.
Fauconnier, Gilles & Mark Turner. 2002. *The way we think. Conceptual blending and the mind's hidden complexities*. New York: Basic Books.
Faust, Miriam & Nira Mashal. 2007. The role of the right cerebral hemisphere in processing novel metaphoric expressions taken from poetry: A divided visual field study. *Neuropsychologia* 45(4). 860–870.
Feynman, Richard P., Leighton Robert B. & Sands Matthew (eds.). 1970. *The Feynman lectures on physics*. London: Addison Wesley Longman.
Foroni, Francesco & Gün R. Semin. 2009. Language that puts you in touch with your bodily feelings: The multimodal responsiveness of affective expressions. *Psychological Science* 20(8). 974–980.
Frank, Roslyn M., Dirven René, Ziemke Tom & Enrique Bernárdez (eds.). 2008. *Body, Language and Mind, Vol. 2: Sociocultural Situatedness*. Berlin: Mouton de Gruyter.
Gallese, Vittorio & Corrado Sinigaglia. 2011. What is so special about embodied simulation? *Trends in Cognitive Science* 15(11). 512–519.
Geary, James. 2010. *I is another: The Secret Life of Metaphor and How It Shapes the Way We See the World*. New York: Harper.
Gibbs, Raymond W. 1994. *The poetics of mind: Figurative thought, language, and understanding*. Cambridge: Cambridge University Press.
Gibbs, Raymond W. 1999. *Intentions in the experience of meaning*. Cambridge: Cambridge University Press.
Gibbs, Raymond W. 2003. Embodied experience and linguistic meaning. *Brain and Language* 84(1). 1–15.
Gibbs, Raymond W. 2006. *Embodiment and cognitive science*. Cambridge: Cambridge University Press.
Gibbs, Raymond W. & Josephine M. Bogdanovich. 1999. Mental imagery in interpreting poetic metaphor. *Metaphor and Symbol* 14(1). 37–54.
Gibbs, Raymond W. Jr. & Herbert L. Colston. 2012. *Interpreting figurative meaning*. Cambridge: Cambridge University Press.
Gibbs, Raymond W. & Teenie Matlock. 2008. Metaphor, imagination, and simulation: Psycholinguistic evidence. In Raymond Gibbs (ed.), *Cambridge handbook of metaphor and thought*, 161–176. New York: Cambridge University Press.

Gibbs, Raymond W. & Marcus Perlman. 2010. Language understanding is grounded in experiential simulations: A response to Weiskopf. *Studies in the History and Philosophy of Science* 41(3). 305–308.

Gilquin, Gaetanelle & Sylviane Granger. 2011. From EFL to ESL: Evidence from the International Corpus of Learner English. In Joybrato Mukherjee & Marianne Hundt (eds.), *Exploring second-language varieties of English and learner Englishes: Bridging a paradigm gap*, 55–78. Amsterdam: John Benjamins.

Giora, Rachel. 2003. *On our mind: Salience, context, and figurative language*. Oxford: Oxford University Press.

Glucksberg, Sam. 2001. *Understanding figurative language: From metaphors to idioms*. New York: Oxford University Press.

Glucksberg, Sam. 2008. How metaphors create categories—quickly. In Raymond W. Gibbs (ed.), *The Cambridge handbook of metaphor and thought*, 67–83. Cambridge: Cambridge University Press.

Gola, Elisabetta & Francesca Ervas. 2016. Metaphors we live twice: A communication approach beyond the conceptual view? In Elisabetta Gola & Francesca Ervas (eds.). *Metaphor and Communication*, 1–22. Amsterdam: John Benjamins.

Grady, Joseph. 2000. Cognitive Mechanisms of Conceptual Integration. *Cognitive Linguistics* 11(3–4). 335–345.

Goodman, Nelson. 1976. *Languages of art*. Indianapolis: Hackett.

Graesser, Arthur C. & Keith Millis. 2011. Discourse and cognition. In Teun Van Dijk (ed.), *Discourse Studies: A Multidisciplinary Introduction*, 126–142. London: Sage.

Hesse, Mary B. 1974. *The structure of scientific inference*. Basingstoke: Palgrave Macmillan.

Holme, Randall. 2004. *Mind, metaphor and language teaching*. Basingstoke: Palgrave Macmillan.

Iljinska, Larisa, Marina Platonova & Tatjana Smirnova. 2015. Coinage and application of metaphoric terms in scientific and technical texts: Contrastive approach. In Karin Maksymski, Silke Gutermuth, Silvia Hansen-Schirra (eds.), *Translation and Comprehensibility*, 139–162. Berlin: Frank & Timme.

Jonides, John, Edward E. Smith, Robert A. Koeppe, Edward Awh, Satoshi Minoshima & Mark A. Mintun. 1993. Spatial working memory in humans as revealed by PET. *Nature* 363. 623–625.

Juchem-Grundmann, Constanze. 2009. *"Dip into your savings!" Applying Cognitive Metaphor Theory in the Business English Classroom. An Empirical Study*. University Koblenz-Landau: Doctoral Dissertation.

Kahneman, Daniel. 2003. A perspective on judgment and choice: Mapping bounded rationality. *American Psychologist* 58. 697–720.

Katz, Albert N., Cristina Cacciari, Raymond W. Gibbs, Mark Turner (eds.). 1998. *Figurative Language and Thought*. Oxford: Oxford University Press.

Kintsch, Walter. 1998. *Comprehension: A Paradigm for Cognition*. Cambridge: Cambridge University Press.

Kövecses, Zoltán. 2005. *Metaphor in Culture. Universality and Variation*. Cambridge: Cambridge University Press.

Kövecses, Zoltán. 2013. The metaphor-metonymy relationship: correlation metaphors are based on metonymy. *Metaphor and Symbol* 28(2). 75–88.

Kuhn, Thomas S. 1979. Metaphor in Science. In Andrew Ortony (ed.), *Metaphor and thought*, 409–419. Cambridge: Cambridge University Press.

Lakoff, George. 1993. The contemporary theory of metaphor. In Andrew Ortony (ed.), *Metaphor and thought*, 202–251. Cambridge: Cambridge University Press.

Lakoff, George & Johnson Mark. 1999. *Philosophy in the flesh. The embodied mind and its challange to Western Thought*. New York: Basic Books.

Lakoff, George & Johnson Mark. 1980. *Metaphors we live by*. Chicago: University of Chicago Press.

Lindblom, Jessica & Tom Ziemke. 2002. Social situatedness: Vygotsky and beyond. In Christopher G. Prince, Yiannis Demiris, Yuval Marom, Hideki Kozima & Christian Balkenius (eds.), *Proceedings of the Second International Workshop on Epigenetic Robotics. Modelling cognitive development in robotic systems*, 71–78. Lund: Lund University Cognitive Studies.

Littlemore, Jeannette & Graham Low. 2006. *Figurative thinking and foreign language learning*. Basingstoke: Palgrave Macmillan.

Littlemore, Jeannette. 2011. *Applying cognitive linguistics to second language learning and teaching*. Basingstoke: Palgrave Macmillan.

Low, Graham D. 2008. Metaphor in education. In Raymond Gibbs (ed.), *The Cambridge handbook of metaphor and thought*, 212–231. Cambridge, UK: Cambridge University Press.

Low, Graham & Lynne Cameron. 2002. Applied-Linguistic Comments on the Metaphor Identification Projects. *Language and Literature* 11(1). 84–90.

Maalej, Zouheir A. & Ning Yu. 2011. Introduction. Embodiment via body parts. In Zouheir A. Maalej & Ning Yu (eds.), *Embodiment via body parts*, 1–20. Amsterdam: John Benjamins.

Macnamara, Danielle S. & Joe Magliano. 2009. Toward a comprehensive model of comprehension. In Brian Ross (ed.), *The Psychology of Learning and Motivation*, 297–384. Burlington: Academic Press.

Matlock, Teenie, Michael Ramscar & Lera Boroditsky. 2005. The experiential link between spatial and temporal language. *Cognitive Science* 29. 655–664.

McCarthy, Gregory, Andrew M. Blamire, Aina Puce, Anna C. Nobre, Gilles Bloch, Fahmeed Hyder & Robert G. Shulman. 1994. Functional magnetic resonance imaging of human prefrontal cortex activation during a spatial working memory task. *Proceedings of the National Academy of Sciences* 91(18). 8690–8694.

McNeill, David. 1992. *Hand and mind: What gestures reveal about thought*. Chicago: University of Chicago Press.

McNeill, David. 2005. *Gesture and thought*. Chicago: University of Chicago Press.

Muller, Cornelia. 2008. *Metaphors dead and alive, sleeping and waking*. Chicago/London: University of Chicago Press.

Musolff, Andreas. 2004. *Metaphor and political discourse. Analogical reasoning in debates about Europe*. Basingstoke: Palgrave-Macmillan.

Neisser, Ulric. 1976. *Cognition and reality: Principles and implications of cognitive psychology*. San Francisco: W. H. Freeman.

Ping, Raedy, Susan Goldin-Meadow & Sian Beilock. 2014. Understanding gesture: Is the listener's motor system involved. *Journal of Experimental Psychology: General* 143(1). 195–204.

Pragglejaz Group. 2007. MIP: A method for identifying metaphorically used words in discourse. *Metaphor and Symbol* 22(1). 1–39.

Rapp, Alexander M., Dirk T. Leube, Michael Erb, Wolfgang Grodd & Tilo T. Kircher. 2004. Neural correlates of metaphor processing. *Cognitive Brain Research* 20(3). 395–402.

Reichenbach, Hans. 1944. *Philosophic foundations of quantum mechanics*. Berkeley & Los Angeles: University of California Press.
Ritchie, David L. 2010. "Everybody goes down": Metaphors, stories, and simulations in conversations. *Metaphor and Symbol* 25. 123–143.
Ritchie, David L. & Lynne Cameron. 2014. Open hearts or smoke and mirrors: Metaphorical framing and frame conflicts in a public meeting. *Metaphor and Symbol* 29(3). 204–223.
Rohrer, Tim. 2006. Three dogmas of embodiment: Cognitive linguistics as cognitive science. In Gitte Kristiansen, Michel Achard, René Dirven & Francisco Ruiz de Mendoza Ibáñez (eds.), *Cognitive linguistics: Current applications and future perspectives*, 119–146. Berlin: Mouton de Gruyter.
Rohrer, Tim. 2007. The body in space: Embodiment, experientalism and linguistic conceptualization. In Tom Ziemke, Jordan Zlatev, & Roslyn M. Frank (eds.), *Body, language and mind, Vol. 1: Embodiment*, 339–377. Berlin: Mouton de Gruyter.
Romano, Manuela & Maria Dolores Porto. 2016. Introduction. Discourse, cognition and society. In Manuela Romano & Maria Dolores Porto (eds.), *Exploring Discourse Strategies in Social and Cognitive Interaction: Multimodal and cross-linguistic perspectives*, 1–17. Amsterdam: John Benjamins.
Schlanger, Judith. 1995. *Les métaphores de l'organisme*. Paris: L'Harmattan.
Searle, John. 1979. Metaphor. In Andrew Ortony (ed.), *Metaphor and thought*, 83–111. Cambridge: Cambridge University Press.
Semino, Elena. 2008. *Metaphor in discourse*. Cambridge: Cambridge University Press.
Sharifian, Farzad. 2011. *Cultural conceptualisations and language: Theoretical framework and applications*. Amsterdam: John Benjamins.
Sharifian, Farzad. 2015. Cultural Linguistics. In Farzad Sharifian (ed.), *The Routledge Handbook of language and culture*, 473–492. London: Routledge.
Shibataa, Midori, Jun-Ichi Abe, Atsushi Terao & Tamaki Miyamoto. 2007. Neural mechanisms involved in the comprehension of metaphoric and literal sentences: An fMRI study. *Brain Research* 1166. 92–102.
Steen, Gerard J. 2008. The paradox of metaphor: Why we need a three-dimensional model of metaphor. *Metaphor and Symbol* 23(4). 213–241.
Steen, Gerard J. 2004. Can discourse properties of metaphor affect metaphor recognition? *Journal of Pragmatics* 36(7). 1295–1313.
Steen, Gerard J. 2006. Discourse functions of metaphor: An experiment in affect. In Réka Benczes & Szilvia Csabi (eds.), *The metaphors of sixty: Papers presented on the occasion of the 60th birthday of Zoltan Kövecses*, 236–244. Budapest, Hungary: School of English and American Studies, Eotvos Lorand University.
Steen, Gerard J. 2011. The contemporary theory of metaphor – Now new and improved! *Review of Cognitive Linguistics* 9(1). 26–64.
Steen, Gerard J., Aletta G. Dorst, Berenike J. Herrmann, Anna A. Kaal, Tina Krennmayr & Trijntje Pasma. 2010. *A method for linguistic metaphor identification: From MIP to MIPVU*. Amsterdam: John Benjamins.
Stengers, Isabelle & Judith Schlanger. 1991. *Les Concepts scientifiques: Invention et pouvoir*. Paris: Folio.
Svensson, Henrik & Tom Ziemke. 2004. Making Sense of Embodiment. In Kenneth Forbus, Dedre Gentner & Terry Regier (eds.), *Proceedings of the 26th Annual Conference of the Cognitive Science Society*, 1309–1314. Mahwah, NJ: Lawrence Erlbaum.

Temmerman, Rita. 2007. Les métaphores dans les sciences de la vie et le situé socioculturel. *Cahiers du RIFAL* 26. 72–83.

Thibodeau, Paul. H., Anna Winneg, Cynthia Frantz & Stephen J. Flusberg. 2016. The mind is an ecosystem: Systemic metaphors promote systems thinking. *Metaphor and the Social World* 6(2). 225–242.

Van Dijk, Teun A. & Walter Kintsch. 1983. *Strategies of discourse comprehension*. New York: Academic Press.

Veale, Tony. 2012. From Conceptual mash-ups to "Bad-Ass" blends: A robust computational model of conceptual blending. In *Proceedings of ICCC 2012, the 3rd International Conference on Computational Creativity*. Dublin, Ireland.

Walsh, Paul. 1990. Imagery as a heuristic in the comprehension of metaphorical analogies. In Kenneth J. Gilhooly, Mark T. G. Keane, Robert H. Logie & George Erdos (eds.), *Lines of thinking: Reflections on the psychology of thought. Representation, reasoning, analogy and decision making*, 237–250. New York: Wiley.

Wilson, Margaret. 2002. Six views of embodied cognition. *Psychological Bulletin and Review* 9(4). 625–636.

Ziemke, Tom. 2003. What's that thing called embodiment? In Richard Alterman & David Kirsh (eds.), *Proceedings of the 25th Annual Conference of the Cognitive Science Society*, 1305–1310. Mahwah, NJ: Lawrence Erlbaum.

Ziemke, Tom & Roslyn M. Frank. 2007. Introduction. The body eclectic. In Tom, Ziemke, Jordan Zlatev & Roslyn M. Frank (eds.), *Body, language, and mind, Vol. 1: Embodiment*, 1–13. Berlin: Mouton De Gruyter.

Ziemke, Tom, Zlatev Jordan & Roslyn M. Frank (eds.). 2007. *Body, language, and mind, Vol. 1: Embodiment*. Berlin: Mouton De Gruyter.

Zlatev, Jordan. 1997. *Situated Embodiment. Studies in the Emergence of Spatial Meaning*. Stockholm: Gotab.

Part I: **Theoretical perspectives**

Zoltán Kövecses
Metaphor and metonymy in folk and expert theories of emotion

1 Introduction

The conference where a previous version of this paper was presented had as its major topic: *metaphors in communication, science, and education*. Thus, it seems appropriate to ask the question: What role does metaphor play in folk and expert theories of emotion? What makes the question interesting is that while we would expect folk theories of emotion to use metaphors to a greater or lesser extent, the use of metaphor in expert, or scientific, theories appears to be much less expected or even acceptable, and thus less likely. After all, folk theories are often language-based, and we know that the language of emotions is highly metaphoric. At the same time, we expect expert theories to give us the truth about emotions without the metaphors that pervade everyday language.

And in the context of the present conference on metaphor, the issue is even more interesting because it has implications for how we view metaphor as the object of our study. An applied linguistic view of metaphor (shared by most participants here) assumes, in one form or another, some of the foundational claims of conceptual metaphor theory. One of these is that the metaphors we use are not isolated from each other but are systematic, that is, the claim that the metaphors used often form systematic groups (called "systematic metaphors"). However, other foundational claims of conceptual metaphor theory may not be accepted by the practitioners of metaphor analysis with an applied linguistic orientation. Perhaps chief among these is the idea that metaphors of the kind Lakoff and Johnson (1980) called "conceptual metaphors" are used in thinking about the subject matters they apply to. Such a claim concerning the status of conceptual metaphors in human thought is looked at with suspicion and is commonly regarded as exaggerated and even unfounded by discourse-oriented metaphor scholars (see, e.g., Cameron and Maslen 2010).

And yet this is precisely the view of metaphor that I would like to defend in this paper in an area that is one of the prime examples of human thought: the construction of expert, or scientific, theories. In particular, I would like to show that metaphors not only play a role in the formation of folk theories of emotion

Zoltán Kövecses, Eötvös Loránd University

but also in the construction of expert theories. If it can be shown that both folk and expert theories are commonly based on the same conceptual metaphors, we get very strong additional evidence that conceptual metaphors are used in thought, and that, therefore, this reservation and the general skepticism concerning conceptual metaphor theory is not quite justified.

In the paper, I simply take a folk theory to be a theory implicit in language and an expert theory to be a theory proposed by scientists dealing with a domain, in our case, that of emotion.

2 Emotion language and folk theories/models of emotion

In various previous publications, I argued that folk theories of emotion can be best described as consisting of a number of conceptual metaphors, conceptual metonymies, and "related concepts" (Kövecses 1986, 1990, 2000). These are the conceptual components that give rise to and constitute folk theories, or models, of emotion. Below are some examples of such conceptual components for the emotions in general and specific emotions in particular: (linguistic examples will be provided in later sections)
- General emotion metaphors:
    - EMOTION IS A SUBSTANCE
    - THE BODY IS A CONTAINER
    - EMOTIONS ARE NATURAL/PHYSICAL FORCES
    - EMOTION IS INSANITY
    - EMOTION IS A DISEASE
- General emotion metonymies:
    - BODY TEMPERATURE FOR THE EMOTION
    - EXPRESSIVE RESPONSE FOR THE EMOTION
    - BEHAVIORAL RESPONSE FOR THE EMOTION
- Specific emotion metaphors:
    - Anger
        - ANGER IS A HOT FLUID IN A CONTAINER
    - Love
        - LOVE IS A UNITY OF TWO COMPLEMENTARY PARTS
    - Happiness
        - HAPPINESS IS A NATURAL FORCE

- Pride
    - PRIDE IS A FLUID IN A CONTAINER
    - TO BE PROUD IS TO BE BIG/UP/HIGH
- Specific emotion metonymies:
    - Anger
        - INCREASE IN BODY TEMPERATURE FOR ANGER
    - Love
        - BODILY CLOSENESS FOR LOVE
    - Happiness:
        - BECOMING RED IN THE FACE FOR JOY
        - SMILING FOR HAPPINESS
    - Pride:
        - ERECT POSTURE/HEAD HELD HIGH FOR PRIDE
        - CHEST (THRUST) OUT FOR PRIDE

Emotion-related metonymies serve to capture the physiological, expressive, and behavioral responses associated with emotions.

The relationship between these metaphors and metonymies is that the metaphors are based on the metonymies: for example, ANGER IS A HOT FLUID IN A CONTAINER is based on AN INCREASE IN BODY TEMPERATURE FOR ANGER, LOVE IS A UNITY OF TWO COMPLEMENTARY PARTS is based on BODILY CLOSENESS FOR LOVE, and TO BE PROUD IS TO BE BIG is based on CHEST OUT FOR PRIDE.

The process works like this: an emotion frame consists of a variety of elements, including the participating entities and the responses associated with an emotion. An emotion-specific response is generalized to a concept outside the emotion frame (e.g., BODY HEAT TO HEAT, BODILY CLOSENESS to CLOSENESS, and CHEST OUT to LARGE SIZE/BIGNESS). This generalized concept that is outside the original emotion frame becomes the source domain in the metaphorical conceptualization of the emotion (such as ANGER IS HEAT, LOVE IS UNITY/CLOSENESS, and PRIDE IS BIGNESS) (for more detail on the process, see Kövecses 2013).

In the case of most emotions, we experience changes in the body. This gives rise to the general metonymy THE FEELING OF BODILY CHANGE FOR THE EMOTION. Here the emotion-specific notion of FEELING OF BODILY CHANGE is generalized into the concept of FEELING. This generic concept then becomes the source domain for emotions in general: EMOTIONS ARE FEELINGS.

3 What is the relationship between the folk and expert theories?

It is commonly the case that a conceptual metaphor in everyday language can be found in a corresponding expert theory of emotions; the expert theory typically elaborates the folk theory (partially) constituted by a metaphor. This can happen both in the case of individual folk theories for particular emotions or for groups of expert theories of emotion (examples are taken from my previous work).

3.1 A conceptual metaphor shared by a folk and an expert theory

In this subsection, I briefly analyze particular metaphorical source domains (for particular emotions) that can also be found underlying expert theories for these emotions.

Fluid in a container and large size
As we saw above, the emotions can be conceptualized as fluids inside a container. This metaphor exists in a generic and a specific version for pride: PRIDE IS A FLUID IN A CONTAINER and PRIDE IS A FLUID IN THE HEART. In Davitz's (1969) expert theory, the key component of pride is what he calls "enhancement". This can be noticed when people report experiences related to pride such as "I feel taller, stronger, bigger, strong inside". The notion of enhancement seems to be based, in part, on the FLUID IN A CONTAINER metaphor. A container may grow in size (cf. swell with pride) when it contains a lot of fluid. To make this inference is justified by the behavioral response commonly observed in intense cases of pride: thrusting the chest out. The CHEST OUT FOR PRIDE metonymy and the FLUID IN A CONTAINER metaphor jointly motivate the expert notion of enhancement. Another way in which the notion of enhancement finds support in everyday metaphors is when the proud person is conceived metaphorically as big; i.e., through the metaphor TO BE PROUD IS TO BE BIG/HIGH/UP. This metaphor is in turn based on such metonymies of pride as ERECT POSTURE/HEAD HELD HIGH FOR PRIDE and CHEST (THRUST) OUT FOR PRIDE.

UNITY

A major metaphor for ROMANTIC LOVE is the metaphor LOVE IS A UNITY (see Kövecses 1988, 2000). This metaphor has become the basis for several expert theories of love. A possible reason for this is that the metaphor captures a large number of our experiences in an intense love relationship. The idea that two people somehow form a unity, that they function together, that they are individually incomplete without the other, that they experience a sense of belonging together, and several others, are all implications of this metaphor. Many authors, beginning with Plato, picked up and elaborated on this metaphor in their expert theories (see, for example, Hatfield 1988, Solomon 1981).

RAPTURE

One of the metaphors associated with ROMANTIC LOVE is that LOVE IS A RAPTURE. One can be drunk or intoxicated with love. In addition to experiencing it as a pleasant state, the metaphor's focuses on the notion of lack of control. When in love in an intense way, people are seen as not quite in possession of their powers, that is, they appear to have no control over their emotions and actions. Stanton Peele (1975) elevated this metaphor to the status of an expert theory in his book: in a telling way, the title of the book is LOVE AND ADDICTION.

NATURAL FORCE (storm, wave, flood)

This conceptual metaphor can be found in linguistic examples, such as "*engulfed* by passion", "emotions *swept over* her", "*waves* of passion *came over* him", and "his emotions *subsided*". The metaphor depicts emotions as overwhelming outside forces and people as being helpless and passive in relation to them; the emotions have control over us. Probably this is what Plato had in mind when he thought of emotions as wild horses running away with us. We are still talking about intense emotions as forces that carry us away or can transport us. Characteristically, we use the passive voice in such cases ("be *carried away* by emotion," "be *transported* by a feeling," etc.).

The metaphor LOVE IS A NATURAL or PHYSICAL FORCE is the basis for the most prevalent belief about love; namely, that it is an experience that we undergo in a passive way: "we are *bowled over*" and "*swept away* by it." Expert theories are commonly offered that challenge this metaphor-based assumption. In them, love is not seen as a force acting on us, but, instead, as a rational judgment, a conscious decision on our part (see, for example, Fromm 1956; Solomon 1981; Sternberg 1986). Although such expert theories challenge a conceptual metaphor, they clearly assume its existence.

BODY AS CONTAINER

As mentioned above, the emotions are commonly viewed as substances, usually fluids, in the body as a container. The BODY AS CONTAINER metaphor, together with several of its derivatives, can be found in a number of expert theories. Of these, perhaps the best-known one is Freud's theory of emotions. Freud essentially takes over two CONTAINER metaphors from the language-based folk theory of emotions (see Kövecses 1990): THE BODY IS A CONTAINER and THE MIND IS A CONTAINER. It is in the body container that certain emotional forces rise. These correspond to fluids rising in the container. The additional metaphor that is assumed here is THE EMOTIONS ARE FLUID (IN A CONTAINER). In Talmy's (1988) system of force dynamics, the agonist corresponds to the rising fluids in the lower *body container*, where the rising fluids represent a person's psychological desires, the id in Freud's theory. THE MIND CONTAINER above THE BODY CONTAINER corresponds to the antagonist, representing external social values. This latter is the superego in Freud. Now, the ego is between the mind-antagonist and the body-agonist, being torn between the two. However, it has to be noticed that the emotions in this system cannot be simply identified with the upward-moving fluids in the body container.

Freud's innovation was his subtle change in the body container. Instead of viewing emotions as upward-moving fluids (as in the language-based folk theory), Freud claimed that the upward moving fluids are basic psychological instincts and desires that need to be controlled and that the emotions correspond to a number of outlets, or valves, in the side of the lower container through which the dangerous upward moving fluids (the contents of the id) can leave the container. This was a subtle elaboration on the folk theory, but at the same time it does rely on the folk theory in taking over its general metaphorical structure.

3.2 Conceptual metaphors underlying groups of expert theories

Individual conceptual metaphors may be found to underlie not only particular expert theories of emotion but also *entire groups* of scientific theories. Averill and I (Kövecses 1990) point out that there are several groups of expert theories of emotion that seem to be based on emotion metaphors prevalent in everyday language.

3.2.1 Emotion as disturbance

Several emotion theories regard emotions as disturbances to body and mind. Psychoanalytic and several behaviorist theories are of this kind. They are based on the conceptual metaphors and metonymies below:
- EMOTIONAL DISTURBANCE IS PHYSICAL DISTURBANCE
  - Linguistic examples include *stir up, be shook up, be worked up, upset, disturb, be excited, be paralyzed,* and *calm down.*
- EMOTIONS ARE DISEASES
  - Linguistic examples include *hurt, wounded, tortured, suffer from, be sick from, heart-broken, painful, fevered state, die from* emotion.
- EMOTION IS INSANITY
  - Linguistic examples include *mad/crazy with* emotion, *drive someone crazy, wild, beside* oneself, *send into a frenzy.*
- BODILY AGITATION FOR THE EMOTION
  - Linguistic example include *shake, tremble* with emotion.
- INTERFERENCE WITH ACCURATE PERCEPTION
  - Linguistic examples include *be blind with, be blinded* by an emotion.

3.2.2 Emotion as motivation

Other theories emphasize the motivational character of emotions, and they view emotions as biological instincts, that is, as forces that can compel a person to act in certain ways. Such theories may have evolved from or may have inspired (and in this sense are based on) the metaphors below:
- EMOTION IS A NATURAL FORCE
- EMOTIONAL EFFECT IS PHYSICAL MOVEMENT
  - Linguistic examples include *waves* of passion, *be carried away* by emotion.
- EMOTION IS A PHYSICAL FORCE
  - Linguistic examples include *be hit/struck* by emotion.
- EMOTION IS A SOCIAL FORCE (SUPERIOR)
  - Linguistic examples include *be governed/ruled* by passion.
- ACTION RESULTING FROM AN EMOTION FOR THE EMOTION
  - Linguistic examples include *flee in* terror, *weep in* grief.

3.2.3 Emotion as physiological change

Emotions are here viewed as being constituted by physiological changes in the body, that is, as essential constituents of emotions, sometimes in combination with other factors.

- EMOTIONS ARE PHYSIOLOGICAL REACTIONS
  - Linguistic examples include *gut issue/reaction, visceral response*.
- EMOTIONS ARE IN THE HEART
  - Linguistic examples include *listen to your heart, with all his heart, heart-felt, in his heart, heartless*.
- CHANGE IN HEART RATE FOR THE EMOTION
  - Linguistic examples include *heart throbbing, with one's heart in one's mouth, heart beating faster*.
- CHANGE IN RESPIRATION FOR THE EMOTION
  - Linguistic examples include *heave with* emotion, *take one's breath away, breathless from* emotion.
- CHANGE IN SKIN COLOR ON THE FACE FOR THE EMOTION
  - Linguistic examples include *be flushed, pale, red, blushed*.
- CHANGES IN THE EYES FOR THE EMOTION
  - Linguistic examples include *mean/angry/loving look, icy stare, tears in the eyes*.
- EMOTIONS ARE EXPRESSIVE REACTIONS
  - Linguistic examples include emotions *on one's face, one's face is an open book*.
- CHANGES IN THE FACE FOR THE EMOTION
  - Linguistic examples include *frown, smile, grimace, knitted brows, flaring nostrils, rosy cheeks, bared teeth, tight lips*.

3.2.4 Emotion as physical sensation

Emotion is here identified with the subjective experience of emotion, namely, the perception or feeling of bodily change (which accompanies the perception of an initiating event) (James 1890). The physical sensation, the feeling of the bodily change is the emotion.
- EMOTION IS FEELING
  - Linguistic examples include *feel* angry/sad/happy.
- EMOTION IS FEELING SOMETHING EXTERNAL
  - Linguistic examples include *be touched*.
- EMOTION IS FEELING SOMETHING INTERNAL
  - Linguistic examples include *feel in the heart, have the feeling inside*.

Klaus Scherer (2005) criticizes James for reducing emotions to feelings on the grounds that, this way, James makes a broader definition of emotions impossible or difficult.

3.2.5 Emotion as animal

This is the view that human emotions are instinctive reactions that humans inherited from animals in the course of biological evolution. The major figure behind this view is Darwin (1872), in his *The expression of the emotions in man and animals*. The corresponding conceptual metaphor is:
- EMOTION IS A DANGEROUS ANIMAL
  - Linguistic examples include *arouse* emotion, *wild, fierce, unbridled, insatiable, untamed, violent* emotion, *unleash* emotion, *keep it on short leash, keep it in check, get away from, run away with*.

Interestingly, this conceptual metaphor does not have a clear and obvious metonymic basis. This might indicate that, unlike the other conceptual metaphors, the animal metaphor is a resemblance, rather than a correlation-based, one.

3.2.6 Emotion as nonrational evaluation

"Cognitive" theories of emotion maintain that emotions involve nonrational judgments (positive or negative) concerning a particular emotional target. The judgments may be irrational, intuitive, magical, or evaluative, depending on which cognitive theory we take.
- EMOTION IS RAPTURE
  - Linguistic examples include *be drunk, intoxicated, high on* emotion, *delirious*, and even emotionally *sober*.
- EMOTION IS A TRICKSTER
  - Linguistic examples include (how emotions) *deceive, mislead, lead astray, trick, fool*.
- EMOTION IS A CHANGER
- EMOTION CHANGES HOW THE SELF SEES THE WORLD
  - Linguistic examples include *see* something *through rose-colored glasses*, something *looks dark and blue*.
- EMOTION CHANGES THE (EXTERNAL) WORLD
  - Linguistic examples include love *makes the world go around*, fear *is a great inventor*.
- INTERFERENCE WITH ACCURATE PERCEPTION FOR THE EMOTION
  - Linguistic examples include *be blind with/blinded by* something.

This completes the survey of the possible conceptual relationship between language-based folk theories of emotion and expert theories of emotion. The discussion in this section allows us to bring out some of the implications of what we have found.

4 Some implications

We have seen robust evidence that emotion theories are based on the conceptual metaphors that provide much of the material for folk theories of emotion. In probably all of these cases, the everyday metaphors must have preceded the scientific ones. This is important to recognize since I wish to argue that the conceptual metaphors that "fashion" folk theories also provide part of the content and structure of expert theories. What this means is that the scholars who create the scientific theories appear to be thinking along the lines of the everyday conceptual metaphors. I am not claiming of course that the metaphors as used by the scientists are exactly the same as the ones we find in everyday language. An excellent example of an everyday metaphor that is transformed into a somewhat different but highly influential scientific one is Freud's modification of the most basic everyday metaphor for the emotions: EMOTIONS ARE FLUIDS IN A CONTAINER. As a matter of fact, the very fact that Freud modified this metaphor indicates very clearly that in the course of (probably unconsciously) creating his scientific view of emotions he was thinking along the lines of the folk theory and the everyday metaphor that constitutes it.

Why do scientists use the same metaphors (often in more elaborated forms) as do lay people? I suggest that this is because the metaphors that characterize emotions are based on conceptual metonymies that reflect real or assumed responses associated with the emotions and that the scientists, as members of the same culture as the laymen who use the metaphors, share and find natural those responses. In this sense, the scientists and the lay people inhabit the same world, a world where, to paraphrase Wittgenstein, the limits of my linguistically-defined emotional experiences are the limits of my emotional world. The metaphors are based on the metonymies and they make sense for that reason.

Notice that this account is somewhat different from the "standard" Lakoff-Johnson-Grady (Lakoff and Johnson 1999) account of metaphors, where it is the primary metaphors themselves that are embodied. In the view I presented here there must first be a metonymic stage in the development of metaphors (see Kövecses 2013). This is because the usual emotional responses are parts of the overall emotion frames to begin with. It is only through a metonymic stage that the various parts of the emotion frame, such as the responses, can generalize into concepts that can be conceived of as appropriate source domains for emotions. This might explain why scholars with a discourse orientation emphasize that in real discourse often it is difficult to tell whether a particular linguistic expression is used in a literal, metonymic or metaphoric sense.

Most importantly for my purposes here, the evidence for the shared use of conceptual metaphors by lay people and experts compellingly shows that conceptual metaphors are very clearly present and used in creative thought. For this reason, I cannot accept claims such as the following on the part of applied linguists: "For applied linguists and social scientists there is little acceptable evidence that conceptual metaphors are actually ways of thinking" (Deignan 2010: 56). Neither is there a need for applied linguists to "remain agnostic about the existence or whereabouts of conceptual metaphor" (Cameron 2010: 79). As the data surveyed in the paper seems to indicate, conceptual metaphors are real and exist in the conceptual system; otherwise we would have to regard the presence of many emotion metaphors in expert theories by scientists as utterly chance phenomena. And conceptual metaphors seem also to function in human thought, as when scientists use lay metaphors as expert ones – though often in modified forms. The elaborations and modifications reveal that real cognitive work (i.e., thinking) is performed when scientists propose theories of emotion as based on lay metaphors.

Regarding this issue, to my mind, the moral is this: Just because our concerns as metaphor scholars are different, we should not assume that our concerns are the only valid ones. It seems to me that there are many valid concerns about metaphor research, including the existence of conceptual metaphors and their use in thought, and that some of these are supported by evidence, as I tried to show in the paper.

5 Conclusion

What is the relationship between folk and expert theories of emotion? I showed in this paper that expert theories commonly display content and structure that appear to be shared with language-based folk theories of emotion. I suggested that this is only possible if the conceptual metaphors that constitute the folk theories also play some role in how the expert theories are constructed. It is in this sense that I claimed that in many cases expert theories of emotion are based on the same conceptual metaphors that constitute the corresponding folk theories.

Furthermore, I proposed that the conceptual metaphors that constitute the folk theories of emotion emerge from the metonymic conceptualization of the emotions. Conceptual metonymies serve as the cognitive foundations of many conceptual metaphors. Since the metonymies reflect common physiological, behavioral, and expressive responses associated with emotions, the metonymies will also make the conceptual metaphors look natural – both to lay people and experts.

Finally, I suggested that the phenomenon that folk and expert theories of emotion share certain conceptual metaphors indicates that the metaphors are actively (though not necessarily consciously) present in cognition. Their use in cognition is shown not only by experts commonly borrowing from and relying on conceptual metaphors produced by lay people (i.e., from everyday language), but also by the fact that experts very clearly manipulate, modify, and elaborate on existing conceptual metaphors. This cognitive work implies that metaphors are actively present in creative theory construction – a key aspect of human thought. This result goes against recent views in discourse-oriented work in linguistics and the social sciences that denies the existence and active role of conceptual metaphors in our conceptual system.

References

Cameron, Lynne. 2010. The discourse dynamics framework for metaphor. In Lynne Cameron & Robert Maslen (eds.), *Metaphor Analysis: Research Practice in Applied Linguistics, Social Sciences and the Humanities*, 77–96. London: Equinox.
Cameron, Lynne, & Robert Maslen (eds.). 2010. *Metaphor Analysis: Research Practice in Applied Linguistics, Social Sciences and the Humanities*. London: Equinox.
Darwin, Charles. 1872. *The expression of emotions in man and animals*. Chicago: The University of Chicago Press.
Davitz, Joel R. 1969. *The language of emotion*. New York: Academic Press.
Deignan, Alice. 2010. The cognitive view of metaphor: conceptual metaphor theory. In Lynne Cameron & Robert Maslen (eds.), *Metaphor Analysis: Research Practice in Applied Linguistics, Social Sciences and the Humanities*, 44–56. London: Equinox.
Fromm, Eric. 1956. *The art of loving*. New York: Harper and Row.
Hatfield, Elaine. 1988. Passionate and companionate love. In Robert J. Sternberg & Michael L. Barnes (eds.), *The psychology of love*. New Haven, CT: Yale University Press.
Holland, Dorothy, & Naomi Quinn (eds.). 1987. *Cultural models in language and thought*. New York: Cambridge University Press.
James, William. 1890. *The principles of psychology*. New York: Henry Holt.
Kövecses, Zoltán. 1986. *Metaphors of anger, pride, and love*. Amsterdam: John Benjamins.
Kövecses, Zoltán. 1988. *The language of love*. Lewisburg: Bucknell University Press.
Kövecses, Zoltán. 1990. *Emotion concepts*. New York: Springer-Verlag.
Kövecses, Zoltán. 2000. *Metaphor and emotion*. New York: Cambridge University Press.
Kövecses, Zoltán. 2013. The metaphor-metonymy relationship: correlation metaphors are based on metonymy. *Metaphor and Symbol* 28(2). 75–88.
Lakoff, George & Mark Johnson. 1980. *Metaphors we live by*. Chicago: The University of Chicago Press.
Lakoff, George & Mark Johnson. 1999. *Philosophy in the flesh*. New York: Basic Books.
Peele, Stanton. 1975. *Love and addiction*. New York: Taplinger.

Scherer, Klaus R. 2005. What are emotions? And how can they be measured? *Social Science Information* 44(4). 695–729.
Solomon, Robert. 1981. *Love: emotion, myth, and metaphor*. New York: Doubleday Anchor.
Sternberg, Robert J. 1986. A triangular theory of love. *Psychological Review* 93. 119–135.
Talmy, Leonard. 1988. Force dynamics in language and cognition. *Cognitive Science* 12. 49–100.

Tony Veale
Metaphor and Metamorphosis

1 Metamorphosis

As Gregor Samsa awoke one morning from uneasy dreams, he found himself transformed in his bed into a monstrous vermin. So starts Franz Kafka's novella of transformation, titled *Metamorphosis*, in which the author explores issues of otherness and guilt by exploiting a character's horrific (if unexplained) change into an insect.

Authors from Ovid to Kafka demonstrate the value of transformation – physical, spiritual and metaphorical – as a tool of character development, just as storytellers from Homer to Kubrick demonstrate the value of journeys as support-structures for narratives of becoming and change. Even narratives that are primarily plot-focused or action-centric can, many times, be succinctly summarized by listing key character transformations (Cook 1928, Yorke 2014). Consider *Gladiator*, an Oscar-winning film from 2000. The main villain of that piece, *Emperor Commodus*, summarizes the plot with three successive transformations: "The *general* who became a *slave*. The *slave* who became a *gladiator*. The *gladiator* who defied an *emperor*." Note how the third transformation is implicit, for the gladiator *Maximus* has transformed himself into a potential leader of Rome itself.

Kafka presents his driving transformation as a *fait accompli* in the very first line, while in Ovid's *Metamorphoses*, characters are transformed by gods into trees or animals with magical immediacy. Most narrative transformations occur gradually, however, with a story charting the course of a character's development from a start-state **S** to target-state **T**. In this respect the television drama *Breaking Bad* offers an exemplary model of the slow-burn transformation. We first meet the show's protagonist, Walter White, in his guise as a put-upon high-school chemistry teacher. "*Chemistry*", he tells us, "*is the study of change.*" Though Walter has a brilliant mind, he lives a dull suburban life of quiet desperation, until a diagnosis of lung cancer provides the catalyst to look anew at his life's choices. Walter decides to use his chemistry skills to "cook" and sell the drug *Crystal Meth*, and recruits former student Jessie as his drug-savvy partner. In 62 episodes, the show charts Walter's evolution from dedicated teacher into ruthless drug baron. As Vince Gilligan, the show's creator, put it, "*I wanted to turn my lead character from Mr. Chips into Scarface.*"

Tony Veale, University College Dublin

DOI 10.1515/9783110549928-003

Walter's progress – what Yorke (2015) calls a journey of *dark inversion* – is neither smooth nor monotonic. He becomes an unstable, dynamic blend of his start and end states. Though he commits unspeakable crimes, he never entirely ceases to be a caring parent, husband or teacher. As viewers we witness a true conceptual integration of his two worlds: Walter brings the qualities of a drug baron to his family relationships, just as he brings the qualities of a husband and father-figure to his illicit business dealings. To fully appreciate this nuanced character transformation, we must understand it as more than a monotonic journey between two states: characters must unfold as evolving blends of the states that they move between, and thus exhibit emergent qualities that arise from no single state.

This chapter presents a creative metaphor-generation system – *The Flux Capacitor* – that transmutes metaphorical tension into literal dramatic tension to turn metaphors into "what if" character arcs for use in narrative generation. Though it is a trivial matter to randomly generate narrative arcs between any two conceptual perspectives – say between *teacher* and *drug-baron*, or *terrorist* and *politician* – the *Flux Capacitor* uses metaphor to generate arcs that are well-formed, well-motivated, intuitive and of dramatic interest. It does so by using a rich knowledge-representation of our stereotypical perspectives on humans, knowing e.g. what qualities are exhibited by teachers or criminals. It uses corpus analysis both to acquire a stock of valid start- and end-states and to model the most natural direction of change. And it uses a robust computational model of conceptual blending (Fauconnier and Turner 1998, 2002) to understand the emergent qualities that may arise along the way.

The *Flux Capacitor* builds on a body of related work which will be discussed in the next section. The means by which novel transformative arcs are formulated is then presented, before a model of property-level blending and proposition-level analogy/disanalogy is also described. *The Flux Capacitor* does more than generate a list of possible character arcs: it provides to a third-party story generator a conceptual rationale for each transformation, so a story-teller may properly appreciate the ramifications of a given arc. In effect this rationale is a *pitch* for a story. Before drawing our final conclusions, we describe how such a pitch can be constructed from a blending analysis and packaged concisely as a social media *tweet*.

2 Related work and ideas

What is a hero without a quest? And what is a quest that does not transform its hero in profound ways? The scholar Joseph Campbell has argued that our most steadfast myths persist because they each instantiate, in their own way, a profoundly affecting narrative structure that Campbell calls the *monomyth*. Campbell (1973) sees the monomyth as a productive schema for the generation of heroic stories that, at their root, follow this core pattern either literally or figuratively: "*A hero ventures forth from the world of common day into a region of supernatural wonder: fabulous forces are encountered and a decisive victory is won: the hero comes back from this mysterious adventure with the power to bestow boons on his fellow man.*" Many ancient tales subconsciously instantiate this schema, whilst many modern stories – such as George Lucas's *Star Wars* – are consciously written so as to employ Campbell's monomyth schema as a narrative deep-structure. Indeed, the tremendous financial success of *Star Wars* prompted Hollywood film studios to adopt the Campbellian journey schema as a default structural model for many future films projects (Yorke 2014).

A comparable schematic analysis of the heroic quest is provided by Propp's *Morphology of the Folk Tale* (1968). Like Campbell, Propp identifies an inventory of recurring classes (of characters and events) that make up a traditional Russian folk tale, though Propp's analysis can be applied to many different kinds of heroic tale. Transformative elements in Propp's inventory include *Receipt of Magical Agent*, which newly empowers a hero, *Transfiguration*, in which a hero is rewarded through change, and *Wedding*, through which a hero's social status is elevated. Propp also anticipates that a truly transformed hero may not be recognized on returning home (*Unrecognized Arrival*) and may have to undergo a test of identity (*Recognition*). The basic morphemes of Propp's model can be used either to analyze or to generate stories, in the latter case by using a variant of Zwicky's *Morphological Analysis* (1969). Propp's morphemes have thus been used in the service of automated game design (Fairclough and Cunningham 2004) and automated story generation (Gervás 2013).

Campbell's monomyth and Propp's morphology can each be subsumed under a more abstract mental structure, the *Source-Path-Goal* (SPG) schema analyzed by Johnson (1987). Johnson argues that any purposeful action along a path – from going to the shops to undertaking a quest – activates an instance of the SPG schema in the mind. In cinema the SPG is most obviously activated by "road movies", in which (to quote the marketing campaign for *Dances With Wolves*), a hero goes "*in search of America and finds himself*". Such movies use the SPG to align the literal with the figurative, so that a hero starts from a state that is both geographic and psychological, and reaches an end-point that is similarly dual-natured. The SPG schema is also evident in comic-book tales in which an everyman is transformed into a superheroic form that permits some driving goal (revenge, justice) to be achieved. Forceville (2006) has additionally used the SPG to uncover the transformative-quest structure of less overtly heroic film genres, such as documentaries and autobiographical films.

Storytelling is a purposeful activity with a beginning (*Source*), middle (*Path*) and end (*Goal*) that typically shapes the events of a narrative into a purposeful activity on the part of one or more of its characters. Computer systems that generate stories – as described in e.g. Meehan (1981), Turner (1994), Perez y Perez and Sharples (2001), Riedl and Young (2004) and Gervás (2013) – are thus, implicitly, automated instantiators of the Source-Path-Goal schema. This is especially so of story systems, such as that of Riedl and Young, that employ an explicitly *plan-based* approach to generation. These authors use a planner that is anchored in a model of the beliefs and internal states of the story's characters, so as to construct narrative plans that call for believable, well-motivated actions from their actors. The use of a planner also ensures that these actions create the appearance of an intentional SPG path that is more likely to be viewed as plausible and coherent by the story's intended audience.

Outside the realm of myths and fairy-tales, the deepest transformations are to the beliefs and internal states of a character, though such profound changes may be reflected in outward appearances too, such as via a change of garb, residence, place of work, or choice of tools. Consider the case of a prostitute who becomes a nun, or the altogether rarer case of a nun who *breaks bad* in the other direction. Such transformations are dramatically interesting because they create oppositions at the levels of properties and of propositions. Though frame-level symmetries are present, since each kind of person follows a particular vocation in a particular place of work while wearing a particular kind of clothing, the specific frame-fillers are very different. We can imagine a tabloid headline screaming "*Nun burns habit, buys thong*" or "*Nun flees convent, joins bordello.*" Analogies and disanalogies between the start- and end-states of a transformation provide fodder for the evolving blends that need to be constructed to ferry a protagonist between these two states in a narrative.

Conceptual blending is a knowledge-hungry process *par excellence* (see Fauconnier and Turner 1998, 2002). However, Veale (2012a) presents a computational variant of conceptual blending, called the *conceptual mash-up*, that is robust and scalable. Propositional knowledge is milked from various Web sources – such as query completions from Web search engines – and, using corpus evidence, this knowledge is mapped to more than one concepts. Veale (2012b) also presents a robust method for mining stereotypical properties from Web similes, such as "*as chaste as a nun*" and "*as sleazy as a prostitute*". Used here, these representations allow the *Flux Capacitor* to analyze the blending potential of a transformative arc, and so construct a conceptual rationale as to why a given arc has the potential to underpin an interesting narrative.

3 Opposites attract

At its most reductive, a transformative character arc is an unlabeled directed edge $S\grave{a}T$ that takes a character from a conceptual starting-state **S** to a conceptual endpoint **T**, where **S** and **T** are different lexicalized perspectives on a character (such as e.g. **S**=*activist* and **T**=*terrorist*). To be a truly transformative arc, as opposed to an arbitrarily random pairing of **S** and **T** states, an arc should induce a dramatic change of qualities. Superficially, this change may be reflected in a reversal of affective polarity from **S** to **T**. Thus, if **S** is viewed as a positive state overall, such as *activist*, *saint* or *defender*, and **T** is predominantly seen as a negative state, such as *terrorist*, *prostitute* or *tyrant*, then a character will *break bad* by following this arc. Conversely, if **S** is most often seen as a negative state, and **T** is typically seen as a positive state, then a character will *come good* by following this arc. Naturally, our overall affective view of a concept will be a function of our property-level perception of all its stereotypical qualities. If **S** typically evokes a preponderance of positive qualities then it will be viewed as a positive state overall. Likewise, if **S** typically evokes a preponderance of negative qualities then it will be viewed as a negative state overall. A means of mapping from property-level representations to overall +/− affective polarity scores is presented in Veale (2011).

Stories thrive on conflict and surprise, and surprising transformations arise when the pairing of **S** and **T** gives rise to a clash of opposing properties. Consider again the case of the *prostitute* (=**S**) who becomes a *nun* (=**T**). The transformation **S→T** at the conceptual-level implies the property-level transformations *dirty↔pure, immoral↔moral, promiscuous↔chaste* and *sleazy↔respected*, affording an opportunity for a truly dramatic Proppian transfiguration. Generalizing, we say that a character arc **S→T** implies a direct opposition at the property-level if **S** and **T** each exhibit properties that can produce antonymous pairs. We thus use WordNet (Fellbaum 1998) as a comprehensive source of antonymy relationships (such as *pure↔dirty*), which we apply to any putative arc **S→T** to determine whether it involves a dramatic conflict of properties.

This property-level analysis allows *The Flux Capacitor* to identify nuanced transformations that allow a character to come good *while also* breaking bad. Consider the *rags to riches* arc *beggar→king*. A character following this arc may come good in many ways, by going from *lowly→lordly, poor→lofty, broke→wealthy, impoverished→privileged* and *ragged→regal*. Yet such an arc may induce negative effects too, changing a character from *humble→arrogant, humble→unapproachable* and *humble→arrogant*. Perhaps a beggar that becomes a king may come to rue his change of station, while a king that becomes a beggar may derive some small comfort from his fall from grace?

Yet **S** and **T** need not conflict directly at the property-level to yield an opposition-rich transformation. The clash of properties may be *indirect*, if **S** relates to a concept **S'** in the same way that **T** relates to **T'**, and if a clash of opposing properties can be observed between **S'** and **T'**. For instance, *scientists* and *priests* do not directly oppose one another, but a property-level clash can be found in the stereotypical representations of *science* and *religion*, since science is stereotypically rational while religion is often seen as irrational. Since scientists practice science while priests practice religion, a character that goes from being a scientist to being a priest will, in a leap of faith, reject *rational* science and embrace *irrational* religion instead.

A gifted storyteller can surely make a transformation, no matter how random or illogical, seem interesting. Such is the art of improvisational comedy, after all. However, rather than abdicate its responsibility for making an arc interesting to a subsequent story-telling component, the *Flux Capacitor* applies it own filtering criteria to find the arcs it considers to have dramatic potential. An arc **S→T** is generated only if **S** and **T** possess opposing qualities, or if **S** and **T** are indirectly opposed by virtue of being analogously related to a concept pair **S'** and **T'** that do. We now turn to how **S** and **T** are found in the first place.

4 Charging the Capacitor

We often speak of children in terms of what they may one day become, but speak of adults in terms of what they have *already* become. Some concepts are more naturally thought of as start-states in a transformation, while others are more naturally viewed as end-states. Beyond the clear cut cases, most concepts sit on a continuum of suitability for use on either side of a transformation. To determine the suitability of a given concept **C** as either a start state or an end state, we can simply look to a large text corpus. The frequency of the 2-gram "**C**+*s* become" in a corpus such as the Google n-grams (Brants and Franz 2006) will indicate how often **C** is viewed as a start-state, while the frequency of the 2-gram "become **C**+*s*" will indicate **C**'s suitability as an end-state. Since the n-gram frequency of "*become terrorists*" (7180) is almost 7 times greater than the frequency of "*terrorists become*" (1166), *terrorist* is far more suited to the role of end-point than to start-point.

The *Flux Capacitor* limits its choice of start-states to any stereotype **S** for which the Google n-grams contains the bigram "**S**+*s become*". Similarly, it limits its choice of end-states to any stereotype **T** for which Google provides the bigram "*become* **T**+*s*". Within these constraints, the Google n-grams suggests 1,213 person-concepts to use as start-states, and 1,529 to use as their ultimate end-states. In addition to these arc fragments, the Google n-grams also contains a small number (< 500) of well-established transformations between person-types that can be found via the pattern "**S**-*turned*-**T**". Examples include *friend*-turned-*foe*, *bodybuilder*-turned-*actor* and *actor*-turned-*politician*. Though some turns have dramatic value (like *bully*-turned-*Buddhist*), most are well-trodden paths with little to offer a creative system. Nonetheless, the Google n-grams are a valuable source of inspiration for the generation of novel transformations that combine complementary ideas. For the n-grams can tell us whether two ideas have a history of working well together, either in harmony or as part of an antagonistic double-act.

Consider the 3-gram pattern "**X**+s *and* **Y**+s", which matches all instances of coordinated bare plurals in the Google n-grams. Examples include "*angels and demons*", "*nuns and prostitutes*" and "*scientists and priests*". While these attested coordinations often bring together opposing concepts, they are concepts drawn from the same domains or semantic fields, and thus seem *fitted* to each other. So while a transformation linking two such conflicting states may strike one as a surprising turn of events, it will also likely strike one as a *fitting* turn of events. By mining the Google 3-grams for instances of this pattern that connect a valid start-state to a valid end-state, where these states also exhibit either a direct or indirect conflict of qualities, the *Flux Capacitor* harvests a large collection of potential state-pairs for its own transformative character arcs. The question of which state can best serve as a start-state, and which should serve as the end-state, is decided afterwards.

Coordination constructions offer us a rich source of explicit contrasts between conceptual states, but other n-grams are an even richer source of *implicit* contrasts. Consider the 3-gram "army of dreamers". The typical member of an army is a *soldier*, not a *dreamer*, as borne out by the system's own propositional world-knowledge. This 3-gram thus implies a clash of soldiers and dreamers, which in turn implies the property-level conflicts *disciplined*↔*undisciplined* and *fit*↔*lethargic*. Generalizing, we mine all Google 3-grams that match the construction pattern "<**group**> *of* <**person**>+s", such as "*church of heretics*", "*army of cowards*" and "*religion of sinners*", to identify any cases where the stated member (*sinner*, *coward*, etc.) contrasts with a known stereotypical member of the group. A large pool of contrasting concept pairs is mined in this way from the Google n-grams, to be used to form each side of a transformative character arc.

But what trajectory should each transformation follow? Which concept will serve as the start-point **S** of an arc, and which as its end-point **T**? We infer the most natural direction for an arc by again looking to corpus data. For a pair of contrasting concepts **X** and **Y**, we calculate a score for the arc **X**→**Y** as the sum of the n-gram frequencies for "**X**+*s become*" and "*become* **Y**+*s*". Likewise, we calculate the score for the arc **Y**→**X** as the sum of the n-gram frequencies for "**Y**+*s become*" and "*become* **X**+*s*". We then choose the arc/direction with the greatest score. Consider, for example, the pair *militant* and *politician*, which share, in the world-view of the *Flux Capacitor*, this implicit contrast: militants launch *celebrated* rebellions, whilst politicians launch *hated* wars. Corpus data suggests that *politician* is more suited to be the end-state of an arc than its start-state, perhaps because politicians must be elected, and election is an obvious goal-state in the SPG schema. In contrast, *militant* is slightly more comfortable in the role of start-state than end-state, no doubt because militants fight so as to initiate some future change. Thus, the arc *militant*→*politician* is favored over its inverse, *politician*→*militant*, and so only the former is generated.

5 Blended states

In character-led stories, key transformations often unfold gradually through a build-up of incremental changes. So as characters follow their trajectory along an arc that takes them ever closer to their final state, they will exhibit more of the qualities we stereotypically associate with the endpoint of their arc and fewer of the properties we associate with their starting point. In effect, a changing character becomes a dynamic *blend* of the starting-point and end-point concepts that define its narrative trajectory.

The theory of conceptual integration networks, also known as *conceptual blending* (see Fauconnier and Turner 1998, 2002), offers a principle-driven framework for the interpretation of any blend, while Veale (1997) further explores the workings of character blends that gradually unfold during a narrative. A character blend – a character that moves between two states and thus assumes a mix of the properties and behaviors associated with each – can be modeled computationally at the level of properties and of propositions. To model the former, we explore the space of complex properties that integrate nuances from each of the inputs, while to model the latter we draw on Markman and Gentner's (1993) theory of *alignable differences*.

Consider a proposition-level blend in the shocking case of our *nun-turned-prostitute*. The alignable differences in this example concern the propositions associated with nuns and with prostitutes that can be aligned by virtue of positing exactly the same relationship for each subject, but with different values for their objects. For instance, nuns work and reside in convents or cloisters, under the supervision of a mother superior, while prostitutes work and reside in bordellos under the supervision of madams and pimps. So as this transformation is effected, convents and cloisters will give way to bordellos, while mother superiors will lose out to pimps and madams, just as wimples and habits will transition into an altogether racier style of dress. It is a simple matter to connect propositions with alignable differences such as these, to produce a structural blend that is part analogy and part disanalogy

The *Flux Capacitor* is also sensitive to the reversals of status and power that accompany a given transformation. By attending to the relationships that link a subject A to an object B, and the relationships that reciprocally link B as a subject to A as an object, it learns how to recognize situations where a protagonist's social inter-relationships are dramatically reversed in a blend. Thus, for instance, it observes a fundamental tension between the verbs *obey* and *control*, between *ruling* and *following*, and between *governing* and *electing*. In the case of a *king-turned-slave* then, it perceives an interesting reversal of power, where a once-mighty king goes from being served by respectful followers to being led by haughty and arrogant rulers, just as he may go from appointing fawning servants to being managed by dominant and exalted masters. The scale of each reversal is emphasized by highlighting the most pointed contrasts between the blended states; thus, it also suggests that our deposed king goes from being served by *honorable* knights to being led by *depraved* rulers. While these new rulers need not be depraved, it heightens the drama of the blend to assume that they are.

At the property-level, we strive to understand how a property *A* associated with a start-state **S**, and a property *B* associated with an end-state **T**, might yield an emergent property *AB* that arises from a character's transformation from **S** into **T**. Might our *nun-turned-prostitute* retain a residual sense of *piety*, even if such piety were to be unjustified or even immoral? The Google 2-grams inform us that the phrase "*immoral piety*" denotes an attested state (with a Web frequency of at least 49). Since nuns are typically pious and so practice piety, while prostitutes are typically seen as immoral, *immoral piety* denotes the kind of nuanced state that may arise as one state gives way to the other. The Google n-grams also suggest, in this vein, that a nun-turned-prostitute might be a *moral prostitute*, a *compassionate prostitute*, a *religious prostitute* or, at least, a *spiritual prostitute*, one that commits *pure* or *virtuous sins* despite practicing a *sleazy morality* and a *dirty faith*. Likewise, when intellectuals become zealots, attested 2-grams that bridge both states include "*inspired rant*", "*misguided superiority*", "*uncompromising critique*", "*extreme logic*", "*intellectual obsession*", "*scholarly zeal*" and even "*educated stupidity*".

The Google n-grams attest to the validity of a great many complex states that can be surprising and revealing. By seeking out nuanced states that bridge the properties of the conflicting concepts in a character arc, the *Flux Capacitor* can tap in to the vast, collective imagination of readers and writers as exercised for other, past narratives.

6 Form and content

These blend interpretations serve to advertize the merits of a given transformation: the richer the blend, in terms of aligned propositions and nuanced properties, the richer the narrative it should yield when turned over to a dedicated story-generator. In many ways, these blend interpretations are merely the computational version of a Hollywood story *pitch*, in which a screenwriter *sells* his or her vision of a story to the studio that will make it. Like a commercial studio, which can only afford to make a small number of films per year, a story-generator will need some narratological basis to judge which of numerous plot possibilities to further refine and which to reject outright. So to better *sell* its ideas, the *Flux Capacitor* packages its blend analyses as story pitches. Consider the following pitch, in which each mapping in the blend for *nun→prostitute* is rendered in its own sentence:

> *Nun condemns chastity, wallows in wickedness*
> *Nun criticizes convents, bounces into brothels*
> *Nun chucks crucifixes, gropes for garters*
> *Nun fatigued by fidelity, veers toward vices*
> *Nun hates habits, stockpiles stilettos*
> *Nun mistreated by mother superiors, pulled to pimps*
> *Nun skips out of spectacles, loves latex*
> *Nun vents about veils, crazy for corsets*
> *Nun vents about virginity, seduced by shamelessness*
> *Nun whines about wimples, grabs garters*
> *Nun goes from being managed by abbesses to being controlled by pimps*
> *Nun goes from carrying beads to carrying infections*
> *Nun goes from living in cloisters to working in bawdy houses*
> *Nun goes from practicing chastity to practicing vices*
> *Nun goes from wearing habits and crucifixes to corsets and fishnets*
> *Nun goes from wearing veils and spectacles to latex and stilettos*
> *Nun goes from wearing wimples to wearing hot pants*

Where possible, a tabloid-style headline is employed, using alliteration – as in <u>c</u>ondemns <u>c</u>hastity, <u>w</u>allows in <u>w</u>ickedness – to make each step of a transformation more compelling. Such devices, though simple, embody a strategy that psychologists call the *Keats heuristic*, for the use of even rudimentary rhymes has been empirically shown to heighten the perceived truthfulness of a statement (see McGlone and Tofighbakhsh 2000).

7 Rendering and delivery

Twitter is the ideal midwife for pushing the products of true computational creativity – such as metaphors, jokes, aphorisms and story pitches – into the world. A new *twitterbot* named *MetaphorIsMyBusiness* (handle: *@MetaphorMagnet*) thus employs the *Flux Capacitor* to generate a novel, well-formed, creative metaphor or story pitch every hour or so. As such, *@MetaphorMagnet*'s outputs are the product of a complex reasoning process that combines a large knowledge-base of stereotypical norms with real usage data from the Google n-grams. Though encouraged by the quality of the bot's outputs, we continue to expand its expressive range, to give the twitterbot its own unique voice and identifiable aesthetic. Outputs such as "*What is an accountant but a timid visionary? What is a visionary but a bold accountant?*" show how *@MetaphorMagnet* frames the conceits of the *Flux Capacitor* as though-provoking metaphors, to lend the bot a distinctly hard-boiled persona.

A story-generation system may use a Proppian or Campbellian analysis to impose a dramatic narrative structure on a transformative character arc. For a transformed character effectively undertakes a journey, whether or not this journey takes place entirely within one's mind or social circumstances. By better understanding how the arrow of causality may impose a narrative ordering on the property-changes in a story, a system can better impose the morphology of a folktale or a monomyth on any generated character arc. Consider the following journey into irrationality, as rendered in a 5-act mini-narrative by *@MetaphorMagnet* in 140 characters:

> #Knight=#Madman
> 1. *Go on a crusade*
> 2. *Become a knight*
> 3. *Launch irrational crusades*
> 4. *Become an irrational knight*
> 5. *Get called a "madman"*

The core transformation, of a respected knight into a pitiable madman, is rendered as a Campbellian journey from laudable passion to irrational zeal. The final act – 5. *Get called a "madman"* – renders the metaphor as a pejorative speech act that lends the mini-narrative a tragic form. Metaphor provides an invaluable service to otherwise literal story-telling by allowing a writer to imagine the figurative labels that readers will apply to characters that pursue certain story actions (such as starting an irrational crusade). In this instance, it is the Google 2-grams that attests to the meaningfulness of an "irrational crusade" and thereby provides the pivotal action in the tale.

The following mini-narrative, rendered as two successive 140-character tweets by @*MetaphorMagnet*, uses animal metaphors to impose a moral structure on the underlying *Flux Capacitor* transformation.

> "*I want to be a hipster,*" *squeaked a hip ant.*
> "*I want to reject the status quo too,*" *huffed a panda.*
> #Hipster=#Layabout
>
> *So the panda helped the hip ant to embrace listless fashions.*
> *And that is how the hip ant became a layabout.*
> #Hipster=#Layabout

As indicated by the hashtags appended to each tweet – which serve to link them both into a narrative whole in the mind of a reader – the above mini-story pivots around the transformation of a passionate hipster into a listless layabout. This Aesop-style rendering requires @*MetaphorMagnet* to recruit a pair of complementary animal metaphors to package this arc as a morality tale that is at once fantastical but plausible. Corpus analysis (of Google's Web 2-grams) offers up the phrase "hip ant" to suggest an animal counterpart to a hip human hipster, while pandas, which are stereotypically lazy and listless, serve as an appropriate antagonist for our protagonist. The linguistic rendering is completed by using apt verbs for the reported speech of each character (so e.g. tiny ants "squeak" while hefty pandas "huff" their words). In effect, the system uses its diverse sources of stereotypical knowledge to meaningfully package a striking opposition within layers of apt metaphor. @*MetaphorMagnet* is a sophisticated system that combines multiple sources of normative knowledge of the world with a diversity of linguistic rendering capabilities: each adds an extra dimension to the search space in which the system must navigate to find a meaningful, well-crafted linguistic form. Readers who are interested in learning more of the inner workings of this complex system are directed to Veale (2013, 2015).

8 Evaluating aptness and rendering quality

Some arcs simply demand too much from an audience. Novel arcs may be provocative, but they should rarely be jarring. Arcs that strain credulity, or require an element of cod science to work at all, are best avoided. While it is not possible to predict every fault line along which a narrative may rupture, it is worth considering the most obvious problem-cases here, as these allow us to draw broad generalizations about the quality of our arcs.

The first problem-case concerns gender. Though there exist famous *and* dramatically successful exceptions to this rule, such as Virginia Wolff's *Orlando*, characters rarely change their gender during a transformation. Of the valid start/end states used by the *Flux Capacitor*, 84 are manually annotated as *male*, such as *pope* and *hunk*, while 72 are annotated as *female*, such as *geisha* and *nun*. All other states are assumed to be compatible with both male and female characters. In all, 9,915 of the 63,016 arcs that are generated involve one or more gender-marked states. Of these, only 7% involve a problematic mix of genders (e.g. *pope→mother*). Though a creative story-teller might make lemonade from these lemons (e.g. as in the apocryphal tale of Pope Joan, who passed as a man until made pregnant), the *Flux Capacitor* prefers to filter out these arcs.

The second problem-case concerns age. Once again, though Hollywood may occasionally find a cod-science reason to reverse time's arrow, characters rarely transform into people younger than themselves. Not wishing to paint a story-teller into a corner, where it must appeal to a dust-blown plot device such as time travel, body swapping or family curses to get out, the *Flux Capacitor* aims to avoid generating such arcs altogether. So of its valid start/end states, 52 are manually tagged for age to reflect our strong stereotypical expectations. Elders such as *grandmother*, *pensioner* and *archbishop* are assigned a time point of 60 years, while youths such as *student*, *rookie* and *newcomer* are given a time point of 18. Younger states, such as *baby*, *toddler*, *child*, *kid*, *preteen* and *schoolgirl*, are assigned lower time-points still, while those states unmarked for age are all assumed to have a default time point of 30. In all, 7,892 arcs are generated for which one or more states is explicitly marked for age. Now, if our corpus-based approach to determining the trajectory of an arc is valid, we should expect most of these 7,892 arcs to flow in the expected *younger→older* direction. In fact, 76% of arcs do flow in the right direction. The remaining 24% are not simply discarded however. Rather, these arcs are inverted, turning e.g. *mentor→student* into *student→mentor*. The diversity of the *Flux Capacitor*'s outputs – 63,016 well-formed arcs, pairing 1,213 start-states to 1,529 end-states in ways that suggest both conflict *and* corpus-attested affinities – is a reason to be optimistic about the quality of the stories that may be rendered around these arcs.

A notable benefit of implementing any system for generating metaphors or stories (or stories based on metaphors) as a Twitterbot is that all of the system's outputs – all its hits *and* all its misses – are available for anyone to scrutinize on Twitter. Nonetheless, it is worth quantifying the degree to which typical users find a system's outputs to be meaningful, novel and worth sharing with others. We thus sampled 60 of @*MetaphorMagnet*'s figurative tweets (each of which renders a transformative arc from *The Flux Capacitor* in a pithy linguistic form) and gave these to paid volunteers on *CrowdFlower.com* to rate along the dimensions of *comprehensibility*, *novelty* and *retweetability*. Judges were paid a small fee per judgment but were not informed of the mechanical origin of any tweet; rather, they were simply told that each was taken from Twitter for its figurative content.

We solicited 10 ratings per tweet, though this number of ratings was eventually reduced once the likely scammers – unengaged judges that offer random or unvarying answers or which fail the simple tests interspersed throughout the evaluation – were filtered from the raw results set. For each dimension, judges offered a rating for a given tweet on the following scale: 1=*very low*; 2=*medium low*; 3=*medium high*; 4=*very high*. The aggregate rating for each dimension of each tweet is then calculated as the mean rating from all judges for that dimension of that tweet.

For the dimension of *comprehensibility*, over half (51.5%) of tweets are deemed to have *very-high* aggregate comprehensibility, while 23.7% are deemed to have *medium-high* comprehensibility. Only 11.6% of the system's tweets are judged to have *very low* comprehensibility, and just 13.2% have *medium low* comprehensibility. For the dimension of *novelty*, almost half of @*MetaphorMagnet*'s tweets (49.8%) are judged to exhibit *very high* aggregate novelty, while only 11.9% are judged to exhibit *very low* novelty. For the dimension of *retweetability*, for which judges were asked to speculate about the desirability of sharing a given tweet with one's followers on Twitter, 15.3% of tweets are deemed to have *very high* retweet value on aggregate, while 15.5% are deemed to have *very low* retweet value. Most tweets fall into the two intermediate categories: 49.9% are deemed to have *medium low* retweet value, while 27.4% are deemed to have *medium high* retweet value. Though based on speculative evaluation rather than actual retweet rates, these numbers accord with our own informal experience of the bot on Twitter, as thus far its own designers have favorited approx. 27% of the bot's ~10000 tweets to date. It should also be noted that a 15.3% retweet rate would be considered rather ambitious for most Twitter users, and is thus perhaps an overstatement in the case of @*MetaphorMagnet* too. We thus see this as a speculative but nonetheless encouraging result.

In a second experiment, we make raters work harder, to reconstruct a partial tweet by adding the missing information that would make it whole and apt again. That is, we employ a *cloze* test format for this experiment, by removing from each tweet the pair of key qualities that highlight the start and end properties of a transformative character arc. For example, we blank out the properties *undefeated* and *defeated* from the following tweet:

> *To be rejected by and excluded from a community: This can turn* **undefeated** *winners into* **defeated** *outcasts.*
> #Winner=#Outcast

We also choose 4 distractor pairs for each extracted property pair, by selecting pairs from other tweets from *@MetaphorMagnet*. As in our first experiment, we chose 60 tweets at random from the past outputs of the bot, and solicited 10 ratings for each. Annotators were presented with a partial tweet as above, and given the five randomly ordered pairs of possible fillers (the original pair, and four distractor pairs) to choose from. To make the results of this experiment comparable to those of our earlier experiment, we aggregate the human judgments, so that e.g. if 7 out of 10 raters correctly choose the original pairing, then that tweet is deemed to have an aptness of 0.7. We then place these scores into bands, where the *very low* band corresponds to an aggregate score of 0 to 0.25, *medium low* = 0.26 to 0.5, *medium high* = 0.51 to 0.75, and *very high* = 0.76 to 1. In this way, we can estimate e.g. the percentage of tweets from *@MetaphorMagnet* that will be put into the *very high* aptness band. In this test, 58 % of the sampled tweets were rated as having *medium high* aptness, while 20 % were rated as *very high*, 22 % were rated as having *medium low* aptness, and none at all were rated as *very low*. These results suggest that the plots suggested by *The Flux Capacitor* are plausible without being either obvious or deterministic.

9 Exercises in style

Georges Braque, who co-developed *Cubism* with Pablo Picasso, was less than impressed with the arc of Picasso's career, noting late in life that "*Pablo used to be a good painter, but now he's just a genius.*" If character arcs induce change, such changes are just as likely to remove a desirable quality as add it. For Braque, to go from genuine painter to certified genius was to follow a downward arc, for Picasso was now to be feted more for his politics, his lifestyle and his women than for any of his painterly gifts. Braque's view of Picasso's career is witty because it runs against expectation: to become a genius is often seen as the highest of achievements and not a vulgar booby prize. So as we strive to make the *Flux Capacitor* generate arcs that seem interesting yet plausible, we must remember that it is not just a transformation *per se* that can be original, but the manner in which we choose to interpret it, not to mention the way we ultimately choose to render it in a story.

In his remarkable book *Exercises in Style*, modernist writer Raymond Queneau (1981) showed that the most mundane conflict – for instance, a question of etiquette on a crowded bus – can be transformed by style into a myriad of narrative possibilities. Queneau demonstrates the application of 99 style devices in his book, calling upon overt metaphor, lexical invention, subjectivity, reportage, telegram-syntax (the telegram being the tweet of Queneau's day) and many other linguistic strategies to draw out the diverse potentialities of the same banal event. Queneau's linguistic dexterity and stylistic virtuosity offers an aspirational model for generative systems such as *@MetaphorMagnet*: the received wisdom and normative generalizations that make up the vast bulk of a computer system's knowledge of the world is scarcely more interesting than the trite argument on a bus that forms the central conceit of Queneau's exercises in style. Yet the oppositions deriving from this knowledge, via the figurative mechanisms of the *Flux Capacitor*, can be rendered in a rich diversity of pithy forms that grow very different narratives from the same narrative seed. This, after all, is the real power of metaphor: to entice the imagination, to create sparks from the collision of superficially ill-matched ideas, and to lure us toward a satisfying resolution.

References

Brants, Thorsten & Alex Franz. 2006. Web 1T 5-gram Version 1. *Linguistic Data Consortium*.
Campbell, Joseph. 1973. *The hero with a thousand faces*. Princeton: Princeton University Press.
Cook, William Wallace. 1928. *PLOTTO: The master book of all plots*. Battle Creek, MI: Ellis Publishing Company.
Fairclough, Chris & Pádraig Cunningham. 2004. AI structuralist storytelling in computer games. In *Proceedings of the International conference on computer games: Artificial Intelligence, design and education*.
Fauconnier, Gilles & Mark Turner. 1998. Conceptual integration networks. *Cognitive Science*, 22(2). 133–187.
Fauconnier, Gilles & Mark Turner. 2002. *The way we think. Conceptual blending and the mind's hidden complexities*. New York: Basic Books.
Fellbaum, Christiane (ed.). 2008. *WordNet: An electronic lexical database*. Cambridge, MA: MIT Press.

Forceville, Charles. 2006. The source-path-goal schema in the autobiographical journey documentary: McElwee, Van der Keuken, Cole. *The New Review of Film and Television Studies* 4(3). 241–261.

Gervás, Pablo. 2013. Propp's morphology of the folk tale as a grammar for generation. In *Proceedings of the 2013 Workshop on Computational Models of Narrative*. Dagstuhl, Germany.

Johnson, Mark. 1987. *The body in the mind: The bodily basis of meaning, imagination, and reason*. Chicago: University of Chicago Press.

Markman, Arthur & Derdre Gentner. 1993. Splitting the differences: A structural alignment view of similarity. *Journal of Memory and Language* 32(4). 517–535.

McGlone, Matthew & Jessica Tofighbakhsh. 2000. Birds of a feather flock conjointly (?): rhyme as reason in aphorisms. *Psychological Science* 11(5). 424–428.

Meehan, James. 1981. *TALE-SPIN*. In Roger Schank and Christopher K. Riesbeck (eds.). *Inside computer understanding: Five programs plus miniatures*. Hillsdale, NJ: Lawrence Erlbaum.

Pérez y Pérez, Rafael & Mike Sharples. 2001. MEXICA: A computer model of a cognitive account of creative writing. *The Journal of Experimental and Theoretical Artificial Intelligence*, 13. 119–139.

Propp, Vladimir. 1968. *Morphology of the folk tale*, 2nd edn. Austin: University of Texas Press.

Queneau, Raymond. 1981. *Exercises in style*, 2nd edn. (translated by Barbara Wright). New York: New Direction Books.

Riedl, Mark & Michael Young. 2004. An intent-driven planner for multi-agent story generation. In *Proceedings of the 3rd international joint conference on Autonomous agents and multi-agent systems*. 186–193.

Turner, Scott R. 1994. *The creative process: A computer model of storytelling*, Hillsdale, NJ: Lawrence Erlbaum.

Veale, Tony. 1997. Creativity as pastiche: A computational treatment of metaphoric blends, with special reference to cinematic "borrowing". In *Proc. of Mind II: Computational models of creative cognition*. Dublin, Ireland.

Veale, Tony. 2011. The Agile cliché: using flexible stereotypes as building blocks in the construction of an affective lexicon. In: Alessandro Oltramari, Piek Vossen, Lu Qin, & Edward Hovy (eds.). *New trends of research in ontologies and lexical resources. Springer: Theory and applications of Nat. Lang. Processing*. Heidelberg: Springer.

Veale, Tony. 2012a. From Conceptual mash-ups to "Bad-Ass" blends: A robust computational model of conceptual blending. *In Proceedings of ICCC 2012, the 3rd International Conference on Computational Creativity*. Dublin, Ireland.

Veale, Tony. 2012b. *Exploding the creativity myth: The computational foundations of linguistic creativity*. London: Bloomsbury.

Veale, Tony. 2013. Less rhyme, more reason: Knowledge-based poetry generation with feeling, insight and wit. In *Proceedings of ICCC-2013, the 4th International Conference on Computational Creativity*. Sydney, Australia.

Veale, Tony. 2015. Game of tropes: Exploring the placebo effect in computational creativity. In *Proceedings of ICCC-2015, the 6th International Conference on Computational Creativity*. Park City, Utah.

Yorke, John. 2014. *Into the woods: How stories work and why we tell them*. London: Penguin Books.

Zwicky, Fritz. 1969. *Discovery, invention, research: Through the morphological approach*. Toronto: Macmillan.

Amitash Ojha, Bipin Indurkhya and Minho Lee
Is language necessary to interpret visual metaphors?

1 Introduction

Metaphor is defined as the experience of one thing in terms of another thing. Since Richards (1936) argued, "Thought is metaphoric and proceeds by comparison and the metaphors of language derive therefrom", there have been several approaches to consider metaphor as a conceptual phenomenon (Ortony 1979; Lakoff and Johnson 1980). Recent theories of metaphor suggest that metaphor comprehension requires allocation of various cognitive processes and interaction among different modalities. Several studies have argued (Gibbs and Bogdanovich 1999; Walsh 1990; Neisser 1976) that interpretation of some verbal metaphors require mental images that can produce perception-like experiences.

While presenting contemporary theory of metaphors, Lakoff (1993) discussed a class of metaphors that work by mapping one conventional mental image onto another. He called them *image metaphors*. Similarly, Indurkhya (2007) made a distinction between analytic and synthetic metaphors whereby a class of metaphors namely synthetic metaphors evoke vivid mental images. According to him, certain metaphors cannot be interpreted just by analyzing the meaning constituents of the components of the metaphor, but they require synthesizing subjective mental images evoked by the words and phrases occurring in the metaphor. Neisser (1976) suggested that words are embedded in the perceptual schema associated with the (perceptual) experiences [imagery] that share certain implicit characteristics of the direct perception of the corresponding physical environment. In this framework, he argued that imagery plays a significant role in verbal metaphor comprehension. Similarly, Walsh (1990) conducted behavioral experiments to find that noun-noun metaphors are easier to understand, and are considered more apt, when they evoke some appropriate imagery in the readers' mind. Studies related to gestures and metaphors claim that language is an integration of speech and gesture at the level of the system and of use and a dynamic product of modality specific forms of thought. Thus language and verbal

---

Amitash Ojha, University of Cagliari
Bipin Indurkhya, Jagiellonian University
Minho Lee, Kyungpook National University

DOI 10.1515/9783110549928-004

metaphor is shaped by cognitive processes, such as the flow of attention and foregrounding of information (Muller 2009).

In recent years, brain-imaging studies have further confirmed that brain areas associated with perception, imagery and motor planning are activated during verbal metaphor comprehension. For example, metaphor comprehension studies using visuo-verbal tasks on brain-damaged patients have shown that right-hemisphere-damaged (RHD) subjects tend to choose literal images over metaphorical images compared to normal subjects. RHD subjects' poor performance in the metaphor task is explained as a result of their insensitivity to context, due to visuo-spatial and visuo-perceptual problems, which is well known in RHD patients (Winner and Gardner 1977), and also because of their inability to integrate different representational (visual and verbal) codes (Rinaldi et al. 2004). A significant role of the right hemisphere in perception and integration of various modalities has been established in normal subjects under various experimental conditions (Anaki, Faust, and Kravetz 1998; Faust and Mashal 2007; Arzouan, Goldstein, and Faust 2007; Rapp et al. 2004; Ahrens et. al. 2007; Shibata et. al. 2007). Motivated by these results, some models have proposed that an imagistic or imagery-producing module is needed while comprehending at least some verbal metaphors, if not all (Carston 2010; Indurkhya 2007, 2016). These studies together support the idea that the understanding process of verbal metaphor is mediated by an interaction among different modalities, and, apart from lexical processing, it requires involvement of various other perceptual processes.

If some verbal metaphors evoke mental images for their interpretation, it is interesting to explore the case of visual metaphors. Visual metaphors are visual manifestations of cognitive metaphors (Lakoff and Johnson 1980), where concepts are represented in images (Kennedy 1982; Forceville 1996; Carroll 1994) (see Figure 1b). An intriguing issue is whether visual metaphors evoke verbal and language areas in order to be interpreted. This is the focus of the fMRI study presented here. If metaphors are primarily perceptual, then we expect that there will be little or no activation of language areas for visual metaphors. On the other hand, if we find significant activation in language areas, it will suggest that metaphors are primarily multimodal: information from all different modalities are recruited to make sense of the incongruity posed by a metaphor in order to render it meaningful.

In behavioral experiments on visual metaphors, it is difficult to completely block the role of language because even though the stimulus maybe purely visual, the response required is usually verbal, especially when an interpretation and a list of features are elicited (Indurkhya and Ojha 2013; Van Weelden et al. 2012). However, in an fMRI study, we can image their active brain areas during visual metaphor comprehension without requiring any verbal responses.

We also aim to compare the brain-activation patterns for verbal and visual metaphors with respect to the Left-Hemisphere (LH) and the Right-Hemisphere (RH) dichotomy, and the current debate on the dominating role of the RH in verbal metaphors. It has been hypothesized that the LH is dominant in processing alphabetic languages (Beaumont 1982; Binder et al. 1996; Desmond et al. 1995; Howard et al. 1992), and the RH is specialized for holistic, imagistic and spatial processing (Bryden 1982; Ellis, Young, and Anderson 1988; Jonides et al. 1993; McCarthy et al. 1994). Given that text and images are different modalities, one corresponding to the LH and the other to the RH, it would be instructive to see if metaphors in each of these modalities respect this hemispheric specialization.

2 Objectives and experiment design

The primary objective of this pilot fMRI study is two fold: First, to determine if the conventional language areas are activated during the visual metaphor comprehension task, and, second, to explore the differences and similarities in the brain activation patterns during the verbal and visual metaphor comprehension tasks. In the present study, participants were shown four different kinds of stimuli: (1) Literal sentences, (2) metaphorical sentences, (3) literal images and (4) metaphorical images. In previous studies, different tasks (plausibility judgment, aptness rating, word-relatedness judgment and so on) and kinds of stimuli (conventional and novel metaphor with their familiarity) have produced different results (Kacinik and Chiarello 2007). For instance, novel metaphor such as "the investors were squirrels collecting nuts" and familiar "broken heart" can produce different results in brain activation (Bottini et al. 1994). Similarly, decision of metaphor vs literal meaning such as "Deep: wise vs. lake) can also produce different results (Van Lancker and Kempler 1987). Therefore, we wanted to adopt a methodology that would reduce the effect of task complexity and metaphor kind. To reduce the task complexity, we asked the participants to decide if the given stimulus is literal or metaphorical (Anaki, Faust, and Kravetz 1998; Mashal, Faust, and Handler 2005). This decision task is not as complex as high-level judgment tasks such as deciding meaningfulness (Schmidt, DeBuse and Seger 2007) or plausibility judgment (Bottini et al. 1994). To avoid the familiarity issue (Schmidt and Seger 2009), we used novel metaphors (both visual and verbal). Moreover, all verbal metaphors used were based on semantic incongruity and not syntactic incongruity (for example, semantic: "the young man drank the guitar" vs. syntactic: "the young man slept the guitar") as this factor can also produce differences in the brain activation pattern (Kuperberg et al. 2000).

We acquired brain-imaging data while participants performed the task in all the four conditions, and contrasted them with the baseline rest state for each participant to get significant neural activation pattern for each condition, and used this direct comparison to look into the differences in the activation patterns. In the experiment, if a participant was not sure about a stimulus, she or he was allowed to skip it and move on to the next one. We analyzed only those responses that matched with our previous categorization (literal or metaphor) of the stimuli, which was independently provided by a group of different participants.

2.1 Participants

Seven postgraduate students (Four males and three females; mean age 25.6 years, range 25–27) participated in this pilot study. All participants were fluent in English and all participants were right-handed as assessed by the Edinburgh Handedness survey (Oldfield 1971). The experiment was conducted under a protocol approved by the Ethics committee of the International Institute of Information Technology, Hyderabad. All participants gave their written informed consent before attending the experiment. Participants were paid for their participation.

2.2 Stimulus material

The stimuli were presented in four conditions: (1) Literal verbal, (2) Metaphor verbal, (3) Literal visual and (4) Metaphor visual. We used sixteen copula sentences (A is B) and sixteen images as stimulus material. The material consisted of eight literal sentences (e.g., "A dolphin is an animal."), eight verbal metaphors (e.g., "Education is stairs."), eight literal images (Figure 1 (a)) and eight visual metaphors (Figure 1 (b)). The verbal sentences in 'A is B' format were without any contextual information. The experimental material was selected as follows: We took twenty metaphorical sentences and twenty literal sentences from the work of Shibataa et al., (2007), and asked seven participants to rate the comprehensibility of these sentences on a 1–7 scale. Eight highly-rated metaphorical sentences (mean comprehensibility: 5.7, SD=1.65) and eight literal sentences (Mean comprehensibility: 6.5, SD=1.12) were selected as the experimental stimuli. For visual material, forty images from print advertisements genre (twenty literal images and twenty metaphorical images) were chosen, and the same seven participants were asked to decide if the image was metaphorical or not. Based on the inter-rater agreement score (Kappa=0.85 with $p < 0.001$), eight literal images and eight metaphorical images were selected for the experiment.

Figure 1. (a) literal visual and (b) metaphor visual

2.3 Procedure

Prior to the actual fMRI scanning phase, the participants were briefed about the experiment. They were also given a practice trial, which included two instances each of all the four conditions. After the practice session, the participants were sent to the brain scanner. The scanning phase involved one session with 32 instances of the four conditions (4 blocks). Each block included 8 trials (stimulus and response) from the following four conditions: (1) literal verbal, (2) metaphor verbal, (3) literal visual and (4) metaphor visual. Trials within the blocks were randomized. There was a five-second gap between any two consecutive blocks during which the participants were presented with a white + sign on a black background. Scans of the initial three minutes during the rest state, when participants did not do any task and lied down quietly, were taken as the baseline. The experimental stimuli were presented on a computer screen mounted at the head coil. Participants were asked to look at the sentence or the image and decide if it was metaphorical or literal. They were asked to press one of the two buttons with their right index finger if it was a metaphor and to press the other button with their middle finger if the stimulus was literal. They were also allowed to skip a stimulus if they could not determine the nature of it by pressing a third button with their thumb (during analysis we did not find any such case). The fMRI data was acquired using 3 Tesla Phillips whole-body MRI scanner[1].

---

[1] The 3 Tesla Phillips whole-body scanner collects high-resolution T1-weighted anatomical images and gradient echo-planar T2-weighted images with blood oxygenation level-dependent contract of 16 axial slices. The parameters of the sequence were set as follows: TR=2000 ms, TE=35ms, flip angle=90°, FOV=230×230 mm, matrix=128×128, slice thickness=5mm, slice gap=1mm.

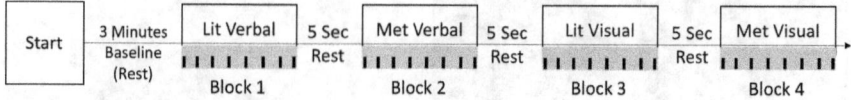

Figure 2. Procedure followed for stimuli presentation

3 Data analysis and results

3.1 fMRI Data Analysis

The data was analyzed using the standard fMRI analysis procedure on SPM[2] software. After initially pre-processing data from each individual participant, a first-level analysis was done by creating four conditions based on the response time, and taking t-contrasts in the SPM in relation to the rest state. The output of this step was contrast images (in relation to the rest state) for individual participants in each of the four conditions. In order to get a generalized result, a second-level analysis of one-sample T testing was done for each condition taking respective contrast images for each participant.

3.2 Behavioral data analysis

We also calculated the mean reaction time for all the responses. The reaction time was defined as the time interval between the onset of the stimulus presentation and pressing of the button by the participant. We found the mean reaction times to be as follows: for literal sentences 2 seconds, for verbal metaphors 2.29 seconds, for literal images 3.25 seconds, and for metaphorical images 4.35 seconds. A one-way ANOVA revealed a significant main effect (F (3,28)=5.28, p<.01) as shown in Figure 3.

---

[2] Statistical Parametric Mapping (SPM 8, by the members & collaborators of the Welcome Trust Centre for Neuroimaging, UK2). In the preprocessing of data, all functional volumes were re-aligned to the first volume of each participant to correct for head motion and were spatially normalized and smoothed.

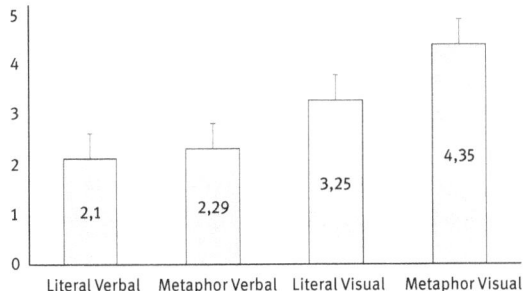

Figure 3. Mean response time in four different experimental conditions

3.3 fMRI results

We contrasted the brain activation patterns for each of the four conditions (literal verbal, literal visual, metaphor verbal, and metaphor visual) with the rest condition, and the results are shown in Table 1. In the **literal verbal** condition, we found activation in *left inferior frontal gyrus*, which is important for processing of syntax in oral and sign languages (Dapretto 1999); *occipital lobe lingual gyrus* and *occipital lobe fusiform gyrus*, both of which are responsible for word recognition and within-category identification (Tan et al. 2000). *Right parietal lobe, precuneus* was also activated, which is involved with episodic memory (Wagner et al. 2005), visuo-spatial processing and aspects of consciousness (Cavanna and Trimbile 2006). For the **metaphor verbal** task, *right temporal sub gyral* was highly activated, which is considered to play a role in auditory processing (Zatorre et al. 1996). We also found high activation in *left caudate*, which is required to monitor and control lexical and language alternatives in production tasks for bilingual individuals (Crinion et al. 2006) and *left middle temporal gyrus*, which is involved in assessing word meaning while reading (Chao, Haxby, and Martin 1999). *Right inferior temporal gyrus*, which is known for the representation of complex object features (Haxby et al. 2001), was highly activated as well. In the **literal visual** condition, significant activations were found in *precuneus, right insula, right inferior frontal gyrus*, all of which are involved in sustaining attention and working memory (McAlonan et al. 2007), and *left cingulate gyrus*, which is mostly considered a part of the limbic lobe and is associated with emotional response (Vogt 2005). In the **metaphor visual** task, we found high activation in *left insula* and *left putamen*, which is responsible for reinforcement and implicit and category learning and switching languages (Cincotta and Seger 2007). Significant activation was also found in *right parahippocampal gyrus*, which is considered to be active in scene recognition, memory recall and contextualizing visual background (Medford et al. 2005). It has been suggested that *parahippocampal gyrus* may play a crucial role in identifying social context as well (Chiao et al. 2009), including paralinguistic elements of verbal communication such as sarcasm (Mashal, Faust, and Hendler 2005). There was a significant activation in *left superior temporal gyrus* and *left temporal lobe, sub gyral*, both of which are responsible for language comprehension (Zatorre et al. 1996). *Left temporal lobe* holds the primary auditory cortex, which is important for the processing of semantics in both speech and vision (Friederici et al. 2003). The details of the activation in different brain areas are presented in the appendix 1.

4 Discussion

The objective of this study was two fold: (1) to determine what language areas, if any, are activated during visual metaphor processing; and (2) to explore the neural differences and similarities in visual and verbal metaphor processing. Our results show a significant activation in *left superior temporal gyrus* and *temporal lobe, sub-gyral* (BA 22) while the participants interpreted presented images metaphorically. These include Broca's and Wernicke's areas, and are primarily responsible for auditory perception, speech and language comprehension. We must emphasize here that there was no text embedded in any of the visual-metaphor stimuli. In contrast, we found no significant activity in these areas during the literal-image comprehension. This finding confirms that the comprehension process of visual metaphors requires activation of language areas.

We directly compared the brain activation patterns for the visual and verbal metaphors to explore the differences and similarities between their respective processing, which led to two observations. First, for visual metaphors, we did not find any exclusive right-hemisphere (RH) deployment as has been reported in several verbal metaphor studies (Winner and Gardner 1977; Bottini et al. 1994; Anaki, Faust, and Kravetz 1998), except significant activation in *right Parahippocampal gyrus*. This part of the brain is considered to be involved in detecting sarcasm from non-verbal cues, inferring speaker's intention (Rankin et al. 2009), and in creating internal images and retrieval of visual knowledge (Mashal, Faust, and Handler 2005). Activation in *Parahippocampal gyrus* during visual metaphor comprehension suggests that the incongruity created by juxtaposing two unrelated images triggers similar mechanisms as in sarcasm, and initiates a search for the author's intentions or some other possible context to render the juxtaposition meaningful. It is not surprising that visual knowledge and image-creating mechanisms are involved in visual metaphors.

Secondly, we found some common activation areas for both verbal and visual metaphor conditions. For instance, *sub gyral* was activated in both conditions in the *right frontal lobe*, which is considered to be involved in verbal memory (Shinoura et al. 2011; della Rocchetta et al. 1995). This suggests that verbal memory plays a role both in visual and verbal metaphors. Similarly, *Occipital lobe Precuneus* was significantly activated in both conditions in the left hemisphere. This area is considered to play an important role in visuo-spatial imagery (Simon et al. 2002). Previous studies (Mashal, Faust, and Handler 2005; Bottini et al. 1994) have also shown significant activation in this area for verbal metaphors (especially novel metaphors). Our study adds to this previous research by noting that the left *Occipital lobe Precuneus* is activated in visual metaphor processing too. So we can conclude that visuo-spatial imagery is important to both visual and verbal metaphors.

On the other hand, we found that though *Putamen* was significantly activated in both visual and verbal metaphor conditions, it was in the left hemisphere for visual metaphors, and in the right hemisphere for verbal metaphors. Activation of *right putamen* has been reported in several verbal metaphor studies (Schmidt, DeBuse and Seger 2007). It is suggested that *right putamen* is activated when the reader attempts to construct a unitary coherent model of a discourse and discover the author's intent (Rapp et al. 2004; Kircher et al. 2001; Cooke et al. 2002). Some recent studies focusing on bilingualism have reported activation in *left putamen* when some cognitive control is required such as switching between languages. (Abutalebi et al. 2007; Crinion et al. 2006) and predicting future motor movements (Aramaki et al. 2011). Besides this hemispheric specialization, bilateral activation in *putamen* is reported in tasks requiring implicit or category learning and motor planning and movement. Thus, our findings suggest that interpreting visual metaphors might require some mechanism analogous to switching between languages and predicting future movement. Obviously, this requires further experimentation before a more detailed model can be articulated.

We also found that the response time for visual metaphors was longer than for verbal metaphors. A longer response time usually indicates a more complex mechanism, and vice versa. For example, in research on verbal metaphors, it is argued that the two-stage anomaly model, which assumes that a failure in literal interpretation triggers the search for a metaphorical meaning, would predict a longer response time. Although, several empirical studies have refuted this prediction (Gerrig 1989; Gibbs 1994; Hoffman and Kemper 1987), still recent ERP studies have shown that metaphors appear anomalous at least initially (Tartter et al. 2002), and take longer to comprehend. So a longer response time for visual metaphors suggests a more complex process. However, we leave a more detailed implication of this result for future research on different kinds of visual metaphors with more participants.

5 Conclusion

The main finding of our pilot fMRI study is that language areas are activated during visual metaphor comprehension process. Together with the existing research that has demonstrated that visual imagery areas are activated during verbal metaphor processing, this shows that both verbal and visual metaphors require interaction across different modalities in order to be interpreted: In order to make sense of seemingly anomalous juxtaposition, whether in language or in images, all different modalities, visual, sensory motor, linguistic, and their associated knowledge is brought into play.

Perhaps more significantly, on the basis of previous theoretical studies on visual metaphor, our study provides an initial empirical data on which brain areas are activated during the visual metaphor processing. As most of the existing empirical studies on metaphor are restricted to verbal metaphors, we argue, to develop a more comprehensive cognitive model of metaphor processing, it is crucial that other modalities like visual, aural and gestural are studied as well. The research presented here takes one small step in this direction. In future, we plan to conduct more experiments with more participants with different kinds of visual metaphors. We would also like to explore the interaction between language and images in multimodal pictorial metaphors.

Acknowledgement: We would like to thank Akshita, IIIT-H for her help for organizing the data. This work was supported by the Industrial Strategic Technology Development Program (10044009, Development of a self-improving bidirectional sustainable HRI technology for 95% of successful responses with understanding user's complex emotion and transactional intent through continuous interactions) funded by the Ministry of Knowledge Economy (MKE, Korea) and by the R&D program of the Korea Ministry of Knowledge and Economy (MKE) and the Korea Evaluation Institute of Industrial Technology (KEIT) [10041826, Development of emotional features sensing, diagnostics and distribution s/w platform for measurement of multiple intelligence from young children].

References

Abutalebi, Jubin, Pasquale A. Della Rosa, Anna K. Castro Gonzaga, Roland Keim, Albert Costa & Daniela Perani. 2012. The role of the left putamen in multilingual language production. *Brain and Language* 125. 307–315.

Ahrens, Kathleen, Ho L. Liu, Chia Y. Lee, Shu Gong, Shin Fang & Yuan-Yu Hsu. 2007. Functional MRI of conventional and anomalous metaphors in mandarin Chinese. *Brain and Language* 100. 163–171.

Anaki, David, Miriam Faust & Shlomo Kravetz. 1998. Cerebral hemispheric asymmetries in processing lexical metaphors. *Neuropsychologia* 36. 353–362.

Aramaki, Yu, Masahiko Haruno, Rieko Osu & Norihiro Sadato. 2011. Movement initiation locked activity of the anterior putamen predicts future movement instability in periodic bimanual movement. *The Journal of Neuroscience* 31(27). 9819–9823.

Arzouan, Yossi, Abraham Goldstein & Miriam Faust. 2007. Dynamics of hemispheric activity during metaphor comprehension: Electrophysiological measures. *Neuroimage* 36(1). 222.

Beaumont, Graham J. 1982. Studies with verbal stimuli. In Graham J. Beaumont (ed.), *Divided visual field studies of cerebral organization*, 57–86. London: Academic.

Binder, Jeffrey R., Sara J. Swanson, Thomas A. Hammeke, George L. Morris, Wade M. Mueller, Mariellen Fischer, Selim R. Benbadis, Julie A. Frost, Stephen M. Rao, Victor M. Haughton. 1996. Determination of language dominance with functional MRI: A comparison with the Wada test. *Neurology* 46. 978–984.

Bottini, Gabriella, Rhiannon Corcoran, Roberto Sterzi, Eraldo S. P. Paulesu, Pietro Schenone, Pina Scarpa, Richard S. J. Frackoviak & Christopher D. Frith. 1994. The role of the right hemisphere in the interpretation of the figurative aspects of language: A positron emission tomography activation study. *Brain* 117. 1241–1253.

Bryden, Mark. P. 1982. *Laterality: Functional asymmetry in the intact brain*. New York: Academic Press.

Carroll, Noel. 1994. Visual Metaphor. In Jaakko Hintikka (ed.), *Aspects of Metaphor*, 189–218. Netherlands: Springer.

Carston, Robyn. 2010. Metaphor: Ad hoc concept, literal meaning and mental images. *Proceedings of the Aristotelian Society* 110(3). 295–321.

Cavanna, Andrea E. & Michael R. Trimble. 2006. The precuneus: a review of its functional anatomy and behavioural correlates. *Brain* 129(3). 564–583.

Chao, Linda L., James V. Haxby & Alex Martin. 1999. Attribute-based neural substrates in temporal cortex for perceiving and knowing about objects. *Nature Neuroscience* 2(10). 913–919.

Chiao, Joan Y., Tokiko Harada, Hidetsugu *Komeda*, Zhang Li, Yoko Mano, Daisuke Saito, Todd B. Parrish, Norihiro Sadato & Tetsuya Iidaka. 2009. Neural basis of individualistic and collectivistic views of self. *Human Brain Mapping* 30(9). 2813–2820.

Cincotta, Corinna M. & Carol A. Seger. 2007. Dissociation between striatal regions while learning to categorize via feedback and via observation. *Journal of Cognitive Neuroscience* 19(2). 249–265.

Cooke, Ayanna, Edgard B. Zurif, Christian DeVita, David Alsop, Phyllis Koenig, John Detre, James Gee, Maria Piñango, Jennifer Balogh & Murray Grossman. 2002. Neural basis for sentence comprehension: Grammatical and short-term memory components. *Human Brain Mapping* 15(2). 80–94.

Crinion, Jenny, Robert Turner, Alice Grogan, Takashi Hanakawa, Uta Noppeney, Joseph T. Devlin & Cathy J. Price. 2006. Language control in the bilingual brain. *Science* 312(5779). 1537–1540.

Dapretto, Mirella & Susan Y. Bookheimer. 1999. Form and content: Dissociating syntax and semantics in sentence comprehension. *Neuron* 24(2). 427–432.

Desmond, John E., John M. Sum, Anthony D. Wagner, Jonathan B. Demb, Paula K. Shear, Gary H. Glover & Martha J. Morrell. 1995. Functional MRI measurement of language lateralization in Wada-tested patients. *Brain* 118(6). 1411–1419.

Ellis, Andrew W., Andrew W. Young, Christine Anderson. 1988. Modes of word recognition in the left and right cerebral hemispheres. *Brain and Language* 35. 254–273.

Faust, Miriam & Nira Mashal. 2007. The role of the right cerebral hemisphere in processing novel metaphoric expressions taken from poetry: A divided visual field study. *Neuropsychologia* 45(4). 860–870.

Forceville, Charles. 1996. *Pictorial metaphor in advertising*. London: Routledge.

Friederici, Angela D., Shirley A. Rüschemeyer, Anja Hahne & Christian J. Fiebach. 2003. The role of left inferior frontal and superior temporal cortex in sentence comprehension: localizing syntactic and semantic processes. *Cerebral Cortex* 13(2). 170–177.

Gerrig, Richard J. 1989. Empirical constraints on computational theories of metaphor: Comments on Indurkhya. *Cognitive Science* 13(2). 235–241.

Gibbs, Raymond W. 1994. *The poetics of mind: Figurative thought, language, and understanding*. Cambridge: Cambridge University Press.

Gibbs, Raymond W. & Josephine M. Bogdanovich. 1999. Mental imagery in interpreting poetic metaphor. *Metaphor and Symbol* 14(1). 37–54.

Haxby, James V., Maria I. Gobbini, Maura L. Furey, Alumit Ishai, Jennifer L. Schouten & Pietro Pietrini. 2001. Distributed and overlapping representations of faces and objects in ventral temporal cortex. *Science* 293(5539). 2425–2430.

Hoffman, Robert R. & Susan Kemper. 1987. What could reaction-time studies be telling us about metaphor comprehension? *Metaphor and Symbol* 2(3). 149–186.

Howard, David, Karalyn Patterson, Richard Wise, W. Douglas Brown, Karl Friston, Cornelius Weiller & Richard Frackowiak. 1992. The cortical localization of the lexicons. *Brain* 115. 1769–1782.

Incisa della Rocchetta, Antonio, David G. Gadian, Alan Connelly, Charles E. Polkey, Graeme D. Jackson, Kate E. Watkins & Faraneh Vargha-Khadem. 1995. Verbal memory impairment after right temporal lobe surgery role of contralateral damage as revealed by Hydrogen-1 magnetic resonance spectroscopy and T sub 2 relaxometry. *Neurology* 45(4). 797–802.

Indurkhya, Bipin. 2016. Toward a model of metaphorical understanding. In Elisabetta Gola & Francesca Ervas (eds.), *Metaphor and communication*, 129–146. Amsterdam: John Benjamin.

Indurkhya, Bipin. 2007. Creativity in interpreting poetic metaphors. In T. Kusumi (ed.), *New directions in metaphor research*, 483–501. Tokyo: Hitsuji Shobo.

Indurkhya, Bipin & Amitash Ojha. 2013. An empirical study on the role of perceptual similarity in visual metaphors and creativity. *Metaphor and Symbol* 28(4). 233–253.

Jonides, John, Edward E. Smith, Robert A. Koeppe, Edward Awh, Satoshi Minoshima & Mark A. Mintun. 1993. Spatial working memory in humans as revealed by PET. *Nature* 363, 623–625.

Kacinik, Natalie A., & Christine Chiarello. 2007. Understanding metaphors: Is the right hemisphere uniquely involved? *Brain and Language* 100(2). 188–207.

Kennedy, John M. 1982. Metaphor in pictures. *Perception* 11(5). 589–605.
Kircher, Tilo T., Michael J. Brammer, Nuria Tous Andreu, Steven C. Williams & Philip K. McGuire. 2001. Engagement of right temporal cortex during processing of linguistic context. *Neuropsychologia* 39(8). 798–809.
Kuperberg, Gina R., Philip K. McGuire, Edward T. Bullmore, Michael J. Brammer, Sophia Rabe-Hesketh, Ian C. Wright & Anthony S. David. 2000. Common and distinct neural substrates for pragmatic, semantic, and syntactic processing of spoken sentences: an fMRI study. *Journal of Cognitive Neuroscience* 12(2), 321–341.
Lakoff, George. 1993. The contemporary theory of metaphor. In Andrew Ortony (ed.), *Metaphor and thought*, 2nd edn., 202–251. Cambridge: Cambridge University press.
Lakoff, George & Mark Johnson. 1980. *Metaphors we live by*. Chicago: University of Chicago Press.
Mashal, Nira, Miriam Faust & Talma Hendler. 2005. The role of the right hemisphere in processing nonsalient metaphorical meanings: Application of principal components analysis to fMRI data. *Neuropsychologia* 43(14). 2084–2100.
McAlonan, Grainne M., Vinci Cheung, Charlton Cheung, Siew E. Chua, Decian G. Murphy, John Suckling & Ting-Po Ho. 2007. Mapping brain structure in attention deficit-hyperactivity disorder: A voxel-based MRI study of regional grey and white matter volume. *Psychiatry Research: Neuroimaging* 154(2). 171–180.
McCarthy, Gregory, Andrew M. Blamire, Aina Puce, Anna C. Nobre, Gilles Bloch, Fahmeed Hyder & Robert G. Shulman. 1994. Functional magnetic resonance imaging of human prefrontal cortex activation during a spatial working memory task. *Proceedings of the National Academy of Sciences* 91(18). 8690–8694.
Medford, Nicholas, Mary L. Phillips, Barbara Brierley, Michael Brammer, Edward T. Bullmore & Anthony S. David. 2005. Emotional memory: Separating content and context. *Psychiatry Research: Neuroimaging* 138(3). 247–258.
Mulken, Margot van, Rob le Pair & Charles Forceville. 2010. The impact of perceived complexity, deviation and comprehension on the appreciation of visual metaphor in advertising across three European countries. *Journal of Pragmatics* 42. 3418–3430.
Müller, Cornelia. 2009. *Metaphors dead and alive, sleeping and waking: A dynamic view*. Midway Plaisance: University of Chicago Press.
Neisser, Ulric. 1976. *Cognition and reality: Principles and implications of cognitive psychology*. San Francisco: W. H. Freeman.
Oldfield, Carolus R. 1971. The assessment and analysis of handedness: The Edinburgh inventory. *Neuropsychologia* 9(1). 97–113.
Ortony, Andrew. 1979. Beyond literal similarity. *Psychological Review* 86. 161–180.
Rankin, Khaterine P., Andrea Salazar, Maria L. Gorno-Tempini, Marc Sollberger, Stephen M. Wilson, Danijela Pavlic & Bruce L. Miller. 2009. Detecting sarcasm from paralinguistic cues: Anatomic and cognitive correlates in neurodegenerative disease. *Neuroimage* 47(4). 2005–2015.
Rapp, Alexander M., Dirk T. Leube, Michael Erb, Wolfgang Grodd & Tilo T. Kircher. 2004. Neural correlates of metaphor processing. *Cognitive Brain Research* 20(3). 395–402.
Richards, Ivor A. 1936. *The philosophy of rhetoric*. Oxford: Clarendon Press.
Rinaldi, Maria C., Paola Marangolo & Francesca Baldassarri. 2004. Metaphor comprehension in right brain-damaged patients with visuo-verbal and verbal material: A dissociation (re)considered. *Cortex* 40. 479–490.

Schmidt, Gwenda L., Casey J. DeBuse & Carol A. Seger. 2007. Right hemisphere metaphor processing? Characterizing the lateralization of semantic processes. *Brain and language* 100(2). 127–141.

Schmidt, Gwenda L. & Carol A. Seger. 2009. Neural correlates of metaphor processing: The roles of figurativeness, familiarity and difficulty. *Brain and cognition* 71(3). 375–386.

Shibataa, Midori, Jun-Ichi *Abe*, Atsushi *Terao* & Tamaki Miyamoto. 2007. Neural mechanisms involved in the comprehension of metaphoric and literal sentences: An fMRI study. *Brain research* 1166. 92–102.

Shinoura, Nobusada, Akira Midorikawa, Kotoyo Kurokawa, Toshiyuki Onodera, Masanobu Tsukada, Ryozi Yamada Yusuke Tabei, Tomoyuki Koizumi, Mizuho Yoshida, Seiko Saito & Kazuo Yagi. 2011. Right temporal lobe plays a role in verbal memory. *Neurological Research* 33(7). 734–738.

Simon, Stéphane R., Martine Meunier, Loÿs Piettre, Anna M. Berardi, Christoph M. Segebarth, & Driss Boussaoud. 2002. Spatial attention and memory versus motor preparation: premotor cortex involvement as revealed by fMRI. *Journal of Neurophysiology* 88(4). 2047–2057.

Tan, Li-Hai, John A. Spinks, Jia-Hong Gao, Ho-Ling Liu, Charles A. Perfetti, Jinhu Xiong, Kathryn A. Stofer, Yonglin Pu, Yijun Liu & Peter T. Fox. 2000. Brain activation in the processing of Chinese characters and words: a functional MRI study. *Human Brain Mapping* 10(1). 16–27.

Tartter, Vivien C., Hilary Gomes, Borsi Dubrovsky, Sophie Molholm & Rosemarie V. Stewart. 2002. Novel metaphors appear anomalous at least momentarily: Evidence from N400. *Brain and Language* 80(3). 488–509.

Van Lancker, Diana R. & Daniel Kempler. 1987. Comprehension of familiar phrases by left-but not by right-hemisphere damaged patients. *Brain and language* 32(2). 265–277.

Van Weelden, Lisanne, Alfons Maes, Joost Schilperoord & Rein Cozijn, R. 2011. The role of shape in comparing objects: How perceptual similarity may affect visual metaphor processing. *Metaphor and Symbol* 26(4). 272–298.

Vogt, Brent A. 2005. Pain and emotion interactions in subregions of the cingulate gyrus. *Nature Reviews Neuroscience* 6(7). 533–544.

Wagner, Anthony D., Benjamin Shannon, Itamar Kahn & Randy L. Buckner. 2005. Parietal lobe contributions to episodic memory retrieval. *Trends in Cognitive Sciences* 9(9). 445–453.

Walsh, Paul. 1990. Imagery as a heuristic in the comprehension of metaphorical analogies. In Kenneth J. Gilhooly, Mark T. G. Keane, Robert H. Logie & George Erdos (eds.), *Lines of thinking: Reflections on the psychology of thought. Representation, reasoning, analogy and decision making*, 237–250. New York: Wiley.

Winner, Ellen & Howard Gardner. 1977. The comprehension of metaphor in brain damaged patients. *Brain* 100. 717–772.

Zatorre, Robert J., Ernst Meyer, Albert Gjedde & Alan C. Evans. 1996. PET studies of phonetic processing of speech: review, replication, and reanalysis. *Cerebral cortex* 6(1). 21–30.

Appendix

Table 1. Coordinates of activation peaks compared with the Rest state in literal verbal and metaphor verbal conditions as compared to rest condition.

Literal Verbal vs. Rest

Regions	Side	BA	Coordinates			
			x	y	z	t
Sub-Lobar, Lentiform Neucleus, Putamen	L	–	−30	−4	1	10.13
Insula	R	13	36	20	1	8.97
Frontal-Temporal Space	R	–	48	11	4	7.57
Parietal Lobe, Precuneus	R	07	21	−49	31	6.95
Occipital Lobe, Lingual Gyrus	L	18	−24	−58	4	6.65
Putamen	R	–	21	−4	10	6.01
Inferior Frontal Gyrus	L	47	−24	23	−5	5.56
Occipital Lobe, Fusiform Gyrus	L	20	−30	−58	−11	5.41

Metaphor Verbal vs. Rest

Regions	Side	BA	x	y	z	t
Temporal Lobe, Sub-Gyral	R	22	33	−52	−2	18.45
Frontal Lobe, Sub-Gyral, White matter	R	–	24	−37	25	17.31
Thalamus	R	–	21	−13	18	15.14
Caudate	L	–	−9	17	10	14.55
Middle Temporal Gyrus	L	39	−39	−58	25	9.97
Claustrum	R	16	30	5	10	8.57
Putamen	R	–	24	17	7	8.48
Inferior Temporal Gyrus	R	20	54	−52	−11	4.50
Occipital Lobe, Precuneus	L	07	−18	−73	19	3.99

Table 2. Coordinates of activation peaks compared with the Rest state in literal visual and metaphor visual conditions as compared to rest condition.

Literal Visual vs. Rest

Regions	Side	BA	Coordinates			
			x	y	z	t
Precuneus	L	31	0	−46	31	21.28
Insula	R	13	38	−22	−2	18.11
Transverse Temporal Gyrus	R	41	36	−25	10	17.88
Inferior Frontal Gyrus	R	46	42	38	7	9.97
Cingulate Gyrus	L	24	−12	−34	40	9.42

Table 2. (continued)

Literal Visual vs. Rest						
Regions	Side	BA	Coordinates			
			x	y	z	t
Limbic Lobe, Cingulate Gyrus	L	23	0	−25	31	6.72
Midbrain	R	−	12	−22	−14	9.27
Occipital Lobe, Cuneus	L	17	−18	−91	7	7.97
Metaphor Visual vs. Rest						
Putamen	L	−	−21	2	13	9.54
Sub-Lobar, Extra Nuclear, White matter	L	−	−18	−43	22	7.22
Insula	L	13	−36	−25	16	8.20
Frontal Lobe, Sub-Gyral, White matter	R	−	24	−22	40	7.16
Parahippocampal Gyrus	R	27	24	−31	−5	7.03
Superior Temporal Gyrus	L	22	−57	−10	7	6.14
Temporal Lobe, Sub−Gyral	L	22	−42	−34	1	6.06
Occipital Lobe, Precuneus	L	07	−21	−67	19	5.63

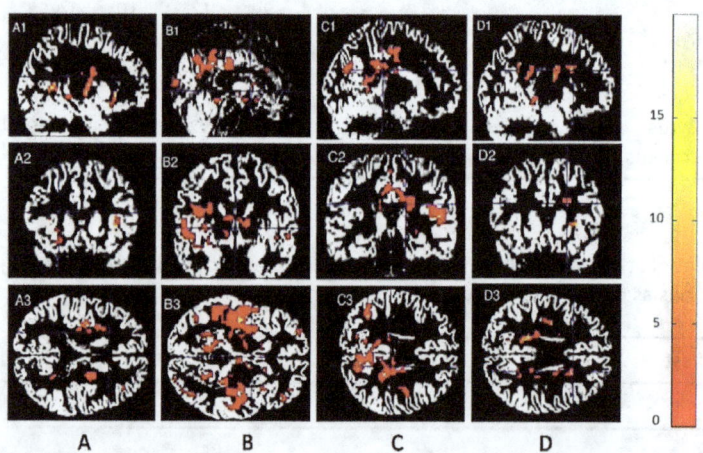

Figure 4. Brain activation elicited by (A) Literal Verbal, (B) Metaphor Verbal, (C) Literal Visual and (D) Metaphor Visual conditions

Valentina Cuccio and Sabina Fontana
Embodied Simulation and metaphorical gestures

1 Introduction

In the past years, many studies have shown that bodily experiences play a crucial role in human cognition and, especially, in language comprehension. In this regard, many findings, from different research paradigms, have suggested that language is embodied at least on two different dimensions. As suggested by Margethis and Bergen (2014, 2002), language is embodied inside and outside. On the inside, language is embodied by virtue of the mechanism of Embodied Simulation. From outside, language is embodied by means of co-speech gestures. Furthermore, the embodied nature of language has been particularly investigated in relation to metaphor studies. Bodily-based metaphors seem to be particularly apt at exploiting the bodily foundation of language in these two dimensions.

In the first part of this paper, we will first discuss separately data supporting the role of the body in the comprehension of language, and specifically in the comprehension of bodily-based metaphors, from the inside and the outside. We will, then, present our proposal on the possible interaction between Embodied Simulation and co-speech gestures during the comprehension of bodily-based metaphors. This proposal relies on a novel definition for the mechanism of Embodied Simulation (Cuccio 2015a, 2015b) on the basis of which we will claim that Embodied Simulation and gestures are not two different dimensions of embodiment. They are the two extremes of a *continuum* process and Embodied Simulation is its core mechanism. We will suggest that, in this view, empirical and theoretical works on Embodied Simulation and gestures, mainly considered as two separate lines of research, should be considered from an integrated and unitary perspective.

Valentina Cuccio, University of Palermo
Sabina Fontana, University of Catania

2 Embodied Simulation and language

In the last few years many empirical studies, carried out with different techniques (e.g. Glenberg and Kaschak 2002; Glenberg et al. 2008; Sato et al. 2008; Hauk, Johnsrude, and Pulvermüller 2004; Kemmerer et al. 2008; Pulvermüller 1999; Tettamanti et al. 2005; Buccino et al. 2005; Papeo et al. 2009) have shown the involvement of the sensorimotor system in language understanding. This means that listening to a sentence such as "John grasps the glass" determines in our brain the activation of hand-related areas of the motor cortex even if we are not carrying out any hand-related action (for reviews and critical discussions: Barsalou 2010; Fisher and Zwaan 2008; Glenberg, Witt, and Metcalfe 2013; Pulvermüller et al. 2014; Jirak et al. 2010). The same holds true also for linguistic descriptions of perception and emotion: in this case, language processing determines the activation of perception or emotion related areas of the brain. With regards to the description of emotions, it has been observed that the processing of verbs that describe facial expressions (e.g. to smile) also determines the activation of the muscles involved in the real occurrence of those facial expressions (Foroni and Semin 2009). This activation of neural circuits in the absence of a corresponding action, perception or emotion has been defined as *Embodied Simulation* (Gallese and Sinigaglia 2011).

Together, these data suggest that language understanding, when language refers to action, emotion and perception, involves the activation of our bodily knowledge. This claim holds true even for the comprehension of bodily metaphors, namely metaphors based on our bodily experiences (e.g Boulenger, Hauk, and Pulvermüller 2009; Boulenger, Shtyrov, and Pulvermüller 2012; Desai et al. 2011; Desai et al. 2013). Thus, the processing of a metaphorical expression such as "John grasps the idea" will determine the activation of hand-related areas of the motor cortex as well. It has been suggested that, in this example, we comprehend the abstract concept of "understanding" (the target domain of the metaphor) resorting to the physical action of "grasping" (the source domain of the metaphor). In this regard, it is important to note that, while cognitive theories of metaphors have usually described metaphor understanding as a conceptual, abstract and disembodied process that happens at the conceptual level, these recent neuroscientific findings support the claim that our bodies directly contribute to the comprehension of metaphors by means of the mechanism of *Embodied Simulation* (Gibbs 2003, 2005; Matlock, Ramscar and Boroditsky 2005; Gibbs and Matlock 2008; Gibbs and Perlman 2010; Ritchie 2010; Semino 2010).

Nevertheless, it is worth noting that divergent findings have also been obtained in another set of studies (e.g. Aziz-Zadeh et al. 2006; Cacciari et al. 2011; Raposo et al. 2009). In these studies, the comprehension of figurative and abstract language did not determine the activation of the mechanism of *Embodied Simulation*. Although it is not easy to make a direct comparison between these studies because they differ in many respects, a meta-analysis study has recently suggested that the involvement of the sensorimotor system in non-literal language comprehension depends on semantic features of language stimuli (Yang and Shu 2015). More specifically, it has also been suggested that the recruitment of the mechanism of simulation, and hence such variability in findings, depends on the level of conventionality and deliberateness of the metaphors used in the studies. A metaphor is conventional when it is so deeply rooted in our culture that it is no longer considered as a comparison between two different domains (e.g. "the table legs"). The more conventional and less deliberate is the metaphor, the less motor activation will be observed in the brain. The reason is that when we use a highly conventional metaphor in a not-deliberate way we go directly to the abstract meaning without resorting to the bodily-based source domain. Theoretical (Bowdle and Gentner 2005; Cuccio and Steen, in press; Gentner and Bowdle 2008; Giora 2003; Steen 2011) and empirical arguments (Tzuyin, Lai, and Curran 2013) have been provided in support of this claim.

Consequentially, a further crucial problem in this debate is to define the contribution *Embodied Simulation* makes to linguistic meaning. Currently, this topic is highly debated by philosophers and neuroscientists with different positions being considered (Shapiro 2011). How does the body interacts with symbols? Is the contribution of the body really necessary and constitutive of linguistic meaning (Pulvermüller 2013) or is it merely causal, that is causally related to the process of the construction of meaning but not part of this process? Or is it just a side-effect due to other phenomena as has been hypothesized by Mahon and Caramazza (2008)? We hope to provide a tentative answer to these questions at the end of this paper.

3 Gestures and language

The strong interconnection between language and gesture was explored since the mid 1970s in early childhood (Bates et al. 1979; Bates 1976; Volterra and Erting 1990; Capirci and Volterra 2005) and later in adults (McNeill 1992, 2000, 2005; Kendon 2004). These studies have shown that gestures are a universal feature of human communication.

In language acquisition, both hearing and deaf children use gesture for communicative purposes. At about one year, there is an equi-potentiality between the visual-gestural modality and the vocal modality (Volterra and Erting 1990) and the choice of one or the other linguistic channel depends on the input (either sign language or speech) the child is exposed to. The strong interconnection between language and movement has deep ontogenetic roots as Iverson and Thelen (1999) have pointed out. During the child development the gesture-language link shifts from the biological to the social as this block gradually acquires a social meaning and a role within a linguistic system. More recently, other studies (Capirci et al. 2005; Pettenati, Stefanini, and Volterra 2010) have indicated that there is a continuity between the production of the first action schemes, the first gestures and the first words. In particular, Pettenati et al. (2010) have shown that co-speech gestures produced by hearing children share functions and forms to the early signs produced by children exposed to a sign language. Gestures and early signs display the same restricted set of 'basic' handshapes and similar locations such as the face/head and neutral space because they are bound to the motoric characteristics of the hand and the arm. Findings show that there is not a clear boundary between linguistic and gestural systems. Indeed, similar forms of gestures support the hypothesis of a common conceptual space, a common image that is shared with speech as well as the activation of hand-mouth motor programs associated with specific objects or actions (Arbib, Oztop, and Zukow-Goldring 2005; Stefanini et al. 2008).

The relationships between gesture and speech in adults' language is explained by three competing views. According to Hadar et al. (1998), gestures and speech are separate communication systems. Following the *Lexical Retrieval Hypothesis*, gesture is a support for the speaker to carry out tasks and plays a cognitive rather than a linguistic role. In another account, gesture and thought form two separate asymmetric communicative systems, where the gestural system is a support for the vocal system. Krauss and colleagues (Krauss et al. 2000) hypothesize reciprocal links between gesture and speech that are located at the phonological and encoding stage or at the moment in which a word is retrieved from lexical memory. Indeed, in Kita and Ozyurek's (2003) *Information Packaging Hypothesis* gesture plays a role in the conceptual planning of speech by supporting the speaker in the expression of spatial information in linguistic units. Following this hypothesis, in the building of linguistic expression, a process of interaction between the linguistic and gestural representation of events takes place. Finally, McNeill (1992) has put forth the hypothesis that gesture and speech are closely linked to one another and convey different aspects of meaning. McNeill (1992, 2005) and Kendon (1997, 2004) argue that the various hypotheses on gestures' functions cannot be considered as opposed to each other because gesture must be analyzed within a theoretical framework which includes the different dimensions of gestures which involve the cognitive and the linguistic-communicative level (Alibali et al. 2001).

Scholars agree on the fact that in spoken language, gestures have precise functions in the organization of sentences and in the construction of thought. More precisely, the notion of gesture that emerges from the domain of Gesture Studies is the following:

> [...] there is a wide range of ways in which visible bodily actions are employed in the accomplishment of expression that, from a functional point of view, are similar to, or even the same as expression in spoken language. At times they are used in conjunction with spoken expressions, at other times as complements, supplements, substitutes or as alternatives to them. These are utterance uses of visible action and it is these uses that constitutes the domain of "gesture" [...] (Kendon, 2004: 1–2).

The gesture we mean are everyday occurrences- the spontaneous unwitting, and regular accompaniments of speech that we see in our moving fingers, hands and arms (McNeill 2005: 3).

In summary, a gesture looks like a productive linguistic element, with a variable degree of conventionalization, which ranges from emblems to gesticulation (Kendon 2004) and plays a functional role with respect to the utterance. Gestures have a function in the process of *thinking for speaking* (Slobin 1987) and constitute a single unit with speech in that they convey another dimension of meaning which is absent from it (McNeill 1992, 2005). Since gestures and sign languages employ the kinesic medium, they can be considered both expression of the strategies of the speaker/signer in expressing their internal motor simulation. The only major difference between signs and gestures lies in their degree of autonomy and structure. Sign language is autonomous whereas gestures have to co-occur with speech to be fully understandable (Kendon 2004).

In the present paper, we start from McNeill's perspective on the gesture-speech relationship in order to explore the imagery-language dialectic. In particular, we will expand upon this third view by reviewing the literature on embodied simulation in order to claim that gestures are the result of simulation that is produced in co-occurrence with speech to convey different dimensions of meaning.

4 Embodied Simulation and gestures

As we have seen in the previous section, gestures play a fundamental role in language production and comprehension. The questions we would like to address now is whether Embodied Simulation is in some way involved in the understanding of gestures and what kind of contribution this mechanism could, then, provide to their comprehension.

In connection with the first question, it is nowadays widely known that Embodied Simulation is triggered by action observation. To give an example, to observe someone else carrying out an hand-related action such as grasping a cup will activate in the observer hand-related areas of the motor cortex as well (for a discussion, see Gallese and Cuccio 2016). The question that has recently been addressed is whether Embodied Simulation is also triggered by the observation of representational actions, that is, actions that do not have a direct effect on the physical environment but that affect our communicative exchanges. Some studies have been lately carried out with the aim of answering this question. Findings from these studies have shown that the observation of other people gestures results in the activation of the observer's motor system (Ping, Goldin-Meadow, and Beilock 2014; Cartmill, Beilock, and Goldin-Meadow 2012). For example, Ping and colleagues' results (2014) suggested that seeing a gesture, while listening to speech, leads to simulation of the observed gesture and, as a consequence, this simulation affects the processing of language. Furthermore, it has been suggested that the mechanism of simulation is at work not only during language comprehension. It seems to be also involved in language production (Sato 2010).

Under this hypothesis, when we produce action-related sentences, a simulation of the described action is triggered in our brain and this activation can affect our co-speech gestures to the extent that such gestures can emerge as a result of the mechanism of simulation (Hostetter and Alibali 2008, 2010). Thus, these and other studies (for a review, see Marghetis and Bergen 2014) have clearly shown that Embodied Simulation plays a role both in gestures production and comprehension during the processing of language. But we still have to deeply understand the specific kind of contribution it provides. With the aim of answering this question, we will now provide a wider and more comprehensive account of the mechanism of Embodied Simulation. Embodied Simulation has been defined, so far, as a "brain-centered" mechanism. This means that Embodied Simulation is described as the activation of some neural circuits in the brain. No contribution of the body, apart from the brain, is taken into consideration. On the opposite, the definition we would like to propose here is "brain and bodily-centered". Embodied Simulation does not only determine a pattern of neural activation. It can also induce the experience of bodily sensations and, in some cases, when it exceeds the threshold of activation, it can lead to real muscular activity or even to action execution, as in the case of co-speech gestures induced by the mechanism of simulation (see Hostetter and Alibali 2008, 2010). To give an example, action verbs that refer to emotional expressions (e.g. to smile) elicit the same facial muscle activity as is elicited during both production and observation of facial expressions (e.g. a smile). Muscular activity has been recorded by means of facial EMG (Foroni and Semin 2009). Hence, comprehension of verbs that refer to emotional expressions directly activates our facial muscles. This study seems to clearly suggest that Embodied Simulation provides us with a brain and bodily disposition and that it seems to be involved in the understanding of action, perception or emotion related linguistic expressions.

To account for the bodily, and not merely neural dimension, of the mechanism of simulation we need to refer to the models for motor control. In the current neuroscientific debate it is widely accepted the idea that the brain can predict the sensory consequences of well know and practiced actions. These "predictions" are initiated exactly in the motor cortex that generate "an internal copy of its output, termed 'efference copy' (Sperry 1950; von Holst and Mittelstaedt 1950), that alerts sensory cortices to upcoming feedback, changing their response properties" (Niziolek et al. 2013: 16110). During action execution this model/anticipation of sensorial effects is constantly updated by real sensorial feedback and contributes to our possibility for action and perception.

Lately, these models have been explicitly connected to Mirror Neurons and to the mechanism of simulation (Carr, Iacoboni, and Dubeau 2003; Kilner, Friston, and Frith 2013; Miall 2003; Iacoboni 2003). The activation of neurons in the premotor cortex, due to Embodied Simulation, determines the activation of "efference copies", that, in turn, allow us to anticipate and recall the sensorial effects of the observed action. To be more precise, Embodied Simulation can be described as the core mechanism of a *continuum* process between inside and outside, because, following Iacoboni (2003) and Miall (2003), we could say that the mechanism of Embodied Simulation lies at the interface between two systems for motor control. On the one hand, during action observation, and thus also during the observation of symbolic gestures, the activation of the Mirror Neuron system leads to the construction of an "inverse model" that allows us to convert visual information into a motor plan. On the other hand, the mechanism of simulation determines the activation of a "forward model" that leads us to convert the motor plan into the sensory outcome of the observed action/gesture. Embodied Simulation, and in particular Mirror Neurons, make us able to understand the actions/gestures we are observing by means of the rehearsal of the motor programme that underpins them and this, in turn, leads to the prediction of the sensorial effects related to the performance of these actions or gestures. Hence, in this proposal, the mechanism of Embodied Simulation determines not only a pattern of neural activation but also a bodily disposition, that can be defined as the prediction of the sensorial effects determined by the observed action. These sensations are, then, involved in the cognitive task we are facing. Thus, the mechanism of Embodied Simulation does not lead only to the activation of neural circuits in the brain (inside) but also to the experience of some bodily sensations and even to the activation of muscular fibers (outside).

With regard to gesture understanding, the mechanism of simulation, exploiting its outside dimension, can re-create in the observer the same multimodal process for the construction of meaning that have been widely discussed in the literature from the speaker's point of view.

5 Embodied Simulation and metaphorical gestures: Inside time lines

In the previous section, we have described gestures as "visible bodily actions" (Kendon 2004) and have highlighted how gestures serve the speaker and the listener. Following McNeill (1992, 2005) we intend gestures as a "window" into cognitive processes, as support of thought and speech. Indeed, their internal structure is composed of different units: conceptual and neuromuscular. The conceptual content is what gives them meaning, the neuromuscular activity is what makes them shared. Put differently, we make sense of the world through the body. Gestures are synthetic actions (outside) that shape and convey meaning (inside). However, our body does not shape only physical actions or events but also abstract experiences and concept like time or love for example. Gestures support the mapping of abstract concepts into more concrete domains. McNeill and Levy (1982) and McNeill (1992) have applied Lakoff and Johnson's (1980) notion of metaphor to the study of gestures and distinguished metaphoric and iconic gestures. Metaphoric gestures express abstract concepts and handle them as objects whereas iconic gestures depict physical entities or events. Nevertheless, the distinction between abstract and concrete is not so straightforward as it seems and may differ across cultures and situation of use. Cienki (2008) maintains that this distinction should be tested through empirical studies. He suggests to frame conceptual metaphors and metaphoric expression following three parameters (Mueller 2004) based on their degree of conventionality in relation to a given instance of use. However, both abstract and concrete concepts rely on the sensorimotor simulation. In particular, we claim that the mechanism of simulation may explain both iconic and metaphoric gestures since they are both rooted in our bodily experiences. Metaphoric mapping is considered multimodal (Mueller 2008) and "non propositional" (Johnson 1992: 349). Indeed, each semiotic mode express its own affordances and limitations. In other words, gestures may embody abstract concepts by shifting from a source domain to a target domain being iconically metaphoric and thus comprising many different dimensions and layers (Mittelberg 2008).

Starting from this conceptual framework, we have focused on the interplay of universal and cultural traits in linguistic description of space to understand how spatial cognition can map abstract concepts like time and express them externally by mean of co-speech gestures or by mean of signs. Given that "gesture and signs are cut of the same cloth" (Kendon 2004), metaphorical signs and gestures can be taken as evidence, to show how embodied simulation shapes them.

Humans have innate core abilities in spatial reasoning, shared with other animals that arise through bodily interaction with the world (Spelke 2003), but language enhances our possibilities of spatial representations by mapping for example time as space within a set of time lines that appear on one side culturally bound, on the other universal. If we look at the human body in the upright position, we can actually see an intersection of axis that potentially conveys the meaning front/back, up/down, left/right. According to Lakoff and Johnson (1980) orientational metaphors are different from other metaphors because instead of structuring one concept in terms of another, they organize a whole system of concepts with respect to another. They function in correlation with the action of our body in the world. Cuccio and Fontana (2013) found that the body is used as a metaphorical referent to organize the system of concepts related to time and superiority/inferiority in primary sign languages that are used by Deaf people isolated from their community. The same orientational metaphors could be found also in the hearing community co-speech gestures and in the deaf community sign language to convey similar information. The interconnection between time and space is quite recurrent in many cultures to the point that Alverson (1994) has advanced a "spatialization of time hypothesis" according to which the experience of time is based on a universal template of spatial experience. Interestingly, time lines appear to occur both in spoken, in sign languages and in primary sign languages[1] although the meaning of each axis is culturally framed. These metaphorical lines can be found in western and eastern languages (eg. English, see Lakoff 1994), in Chinese where moving forward or backward convey the meaning of "future" and "past" (Ning 1998). In other cultures (eg. the Urubu Kapor, in Brazil) what is made relevant is not the movement of the body (which goes naturally forward) but what you can see. In this case, then future is behind because you cannot see it and past is in front since it is known. Nevertheless, time is conceptualized as space and is segmented by an intersection of lines starting from the body. Below, example of time lines in different sign languages (Netherland, British and American sign languages) show the strong similarities among sign languages. Spoken Italian and Italian sign language (LIS) time lines are similar to those of ASL.

---

[1] Sign languages that are "created" by isolated deaf persons (Kendon 2004; Fontana 2008)

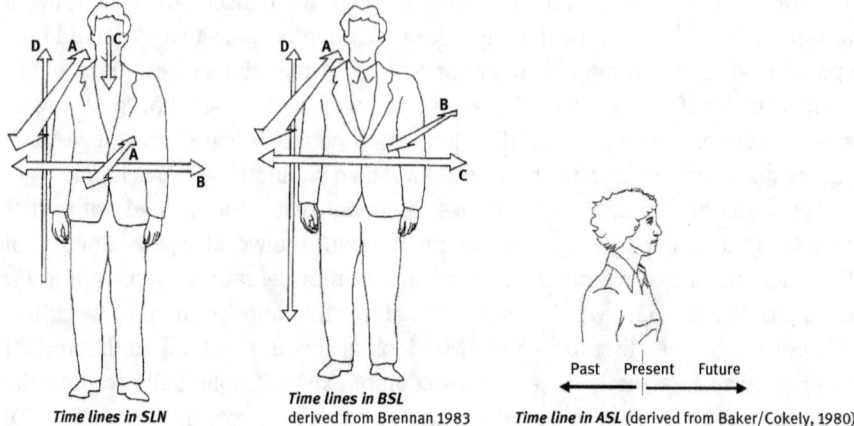

Figure 1. Time lines in Netherland, British and American sign languages

Co-speech gestures and signs move along these lines to express time. This movement is often mirrored in metaphorical expression of spoken languages (eg in Italian: andiamo avanti/let's move forward to mean forget the past).

People's specific intuitions about their bodily experience of time provide the grounding for shared use and understanding of metaphorical expression in many different languages, spoken or signed. Time is experienced as body motion and understood by listeners as such. Recurring bodily experiences in terms of event perceptions contribute to the development of specific metaphorical mapping. Simulation is brain and bodily-centered because people often move in similar patterns to others around them without being necessarily aware of this. Gestures and signs are the visible expression of the inner mechanism of simulation that shape our representations.

6 Conclusion

Concluding, in this paper we analysed the role Embodied Simulation plays in the understanding of gestures, with specific regard to metaphorical gestures. This analysis has been carried out in the light of a new definition of the mechanism simulation. Embodied Simulation has been defined as a brain and bodily-centered mechanism and this definition has led us to claim that this mechanism and the gestures system are not two different dimensions of embodiment. They are, instead, the two extremes of a *continuum* process. Researchers working on language and embodiment should then rethink their empirical and theoretical works in the light of this consideration to provide an integrated and unitary perspective of this phenomenon. The real involvement of the body apart the brain in the mechanism of simulation allows the re-creation in the observer of the same multimodal process for the construction of meaning that has been described from the speaker's point of view.

The definition of the mechanism of simulation that has been here provided makes us able to reach a better understanding of the contribution Embodied Simulation provides to the comprehension of the gestures-speech and the signed systems and suggests the fact that Embodied Simulation and gestures are a unitary system.

References

Alverson, Hoyt. 1994. *Semantics of experience. Universal metaphors of time in English, Mandarin, Hindi and Sesotho*. Baltimore, MD: John Hopkins University Press.
Arbib, Michael A., Erhan Oztop & Patricia Zukow-Goldring. 2005. Language and the mirror system: a perception/action based approach to communicative development. *Cognition, Brain, Behavior* 9(3). 239–272.
Alibali, Martyha W., Dana C. Heath & Heather J. Myers. 2001. Effects of visibility between speaker and listener on gesture production: Some gestures are meant to be seen. *Journal of Memory and Language* 44. 169–188.
Aziz-Zadeh, Lisa, Stephen M. Wilson, Giacomo Rizzolatti & Marco Iacoboni. 2006. Congruent embodied representations for visually presented actions and linguistic phrases describing actions. *Current Biology* 16(18). 1818–1823.
Barsalou, Lawrence. W. 2010. Grounded cognition: Past, present, and future. *Topics in Cognitive Science* 2(4). 716–724.
Bates, Elizabeth, Luigia Camaioni & Virginia Volterra. 1975. The acquisition of performatives prior to speech. *Merrill-Palmer Quarterly* 21. 205–226.
Bates, Elizabeth. 1976. Pragmatics and sociolinguistics in child language. In Donald M. Morehead & Ann W. Morehead (eds.), *Normal and deficient child language*, 411–463. Baltimore, MD: University Park Press.
Bates, Elizabeth., Laura Benigni, Inge Bretherton, Luigia Camaioni, & Virginia Volterra. 1979. *The emergence of symbols: Cognition and communication in infancy*. New York: Academic Press.
Boulenger, Véronique, Olaf Hauk & Friedemann Pulvermüller. 2009. Grasping ideas with the motor system: Semantic somatotopy in idiom comprehension. *Cerebral Cortex* 19(8). 1905–1914.
Boulenger, Véronique, Yury Shtyrov & Friedemann Pulvermüller. 2012. When do you grasp the idea? MEG evidence for instantaneous idiom understanding. *Neuroimage* 59(4). 3502–3513.

Bowdle, Brian F. & Dedre Gentner. 2005. The career of metaphor. *Psychological Review* 112(1). 193–216.
Buccino, Giovanni, Lucia Riggio, Giorgia Melli & Ferdinand Binkofski, Vittorio Gallese & Giacomo Rizzolatti. 2005. Listening to action-related sentences modulates the activity of the motor system: A combined TMS and behavioral study. *Brain Research* 24(3). 355–363.
Cacciari, Cristina, Nadia Bolognini, Irene Senna, Maria C. Pellicciari, Carlo Miniussi & Costanza Papagno. 2011. Literal, fictive and metaphorical motion sentences preserve the motion component of the verb: A TMS study. *Brain and Language* 119(3). 149–157.
Capirci, Olga, Contaldo, A., Caselli, M. C. & Virginia Volterra. 2005. From action to language through gesture: A longitudinal perspective. *Gesture* 5. 155–177.
Cartmill, Erica A., Sian Beilock & Susan Goldin-Meadow. 2012. A word in the hand: Action, gesture, and metal representation in human evolutions. *Philosophical Transaction of the Royal Society, Series B* 367. 129–143.
Cienki, Alan. 2008. Why study metaphor and gesture. In Alan Cienki & Cornelia Müller, *Metaphor and gesture*, 5–26. Amsterdam: John Benjamins.
Cuccio, Valentina. 2015a. The notion of representation and the brain. *Phenomenology and Mind* 7. 247–258.
Cuccio, Valentina. 2015b. Embodied simulation and metaphors. On the role of the body in the interpretation of bodily-based metaphors. *Epistemologia* 1. 99–113.
Cuccio, Valentina & Gerard, J. Steen (in press). Attention to Metaphor. From neurons to representations. Amsterdam: John Benjamins.
Desai, Rutvik H., Jeffrey R. Binder, Lisa L. Conant, Quintino R. Mano & Mark S. Seidenberg. 2011. The neural career of sensory-motor metaphors. *Journal of Cognitive Neuroscience* 23(9). 2376–2386.
Desai, Rutvik H., Lisa L. Conant, Jeffrey R. Binder, Haeil Park & Mark S. Seidenberg. 2013. A piece of the action: Modulation of sensory-motor regions by action idioms and metaphors. *Neuroimage* 83. 862–869.
Fischer, Martin H. & Rolf A. Zwaan 2008. Embodied language: A review of the role of the motor system in language comprehension. *Quarterly Journal of Experimental Psychology* 61(6). 825–850.
Foroni, Francesco & Gün R. Semin. 2009. Language that puts you in touch with your bodily feelings: The multimodal responsiveness of affective expressions. *Psychological Science* 20(8). 974–980.
Gallese, Vittorio & Valentina Cuccio. 2016. The paradigmatic body. Embodied simulation, intersubjectivity and the bodily self. In Thomas Metzinger & Jennifer Windt (eds.), *Open MIND*. Cambridge, Massachussets: The MIT Press.
Gallese, Vittorio & Corrado Sinigaglia. 2011. What is so special about embodied simulation? *Trends in Cognitive Science* 15(11). 512–519.
Gentner, Dedre & Brian Bowdle. 2008. Metaphor as structure-mapping. In Raymond W. Gibbs (ed.), *The Cambridge handbook of metaphor and thought*, 109–128. Cambridge: Cambridge University Press.
Gibbs, Raymond W. 2003. Embodied experience and linguistic meaning. *Brain and Language* 84(1). 1–15.
Gibbs, Raymond W. 2005. *Embodiment and cognitive science*. Cambridge: Cambridge University Press.
Gibbs, Raymond W. 2006. Metaphor interpretation as embodied simulation. *Mind and Language* 21. 434–458.

Gibbs, Raymond W. 2013. Walking the walk while thinking about the talk: Embodied interpretation of metaphorical narratives. *Journal of Psycholinguistic Research* 42(4). 363–378.

Gibbs, Raymond W. & Teenie Matlock. 2008. Metaphor, imagination, and simulation: Psycholinguistic evidence. In Raymond Gibbs (ed.), *Cambridge handbook of metaphor and thought*, 161–176. New York: Cambridge University Press.

Gibbs, Raymond W. & Marcus Perlman. 2010. Language understanding is grounded in experiential simulations: A response to Weiskopf. *Studies in the History and Philosophy of Science* 41(3). 305–308.

Giora, Rachel. 2003. *On our mind: Salience, context, and figurative language*. New York: Oxford University Press.

Glenberg, Arthur M. & Michael P. Kaschak. 2002. Grounding language in action. *Psychonomic Bulletin & Review* 9(3). 558–565.

Glenberg, Arthur M., Marc Sato, Luigi Cattaneo, Lucia Riggio, Daniele Palumbo & Giovanni Buccino. 2008. Processing abstract language modulates motor system activity. *Quarterly Journal of Experimental Psychology* 61(6). 905–919.

Glenberg, Arthur M., Jessica K. Witt, & Janet Metcalfe. 2013. From the revolution to embodiment: 25 years of cognitive psychology. *Perspectives on Psychological Science* 8. 573–585.

Iverson, Jana M. & Esther Thelen. 1999. Hand, mouth and brain: The dynamic emergence of speech and gesture. *Journal of Conscoiusness Studies* 6(11–12). 19–40.

Hadar Uri, Dafna Wenkert-Olenik, Robert Krauss & Nachum Soroker. 1998. Gesture and the processing of speech: Neuropsychological evidence. *Brain and Language* 62. 107–126.

Hauk, Olaf, Ingrid Johnsrude & Friedemann Pulvermüller. 2004. Somatotopic representation of action words in human motor and premotor cortex. *Neuron* 41(2). 301–307.

Hostetter, Autumn B. & Martha Alibali. 2008. Visible embodiment: Gestures as simulated action. *Psychonomic Bulletin and Review* 15(3). 495–514.

Hostetter, Autumn B. & Martha Alibali. 2010. Language, gesture, action! A test of the gesture as simulated action framework. *Journal of Memory and Language* 63(2). 245–257.

Jirak, Doreen, Mareike M. Menz, Giovanni Buccino, Anna M. Borghi & Ferdinand Binkofski. 2010. Grasping language–A short story on embodiment. *Consciousness and Cognition* 19(3). 711–720.

Kemmerer, David, Javier Gonzalez Castillo, Thomas Talavage, Stephanie Patterson & Cynthia Wiley. 2008. Neuroanatomical distribution of five semantic components of verbs: evidence from fMRI. *Brain and Language* 107(1). 16–43.

Kendon, Adam. 1997. Gesture. *Annual Revue of Antropology* 26. 109–128.

Kendon, Adam. 2004. *Gesture: Visible action as utterance*. Cambridge: Cambridge University Press.

Kita, Sotaro & Asli Ozyurek. 2003. What does cross-linguistic variation in semantic coordination of speech and gesture reveal? Evidence for an interface representation of spatial thinking and speaking. *Journal of Memory and Language* 48. 16–32.

Krauss, Robert M., Yihsiu Chen & Rebecca F. Gottesman. 2000. Lexical gestures and lexical access: A process model. In David McNeill (ed.), *Language and gesture*, 261–283. Cambridge: Cambridge University Press.

Lakoff, George & Mark Johnson. 1980. *Metaphors we live by*. Chicago: University of Chicago Press.

Mahon, Bradford Z. & Alfonso Caramazza. 2008. A critical look at the embodied cognition hypothesis and a new proposal for grounding conceptual content. *Journal of Physiology* 102(1–3). 59–70.

Marghetis, Tyler & Benjamin Bergen. 2014. Embodied meaning, inside and out: The coupling of gesture and mental simulation. In Cornelia Müller, Alan Cienki, Ellen Fricke, Silva H. Ladewig, David McNeill & Sedinha Tessendorf (eds.), *Body-Language-Communication*, 2000–2007. New York: Mouton de Gruyter.

Matlock, Teenie, Michael Ramscar & Lera Boroditsky. 2005. The experiential link between spatial and temporal language. *Cognitive Science* 29. 655–664.

McNeill, David. 1992. *Hand and mind: What gestures reveal about thought*. Chicago: University of Chicago Press.

McNeill, David. 2000. *Language and gesture*. Cambridge: Cambridge University Press.

McNeill, David. 2005. *Gesture and thought*. Chicago: University of Chicago Press.

Mittelberg, Irene. 2008. Peircean semiotics meets conceptual metaphor: Iconic modes in gestural representations of grammar. In Alan Cienki & Cornelia Müller, *Metaphor and Gesture*, 115–154. Amsterdam: John Benjamins.

Papeo, Liuba, Antonino Vallesi, Alesio Isaja & Raffaella I. Rumiati. 2009. Effects of TMS on different stages of motor and non-motor verb processing in the primary motor cortex. *PLoS One* 4(2). e4508.

Pettenati, Paolo, Silvia Stefanini & Virginia Volterra. (2010). Motoric characteristics of representational gestures produced by young children in a naming task. *Journal of Child Language* 37(4). 887–911.

Ping, Raedy, Susan Goldin-Meadow & Sian Beilock. 2014. Understanding gesture: Is the listener's motor system involved. *Journal of Experimental Psychology: General* 143(1). 195–204.

Pulvermüller, Friedemann. 1999. Words in the brain's language. *Behavioural and Brain Science* 22(2). 253–279, 280–336.

Pulvermüller, Friedemann, Rachel L. Moseley, Natalia Egorova, Zubaida Shebani & Véronique Boulenger. 2014. Motor cognition-motor semantics: action perception theory of cognition and communication. *Neuropsychologia* 55. 71–84.

Raposo, Ana, Helen E. Moss, Emmanuel A. Stamatakis & Lorraine K. Tyler. 2009. Modulation of motor and premotor cortices by actions, action words and action sentences. *Neuropsychologia* 47(2). 388–396.

Ritchie, David L. 2010. "Everybody goes down": Metaphors, stories, and simulations in conversations. *Metaphor and Symbol* 25. 123–143.

Sato, Marc. 2010. Message in the body: Effects of simulation in sentence production. Unpublished Ph.D. dissertation, University of Hawaii at Manoa.

Sato, Marc, Marisa Mengarelli, Lucia Riggio, Vittorio Gallese & Giovanni Buccino. 2008. Task related modulation of the motor system during language processing. *Brain and Language* 105(2). 83–90.

Semino, Elena. 2010. Descriptions of pain, metaphors, and embodied simulation. *Metaphor & Symbol* 25(4). 205–226.

Shapiro, Larry. 2011. *Embodied cognition*. London: Routledge.

Steen, Gerard J. 2011. The contemporary theory of metaphor – now new and improved! *Review of Cognitive Linguistics* 9(1). 26–64.

Slobin, Dan. 1987. Thinking for speaking. In Jon Aske, Natasha Beery, Laura Michaelis & Hana Filip (eds.), *Berkeley Linguistics Society: Proceedings of the Thirteenth Annual Meeting*, 435–445. Berkeley, CA: Berkeley Linguistics Society.

Stefanini, Silvia, Arianna Bello, Maria C. Caselli, Jana M. Iverson & Virginia Volterra. 2009. Co-speech gestures in a naming task: Develepomental data. *Language and Cognitive Processes* 24(2). 168–189.

Tettamanti, Marco, Giovanni Buccino, Maria C. Saccuman, Vittorio Gallese, Massimo Danna, Paola Scifo, Ferruccio Fazio, Giacomo Rizzolatti, Stefano F. Cappa & Daniela Perani. 2005. Listening to action-related sentences activates fronto-parietal motor circuits. *Journal of Cognitive Neuroscience* 17(2). 273–281.

Tzuyin Lai, Vicky & Tim Curran. 2013. ERP evidence for conceptual mappings and comparison processes during the comprehension of conventional and novel metaphors. *Brain and Language* 127(3). 484–496.

Volterra, Virginia & Carol J. Erting. 1994. *From gesture to language in hearing and deaf children*. Washington, DC: Gallaudet University Press.

Zajonc, Robert B., Sheila T. Murphy & Marita Inglehart. 1989. Feeling and facial efference: Implications of the vascular theory of emotion. *Psychological Review* 96(3). 395–416.

Wojciehowski, Hannah C. & Vittorio Gallese. 2011. How stories make us feel. Toward an embodied narratology. *California Italian Studies* 2(1). 3–37.

Yang, Jie & Hua Shu. 2015. Involvement of the motor system in comprehension of non-literal action language: A meta-analysis study. *Brain Topography* 29(1). 94–107.

Part II: **Communication**

Kathrin Fahlenbrach
Audiovisual metaphors and metonymies of emotions and depression in moving images

1 Audiovisual metaphors: A short outline

In cognitive research, metaphors have been shown to act as elementary structures of human thinking and mental imagination (Lakoff 1987; Johnson 1987; Danesi 1989; Boroditzky and Ramscar 2002; Gallese and Lakoff 2005). They help us to imagine complex, abstract or invisible ideas, concepts, or emotions in terms of embodied schemata and gestalts, like exploding containers (EMOTION IS A CONTAINER, e.g. "bursting with joy"), paths (LIFE IS A PATH, e.g. "at the end of life"), or spatial hierarchies (GOOD IS UP – BAD IS DOWN). As "intermediary structures" in our minds (Danesi 1989), they integrate cultural knowledge with embodied meanings, based on gestalt perception and image schemata.

Given the cognitive character of metaphorical understanding and imagination, it seems obvious that not only language (Lakoff 1987; Johnson 1987; Kövecses 2002), but also visual and multimodal media refer to the metaphoric schemata and mechanisms that are anchored in our minds. Also nonverbal human gestures (Müller and Cienki 2008) and pictures (Forceville 2005, 2006) can refer to mentally based metaphoric concepts. This also is true for audiovisual media such as movies, advertisement spots, or television shows (Forceville 2009, 2011; Fahlenbrach 2007, 2010, 2014; Kappelhoff and Müller 2011; Coëgnarts and Kravanja 2012). As Forceville (e.g. 2009) and Fahlenbrach (2010, 2014a,b) argue, this is especially evident in entertainment media, as well as in press and advertisements, which tend to strategically "sell" their products by addressing their viewers' immediate, reflexive understanding and their affects multi-modally through pictures, sounds, and language. Drawing on conceptual metaphors allows creators of audiovisual media products to communicate complex meanings in an embodied gestalt that their public understands in a reflexive manner.

Based on these premises I take it that audiovisual media implicitly and explicitly draw on conceptual metaphors and the mechanisms of conceptual mappings, thereby creating audiovisual metaphors. Audiovisual metaphors are understood here as intentionally created symbolic forms and relevant elements of genre specific styles in audiovisual media (Fahlenbrach 2010). Audiovisual metaphors transfer cultural meanings in conceptual and mentally based meta-

---

Kathrin Fahlenbrach, Universität Hamburg

DOI 10.1515/9783110549928-006

phoric gestalts. Thereby they use salient gestalt patterns in image, sound, and movement that are closely related to embodied image schemata in our minds as metaphoric source domains. Audiovisual metaphors thereby generate cross-modal mappings of different conceptual domains. They address multi-sensorial qualities of the related image schemata, which are manifested in the visual composition, sound design, music, and movements (produced by the camera and the montage as well as performed by represented movements of the objects in the pictures). The audiovisual compositions use such multi-sensorial gestalts as source domains of specific concepts in order to give their public an audiovisual impression of abstract or otherwise difficult to grasp target domains in the narrative. Thereby they integrate different conceptual source- and target domains into cross-modal gestalts. This is realized by synchronically relating within one shot cross-modal qualities in picture, sound, and movement such as rhythm, duration, intensity, and direction of movement.[1] As a result a cross-modal intensity of picture and sound can, e.g., address the mental image schema of force as a source domain in order to get viewers a sensorially concrete idea of narrative target domains, such as *liberty*, *the evil*, or *the good*.

As I have argued elsewhere (Fahlenbrach 2007, 2010, 2014a, b), moving images build complex metaphorical networks, referring to all types of *conceptual mappings*, and integrating perceptive, cognitive, and affective meanings. Drawing on the typology of conceptual mappings, identified by Kövecses (2002), I have shown that the broad spectrum is realized in audiovisual compositions: e.g. structural metaphors with complex source domains (system-, and event structure metaphors), as well as structurally less rich orientational (e.g. up-down-metaphors) and ontological metaphors (e.g. EMOTION IS A PHYSICAL FORCE). Most significantly, moving images can generate such different mappings even in one single shot by the use of a variety of aspects of audiovisual composition, including movement. Furthermore, metaphorical relations are established between the depicted motifs and their composition in the montage of different shots (cf. Metz 1974; Whittock 1990; Carroll 1996). Consequently, Urios-Aparisi (2010) understands the complex interrelations of metaphorical mappings in movies as "metaphoric scenarios" that are generated by the complete network of metaphors in a film.

The complexity of metaphoric networks, or scenarios, requires categories to identify different mapping types in the composition of single shots and throughout the global texture of a piece. Applying the typology of different mapping

---

[1] The cross-modal association as a general principle to unify multi-sensorial date to coherent impressions has been shown a relevant mechanism for metaphorical imagination by e.g. Cytowic 1993, and Marks and Hammeal 1987.

types to moving images is useful to discern on the local scale different types of audiovisual metaphors; it further helps to observe different cognitive and the deictic elements of these metaphors on the global scale of a piece and within its whole metaphoric network.² As previously mentioned, they thereby either refer to already existing conceptual metaphors or they generate new mappings by the use of vision and sound. Thus we are confronted in audiovisual media with metaphorical networks that are densely composed even in one single shot.

As will be demonstrated in the study below, audiovisual metaphors in moving images are relevant elements of genre typical conventions and strategies (Fahlenbrach 2010, 2014a,b, 2016) that effectively structure both the cognitive and affective reception of viewers. Moving images can generate audiovisual metaphors by a) referring in the audiovisual composition to conceptual metaphors already established in culture (including film culture and genre conventions) and in our minds; and b) they can produce original mappings between image schemata in pictures, sounds, and movements as source domains and abstract concepts anchored in the narration (or other semantic frames) as target domains.

2 Audiovisual metaphors and metonymies of emotions

Representing emotions in moving images requires a depiction of largely invisible and complex inner states. Viewers have to infer the inner feelings of characters in most mainstream genres, since these are in large part not directly accessible. Certainly the performance of significant emotion expressions in mimics and gestures already act as relevant affective cues for the empathic anticipation of character emotions (cf. Tan 2005). But especially fictional media genres as movies or TV shows further aim to communicate their public the inner affective experience of the protagonists in order to intensify empathic feelings in the viewers. Therefore they have to give emotional conflicts of a character a deictically focused audiovisual gestalt that communicate viewers how to potentially interpret and evaluate the situation the character is coping with.

In my approach I start from the premise that popular films make use of established emotion metaphors in order to create affectively loaded scenarios, aiming to initiate in the viewers intense empathic feelings and structuring their

---

2 Elsewhere I proposed the distinction between audiovisual key-, and sub-metaphors in narrative genres in order to distinguish audiovisual metaphors both in terms of their structural richness and of their narrative and deictic status (Fahlenbrach 2009, 2010, 2016).

affective appraisal of an emotional episode on the screen (Fahlenbrach 2014a). Thereby "invisible" character emotions are, of course, not only conveyed through metaphoric representation. The photographic and iconic representation of an emotional expression is per se metonymic: the facial expression is part of the emotion and can be conceptualized in the representation as a pars-pro-toto for an emotion (e.g. ANGRY MIMIC STANDS FOR ANGER in close shots of an enraged face). Hence metonymic mappings are sure to abound. Audiovisual metonymies act as hyperbolic forms that elaborate specific aspects of a very emotion state, without relating them with other experiential domains – as is the case for metaphors. By the use of close-ups or even detail shots focussing on emotion expressions of a character (e.g. crying eyes or a laughing mouth) her inner experience is put in the foreground of the viewer's attention in a saliently deictic manner. Such representations let viewers not just infer from the represented emotion to the inner state of a character in an indexical manner; rather they are confronted with a representation that is strongly guided by a certain deictic intention of the creators to emphasise a quite specific characteristic of the depicted emotion.

In contrast, audiovisual metaphors of emotions further elaborate on an emotion by relating the depiction of prototypic emotion expressions with concepts of a different experiential domain in the filmmaking (e.g. in the editing) and the setting (e.g. the experience of "feeling enclosed by a natural force" in the generic rain-metaphor, see below). Accordingly audiovisual metaphors of emotions convey the more complex inner state of a person or character which cannot be seen or heard by her emotion expression. These invisible aspects include somatic states (e.g. arousal), affective appraisal (e.g. pleasant/unpleasant), moral cognition ("good vs. bad") and the personal dimension of an emotion (e.g. traumatic memories or associations).

Furthermore audiovisual metaphors of emotion not only create deictically structured symbolic performances of *character emotions*; they also address *viewer emotions* by providing them with multi-sensorial scenarios, offering them evaluative cues beyond what metonymy can do. Instead of just highlighting significant aspects of an emotional reaction in metonymies, audiovisual metaphors also offer cross-modal interpretations of the invisible experiences and cognitions of the emotional states (cf. also Bartsch 2010).

The metaphoric display of emotions in moving images can be analysed more specifically by drawing on Zóltan Kövecses' work on emotion metaphors (2003). Accordingly emotion metaphors are a specific category of *conceptual metaphors* that have emotions as their target domain. Emotion metaphors significantly draw on prototypical elements of basic emotions (like anger or fear, cf. Frijda 1986; Scherer 2001), e.g. the prototypical cause of an emotion and the related prototypical behavioural reactions and coping strategies being characteristic for the state of a certain emotion. The cause of an emotion is mostly conceptualised metaphorically as a "force", for example the CAUSE OF FEAR IS A BURDEN; the state of an emotion implies aspects of appraisal and of coping strategies. The state of sadness for example is often appraised as *dark* while coping with anger is often experiences as an *explosion* (cf. Kövecses 2003).

Not only in language, but also in audiovisual media, emotion metaphors lend nuance to the representation of what the situation means to a person or character. They help viewers to categorise and label feelings that others may have (Fahlenbrach 2010, 2014b; Bartsch 2010). Hence audiovisual media may use such metaphors in order to intensify emotions on the screen and to offer evaluative cues for the viewers by interpreting the invisible aspects of the emotional states in pictures, sound and movements.

3 Metaphors of depression in psychology

Psychological studies on depression (Solomon 2001; Ratcliff 2013) demonstrate that it is a highly complex psychic state, which is difficult to articulate for patients who are suffering from it.[3] Although it includes distinctive emotions like sadness and fear, it also implies long-term moods and, according to Matthew Ratcliff (2013) "existential feelings": feelings of being insufficient, worthless, and useless. Depressive persons tend to imaginatively project such existential feelings to the pessimistic anticipation of events, driving to despair and, sometimes, even to catastrophes. Consequently depression is ubiquitously experienced: as physical pain, including intensive negative feelings and moods, and cognitively, as a pessimistic and desperate existential attitude towards the self and the world. Given this complexity, it seems evident that psychologists report that depressive patients explain their feelings and pains in metaphoric expressions. Andrew Salomon even states: "Depression is a condition that is almost unimaginable to anyone who has not known it. A sequence of metaphors – vines, trees, cliffs, etc. – is the only way to talk about the experience." (Solomon 2001: 29).

It seems that metaphors of depression also imply transcultural concepts. In her comparative studies on metaphors of depression in English and in Chinese, Sonya Pritzker (2003, 2007) demonstrates that similar metaphoric concepts do

---

[3] The *Merriam Webster Encyclopedia* defines depression as: "a state of feeling sad; a serious medical condition in which a person feels very sad, hopeless, and unimportant and often is unable to live in a normal way." http://www.merriam-webster.com/dictionary/depression [access: 04.03.2015].

exist in both everyday language and in medical discourses. She comprehensively investigated logo syllabic expressions of depression in Chinese and their calligraphic representation. Comparing them with English expressions she demonstrates that both languages refer to some of the same basic emotion metaphors, which are:

- DEPRESSION IS DARK
- DEPRESSION IS HEAVY
- DEPRESSION IS DOWN
- DEPRESSION IS LACK OF CONTROL (Pritzker 2003)

If we take the manifestation of these basic emotion metaphors in different languages and cultures as a strong evidence also for their *cognitive* valence it seems obvious that they are not only used to articulate depressive states in languages, but also in audiovisual media. In the following analysis I will compare the creation of audiovisual metaphors of depression in two different media genres: a) three informative animation videos and b) a movie, respectively the prologue to Lars von Trier's film *Melancholia* (DK 2011).

4 Case study: Audiovisual metaphors and metonymies of depression in moving images

4.1 Corpus and method

The following case study intends to compare audiovisual metaphors and metonymies of depression in informative videos published on YouTube with those in the entertaining and artistically shaped opener of the movie "Melancholia" by Lars von Trier.

A corpus of 10 informative animation videos has been selected[4] that have been put on YouTube by different kinds of actors, e.g. by private persons, suffering from depression, by medical institutions and organizations providing clinical information on depression, or by psychologists, offering patients their service, and user-generated videos by people that suffer from this disease. Although the corpus is certainly not representative in a quantitative sense, it represents the typical producers and distributors of animation videos on depression on YouTube.

---

4 Cf. list of videos at the end of the article.

In general the method is based on the theory of audiovisual metaphors (Fahlenbrach 2010, 2014b, 2016), introduced before that includes a multi-level procedure. In a first step, the communicative framing of each of the ten videos has been identified by considering its title, its mottos during the first sequences, and the linguistic statements and comments within the videos. Thereby the explicit communicative intention, the addressed public, and the main messages of the videos have been identified. By considering the communicative framing *depression* has been recognized as a salient target of potential metaphoric and metonymic depiction in all videos. In a second step, the filmmaking of each video has been studied by scrutinizing metaphorical and metonymic mappings both on the local scale (single shots and sequences) and on the global scale (redundancies, variations, and differences of mappings throughout a whole piece). Having identified different types of metaphors and metonymies in the ten videos, three representative examples have been chosen for an in-depth-analysis. Accordingly in a third step, each sequence and each shot of these selected videos has been analysed in detail by answering the following questions: what prototypical emotion signals are depicted in vision, sound, and movement (including body posture)? Which explicit information about the depicted state of depression is given by the linguistic comments? Having thus clearly identified, again, *depression* as target domain, it has been studied how visual, acoustic, and movement-based elements in a) the depicted motifs, and b) in the filmmaking (e.g. setting, lightning, colour use, editing etc.) are being used as source domains either for metonymic or metaphoric mappings. By referring to Kövecses's work on emotion metaphors, as well as to the before mentioned studies of Pritzker on metaphors of depression it has been analyzed how a) already established metaphors and metonymies of emotion and depression have been performed audio-visually and b) if and how original audiovisual metaphors and metonymies have been realized.

In a similar manner, also the opener of "Melancholia" has been scrutinized, while also considering specific cinematic conventions and cultural iconographies that act as relevant communicative frames of the metaphors and metonymies in this piece.

4.2 Audiovisual metaphors of depression in informative animation videos

The examination of the communicative frame (first step) and of the most salient mapping types in the complete corpus (second step) offered the following results: all videos refer to medical knowledge on depression. Hence in contrast to movies, they all have a specific informative, and not an entertaining scope. However they often frame their information in short micro-narratives focused on a single protagonist. Thereby they often use standard conventions of cinematic styles in order to give their viewers vivid impressions of the causes and the state of depression and how to cope with them. Even more so, with animation they use a technique that allows not only for a non-personal and anonymous documentation; as a highly artificial technique, animation allows to strategically condense significant experiential aspects in the filmmaking and thereby to focus the attention of their consumers on specific aspects of a represented emotion state.

The two most frequent metaphors in the use of visual motifs of all 10 videos are: DEPRESSION IS BEING ENCLOSED BY RAIN (in 5 of 10), and DEPRESSION IS A DARK PLACE (in 6 of 10). The first generates the primary mapping of DEPRESSION IS A PHYSICAL FORCE; the primary mapping of the second is DEPRESSION IS A DARK CONTAINER.

Using three representative animation videos of the corpus I will analyse more closely how these metaphors and others, including potential metonymies, are shaped in visual and audiovisual motifs and compositions (third step of the analysis).

The first video: *Depression. Animation* (length: 1,07 minutes) has been produced by an aid agency for depressed children (kids helpline.com.au). It shows a girl walking slowly and with a crooked body posture the empty streets of a town by night. Depicting her walk in the pictures is paralleled by the sound of two female off-voices. One of them is the voice of a girl describing in a sad tone her feelings of depression such as: "Nothing good ever happens to me", "I feel like a failure" – "I can't do anything right", "I feel worthless. I just want it to end"; her sentences are alternated by the other girl's voice, who describes how her friend has changed lately: "At first I thought she was just a bit sad", "I think she's depressed", "I try to talk to her". The pictures of the girl's slow walk and crooked body posture act here as audiovisual metonymies for depression, being cross-modally paralleled by the depressed sentences and the slow rhythm of the music score generating the cross-modal gestalt of audiovisual metonymies: SLOW WALK FOR DEPRESSION, SAD MIMICS FOR DEPRESSION, CROOKED BODY POSTURE FOR DEPRESSION. They help to identify DEPRESSION as the explicit target here.

At the same time the animation video performs in its composition many metaphoric mappings to give more specific impressions of what cannot be seen *inside* of her. This first of all concerns the animated setting: showing the depressed girl walking the streets of a town by night features the image schemata DARKNESS and CONTAINER as salient source domains, generating the mapping DEPRESSION IS A DARK PLACE. This goes ahead with an orientational mapping at the beginning of the spot, presenting the girl on the street from above with a top-view-perspective of the camera: DEPRESSION IS DOWN. This establishing shot of the scene also specifies the CONTAINER-metaphor, showing the girl from above as being 'enclosed' at this town with its many streets, like in a maze. Accordingly the camera perspective specifies the mappings here in terms of DEPRESSION IS BEING ENCLOSED AT A DARK PLACE and DEPRESSION IS BEING ENCLOSED AT A MAZY PLACE. The primary metaphoric concept of BEING SPATIALLY ENCLOSED BY AN EMOTION is supported by yet another audiovisual metaphor: throughout the whole spot we see the place in heavy rain, loudly falling on the streets and embracing the girl who is committed to it without any protection. As *a natural force* the rain visually and acoustically acts as another metaphoric source domain: DEPRESSION IS A NATURAL FORCE. This ontological mapping is equally continued with a subsequent motif. When towards the end of the video the girl walks through a gate that has the gestalt of a monster with a toothed mouth, the size of which is seemingly increased by a camera view from below, this place is further specified visually as: DEPRESSION IS A HUGE WILD ANIMAL.

At the end of the spot the girl's friend appears on her side taking her under her umbrella, accompanied by the off-voice stating: "Talking is the first step". In the last shot we see the two girls leaving the town, the rain stops and a final appeal is mentioned: "Depression doesn't discriminate!" Obviously the medical help line uses the presented audiovisual metaphors not only in order to give a vivid idea of this psychic state, but also how it feels when you are released from it: being protected from a natural force (umbrella and company) and finding the exit of a mazy and dark place.

Figure 1. DEPRESSION IS BEING ENCLOSED AT A DARK SPACE

The second example is the video *Depression. Animation* produced by the British illustrator Eileen Hai Hing Kwan who published it on YouTube in 2012 as a contribution to "Mental Illness Awareness" activities featured by the Mental Health Foundation in Britain, other institutions, and also by several artists. It is 02:31 minutes long and is based on pencil-drawn animated pictures.

Figure 2. DEPRESSION IS A SUDDEN FALL

The artist already clearly indicates the goal to enhance public awareness for depression during the first 20 seconds, presenting people walking down a street who all have depressed expressions on their faces. This scene is interrupted when a table with white letters appears: "Mental Health Illness, commonly called depression or anxiety affects in 1 of 4 people in Brittan. Mental health problems can occur at any time, to anyone" appears on the screen. We then return to the fictional scenario showing pedestrians in a street. In the background we hear the sounds of a café with people chatting vividly. While all people are drawn in grey pencil-lines, one girl is contrasting them with her long red hair and her red shoes. Smiling, she is walking the side of another 'grey' girl, linking arms with her. Suddenly the sound of the chatting people stops and in silence the red-haired girl is turning her body in slow motion towards the camera, showing her face now covered with a white mask. The next moment, the ground opens up beneath her feet and accompanied by a slow piano music (*Solitude* from Ruichi Sakamoto) as she slowly falls down into a space below the street while above her the other pedestrians obliviously continue their walks.

According to the textual information on the table we are introduced at the beginning to metonymies of depression depicted by many sad-looking characters, contrasted by the single happy looking red-haired girl. It is by the use of movement and rhythm, as well as by the scale of acoustic intensity between the loud and vivid chatting and the slow and reduced music that her sudden change from a happy to a depressed person is cross-modally performed on the base of embodied source domains: *slow movement – loss of motion control – falling down – deceleration of movement and intensity*. While *moving forward along a path* is a primary source domain to conceptualize metaphorically goal-directed intentionality and identity,[5] the sudden reduction of tempo, the slow rhythm and, finally the fall of the former happy looking girl, suggest that each of us can suddenly lose control about our intentions and feelings. The composition thereby generates audiovisual metaphors of DEPRESSION IS A SUDDEN DECELERATION, DEPRESSION IS SUDDEN LOSS OF CONTROL and OF MOVEMENT, DEPRESSION IS A SUDDEN FALL. Seeing her in single shots rotating around herself during her fall further reinforces the *loss-about-movement*-metaphor. Similar as in the first example the metaphor DEPRESSION IS BEING DOWN is performed here, also in combination with a dark place (DEPRESSION IS BEING ENCLOSED IN A DARK PLACE): Arrived at the bottom of the space under the ground she walks into a dark wood with bare-branched trees (DEPRESSION IS ENTERING A WOOD). A subsequent detail shot of her eye indicates that we are approaching in the following pictures more closely her inner state: her lens changes into a red spot which becomes bigger with the approach of the camera and finally shapes into a red bear. The enraged animal is crying with a toothed and salivating mouth, slowly straightening up its huge body and hitting itself with its paws. Then a woman appears from below the frame and caresses the bear. It gets back to its feet, also getting smaller. In a close shot we see the woman linking her arm with the animal. In a match cut this is followed by the picture of two girls linking arms with each other – at which time the animal is replaced by the girl with the red hair. We return back to the moment before her fall, the two girls are walking along the street, the red-haired girl is smiling again, the background sound of chatting people has returned.

The audiovisual composition that closely relates the girl with the bear, making it a part of her body (eye-sequence) and, via the match-cut, even a substitute strongly associates her inner psychic state with the bear as a *wild animal*, creating the mapping DEPRESSION IS A WILD ANIMAL, DEPRESSION IS AN ENRAGED WILD ANIMAL. As in the first example, the curing of depression is also metaphorically depicted by continuing the metaphoric scenario: COPING DEPRESSION IS CARESSING A WILD ANIMAL, COPING DEPRESSION IS WALKING WITH A WILD ANIMAL.

---

[5] The metaphoric use of this pattern is also made evident for animation films by Forceville and Jeulink (2011); cf. also Forceville 2011.

Obviously the artist suggests here to accept depression as part of everyday life not only of individuals but also in society.

Similar audiovisual metaphors, which depict the very state of depression and its emotional and bodily experiences, can be found in the third example. This especially regards the conceptualizing of depression as a huge animal dominating a depressed person. However, the video entitled *Black Dog*, produced by Matthew Johnston for the World Health Organization (2012) focuses much more than the previous examples on suggesting coping strategies. It consists of painted still pictures presented in an animated slide show and paralleled by a constant music score and male off-comment, narrating from a subjective perspective from his disease and his curing. Hence it rather presents visual than audiovisual metaphors of depression.

During the first half of the video (total duration: 4,18 minutes) The first half of the video shows a depressed man permanently accompanied by a dark grey dog. Using orientational mappings the size of the dog metaphorically conceptualizes the experienced intensity and presence of the depression (DEPRESSION IS A HUGE ANIMAL). By ontological mappings the dog is also shown sometimes lying on the man's head, pushing him down (DEPRESSION IS A BURDEN, DEPRESSION IS A HEAVY ANIMAL). In the second half of the video we than see him discovering how to cope with the dog: it is by *showing animal to others* instead of hiding it, by *hugging the animal* and accepting it as part of his life, by doing sports and *getting the animal exhausted*, or by keeping *the animal outside the house* during meditation that the man in the video finally copes with it successfully. Hence all these depicted actions serve as source domains in the pictures' motifs for conceptualizing metaphorically different strategies of *coping with depression*. The success of these metaphorically represented coping strategies is equally demonstrated by orientational mappings and the reversal of size-relations between the two, showing the dog now being *small* and the man being *big*, and at the end the dog is even leashed (COPING WITH DEPRESSION IS LEASHING THE ANIMAL; COPING WITH DEPRESSION IS CONTROL OVER ANIMAL)

To conclude, the selected videos refer on one hand to metaphors of depression already established in different cultures, such as:
- DEPRESSION IS DARK
- DEPRESSION IS HEAVY
- DEPRESSION IS DOWN
- DEPRESSION IS LACK OF CONTROL

Most of them also provide the primary emotion metaphor EMOTION IS A PHYSICAL FORCE that Kövecses (2003) observed in his study. However through the use of pictures, movements, and sometime sound the videos create more specific mappings. Thereby not only the state of depression is their target domain but also, according to their communicative function, coping with depression. The two following tables present the results in an overview:

Table 1. Audiovisual metaphors conceptualizing the state of depression in informative animation videos

Metaphors of Depression identified in Psychology and CMT	Audiovisual Metaphors of Depression created in Informative Animation Videos
DEPRESSION IS **DARK** (State of Depression)	DEPRESSION IS A **DARK SPACE** DEPRESSION IS A **DARK TOWN** DEPRESSION IS A **DARK ANIMAL** DEPRESSION IS A **DARK SHADOW**
DEPRESSION IS **HEAVY** (State of Depression)	DEPRESSION IS A **HEAVY FORCE** DEPRESSION IS A **HEAVY ANIMAL**
DEPRESSION IS **DOWN** (State of Depression)	DEPRESSION IS **FALLING DOWN** DEPRESSION IS **SHRINKING**
DEPRESSION IS **LACK OF CONTROL** (State of Depression)	DEPRESSION IS **LACK OF MOVEMENT**
DEPRESSION IS **LACK OF VITALITY** (State of Depression)	DEPRESSION IS **SLOW MOVEMENT**

Table 2. Audiovisual metaphors conceptualizing the coping of depression in informative animation videos

COPING DEPRESSION	IS **COPING WITH AN ANIMAL** IS **GETTING ANIMAL EXHAUSTED** IS **LEASHING AN ANIMAL** IS **SHOWING AN ANIMAL** IS **DOCUMENTING AN ANIMAL**
	IS **HUGGING AN ANIMAL** IS **CARESSING AN ANIMAL** IS **WALKING WITH AN ANIMAL**
	IS **INCREASING BODY SIZE**
	IS **ACQUIRING BODY BALANCE**
	IS **PROTECTING BODY**

As has been demonstrated, both audiovisual metonymies and metaphors of depression are produced in informative animation videos in order to enhance understanding and acceptance for this mental disease. While metonymies are used to audio-visually foregrounding specific experiential characteristics of the very expression of depression (e.g. crooked body posture, passivity etc.)[6], audiovisual metaphors provide a more comprehensive impression of it by relating it with experiential domains *outside* depression. Thereby they offer evaluative cues how to cognitively and affectively appraise and cope this disease.

Metaphoric mappings create rich structural elements for short micro-narratives, presenting emotional actors in conflict with each other at a certain action space: the subject and the object of depression. Realizing such scenarios by the use of animation allows its creators to give these conflicts and inner psychic processes the gestalt of many, sometimes even fantastic events (e.g. falling into a green space below the ground of a street or being confronted with a monumental dog).

In the next paragraph I will analyse how photographically filmed movies can equally create such "metaphoric scenarios" (Urios-Aparisi 2010) while following less an informative and appellative goal than an entertaining and artistic one.

4.3 Audiovisual metaphors of depression in movies: The opener of *Melancholia*

An appealing example for the cinematic creation of audiovisual metaphors of depression is the opener of Lars von Trier's movie "Melancholia" (Lars von Trier, DK/S/F/D 2011). As a prologue to the film it acts as a paratext (Genette 1997), priming the viewer affectively for the emotion states and moods of the main story.[7] In this case we are introduced to the psychic reality of Justine, the main character of the story who suffers from a strong, probably even cureless depression. Already the first shot establishes a close relation between Justine and the dense surrealist pictures that follow: we first see her in a close-up, eyes closed. Rhythmically accompanied by the grievous music of Richard Wagner (*Tristan and Isolde*), she slowly opens her eyes, looking straight into the camera, while behind her dead birds are falling from the sky.

---

6 Given their pervasiveness in the videos on the global scale, they are not listed in another table.
7 Cf. Fahlenbrach and Flückiger (2014) on emotional priming of "immersive trailer sequences" in television series.

Figure 3. DEPRESSION IS A FALLING ANIMAL

This introducing picture uses a motif from Christian iconography of the Apocalypse as a metaphor of depression: while the apocalyptic scenario happens in the background of the image, the deictic focus in the foreground lies on the face of Justine, expressing deep sadness and lack of vitality. With her pale skin, the grey lips, her immobile body posture and fixed glance she even resembles a dead body. If the filmmaking would only show her face in the close-up, it would produce a pure metonymy of sadness and depression, taking the selective body language as pars-pro-toto for the psychic state (SAD FACE FOR DEPRESSION, CLOSED EYES FOR DEPRESSION). But the background scenario offers another, symbolic dimension to the depicted situation that provides viewers with a more specific interpretation of her inner state by drawing on mental domains outside the depression-domain. Without her reacting to the background-scenario, the filmmaking invites us to interpret it as a mental image of Justine, be it a nightmare or a catastrophic vision. In this case the *falling of the dead birds* acts as a metaphoric source domain, projected onto the inner emotion state of the protagonist in the close-up of the foreground. As a metaphoric picture it includes two basic metaphors of depression that make the viewer intensively participate the psychic reality of Justine affectively and bodily in the first shot. Thereby these salient audiovisual metaphors of depression are generated:

– DEPRESSION IS LACK OF VITALITY
– DEPRESSION IS LACK OF MOVEMENT
– DEPRESSION IS SILENCE
– DEPRESSION IS A FALLING ANIMAL

The motif of the dead birds in the background act both as a source domain for *lack of vitality* and for *falling down*. The embodied gestalt of their inanimate appearance and of their falling is mapped by the filmmaking onto the concept of *sadness*, which is expressed in the face of the character in the foreground.

Given, that the falling birds are also a conventionally established symbol for the apocalypse, the metaphorical setting prepares the viewers at the same time for the psychic reality of the character, projecting her "existential feelings" (Ratcliff 2013) of depression to the anticipation of an apocalyptic event.

After this metaphoric manifestation of an inner, mental space of depression by the filmmaking, we are prompted to interpret the following sequences as imaginations of the sad and depressed character from the first picture. Thereby the use of extreme slow motion is a strong cinematic cue for a subjective perspective, indicating conventionally dreams, visions, or memories (Reinerth 2010).

During the opener two key spatial motifs are represented: firstly, outer space, where a huge planet slowly approaches the earth and finally swallows it; and secondly, a huge park adjacent to an old castle, the place where the main story of the movie takes place. The castle and its garden is presented in the opener as a surrealistic place, using popular associations of this motif, conventionalized in fairy tales, in fantastic films and horror movies: we know castles from these genres as imaginary and enigmatic places and as symbols of both wishful imaginations and of anxieties. Another art-house film, *L'année dernière à Marienbad* (Alain Resnais, F/I 1961), explicitly plays with the imaginary dimension of this symbolic spatial motif: its protagonist desperately tries to figure out whether his memories of such a place refer to real experiences or only to his imaginations. The opener of *Melancholia* even refers explicitly to the surrealist atmosphere of this film: the first shot of the garden resembles similar shots in Resnais' film. The surrealist connotations of this picture are put forward by the giant sundial (another well known surrealist motif, established by Salvador Dalí) and the double shadows, produced by the two planets: the moon and the foreign planet. The disturbing effect of this picture is enhanced by agoraphobic associations, produced in the wide angle perspective and by the contrast between the huge size of the palace garden with its monumental and symmetrical architecture, and the diminutive size of a person in a white dress, slowly moving around herself. During the prologue the entire garden and its surroundings are shown as a place where humans and animals lose control of their motion. By using the contrast of size between the place and the depicted person in the full shot of the camera as source domain the following metaphors are created:
- DEPRESSION IS BEING SMALL AT A HUGE PLACE
- DEPRESSION IS BEING SURROUNDED BY A HUGE PLACE

In one of the subsequent sequences we see a women with a child (Claire with her son), desperately trying to run and, obviously, to escape this place. Her face crying soundlessly is a strong metonymic emotion cue for fear, multi-modally reinforced by the grievous music. In an extreme slow motion we see her legs deeply sinking into the grass ground and hindering her run. Another shot shows a horse, loosing balance and slowly falling down. Similarly in a proceeding sequence a bride in a white wedding dress (Justine), is trying to run but is hindered by root-like ties from the ground in the woods, entangling her feet.

Figure 4. DEPRESSION IS LOSS OF CONTROL OVER MOVEMENT

Shortly after, we see her, similar to the well-known motif of Ophelia, being passively transported by the water of a little river, dead-like and immobile, eyes closed.

Framed by the initial close-up on Justine's depressed face, all these images might be considered as a sequence of densely composed emotion metaphors of depression. The predominant and commonly shared embodied image schema of all these metaphors is *movement*, performed both by the represented movements of characters and by the extreme slow rhythm, produced by the slow motion tempo of the camera, by the slow rhythm of the music, and, in the editing, by the long duration of the single shots. Accordingly cross-modal gestalts of the metaphor DEPRESSION IS SLOW MOTION, DEPRESSION IS LOSS OF CONTROL OVER MOVEMENT are primarily generated in these sequences. In some of the pictures, movements of the characters are even completely frozen, mapping DEPRESSION IS LACK OF MOTION. Both in the representation of immobility and by the slow rhythm, created by the filmmaking, 'movement' in time and space is concerned, as a basic multimodal embodied experience.

Another prominent source domain here is *darkness*. The darkness of these sequences is not just a natural *nocturnal* darkness; in the editing, scenes of the foreign planet, approaching earth and overshadowing it, are crosscut with the scenes of the park, indicating simultaneity between the events happening both on earth and in outer space. Outer space is represented during the single shots as a dark and threatening space. It is a place that humans cannot control by its very nature and therefore it is a constant object of collective anxieties in human cultures – as literature on Science Fiction demonstrates (e.g. Sobchack 1997). Showing our planet being approached and finally swallowed up by another giant planet creates an apocalyptic scenario, which increases the fear of being exposed to an extra-terrestrial power that cannot be controlled.

On the one hand, we might of course interpret this scenario as a fantastic one, as we know it from science fiction or disaster films. But considering, again, the first sequence of the opener as a priming cue, indicating the mental perspective of a sad and depressive character, this apocalyptic scenario might, on the other hand, also be part of her imagination and negative existential feelings. In this case the huge and dark planet, significantly called "Melancholia", might be understood as another strong emotion metaphor for depression: DEPRESSION IS A HUGE PHYSICAL FORCE. Its embodied image schemata are its big size, which is effectively contrasted with the small size of the earth; its darkness, and, finally, its slow but constantly earth approaching movements, which gives it the impression of a strong physical force. Even if the main story of the film plays with the ambiguity of an apocalypse that might both happen in fact or be anticipated by a depressed person, the prologue establishes a metaphoric scenario that affectively and bodily primes the viewers for the psychic reality of the protagonist, performed in the main story of the film.

To conclude, the most relevant mappings generated by the filmmaking in the opener creating cross-modal gestalts of depression, are:

Table 3. Audiovisual metaphors of depression in *Melancholia*

DEPRESSION	*intensity* as source domain:
	IS LACK OF VITALITY
	IS SLOW MOVEMENT
	movement as source domain:
	IS SLOW MOVEMENT
	IS LACK OF CONTROL – IS LACK OF CONTROL OVER MOVEMENT:
	IS PARALYZED MOVEMENT
	IS RESTRAINED MOVEMENT
	IS BEING TRANSPORTED
	physical force as source domain:
	IS A HUGE PHYSICAL FORCE
	IS A FALLING ANIMAL
	place/container as source domain:
	IS A DARK PLACE
	IS A HUGE PLACE
	IS BEING SMALL IN A HUGE PLACE
	IS BEING SURROUNDED BY A HUGE PLACE
	weight as source domain:
	IS HEAVY
	IS DARKNESS

4.4 Discussion of the results

Obviously emotion metaphors of depression are generated in different audiovisual genres – both in informative and fictional ones. Comparing the results of the two case studies we can conclude, on the one hand, that similar audiovisual metaphors of depression are generated in both genres. Especially by using significant elements of audiovisual composition, such as movement based elements, colours, size, fore- and background etc. as manifestations of embodied image schemata (e.g. slow rhythm, darkness, etc.) this similarity between the genres seems evident. On the other hand the examples greatly differ in their artistic elaboration of these audiovisual metaphors. While the informative videos use rather clear-cut metaphoric scenarios aiming to be understood quickly by a general public, the cinematic example from filmmaker Lars von Trier performs a much more complex metaphoric display of depression, also referring to specific cultural and cinematic knowledge of viewers. While the depression state of the protagonist is framed ambivalently in the narrative, oscillating in its representation between a psychic state and an actual apocalyptic scenario, viewers have to cope with this open ambivalence which is, following Ratcliffe (2013), characteristic of the depression state itself. Accordingly von Trier lets his viewers experience the significant existential uncertainty by themselves.

Furthermore he refers in his opening pictures to a long iconographical tradition in Western culture. By using them, he also includes cultural interpretations and attitudes related to "melancholia" and depression. Accordingly his metaphoric displays also imply the analysis of the very discourse on depression and its iconography in Western cultures. Evidently *Melancholia* thereby addresses not a broad mainstream public and hence is not representative for entertaining feature films. However in its dense artistic compositions it marks the possibilities of movies to create audiovisual metaphors that both create and reflect image based metaphors of depression in our culture.

All examples refer on the one hand evidently to already established conceptual metaphors of depression, used in different cultures (cf. Pritzker 2003, 2007). However by performing them in vision and sound, they create audiovisual metaphors, which are specific for audiovisual media – especially because they provide viewers with sensorially concrete, cross-modal gestalts of metaphoric mappings in vision, sound, and movement. Furthermore, and most significantly for audiovisual media, single shots and scenes might imply several conceptual mappings at the same time: the depicted spaces, objects, and persons include visual and acoustic manifestations of different image schemata which refer to the same target domain, saliently established in the narrative or informative framing (e.g. in medical information videos). Depression is than performed for example at the same time as a huge and dark animal, acting as a natural force, and restraining self-movement of the depicted character.

Furthermore all examples demonstrate that audiovisual metonymies act as deictically created emotion cues that communicate viewers the specific emotion state of a represented person in a focussed way. In the interplay with metaphors, metonymies further help to identify a specific emotion state as target domain in the global network of a piece. Filmmakers intuitively create audio-visual texts which are dense of 'invisible' feelings and mental states through metonymic and metaphoric representation. As my case studies have shown, they build conceptually coherent scenarios of audiovisual metaphors, which allow viewers to not only anticipate complex inner states, but also to learn how to evaluate them and to cope with them.

5 Conclusion

As both case studies have shown, the analysis of audiovisual metaphors and metonymies has to consider not only mappings on the local scale of single shots and sequences; also the global informative and narrative framing has to be recognized to identify salient target domains. Furthermore it is by observing metaphoric and metonymic redundancies and variations in the whole piece that we might identify relevant strategies and dramaturgies of creators to address viewers thinking, feeling, and bodily experiencing for a specific communicative intention.

Also it has been evidenced that metonymies and metaphors serve different functions in the audiovisual depiction of emotions – either to elaborate in the filmmaking a specific emotion expression (metonymy), or to relate in the filmmaking an emotion with a different domain (metaphor) which offers viewers evaluative cues how to appraise of and, sometimes, how to cope with the depicted emotion.

Analyzing audiovisual metaphors and metonymies in informative and fictional moving images help to systematically seize multi-modal and embodied expressions and communications of embodied cultural and emotional meanings in different media discourses and genres and with specific communicative goals.

References

Barkfelt, Judith. 2003. *Bilder (aus) der Depression. Metaphorische Episoden über depressive Episoden: Szenarien des Depressionserlebens*. Konstanz: Hartung-Gorre.

Bartsch, Anne. 2010. Vivid abstractions: On the role of emotion metaphors in film viewers' search for deeper insight and meaning. *Midwest Studies in Philosophy* 34(1). 240–260.

Boroditsky, Lera & Michael Ramscar. 2002. The roles of body and mind in abstract thought. *Psychological Science* 13(2). 185–189.

Carroll, Noël. 1996. *Theorizing the moving image*. Cambridge: Cambridge University Press.

Coëgnarts, Marten & Peter Kravanja. 2012. Embodied visual meaning: Image schemas in film. *Projections: The Journal of Movies and Mind* 6(2). 84–101.

Cytowic, Richard. 1993. *The man who tasted shapes. A bizarre medical mystery offers revolutionary insights into emotions, reasoning, and consciousness*. New York: G.P. Putnam's.

Danesi, Marcel. 1989. The neurological coordinates of metaphor. *Communication & Cognition* 1. 73–86.

Eder, Jens. 2012. Depressionsdarstellung und Zuschauergefühle im Film. In Sandra Poppe (ed.), *Emotionen in literatur und film*, 219–247. Würzburg: Königshausen & Neumann.

Fahlenbrach, Kathrin. 2007. Embodied spaces. Film spaces as leading audiovisual metaphors. In Joseph D. Anderson & Barbara Fisher Anderson (eds.), *Narration and Spectatorship*, 105–124. Cambridge: Cambridge Scholar Press.

Fahlenbrach, Kathrin. 2010. *Audiovisuelle Metaphern. Zur Körper- und Affektästhetik in Film und Fernsehen*. Marburg: Schüren.

Fahlenbrach, Kathrin. 2014a. Embodying utopia and dystopia in vision and sounds of moving images. Metaphoric performances in science-siction-films around 1968. In Timothy Brown & Andrew E. Lison (eds.), *Sound and Visions. Counterculture and the Global 1968*, 83–100. Basingstoke: Palgrave Macmillan.

Fahlenbrach, Kathrin. 2014b. Metaphoric narratives. Paradigm scenarios and metaphors of shame in entertainment films. *Image [&] Narrative*. Special Issue: Marten Coëgnarts & Peter Kravanja (eds.), *Metaphor, Bodily Meaning, and Cinema*. 56–70.

Fahlenbrach, Kathrin. 2016. Audiovisual metaphors as embodied narratives in moving images. In Kathrin Fahlenbrach (ed.), *Embodied Metaphors in Film, Television, and Video Games– Cognitive Approaches*, 33–50. New York and London: Routledge.

Fahlenbrach, Kathrin & Barbara Flückiger. 2014. Immersive entryways into tele-visual worlds. Affective and aesthetic functions of title sequences in quality series. *Projections. Journal for Movies and Mind* 8(1). 84–103.

Forceville, Charles. 2005. Cognitive linguistics and multimodal metaphor. In Klaus Sachs-Hombach (ed.), *Bildwissenschaft: Zwischen Reflektion und Anwendung*, 264–284. Köln: von Halem.

Forceville, Charles. 2006. Non-verbal and multimodal metaphor in a cognitivist framework: agendas for research. In Gitte Kristiansen, Michel Achard, René Dirven & Francisco Ruiz de Mendoza Ibàñez (eds.), *Cognitive linguistics: Current applications and future perspectives*, 379–402. Berlin: Mouton de Gruyter.

Forceville, Charles. 2009. Metonymy in visual and audiovisual discourse. In Eija Ventola & Arsenio Jésus Moya Guijarro (eds.), *The World Told and the World Shown: Issues in Multisemiotics*, 56–74. Basingstoke: Palgrave.

Forceville, Charles. 2011. The Source-Path-Goal schema in Agnès Varda's Les Glaneurs et la Glaneuse and deux ans après. In Monika Fludernik (ed.), *Beyond Cognitive Metaphor Theory: Perspectives on Literary Metaphor*, 281–297. London: Routledge.

Forceville, Charles and Marloes Jeulink. 2011. The flesh and blood of embodied understanding: The Source-Path-Goal schema in animation film. *Pragmatics & Cognition* 19(1). 37–59.

Frijda, Nico. 1986. *The emotions*. Cambridge: Cambridge University Press.

Genette, Gérard. 1997. *Paratexts. Thresholds of interpretation*. Cambridge: Cambridge University Press.

Johnson, Mark. 1987. *The body in the mind. The bodily basis of meaning, imagination, and reason*. Chicago: Chicago University Press.

Kappelhoff, Hermann & Claudia Müller. 2011. Embodied meaning construction. Multimodal metaphor and expressive movement in speech, gesture, and feature film. *Metaphor and the Social World* 1(2). 121–153.

Kövecses, Zóltan. 2002. *Metaphor. A practical introduction*. Oxford and New York: Oxford University Press.

Kövecses, Zóltan. 2003. *Metaphor and emotion. Language, culture, and body in human feeling*. Cambridge: Cambridge University Press.

Lakoff, George. 1987. *Woman, fire, and dangerous things. What categories reveal about the mind*. Chicago: Chicago University Press.

Marks, Lawrence & Robin Hammeal. 1987. *Perceiving similarity and comprehending metaphor*. Chicago: University of Chicago Press.

Metz, Christian. 1974. *Film language. A semiotics of cinema*. New York: University Press.

Müller, Cornelia & Alan Cienki. 2009. Words, gestures, and beyond. Forms of multimodal metaphor in the use of spoken language. In Charles Forceville & Eduardo Urios-Aparisi (eds.), *Multimodal Metaphor*, 297–328. Berlin and New York: Mouton de Gruyter.

Pritzker, Sonya. 2003. The role of metaphor in culture, consciousness, and medicine: A preliminary inquiry into the metaphors of depression in Chinese and western medical and common languages. *Clinical Acupuncture & Oriental Medicine* 4(1). 11–28.

Pritzker, Sonya. 2007. Thinking hearts, feeling brains: Metaphor, culture, and the self in chinese narratives of depression. *Metaphor and Symbol* 22(3). 251–274.

Ratcliffe, Matthew. 2013. Depression and the phenomenology of free will. In K.W.M. Fulford, Martin Davies, Richard G.T. Gipps, George Graham, John Z. Sadler, Giovanni Stanghellini & Tim Thornton (eds.), *Oxford Handbook of Philosophy and Psychiatry*, 574–591. Oxford: Oxford University Press.

Reinerth, Maike. 2010. Intersubjective subjectivity? Transdisciplinary challenges in analysing cinematic representations of character interiority, *Amsterdam International Electronic Journal for Cultural Narratology* 6 (Autumn 2010/2011). URL: http://cf.hum.uva.nl/narratology/a11_reinert.htm.

Scherer, Klaus R. 2001. Appraisal considered as a process of multilevel sequential checking. In Klaus Scherer, Angela Schorr & Tom Johnstone (eds.), *Appraisal processes in emotion*, 92–120. Oxford: Oxford University Press.

Sobchack, Vivian. 1997. *Screening space. The American science fiction film*. New York: Rutgers University Press.

Solomon, Andrew. 2001. *The noonday demon: An atlas of depression*. New York: Touchstone.

Tan, Ed S. 2005. Three views of facial expression and its understanding in the cinema. In by Joseph D. Anderson & Barbara Fisher Anderson (eds.), *Moving image theory. Ecological considerations*, 107–128. Carbondale: Southern Illinois University Press.

Urios-Aparisi, Eduardo. 2010. The body of love in Almodóvar's cinema: Metaphor and metonymy of the body and body parts. *Metaphor and Symbol*, 25(3). 181–203.

Whittock, Trevor. 1990. *Metaphor and film*. Cambridge: Cambridge University Press.

Films and videos

Acceptance – Living with Depression. Helen Macklin (21.08.2011) https://www.youtube.com/watch?v=hYM8LhnFi0E [10.04.2014]
Black Dog, Matthew Johnston/ World Health Organization (02.10.12) https://www.youtube.com/watch?v=XiCrniLQGYc
Black Cloud, by Ross Hendrick (27.09.2014) https://www.youtube.com/watch?v=f1R0qLh61Yw [12.10.2014]
Depression, by Royal College of Psychiatrists (27.1.2015) https://www.youtube.com/watch?v=qC8SUmYcOvs
Depression. Animation. kids helpline.com.au (01.11.2009) https://www.youtube.com/watch?v=KHQmQSUGIT8
Depression. Animation. Eileen Hai Hing Kwan (08.06.2012) https://www.youtube.com/watch?v=Frjd48hnuD4
Depression Animation, Adam Campion, 17.12.2007. https://www.youtube.com/watch?v=IEuwjpAuXAA
Depression. Short Animation. Johnny Clyde, 1.9.2014 https://www.youtube.com/watch?v=zVmClo8u4Kk
Depression – Understand the causes, Recognize the Signs, IHEAD, Digital Designers Responding to Global Health Challenges (26.02.2013) https://www.youtube.com/watch?v=Gp_EFelilZw [12.10.2014]
L'Année Dernière à Marienbad (Alain Resnais, F/I 1961)
Melancholia (Lars von Trier, DK/S/F/D 2011)
Secret: A Postpartum Depression Story, Mario Miamoto, 8.12.2011 https://www.youtube.com/watch?v=XEr5L8yKHhA
Soul in Depression, Febian Nurrahman Saktinegara, 24.01.2010 https://www.youtube.com/watch?v=a5xdoeJeawA

Elena Negrea-Busuioc
Leading the war at home and winning the race abroad: Metaphors used by President Obama to frame the fight against climate change

1 Introduction

Increasingly alarming reports on the devastating effects that climate change has on the future of our planet raise serious concerns over what measures should be taken to reduce the negative impact on the environment and who should take responsibility for putting these measures in practice. Climate change is no longer just a problem of the natural world, for which solutions are likely to come from within the scientific community; its scope has extended to social, political, even group or individual areas, and affects various interests, in accordance to the diversity and complexity of actors involved. For instance, well known world leaders publicly address the issue of the changing climate from a domestic (the immediate effects on the lives of their fellow countrymen) and a global prospective, respectively (the impact on the entire planet), and frequently use metaphors to describe the utmost gravity of the problem and the actions necessary to combat this threat. In a 2013 speech delivered at Georgetown University, President Barack Obama uses a wide range of climate change metaphors to convey to the audience the need to take urgent action. The U.S. President's speech is built around popular climate change metaphors (e.g. "low carbon pollution", "greenhouse gases", "trap heat", "clear/dirty energy") and American and internationally-sensitive stories (e.g. the Dust Bowl, biblical droughts, fires and floods, the photo of the Earth taken by the crew of Apollo 8 while orbiting the moon) about how we perceive the planet we live on. Furthermore, the President discusses the need to take responsibility for combating climate change and ensuring the future of the planet. This paper draws on a discursive approach to metaphor use in an attempt to examine the way in which responsibility in fighting climate change is metaphorically assigned to America, the global leader called upon to "solve this challenge", "fix" the planet and "lead by the power of example". To identify and analyze metaphors associated with climate change and particularly with measures to fight it, in the context of this political speech, a discourse dynamics

Elena Negrea-Busuioc, National University of Political Studies and Public Administration

DOI 10.1515/9783110549928-007

approach to metaphor (Cameron 2007, 2010) will be used. Particular attention will be given to the 'war' and 'race' metaphors – two of the most frequently used frames to discuss climate change – as tools used by politicians to convey to the public that they are in control of the issue and to emphasize their commitment to solving the problem.

There are at least three audiences targeted by Obama's speech: college students, US politicians and decision-makers, but also the leaders of other countries, as the changing climate affects everyone. The use of metaphors to express and construct the relationship between the speaker and the different audiences is investigated alongside the analysis of metaphor choices used to evaluate and promote the USA's vanguard role in leading the world's combat effort against climate change.

2 Functions of metaphor in politics

Metaphor is prevalent in many forms of communication (Lakoff 1987; Gibbs 1994; Kövecses 2002, 2005; Steen 2001, 2007; Forceville 1996), therefore, it is not very surprising that it is pervasive in political communication (Lakoff 1996; Mio 1997; Musolff 2004; Semino 2008). Politicians use metaphors to describe themselves (e.g. Sarah Palin as "mamma grizzly"), their opponents (e.g. Mitt Romney as "vulture capitalist", Margaret Thatcher as "iron lady"), or their political agendas or the policies they support or reject (e.g. Obama's "Forward", F.D. Roosevelt's "New Deal").

Politics is still a distant realm for many people, and politicians use metaphorical expressions to translate abstract topics into more familiar ones, which people can understand and connect to more easily. Examining the metaphors used to conceptualize Europe and the European Union, Musolff (2004) shows how elements of the HUMAN BODY/ORGANISM domains are mapped onto the institutions and the functioning of the Union. The corporeal conceptualization of political entities is widely spread and popular in both political and media discourse on the European Union.

Issues such as decision-making, legislation, elections and electoral campaigns, budget and taxation, social policies, education, national interest, globalization or, more recently, climate change are only a few of the heavy concepts lying at the core of politics, and which politicians need to communicate about in their speeches and public interventions. When using metaphors to talk about any of the abovementioned topics, they do not only aim to better describe them or to explain their nature and functioning. More often than not, politicians seek to exploit the highly persuasive power of metaphors (Mio 1997; Chilton 2004; Charteris-Black 2005; Semino 2008) in order to promote and impose preferred interpretations of these ideas in accordance to their own or their parties' political interests. In addition to exploiting the underlying persuasive potential of metaphors, politicians also rely on the narrative potential of metaphors (Cameron, Maslen, and Low 2010) to frame heavy political issues and to build up scenarios (Musollf 2004, 2006) or stories (Ritchie 2006, 2010) to which their audiences can connect cognitively and discursively. Metaphor scenarios or "mininarratives" are discourse equivalents of conceptual domains (namely, source domains) that help us conceptualize target domains, while at the same time providing the public with evaluative interpretations of the topic (Musollf 2006). Metaphorical scenarios favor source-based interpretations of the target that have a "sufficiently rich conceptual structure to be argumentatively and rhetorically exploitable" (Musollf 2006: 35). In this paper, two metaphorical scenarios derived from the analysis of metaphor vehicles and their groupings in Obama's speech will be examined. The WAR and RACE scenarios are used to conceptualize the fight against climate change, but, at the same time, they also inform on the functions that the speaker might have looked for, namely to legitimize action on climate change and to consolidate the position of the U.S. as a world leader.

3 Metaphors of climate change: From science to politics via media

Undoubtedly, climate change has generated heated debates that have gone beyond the boundaries of scientific communities. The wider, non-scientific public has become more aware and more interested in the topic, which has led to a sophistication and diversification of the discourse on climate change. Given its technological, economic, ethical and political implications, climate change has never been an easy topic to understand and communicate about, either inside or outside the scientific community (Hulme 2009; Deignan, Littlemore, and Semino 2013). What is almost unanimously agreed about climate change is that one cannot *not* communicate about it. Furthermore, in light of recent scientific evidence, the goal of climate change communication has shifted from merely persuading people that this process is undeniable and happening to persuading them to take urgent action against climate change (Nerlich, Koteyko, and Brown 2010).

The complexity of the topic impacts on the language used to communicate about it. Climate change is an abstract scientific concept that needs to be made understandable and manageable by people in order for them to be able to deal with its visible and less visible consequences. Figurative language and thinking, especially metaphors, play a crucial role in mapping climate change onto more familiar, more tangible aspects of human life that people find easier to relate to and use in their everyday life. Metaphors of climate change make various dimensions of this concept cognitively available and discursively usable by means of "boiling them down to "human scale" and connecting them up to established cultural knowledge" (Nerlich, Evans, and Koteyko 2011: 46). Much of the debate on climate change has been impregnated (and dominated, for that matter) by what has been dubbed as "carbon compounds" (Nerlich 2012; Nerlich, Evans, and Koteyko 2011; Nerlich and Koteyko 2009). Carbon compounds are collocations or lexical combinations of a least two words, which are crucial to framing climate change and climate change mitigation, at least in English-speaking countries (Nerlich 2012). Examples include: "carbon footprint", "low carbon diet", "carbon finance", "carbon sinner", "(low) carbon economy", "carbon market", "low carbon future". In their analysis of the discourse of UK Carbon Rationing Action Group (CRAG), available on their website, and of media coverage of this CRAG, Nerlich and Koteyko (2009) show that carbon compounds such as those listed above are used to metaphorically frame climate change action in terms of dieting, wartime rationing, financing or religious imperatives, which may impact substantially on people's attitudes and behavior related to climate change. In addition to carbon compounds, other metaphorical expressions are used to frame climate change. "Greenhouse gas", "greenhouse emissions" or the "notorious 'greenhouse effect'" (Nerlich and Hellsten 2014; Jaspal and Nerlich 2014), alongside the scientifically sound and famous "tipping point" metaphor (Deignan, Littlemore, and Semino 2013) are also frequently used for explanatory and, sometimes, warning purposes by scientists, to alert the public about the irreversibility of climate change and to urge them to take rapid action.

These established climate change metaphors and many others that are used to communicate the complexity and intricacies of the topic not only populate the scientific discourse on climate change, but they also permeate media coverage of the issue or influence the way in which politicians talk about climate change. Currently, the real battle over climate change seems to be economic and political rather than technological. At this point, the role of the media is paramount, since they convey metaphorical scenarios and stories about climate change that "can easily be driven in any direction" (Hulme 2009: 271) to a very large public. Thus, depending on availability of information, newsworthiness and affinity or even preference for certain policies or government views, media might use different metaphors to frame climate change. For instance, Nerlich and Jaspal (2013) analyzed how Carbon Capture and Storage (CCS) was covered in two British newspapers, in 2011, and observed that this climate change mitigation technology was metaphorically framed in terms of "war" or "race", the choice being motivated by the negative or positive attitudes held by the media towards the financial and economic implications of implementing CCS. Furthermore, a study of the career of the "low carbon" compound in news coverage in English from 1985 to 2010 revealed that the popularity of this metaphorical compound increased as result of the market-framed economic approach to climate change endorsed by politicians, which the media covered positively (Nerlich 2012). With the proliferation and diversification of online media, the debate over climate change has extended on websites, blogs and other online platforms. Generally, the use of "low carbon diet", "carbon sinner", and of other more or less creative versions of metaphorical compounds used in online may contribute to the dynamics of climate change debate (Nerlich, Thelwall, and Nerlich 2010), while, at the same time, spurring action on global warming (Nerlich and Koteyko 2009). However, metaphorical framings of climate change found online are not always beneficial to a better understanding of the topic. Nerlich (2010) warns of the dangers of excessive and paradoxical uses of metaphorical framings of climate science as religion, seeking absolute certainty and universal truth. The author suggests that these framings may lead to social apathy and political disregard for climate change and, ultimately, to what she calls "political paralysis" (Nerlich 2010: 437).

The politicization of climate change and climate change mitigation have become more and more visible given the serious impact that climate change has on economies and societies at a global level. With the establishment of the Intergovernmental Panel on Climate Change (IPCC), in 1988, debate on how to deal with the transformations brought by global warming has stepped out the confinement of the scientific discourse and has entered the political spheres of participating governments (Jaspal and Nerlich 2014). As a worldwide recognized authority on climate change, the IPCC regularly issues reports whose findings cannot go unnoticed by politicians and policy makers across the world. How do politicians talk about climate change? How do they convey climate change-related information to their audiences? This paper aims to contribute to the scholarly literature on analyzing climate change discourse by examining President Obama's speech on climate change delivered in 2013 at Georgetown University. My primary focus in analyzing Obama's speech is to identify and examine metaphors used to frame climate change and solutions to deal with it. Furthermore, I also discuss the metaphorical scenarios used by the U.S. President to present his agenda on climate change, as well as the functions that the metaphors used might have within the overall goal of his forceful push for action.

4 Methodology

4.1 Corpus

As already mentioned, this paper analyzes metaphors used by Barack Obama to talk about climate change and solutions to combat its negative effects on the planet, human life, economy and society at large. The corpus of the analysis consists of a speech delivered by Obama on June 25, 2013 to college students and environmental activists at Georgetown University in Washington D.C. Since this was a speech given by the President of the U.S. on a topical subject of global interest and given that the speech was widely covered by the media, one may speculate that it reached a larger, international audience. For the purpose of this analysis, I used the transcript of the speech (counting roughly 6124 words) made available on the website of the White House.

4.2 Method

The political speech examined here is considered a discourse event and, in order to identify, group and label the climate change metaphors that it contains, a discourse dynamics approach to metaphor (Cameron 2007, 2010) was used. This framework for analyzing metaphors in discourse builds on the premise that different dimensions (linguistic, conceptual, cultural, etc.) of metaphor in use are interconnected and they can be reflected across the discourse event and across discourse participants. The interconnectedness of metaphors in discourse made available by the discourse dynamics framework reveals connections between metaphors and discourse contexts, between metaphors used in particular discourse events or between particular metaphors used in some discourse events and metaphors entrenched in societies over time (Cameron 2010). Thus, using this theoretical framework to identify and analyze metaphors in Obama's speech, one can make connections between these metaphors and established metaphors of climate change used across discourse genres and over time, between the way in which the fight against climate change is metaphorically framed in this speech and the context of its production and reception. Moreover, a discourse approach to metaphor analysis could also provide the analyst with more grounds to make predictions about the functions of metaphors and the possible intentions underlying their use in Obama's speech.

Methodologically, the analysis presented here follows the steps described in the literature (Cameron 2010; Cameron and Maslen 2010). Metaphor vehicle terms have been identified and coded, that is words or phrases used metaphorically in the speech to talk about climate change. However, in the rare cases when a clear decision couldn't be made on whether or not an individual word (counted as one, or as part of a vehicle) was used metaphorically, coders applied the Pragglejaz group procedure (Pragglejaz Group 2007) for metaphor identification. Six coders, the author included, coded the transcript and made decisions regarding the identification of metaphor vehicles, the beginning and ending of a vehicle term, the grouping of vehicle terms, the identification of systematic metaphor and the metaphor scenarios prompted by systematic connections between vehicles and topics in the speech. The coding decisions were discussed and unanimously agreed during a research workshop on metaphor analysis conducted by Dr. David Ritchie and held at the Department of Communication, Portland State University, in December 2013.

In the following sections, a brief overview of the identified climate change metaphors and groupings will be outlined, with a particular focus on the "war" and "race" clusters that are discursively used to metaphorically frame combat against climate change.

5 Analysis

5.1 Climate change metaphors in Obama's speech: The obsessive use of 'clean/dirty energy'

The analysis focuses on climate change metaphors used by Obama to announce an ambitious agenda to fight climate change. As expected, the President used lots of metaphors to talk about climate change and its grave consequences. His speech abounds in established metaphors for climate change, and one can even spot some preferences for certain metaphorical expressions that are central to the President's politically charged rhetoric.

> 8   [...] Now, scientists had known since the 1800s that *greenhouse gases* like carbon dioxide *trap heat*, and that burning fossil fuels release those gases into the air. [...][1]

---

[1] Metaphorical vehicles are underlined in the data set according to formatting conventions described in Cameron and Maslen (2010). When extracted from the data and used in the text of the paper, metaphor vehicles will be both italicized and underlined (as it can be seen on the next page).

> 24 This plan begins with *cutting carbon pollution* by changing the way we use energy – using *less dirty energy*, using *more clean energy*, *wasting less energy* throughout our economy.

Taking off his suit jacket under a torrid summer sun, President Obama warned about the rising temperatures and rising sea level as result of the uncontrolled burning of fossil fuels, which releases heat-trapping greenhouse gases that accelerate global warming. Fossil fuel-based industry, especially power plants, is the main target of the Obama's bold attacks. Throughout the speech, he repeatedly refers to the need to urgently reduce the "*limitless dumping* of carbon pollution from power plants and shift to burning *cleaner natural gas* instead of *dirtier fuel sources*."

> 41 Today, we use *more clean energy* – more renewables and natural gas – which is supporting hundreds of thousands of good jobs. We *waste less energy*, which saves you money at the pump and in your pocketbooks.

> 44 A *low-carbon, clean energy economy* can be an engine of growth for decades to come.

> 45 ... And transitioning to a *clean energy economy* takes time...

The pair of metaphorical vehicles *clean/dirty energy* lies at the core of the President's strategy to communicate his plan to combat climate change at the risk of directly attacking the fossil fuel industry. He openly acknowledges the confrontation and announces to aggressively suppress any measure that would lead to increasing levels of carbon pollution: "I'm calling for an *end of public financing* for new coal plants overseas – unless they *deploy carbon-capture technologies*."

Obama's obsession with clean energy is motivated by a market-based approach to climate change. The federally supported plan to reduce carbon pollution is based on both technological developments and economic predictions regarding the alternative solutions. Not only does technology provide the necessary instruments to *make drilling safer and cleaner*, but investing in natural gas is *creating jobs*.

> 62 So using *less dirty energy, transitioning to cleaner sources of energy, wasting less energy through our economy* is where we need to go. And this plan will get us there faster.

The goal is set; how it will be implemented remains to be seen. Nonetheless, the President alludes to certain measures that will encourage private companies to invest in energy-saving business and federal buildings will increase their energy efficiency by switching to renewable sources. If needed, Obama will bypass the Congress to put in practice this ambitious plan to reshape the American energy sector. Such an action will be mainly justified by the "need to invest in the *clean-energy companies* that will *fuel our future*."

5.2 Fighting climate change is preparing for war

An overt component of Obama's speech at Georgetown is the call to urgent action against the dangers of global warming. Admittedly, the entire speech is organized around measures to combat climate change. When organizing metaphor vehicles into groups, two categories stand out: WAR *and* RACE. These categories also collect the majority of the connections between the topic – fighting climate change – and the vehicles identified in the analysis. Thus, data suggests that FIGHTING CLIMATE CHANGE IS WAR and FIGHTING CLIMATE CHANGE IS A RACE are the two prominent metaphors that are used systematically in the speech. Furthermore, these systematic metaphors build up metaphorical scenarios used to frame Obama's solutions to combating global warming. I use the next section to discuss in more detail these scenarios and their functions. For now, let me give some examples of war-related metaphorical vehicles retrieved from the analyzed data.

The President's speech revolves around the need to take urgent action against climate change. Throughout his address, Obama repeatedly issues a metaphorical call to arms, emphasizing almost all key stages of war: preparing for war, assigning responsibilities, ensuring public support, disparaging criticism, leading the assault.

First, he sets the goal of the war action:

23   ... plan to *lead the world* in *a coordinated assault* on a changing climate.

then, he moves to gathering the army

18   [...] And that's why, today, I'm announcing a new national climate action plan, and I'm here *to enlist* your generation's help in keeping the United States of America a leader – a global leader – *in the fight against* climate change.

85   [...] I am willing *to work with anybody* – Republicans, Democrats, independents, libertarians, greens – anybody – *to combat this threat* on behalf of our kids.[...]

When the army is ready, its commander-in-chief will lead and motivate it to the victory

81   I am convinced this is *the fight* America can, and will, *lead* in the 21st century. And I'm convinced this is *a fight* that America must *lead*. [...]

As with many wars, the combat against the changing climate is not easy to justify to the people and, consequently, public support for wartime efforts might be difficult to obtain. The problem with fighting climate change, as President Obama himself acknowledges it, resides mainly in the diffuse nature of the aggressor. Who is the enemy in a war against climate change?

> 92 [...] The challenge we must accept will not reward us with a *clear moment of victory*. There's no *gathering army to defeat*. There's no *peace treaty* to sign. [...]

America needs to be aware of and accept that (total) victory may not be possible in the war against climate change. However, the utmost battle that exists is that fought against an invisible, sneaky enemy. Every line defended, every outpost captured in the fight against climate change is a step forward towards a greater goal – the preservation of the planet. The supreme motivating factor driving the combatants' actions resides in the fact that "while we may not live to see the full realization of our ambition, we will have the satisfaction of knowing that the world we leave to our children will be better off for what we did."

5.3 Fighting climate change is entering a race

Another considerable number of metaphor vehicles identified in the analyzed speech can be grouped into the category of RACE, which is also prominent when metaphorically framing measures taken to mitigate climate change (Nerlich and Jaspal, 2013). Similarly to WAR, the metaphors falling into the category of RACE are used by Obama to emphasize the need for urgent action against climate change and to justify his plan to combat it. Interestingly, when he uses sports metaphors to consolidate the confrontation/conflict schema describing the fight against climate change, Obama apparently switches from an explicit public (students at Georgetown) to a larger audience (Americans and people from other countries, especially foreign politicians, journalists, etc.) who might watch the speech or read reports of it. The use of RACE metaphors in addition to WAR seems to have been partially motivated by the need to take into consideration multiple audiences (Ritchie and Cameron, 2014) that the speech might reached out to due to the notoriety of the speaker and the salience of the topic addressed.

> 53 And countries like China and Germany *are going all in the race* for *clean energy*. I believe Americans build things better than anybody else. I want America *to win that race*, but *we can't win* it if *we're not in it*.

The changing climate is a pressing global problem and solutions to deal with it have to be adopted and implemented globally. Countries around the world must cooperate in order to ensure the success of the measures taken to reduce the negative impact of climate change. These countries must work as a team, whose uncontested leader has to be the U.S. Here is how America's leadership in the race against climate change is metaphorically framed: first, the U.S. is responsible for building partnerships in the race,

> 76   We've also *intensified* our *climate cooperation* with major emerging economies like India and Brazil, and China – the world's largest *emitter*. […]

and for ensuring teamwork, because "every country *has to play its part*." Given the gravity and the urgency of the situation, America "can't *stand on the sidelines*."

As the leader of the team, the U.S. are setting an example for other team members, some of which may suffer even more from devastating effects of climate change .

> 69   […] the world still *looks to* America *to lead*. […]

> 71   […] these same countries are also *more vulnerable* to the effects of climate change than we are. They *don't just have as much to lose*, they probably *have more to lose*.

> 80   […] We will continue *to lead by the power of our example*, because that's what the United States of America has always done.

America's readiness to make sure that other teams also act accordingly and all *shoulder the responsibility* for fighting climate change is illustrated by employing a baseball-inspired metaphor used to convey preparedness to take responsibility for action, *stepping up to the plate*. This metaphor suggests that each country needs to take individual responsibility for its own actions in fighting climate change.

> 72   […] They're *watching what we do*, but we've got to make sure that *they're stepping up to the plate* as well. […]

Finally, the last phase of the race is securing the victory, and the President clearly states that America has to win the race against climate change as long as it is *in it*.

6 Discussion and conclusion

As emphasized in the previous section, systematic metaphors like FIGHTING CLIMATE CHANGE IS WAR and FIGHTING CLIMATE CHANGE IS A RACE emerge from the analysis as ways in which the President frames combat against climate change. Obama uses these frames to legitimize his political agenda on the issue, but also to emphasize the need to overcome political inertia regarding fight against climate change. Interestingly, it may be argued that these metaphorical framings suggest a certain positioning of the speaker with respect to his audience. Thus, Obama seems to frame his plan against climate change as a 'war to be fought at home', when he addresses mainly Americans and fellow American politicians (Republicans, Democrats, greens, etc.). However, when taking into consideration an extended audience (broader than those present on campus at Georgetown at the time of his address), the President frames the actions against the changing climate as a 'race abroad' that America must to win.

These two framings bring up metaphorical scenarios, "overarching conceptual metaphor frames" (Cameron, Maslen, and Low 2010: 138) that allow Obama not only to map the source domain of WAR or RACE, respectively, to the target, but also "to draw on them (i.e. on source and target concepts) to build narrative frames for the conceptualization and assessment of sociopolitical issues" (Musollf 2006: 36), such as combating climate change. These metaphorical scenarios used in this speech are culturally and contextually sensitive and they make use of narratives that are particular to the respective discourse community (Musollf 2006). The war scenario allows the public to infer that climate change is an enemy, albeit an invisible one, that still needs to be fought against. While it may be widely acknowledged that the war metaphor is one of the oldest and most pervasive way to frame climate change (Oreskes 2011), the warfare scenario may also be preferred because it flags the audience's familiarity with military conflicts and its understanding of the implications and efforts required to plan and carry out (even metaphorically) military campaigns.

A far as the RACE metaphorical scenario is concerned, this is complementary to the WAR framing of combat against climate change. Both war and race share an underlying confrontation/competition basis. However, unlike warfare, the RACE framing is more likely to suggest a positive understanding of the fight against climate change, one that focuses on the emergency of action and on the conceivability of results. Furthermore, sports metaphors may be preferred by politicians because they describe a situation where victory and winners could be determined and, subsequently, prizes and recognition could be awarded (Cudd 2007). Such an interpretation of the metaphor used in his speech might be deliberately sought by Obama, if we consider his address as a form of political engagement and commitment towards climate change. While it may not possible to identify and, consequently, pursue the culprit for global warming, chances are high that America wins the race to combat climate change. It may be the case that the President does not necessarily (or not solely) seek to persuade the public of the emergency of action against global warming. By using war and sports metaphors, Obama assigns responsibility to his country in leading the fight against climate change.

Additionally, he also relies on the RACE metaphorical scenario to boost national pride and to consolidate America's leadership role in the world.

Despite the fact that we do not have access to Obama's intentions with respect to this speech, but given the fact that political speeches are usually carefully crafted materials, it is a tenable assumption to consider that the metaphorical framings he uses emerged from a deliberation process. A further analysis of the communicative dimension of WAR and RACE metaphors corroborated with a thoroughly conducted discourse analysis might add valuable insights to the study of metaphor in real-world discourse.

Acknowledgements: I would like to thank the Department of Communication at Portland State University and dr. David Ritchie for hosting and organizing the workshop on metaphor analysis. I would also like to thank the other coders, Serena McIntire, Benjamin Smith, Mariko Thomas and Roya Yazhari for their effort and valuable contributions to metaphor identification. My participation to this workshop was possible thanks to a Fulbright Fellowship for which I am grateful to the Fulbright Program and the Romanian-U.S. Fulbright Commission.

References

Cameron, Lynne. 2010. The discourse dynamics framework for metaphor. In Lynne Cameron and Robert Maslen (eds.), *Metaphor analysis. Research practice in applied linguistics, social sciences and the humanities*, 77–94. London: Equinox.

Cameron, Lynne. 2007. Patterns of metaphor use in reconciliation talk. *Discourse & Society* 18(2). 197–222.

Cameron, Lynne & Robert Maslen. 2010. Identifying metaphors in discourse data. In Lynne Cameron & Robert Maslen (eds.). *Metaphor analysis. Research practice in applied linguistics, social sciences and the humanities*, 97–115. London: Equinox.

Cameron, Lynne, Robert Maslen & Graham Low. 2010. Finding systematicity in metaphor use. In L. Cameron and R. Maslen (eds.). *Metaphor analysis. Research practice in applied linguistics, social sciences and the humanities*, 116–146. London: Equinox.

Charteris-Black, Jonathan. 2005. *Politicians and rhetoric. The persuasive power of metaphor.* Basingstoke: Palgrave Macmillan.

Chilton, Paul. 2004. *Analysing political discourse: Theory and practice.* Lomdon: Routledge.

Cudd, E. Ann. 2007. Sporting metaphors: Competition and the ethos of capitalism. *Journal of the Philosophy of Sport* 34(1). 52–67.

Deignan, Alice, Janette Littlemore & Elena Semino. 2013. *Figurative language, genre and register.* Cambridge: Cambridge University Press.

Forceville, Charles. 1996. *Pictorial metaphors in advertising.* London: Routledge.

Gibbs, Ray. 1994. *The poetics of mind: Figurative thought, language, and understanding.* Cambridge: Cambridge University Press.

Hulme, Mike. 2009. *Why we disagree about climate change: Understanding controversy, inaction and opportunity*. Cambridge: Cambridge University Press.
Jaspal, Rusi & Brigitte Nerlich. 2014. When climate science became climate politics: British media representations of climate change in 1988. *Public Understanding of Science* 23(2). 122–141.
Koteyko, Nelya, Mike Thelwall & Brigitte Nerlich. 2010. From carbon markets to carbon morality: Creative compounds as framing devices in online discourses on climate change mitigation. *Science Communication* 32(1). 25–54.
Kövecses, Zoltán. 2005. *Metaphor in culture. Universality and variation*. Cambridge: Cambridge University Press.
Kövecses, Zoltán. 2002. *Metaphor: A practical introduction*. Oxford: Oxford University Press.
Lakoff, George. 1996. *Moral Politics: What conservatives know that liberals don't*. Chicago and London: University of Chicago Press.
Lakoff, George. 1987. *Women, fire and dangerous things. What categories reveal about the mind*. Chicago and London: University of Chicago Press.
Mio, Jeffery Scott. 1997. Metaphor and politics. *Metaphor and Symbol* 12. 113–133.
Musolff, Andreas. 2006. Metaphor scenarios in public discourse. *Metaphor and Symbol* 21(1). 23–38.
Musolff, Andreas. 2004. *Metaphor and political discourse: Analogical reasoning in debates about Europe*. Basingstoke: Palgrave Macmillan.
Nerlich, Brigitte & Iina Hellsten. 2014. The greenhouse metaphor and the footprint metaphor. Climate change risk assessment and risk management seen through the lens of two prominent metaphors. *Technikfolgenabschätzung. Theorie und Praxis* 2. 27–33.
Nerlich, Brigitte & Rusi Jaspal. 2013. UK media representations of carbon capture and storage: Actors, frames and metaphors. *Metaphor and the Social World* 3(1). 35–53.
Nerlich, Brigitte. 2012. "Low Carbon" metals, markets and metaphors: The creation of economic expectations about climate change mitigation. *Climatic Change* 110(1–2). 31–51.
Nerlich, Brigitte. 2010. "Climategate": Paradoxical metaphors and political paralysis. *Environmental Values* 19 (2010). 421–422.
Nerlich, Brigitte, Vyvyan Evans & Nelya Koteyko. 2011. Low carbon diet: Reducing the complexities of climate change to human scale. *Language and Cognition* 3(1). 45–82.
Nerlich, Brigitte, Nelya Koteyko & Brian Brown. 2010. Theory and language of climate change communication. *Wiley Interdisciplinary Reviews: Climate Change* 1(1). 97–110.
Nerlich, Brigitte & Nelya Koteyko. 2009. Carbon reduction activism in the UK: Lexical creativity and lexical framing in the context of climate change. *Environmental Communication* 3(2). 206–223.
Oreskes, Naomi. 2011. Metaphors of warfare and the lessons of history: time to revisit a carbon tax? *Climatic Change* 104. 223–230.
Pragglejaz Group. 2007. MIP: A Method for identifying metaphorically used words in discourse. *Metaphor and Symbol* 22(1). 1–39.
Ritchie, L. David. 2010. "Everybody goes down": Metaphors, stories, and simulations in conversations. *Metaphor & Symbol* 25. 123–143.
Ritchie, L. David. 2006. *Context and connection in metaphor*. Basingstoke: Palgrave Macmillan.
Ritchie, L. David & Lynne Cameron. 2014. Open hearts or smoke and mirrors: Metaphorical framing and frame conflicts in a public meeting. *Metaphor and Symbol* 29(3). 204–223.
Semino, Elena. 2008. *Metaphor in discourse*. Cambridge: Cambridge University Press.

Steen, J. Gerard. 2007. *Finding metaphor in grammar and usage. A methodological analysis of theory and research*. Amsterdam and Philadelphia: John Benjamins.

Steen, J. Gerard. 2001. A rhetoric of metaphor. Conceptual and linguistic metaphor and the psychology of literature. In Dick Schram and Gerard Steen (eds.), *The psychology and sociology of literature: In honor of Elrud Ibsch*, 145–163. Amsterdam and Philadelphia: John Benjamins.

Larisa Iljinska, Marina Platonova and Tatjana Smirnova
Secret codes of metaphor: Anatomy of architecture

1 Introduction

Contemporary professional language is one of the most rapidly developing varieties of language that gives rise to a great number of new lexical units, consequently contributing to the enrichment of the general vocabulary. Many of these lexical items are formed by meaning extension based on metaphorical meaning shift, "reinforcing the claim that metaphor-induced terminologization is a widespread phenomenon that occurs to some extent in all specialized domains" (Ureña 2012: 239).

The challenges associated with decoding of the meaning of the terms coined by means of metaphorical meaning extension are most apparent when the message should not only be interpreted by the text recipient in the monolingual environment, but also mediated to and re-encoded in another language, accommodating the realia of other culture setting a clear frame for cognition. Hence, the relations between meaning representation and context are viewed as an interactive process that promotes cognition and communication. The process of cognition and symbolic representation of meaning stimulates the evolution of meaning of conceptual metaphors, which has a considerable impact on the way how people understand and represent reality.

The present article focuses on the mechanism of metaphorical meaning extension studied within the framework of the cognitive theory of metaphor, and reflecting on the key role of semiotic representation of meaning (re)construction. The study is a part of the ongoing research on the contemporary tendencies in term formation patterns in the working languages and the principles of knowledge representation in scientific and technical communication (Iljinska, Platonova, and Smirnova 2014; Iljinska & Smirnova 2012; Platonova 2013).

In order to illustrate the processes characteristic of the contemporary professional language in such fields as civil engineering and architecture, and to analyze the terms based on a definite conceptual model in contrastive perspective in three working languages: English, Latvian, and Russian, a conceptual metaphor BUILDING IS A BODY has been chosen.

Larisa Iljinska, Riga Technical University
Marina Platonova, Riga Technical University
Tatjana Smirnova, Riga Technical University

DOI 10.1515/9783110549928-008

The metaphor under discussion is one of the most ancient metaphors demonstrating a universal character, which has given rise to a vast number of terms in many scientific and technical fields. This assumption is well-substantiated by the fact that the human body was considered in many cultures to be the microcosm of the universe and most cultures allocated symbolism to every part of the body and gave these parts meaning beyond their biological functions (cf. Wilkinson 2008: 114). In the Western civilization, the inherent connection between the proportions of the human body and ideal proportions of a building (Golden Ratio) became a fundamental idea of architecture. *De Architectura* by Vitruvius, one of the most important and still widely quoted books dedicated to the issue, became the source of inspiration for Leonardo da Vinci in developing his concept of Vitruvian Man, an ideally symmetrical human body, a universal symbol of harmony. Da Vinci's drawing, setting clear relations between the shapes of a square and a circle, has become an icon in the contemporary art (cf. Panzera 2009: 36–37).

The fact that the concept BODY, i.e. the source domain of the metaphor, is the fundamental concept in terms of which humans understand and explain phenomena surrounding them to a great extent determines the universality and productivity of the metaphor in question. This has conditioned the appearance of numerous conceptual metaphors based on the source domain of BODY: MACHINE IS A BODY, CITY IS A BODY, ORGANIZATION IS A BODY (Musolff 2005; Goschler 2005; Jakob 1991).

Considering the conceptual metaphor BUILDING IS A BODY, it is necessary to analyze it not only as a cognitive model, but also as an element of different semiotic systems. According to Hiraga (1994: 5–6), the approach adopted by cognitive linguistics and the semiotic theory of iconicity can be integrated in a single model. The author maintains that linguistic motivation is iconic in nature, and thus metaphor should be treated as the sub-category of icons. Thus, the present analysis is based on the premise that there is an inner relationship of similarity between the meanings of metaphors and the icons from which they derive.

Langacker (1987: 149), in his turn, claims that visual perception is the key channel to cognize the world, that is why a vast majority of metaphors are based on visual images. The interaction between the system of visual signs of civil engineering and architecture and the system of verbal signs allows creating new complex images and explaining some phenomena in terms of other semiotic systems, as "it becomes increasingly clear that every code contains formative elements whose meaningfulness is ambiguous without indexical correlations to sign formations in other codes" (Preziosi 1979: 1).

This means that each sign system has its limitations and in order to interpret the information and communicate the message precisely and to full extent, it is necessary to consider it within several semiotic systems simultaneously. Adhering to this approach, since the dawn of human civilization artists tried to find new sources to broaden the scope of perception and extend the existing and/or create new meanings. In this sense, architecture, if seen as the process of organizing space, elements of material, and reflection of spiritual needs of human beings, creates a unique language. We give tribute to Jencks's theory (semiotic approach), which states that as architecture can be understood in direct analogy with language, then it can be reconceptualized in semiotic terms (Jencks 1984: 40).

Discussing the interconnection between language and architecture Eco (1997: 176) maintains,

> Significative forms, codes worked out on the strength of inferences from usages and proposed as structural models of given communicative relations, denotative and connotative meanings attached to the sign vehicles on the basis of the codes—this is the semiotic universe in which a reading of architecture as communication becomes viable [...].

A range of metaphorical lexical units created as a result of the interconnection between language and architecture is constantly growing and they are frequently used in novel language use. To make comprehensive conclusions on the nature of metaphoric meaning transfer and the way how the meaning of metaphors is interpreted in different contexts, different modes of knowledge representation should be considered.

2 Cognitive approach to metaphor

Metaphor as both a linguistic and cognitive tool establishes certain relationships between unrelated concepts based on certain similarity, either obvious or implicit, it is a mode of creative human thinking, which is built on "natural human propensity to make metaphorical associations" (Morçöl 2007: 581). Metaphor is frequently used to denote highly abstract concepts, i.e. to explain the unknown in terms of the known. However, metaphor is not based on similarity only. Fiske (2011: 86–87) points out, "a metaphor exploits simultaneous similarity and difference. Thus we can say it works paradigmatically, for vehicle and tenor must have enough similarity to place them in the same paradigms, but enough difference for the comparison to have this necessary element of contrast." The comparison theories arise from Aristotle's classical theory of metaphorical meaning, where metaphor is defined as implicit or indirect comparison. According to Davidson (1984), the literal semantic meaning of the simile is the basic pragmatic meaning of the metaphor. Thus, the decoding of metaphors should be done accounting for the similarity and difference in the mapping of meaning in both target and source domains, as a metaphor is "[...] a cross-domain mapping in the conceptual system [...]" (Lakoff 1993: 203).

It is important to make a distinction between the conceptual metaphor as a conceptual mapping and its linguistic realization. It should be noted that different scholars adopt different terminology to represent this dichotomy. For example, Evans (2010: 604) differentiates between "a conceptual metaphor" and "a linguistic metaphor", whereas Lakoff and Johnson (1980) distinguish between "metaphor" as a conceptual mapping and "metaphorical expression" as its linguistic manifestation. Within the framework of the present article, we adopt the latter definitions.

Language becomes one of the ways of expression of our cognitive models, as our concepts are metaphorically structured. Tendhal and Gibbs (2008) argue that metaphor is a major and indispensable part of the conventional way how people conceptualize the world, and how their everyday behavior reflects their metaphorical interpretation of life experience. They state,

> the analysis of the conceptual and experiential basis of linguistic categories and constructs is of primary importance: the formal structures of language are studied not as if they were autonomous, but as reflections of general conceptual organization, categorization principles, and processing mechanisms (Tendhal and Gibbs 2008: 1825).

Conceptual metaphors can be realized in the language in different ways, for example, they can be a basis for novel, creative metaphorical expressions, or can be used unconsciously following the conventional patterns of expression, because the users are not always aware that they think and speak in metaphors. Lakoff (1993) discussing the relationship of conventionalized and creative metaphors distinguishes the following categories: 1) novel extension of a conventional metaphor; 2) non-conventional elaboration of image-schemes to represent unusual cases; 3) overcoming the limitations of conventional metaphors by offering of new ones; 4) formation of composite metaphors by the non-conventional combination of multiple conventional metaphors for a given target domain. When a metaphor is novel and creative, we are more dependent on imagination as a creative metaphor is ambiguous due to the multiple possibilities of interpretation. Analysis of the mechanisms of conceptual mapping may significantly contribute to the understanding of the patterns of metaphorical term formation, both conventional and creative.

Considering an inherent relationship of similarity between the meanings of metaphors and the icons on which they are based, the visual signs of architecture extend the restricted focus on verbal signs by including the visual context, thus integrating the semiotic approach into investigation of the modes of meaning representation. Eco (1997: 175) argues that within the semiotic framework, a sign is "characterized only on the basis of codified meaning that in a given cultural context is attributed to the sign vehicle". He considers that architectural signs as denotative and connotative according to codes can have different readings in the course of history. At the same time, he stresses that when considering "codes in architecture for one might be tempted to attribute to architectural code articulations that belong really to some code, either more analytic or more synthetic, lying outside architecture." (Eco 1997: 182.) He further maintains that architectural language is an authentic linguistic system obeying the same rules that govern the articulation of natural languages. The examples considered in the present study demonstrate this tendency of interrelation between different sign systems, as they are manifested in different semiotic systems – verbal and visual.

3 Metaphoric terms

The role of metaphorization as an essential process of human cognitive activity is significant in professional communication. Metaphoric terms expand the scope of information communicated, and at the same time compress it, as much information is often concentrated within one lexical item. The tendency to widen the meaning of the existing lexical units is characteristic of the English language in particular, and this is the major reason for proliferation of polysemic words in scientific and technical texts written in English (Iljinska, Platonova, and Smirnova 2015). It should be noted that this phenomenon is also more or less evident in other contemporary languages.

Metaphoric terms, irrespective of their *degree of lexicalization* (i.e. live, novel, original, active or dead, stock, frozen; see Saeed 2004; Lipka 2002 [1990]) or their *status* within specialized vocabularies (i.e. jargonism, professionalism, term), should be studied in context to resolve ambiguities caused by their polysemic nature (Iljinska, Platonova, and Smirnova 2014). Metaphoric polysemy is based on the similarity between two concepts that belong to different conceptual domains (semantic or thematic fields). Metaphor is seen as the main source of polysemic terms in the contemporary scientific and technical language. Temmerman (2000: 138) suggests viewing polysemy as a result of meaning evolution, in the process of which many frequently used lexical items acquire additional layers of meaning. Gibbs (1999: 35) states that "metaphor [...] plays a major role in our understanding of individual words, especially in making sense of how a single word can express a multitude of related meanings (i.e. polysemy)".

Polysemy can be classified depending on the aspect considered, but in synchronic perspective two major types of polysemy are distinguished: *contras-

tive polysemy (homonymy) and *complementary polysemy* (interrelated semantic aspects). Contrastive polysemy is a context-dependent phenomenon, which requires considering the particular communicative setting (context of situation) in order to avoid ambiguity, whereas complementary polysemy is rooted in the background knowledge of the user (context of culture). Therefore, connections are established to the information previously expressed in other texts, ranging from the direct reference or quotation to the indirect and hidden association (Johnstone 2008: 164).

The most frequently applied type of complementary polysemy is metaphoric polysemy, which "derives in most cases from metaphor as a diachronic process" (Blank in Nerlich et al. 2003: 268). Metaphoric polysemy is based on the apparent/obvious or obscure/hidden, but still well-known and understandable similarity between two concepts that belong to different conceptual domains (semantic or thematic fields) (Platonova 2011).

Depending on the degree of lexicalization, metaphoric term can be applied not only in metaphoric, but also in non-metaphoric use. Irrespective of the particular nature of the metaphoric term, it creates a complex network of senses and interconnected meanings (associative, etymological, cultural, historical, etc.), which can be communicated simultaneously.

Metaphoric terms in a contemporary technical vocabulary can be conditionally grouped into two categories – fully lexicalized items and nonce creations that have not fully lost their figurative meaning. Many lexicalized metaphoric terms are based on certain fundamental cognitive metaphors, such as BUILDING IS A BODY. For example, a term or an element in a compound terms *leg* is used to denote a support, *eye* is used to denote a window or an element on the façade (*face*), whereas *head* is frequently used to refer to the top or upper part of a structure. This conceptual metaphor is a perfect example to analyze the trends of the evolution of meaning since the ancient times.

When the notions connected with the concept BODY are used in creation of metaphoric terms, their symbolical connotations are sometimes communicated along with their denotations, e.g. head is symbolic of the life force, it may signify reason, wisdom, intellect, spirituality, sign of respect towards people in authority (Wilkinson, 2008: 106). These symbolic connotations are reflected in such terms as *scanning head, power head,* and *head office* (MW).

Another instance of symbolism reflected in terms is the lexical unit *feet*, which may represent balance, the power of mobility, a solid foundation. Feet are seen as a point of divine contact between beings and the Earth. Hands may signify protection, creation, blessing, power, strength, love, and affection, help and teaching, an instrument of justice (Wilkinson 2008: 116).

Many conceptual metaphors are asymmetrical (cf. Evans 2013: 80), whereas a conceptual metaphor BUILDING IS A BODY is symmetrical, i.e. BODY IS A BUILDING is also in operation and has given ground to such expressions as *blow one's roof, to have rats in the attic, there is nobody home, hit home* (GDS), etc. The reverse metaphor can be even seen as being a separate conceptual metaphor. Lionarons (1994: 43) investigates the presence of this metaphor as far back as medieval English, "That the human body may be figured as a building erected to house the spirit is a commonplace of medieval literature: the metaphor recurs in poems and sermons, legends and sagas."

The reverse metaphor is particularly productive in Russian, e.g. face is referred to as façade (Russian: фасад – лицо), mind is referred to as attic or roof (Russian: чердак, крыша), make-up put on the face is referred to as plaster (Russian: штукатурка) (DRA). It is interesting to note that the *attic* is a fairly universal representation of mind, particularly used in a negative sense. The expressions based on the notion of *deficient or damaged attic* meaning being *out of mind* can be found in all three working languages: ENG: rats in the attic, RUS: чердак протекает (DRA)(attic is leaking), LAT: bardaks bēniņos (mess in the attic).

The knowledge of the conceptual system of a language, the awareness of the relationships existing among the concepts, meanings and their manifestations in the language are the necessary preconditions for successful professional communication.

The more fundamental a conceptual metaphor is, the more widely its linguistic manifestations are represented in a language. Moreover, the mapping may be organized taxonomically, i.e. not only the original superordinate conceptual metaphor is realized in the language, the hyponymic concepts that belong to the same taxonomy may also become source domains for further mapping. Tendahl and Gibbs (2008: 1825) stress, "Among the most important insights from conceptual metaphor theory is the observation that metaphors do not just map single elements from a source to a target, but relational structures and inferences."

Thus, the idea to consider *the building as a body* gives the opportunity to demonstrate how a mapping of a superordinate concept BODY conditions the mapping of the hyponymic concepts that are members of the same taxonomy, i.e. the analysis is performed considering the taxonomy of the semantic field of this concept. The elements of the taxonomy are used as the basis of nomination of many metaphorical terms in civil engineering and architecture. The human body is represented schematically and mapped on the structure of the building, therefore, within the framework of the present article the relationships between a part and the whole as well as between general and specific will be analyzed at semantic, pragmatic and semiotic levels.

Conceptual metaphors in their majority are culture-bound, they induce a whole range of associations thus having a considerable impact on the evolution of figurative language. These concepts are extended as the creative cognition process is never-ending.

As mentioned above, metaphoric expressions based on the conceptual metaphor BUILDING IS A BODY can be of two types – fully lexicalized stock metaphors and genuine metaphors continuously created as a realization of the concept. The majority of terms based on metaphoric mapping of either the superordinate BODY or its hyponyms (parts of body) belong to the first group, i.e. they are stock metaphors, frequently not even perceived as being ones (e.g. *leg of the tower, foot of the bridge*). In the present chapter, both types of metaphorical expressions will be considered and exemplified. Metaphoric terms presented are collected from several sources: Dictionary of Construction, Surveying and Civil Engineering (DCSCE 2012), Celtniecības terminu vārdnīca (Dictionary of Terms in Civil Engineering, DTCE 2004), Merriam-Webster © 2015 (MW).

As previously discussed, the domain *human body* is the most productive because it is one of the most universal symbolic systems. A conceptual metaphor BUILDING IS A BODY is a source for a large number of metaphoric terms, e.g. *tunnel face support, eye-lid windows, winch drum shoulder*, etc. (see Iljinska and Smirnova 2012: 119–128). Metaphoric mapping occurs along several lines: based on the similarity of form (shape, appearance, colour), similarity of function, and based on symbolic representation of certain features. For example, *head* regarded as the chief member of the body, the seat of life force denoting wisdom, mind, control and rule (cf. Cooper 2004: 80) is the source domain for such meanings as *head as a leader* and *head as control panel or device*.

Considering the productivity of hyponyms of the concept BODY, concept HEAD is by far the most productive and universal across the languages. Oxford English Dictionary ranks the lexical item *head* as being included in top 1,000 of frequently used words. The terms based on this concept are abundant in English (more than 400 compounds in the field of civil engineering and architecture in particular, and more than 1,200 compounds in the field of technology in general). The lexical unit *head* is also frequently used in Russian both in its free form and as a stem in many derivatives (e.g. Russian: *голова, головка, наголовник (сваи), оголовок, подголовник*). In Latvian, the unit *head* is one of the rare instances when metaphoric meaning transfer is used in term formation (e.g. Latvian: galva, galviņa, uzgalvis). At the same time, such ubiquity and universality of the lexical unit *head* leads to the fact that it is highly polysemic and thus dependent on the context. Analyzing the possible meanings of the term *head* in the fields under discussion, to mention just a few, they include *the top, upper, front or flank part of a building, structure or piece of equipment*; *a key brick*; *capping*; *a cap*; *a wrench*; *a leader or a manager* and many more.

The element *head* may also appear in compounds, which contain one more element based on metaphoric meaning transfer, e.g. *red head* (anchor bolt); *cheese head* (fillister head of a bolt); *cat head* (capstan); *bull head* (type of brick bond or a voussoir); *mushroom head* (bulging bolt head).

Another hyponym of the concept BODY that is extremely productive in the field of civil engineering and architecture is the concept EYE: *eyebolt*; *eyehook*; *eye nut*; *eye ring*, *eye bar*, *eyelet*, etc. Apart from the lexicalized terms, the element *eye* is also used in creating professionalisms, such as *fisheyes* or *eye-lid window*. In most cases the mapping is based on iconic relationships between the source and target, that is, in all cases the metaphor is based on the similarity of form. It should be mentioned that metaphoric transfer based on the concept EYE is language specific – the concept is not used as a source in Latvian at all, whereas in Russian the corresponding form is represented by metaphors based on the concept EAR, e.g. *болт с проушиной* (literally, a bolt with an ear segment) is the equivalent to the English term *eye bolt*.

The majority of metaphors based on the concept LEG are also distinctly iconic in nature, as metaphoric meaning transfer primarily occurs on the basis of the similarity of form – prolonged support at the bottom of the structure. The mapping is more comprehensive if the transfer is based on both similarity of form and function – a support that holds a structure in place, such as a cable or anchor stay. The metaphoric terms that are based on the concept LEG include *air leg, feed leg, nose undercarriage leg, batter leg tower, sheer leg, guy leg*, etc. However, in the fields of civil engineering and architecture, the lexical unit *leg* demonstrates a polysemic character, so the metaphoric terms based on the secondary meanings are not always transparent. Apart from its primary meaning of *support*, the unit *leg* may mean a section of the pipe (*dead-leg area, cold leg, middle leg*), a channel in a main (*active leg*), a stage or a phase (*first leg, second leg*), and a road (*three-leg junction*). In Latvian and Russian, metaphoric terms based on the concept LEG are also numerous in the fields in question: LAT: kāja (leg), kājiņa (little leg), ķepa (paw); RUS: нога (leg), ножка (little leg), лапа (paw).

Metaphoric meaning transfer based on the concept ARM may occur along two lines: based on similarity of form or based on the similarity of function, e.g. *cross arm, blade arm, rotor arm, anchor arm, clutch arm, distribution arm, skipper arm*, etc.

The following selection lists a collection of terms based on the mapping of other parts of body. The definitions of terms are given with the reference to Merriam-Webster © 2015 dictionary and compound terms – with the reference to DCSCE and DTCE.

(1) Cheek – something suggestive of the human cheek in position or form; *especially*: one of two laterally paired parts; terms: *cheek plate, dormer cheek, groove cheek, cheek valve, cheek bolt*;

(2) Finger – something that is long and thin and looks like a finger; terms: *finger bit, finger joint, finger plate, finger screw, finger dam;*

(3) Foot – something resembling a foot in position or use; terms: *foot bearing, foot block, foot bridge, foot valve, jib foot, crane foot*;

(4) Knee – something resembling the human knee; terms: *beam knee, square knee, knee pad, knee pipe, knee bracing, knee bolt*;

(5) Neck – a relatively narrow part suggestive of a neck; terms: *neck strap, neck gutter, siphon neck, erection neck*;

(6) Rib – something resembling a rib in shape or function; terms: *rib arch, rib vault, wall rib, ridge rib, jack rib, rib joint;*

(7) Shoulder – an area adjacent to or along the edge of a higher, more prominent, or more important part; terms: *shoulder plane, shoulder piece, soft shoulder, track shoulder, gable shoulder, bevel shoulder.*

It is interesting to note that metaphorical expressions based on the conceptual metaphor BUILDING IS A BODY can be manifested not only in the nominal form, they can also be realized in the form of verbs and gerunds. The processes characteristic of human body are attributed to buildings, for example, *crawling* as a defect in which a wet coat recedes from small areas of the surface leaving them uncoated[1], autogenous *healing* is a natural process of closing and filling cracks in concrete or mortar when the concrete or mortar is kept damp[2], *making a face lift* is a colloquial synonym for renovation. Buildings are also discussed in terms of ageing and dying. Such figurative attribution of the processes characteristic of humans to the buildings is also traceable in two other working languages: LAT: *māja nosēžas*[3] (the house sits down); RUS: *дом осел*[4] (the house has sat down); *фундамент поплыл*[5] (the foundation has swam); *краска легла*[6] (the paint has lied). The presence of such metaphorical expressions repeatedly attests that the conceptual metaphor in question is deeply rooted in many languages and is realized in various linguistic forms.

---

1 Jan W. Gooch. Encyclopedic Dictionary of Polymers, Springer Science & Business Media, 2010: 177
2 Roger Dodge Woodson. Concrete Portable Handbook. Elsevier, 2011: 443
3 http://www.intergaz.lv/lv/ka-izveleties-fasada-apdares-materialu#.VeAPBpeLEY0
4 http://dic.academic.ru/dic.nsf/ogegova/141494
5 http://www.know-house.ru/avtor/28072014-2.html
6 http://dic.academic.ru/dic.nsf/ushakov/843014/%D0%9A%D0%A0%D0%90%D0%A1%D0%9A%D0%90

Having conducted empirical research, it may be stated that the majority of metaphoric terms based on the hyponyms of the concept BODY are formed based on the similarity of form, so their relationship with the source is primarily of iconic nature.

In general, the process of metaphorical meaning extension is endless, and new terms keep appearing first in the form of professionalisms and jargonisms, and then, going through standardization procedures, they may become inherent part of the domain terminology. Many terms based on the hyponyms of the concept BODY have fully lost their metaphoric character and are not perceived as metaphors anymore. However, as it has been mentioned, BUILDING IS A BODY is still productive and many genuine metaphorical expressions or creative occasionalisms are formed on its basis. It should be noted that houses have often been ascribed the features of human personality, having the character and soul of their own. Houses become protagonists in literary works, they are uncanny, eccentric, weird, morbid and friendly. Vidler (2009: 17–44) in his essays discusses the manifestations of personification and synesthetic analogy made between the houses and human personalities. His observations are of particular relevance in analyzing fiction, but can be of use also in understanding of the mechanisms of metaphoric meaning transfer.

For example, in the following excerpt, the building is described as having a *soul*, that is, it is not treated merely as a living body, but as a spiritual being, as a compartment of the soul:

(1) It is just this – the *soul* in building – that makes all the effort worthwhile, much more than just a cut-price roof. And self-built homes have infinitely more *soul-potential* than contractor-built houses. If we cannot build a house ourselves, how can we build-in *soul* through design and, once constructed, how do we introduce "*soul*" into the way we live in buildings? (Roaf et al. 2001: 87)

In the next example, the building frame is referred to as *skeleton*, whereas the envelope is referred to as *flesh*. Although the metaphorical expression *skeleton* is quite frequently used to denote building carcass, the application of *flesh* is an instance of a genuine metaphor evidently based on the concept of building treated as a body.

(2) Brick may be used as the building's structural material, or it might be used as an enclosing material to *flesh out a skeleton* constructed of wood and steel. (Roaf et al. 2001: 55)

The application of a metaphoric expression *skin* with the reference to the envelope of the building is quite common in the field of civil engineering, however, the authors extend the meaning of a lexicalized metaphor to include additional meanings. In such case, the expressions manifest creative use of language resources.

(3) In areas with driving rain care should be taken to place a cavity between the insulation and the *outer skin* of the building down which water can run without soaking the insulation. [...] If there is a parapet wall around the roof, the ends of the roof joists may be built into the *inner skin* of cavity walls or supported in metal hangers. [...] Buildings are our *third skin*. (Roaf et al. 2001: 58–59)

Sometimes metaphorical expressions mapped from the conceptual metaphor BUILDING IS A BODY may be communicated not in the form of separate metaphorical expressions, but rather as extended metaphors in a wider context. The following passage is a vivid example of how implicit comparison of a building to a living body may create a distinct aesthetic and stylistic effect.

(4) The church itself, *serene* in plan, resembles in its *immediate presence a body broken on the rack*. It is framed by disjointed backward-*facing* prisms that turn out to be stairs. Over the entrance a distorted gable sticks up like a *twisted tongue, pierced* by a sword-shaped window. (Harbison 2009: 188)

The last example in the selection does not only present the instance of mapping based on the concept in question, it also demonstrates the interaction between different semiotic systems – verbal and visual.

(5) The Old Sacristy is the first integral and enveloping realization of the new vision, formed of the purest geometric elements, *a series of circles and squares that assume body as cubes and spheres of air, practically uninterrupted by any obstructing furniture* (Harbison 2009: 139).

The images of architecture are visible and expressive, they can be perceived differently depending on national, historical and individual aesthetic values. The empirical study demonstrates that at present users of texts on civil engineering and architecture should rely upon corresponding background knowledge, which includes linguistic competence, the knowledge of a special subject field, metaphorical competence, and awareness of situational, cultural, and social contexts, as well as understanding of the pragmatic and semiotic aspects of the contemporary technical text.

4 Concluding remarks

The more ancient is the cognitive concept, the more frequently and extensively it is used as a source in the process of meaning extension and, hence, term creation. This is a never-ending cognitive process, which promotes creative thinking and stimulates the emergence of new ideas described in the categories of other concept systems, thus resulting in the constant evolution of meaning.

BUILDING IS A BODY is one of the primary conceptual metaphors that has significantly influenced the development of professional vocabulary in such fields as civil engineering and architecture. The linguistic manifestations of this conceptual metaphor may take different forms contributing to the emergence of new terms in various semiotic systems and triggering various associations framed within one cognitive model. The use of verbal and visual signs joins two different modes of experience. Therefore, the relationships between verbal and visual signs should be investigated with respect to their common features, specific differences and mutual influence.

The terms based on the hyponyms of the concept BODY demonstrate a tendency for both inter- and intra-disciplinary polysemy, thus creating their unique inner context and contributing to meaning change in the context of use.

Having analyzed the given conceptual metaphor in contrastive perspective, it has been observed that the metaphor under discussion demonstrates a universal character across the working languages. It can be noted, however, that currently many English terms formed by means of metaphoric meaning extension have no established equivalents in Latvian and Russian due to different degree of acceptability concerning this method of term formation among different linguistic communities.

References

Blank, Andreas. 2003. Polysemy in the lexicon and in discourse. In Nerlich Brigitte, Todd Zazie, Herman Vimala & David Clarke (eds.), *Trends in linguistics: polysemy – Flexible patterns of meaning in mind and language*, 267–297. Berlin: De Gruyter.

Cooper, Jean C. 2004. *An illustrated encyclopaedia of traditional symbols*. London: Thames and Hudson Ltd.

Davidson, Donald. 1984. What metaphors mean. In *Inquiries into truth and interpretation*. Oxford: Oxford University Press.

Eco, Umberto. 1997. Function and sign: The semiotics of architecture. In Leach Neil (ed.), *Rethinking architecture – A reader in cultural theory*, 173–185. New York: Routledge.

Evans, Vyvyan. 2010. Figurative language understanding in LMCC Theory. *Cognitive Linguistics* 21(4). 601–622.
Evans, Vyvyan. 2013. Metaphor, lexical concepts, and figurative meaning construction. *Journal of Cognitive Semiotics* 5(1–2). 73–107.
Fiske, John. 2011. *Introduction into communication studies*. London: Routledge.
Gibbs, Raymond W. 1999. Researching metaphor. In Graham Low & Lynne Cameron (eds.), *Researching and Applying Metaphor*, 29–47. Cambridge: Cambridge University Press.
Gibbs, Raymond W. 1994. *The poetics of mind: Figurative thought, language, and understanding*. Cambridge: Cambridge University Press.
Goschler, Juliana. 2005. Embodiment and body metaphors. *metaphorik.de* 9. 33–52. Accessed January 24, 2017. http://www.metaphorik.de/sites/www.metaphorik.de/files/journal-pdf/09_2005_goschler.pdf.
Harbison, Robert. 2009. *Travels into the history of architecture*. Chicago: The University of Chicago Press.
Hiraga, Masako K. 1994. Diagrams and metaphors: Iconic aspects in language. *Journal of Pragmatics* 22. 5–21.
Iljinska, Larisa, Marina Platonova & Tatjana Smirnova. 2015. Coinage and application of metaphoric terms in scientific and technical texts: Contrastive approach. In Maksymski Karin, Gutermuth Silke, Hansen-Schirra Silvia (eds.), *Translation and Comprehensibility*, 139–162. Berlin: Frank & Timme.
Iljinska, Larisa, Marina Platonova & Tatjana Smirnova. 2014. Metaphoric terms: Elusive magic of meaning transformation. In Budin Gerhard & Lušicky Vesna (eds.), *Language for special purposes in multilingual, transcultural world*, Proceedings of the 19th European Symposium on Language for Special Purposes, 442–451. Vienna: University of Vienna.
Iljinska, Larisa & Tatjana Smirnova. 2012. Metaphoric terms in architecture and civil engineering: taxonomy of the concept 'Body'. *Vārds un tā pētīšanas aspekti rakstu krājums* 16(2). 119–128. Liepāja: Liepāja University.
Jakob, Karlheinz. 1991. *Maschine, mentales modell, metapher. Studien zur semantik und geschichte der techniksprache*. Germany: De Gruyter.
Jencks, Charles. 1984. *The Language of post-modern architecture*. New York: Rizzoli.
Johnstone, Barbara. 2008. *Discourse analysis*. Oxford: Blackwell.
Lakoff, George & Mark Johnson. 1980. *Metaphors we live by*. Chicago: University of Chicago Press.
Lakoff, George. 1993. The contemporary theory of metaphor. In Andrew Ortony (ed.), *Metaphor and thought*, 202–252. Cambridge: Cambridge University Press.
Langacker, Ronald W. 1987. *Foundations of cognitive grammar: Theoretical prerequisites*. Stanford: Stanford University Press.
Lionarons, Joyce Tally. 1994. Bodies, buildings, and boundaries: Metaphors of liminality in old English and old norse literature. *Essays in Medieval Studies* 11. Accessed January 24, 2017. http://www.illinoismedieval.org/ems/emsv11.html
Lipka, Leonhard. 2002 [1990]. *English lexicology: Lexical structure, word semantics and word-formation*. Tübingen: Max Niemeyer Verlag.
Morçöl, Gök, T.U.G. 2007. Methods of assessing and enhancing creativity for public policy decision making. In Gök Morçöl (ed.), *Handbook of Decision Making*, 565–585. Boca Raton, FL: CRC Press.
Musolff, Andreas. 2004. Metaphor and conceptual evolution. *Metaphorik.de* 7. 55–77. Accessed January 24, 2017. http://www.metaphorik.de/07/musolff.pdf.

Panzera, Anthony. 2009. Learning from Leonardo's the vitruvian man. *Drawing*. 34–41.
Platonova, Marina. 2013. Contemporary principles of terminology research. *Vārds un tā pētīšanas aspekti* 17(2). 154–167.
Platonova, Marina. 2011. *Term formation and application: Contrastive analysis*. Rīga: RTU Publishing House.
Preziosi, Donald. 1979. *Architecture, language, and meaning: The origins of the built world and its semiotic organization*. Hague: De Gruyter.
Roaf, Sue, Manuel Fuentes & Stephanie Thomas. 2001. *Ecohouse*. Oxford: Architectural Press.
Saeed, John. *Semantics*. 2004. Malden and Oxford: Wiley Blackwell.
Temmerman, Rita. 2000. *Towards new ways of terminological description. The sociocognitive approach*. Amsterdam and Philadelphia: John Benjamins.
Tendahl, Markus & Raymond W. Gibbs. 2008. Complementary perspectives on metaphor: Cognitive linguistics and relevance theory. *Journal of Pragmatics* 3. 1823–1864.
Ureña, José Manuel. 2012. Conceptual types of terminological metaphors in marine biology: An English-Spanish contrastive analysis from an experientialist perspective. In MacArthur Fiona, Oncins-Martínez José Luis, Sánchez-García Manuel and Piquer-Píriz Ana María (eds.). *Metaphor in Use. Context, culture, and communication*, 239–260. Amsterdam and Philadelphia: John Benjamins.
Vidler, Anthony. 1996. Unhomely Houses. *The architectural uncanny. Essays in the modern unhomely*, 17–44. Boston: The MIT Press.
Wilkinson, Kathryn (ed.). 2008. *Signs and symbols, An illustrated guide to their origins and meanings*. London: Dorling Kindersley Limited, A Penguin Company.

Dictionaries

DGA – Green's Dictionary of Slang//Green, Jonathon. UK: Chambers Harrap Publishers, 2010.
MW – Merriam-Webster Dictionary. Accessed: http://www.merriam-webster.com [8 February, 2015]
DTCE – Dictionary of Terms in Civil Engineering //Celtniecības terminu vārdnīca. Krauklis, Vilis. Rīga: Telamons, 2003.
DCSCE – Dictionary of Construction, Surveying and Civil Engineering // Gorse, Christopher, Johnston, David, Pritchard, Martin. UK: Oxford University Press, 2012.
DRA – Dictionary of Russian Argo. Accessed: http://russian_argo.academic.ru/ [10 March, 2015]

Micaela Rossi
Some observations about metaphors in specialised languages

1 Terminological metaphors at an interdisciplinary crossroads

The main studies about the semiotic status of metaphorical terms in Languages for Special Purposes (hereafter LSP) in recent decades have been essentially carried out by terminologists. In the French field, the short essay by Assal (1994) can be considered as a starting point for this scientific trend: in this article, Assal explicitly puts the emphasis on the progressive lexicalization that metaphor has undergone in special languages, emphasising the evolution of metaphors from rhetorical devices to mature technical terms in LSP:

> La métaphore terminologique est loin d'être une simple façon de parler, elle est essentiellement une façon de penser. Certes elle est un emprunt imagé, mais une fois que cet emprunt est réinvesti dans une pratique sociale, une fois que sa signification est réglée par les acteurs agissant dans le cadre de cette pratique, elle devient l'expression d'un nouveau concept (Assal 1994: 23).[1]

The use of technical and scientific terms derived from metaphors had long been a crucial subject in the field of studies on specialised languages; in Kocourek's fundamental study about LSP characteristics (1991), a paragraph is devoted to the description of specialised vocabularies, and to the role of metaphors in technical and scientific terminologies. However, the first period of studies on terminological metaphors seems to relegate this phenomenon to the simple case of isolated, episodic catachresis, based on a formal analogy between concrete referents in a source domain and a target domain, or simply on the need to find simple and comprehensible denominations for complex concepts which could be too difficult to express. This initial trend is in line with the traditional theory, or general theory, of terminology, which dominates this scientific field ever since Wüster's first works and till the end of the 90s. According to this first paradigm, terms – including

---

[1] "Terminological metaphor, far from being a simple way of speaking, is essentially a way of thinking. It is a borrowed image, but once this borrowing is reinvested in a social practice, once its meaning is regulated by the actors acting within the framework of this practice, it becomes the expression of a new concept" (our translation).

Micaela Rossi, University of Genoa

metaphorical terms – are considered just as labels for universally shared concepts. This first theory of terminology does not take into proper account the complex cognitive strategies necessary to give a structure to specialised domains in different languages and cultures, with due regard to anisomorphism and variation.

On the other hand, and during the same period, epistemologists and philosophers' main interest in terminological metaphor is focused on an opposite and at the same time complementary aspect of this phenomenon, *i.e.* the metaphorical projective mechanism and its potential in terms of theoretical modelling. Epistemologists focus on the function of metaphor as a tool for creating, modelling and promoting new scientific theories. Schlanger and Stengers' (1991), then Schlanger's (1995) studies, are an interesting example of this trend that, following Boyd and Kuhn's tradition, puts a particular emphasis on the heuristic function of metaphor. Metaphor thus becomes a figure of concept that generates an interaction between two separate conceptual domains, through allotopic predication, causing a redefinition of the concepts involved, both in the source domain and in the target domain:

> Ce qui se produit est un phénomène que Koestler nomme bissociation : une synthèse immédiate entre deux zones ou matrices. Les deux matrices étaient séparées : soit dans l'espace des disciplines, soit même dans le temps. [...] Le saut dramatique qu'est le rapprochement est l'acte même de la créativité [...] L'activité métaphorique se présente comme la face verbale de la conceptualisation inventive (Stengers 1995: 80–87).[2]

Metaphor according to these authors is a founder tool of a scientific paradigm, rather than a simple catachresis strategy of denomination for technical concepts. We should also mention here Evelyn Fox-Keller's studies (1995), as well as Stengers' analysis of organicist and mechanistic metaphors in science and philosophy (1995), and the previous essay by Claudine Normand, *Métaphore et concept* (1978), where the author underlines the main expressions of conceptual metaphor in scientific theories from the late nineteenth to the early twentieth century, from Nietzsche to Freud, to Ferdinand de Saussure.

Since the 2000s, these different research fields begin to be interested in a wider sense to all the achievements of conceptual metaphor in special languages. We can recognize in the advent of the new paradigms of terminological description a fundamental turning point, marked by the formulation of new theoretical approaches, diverging from the general theory of terminology formulated by

---

[2] "What happens is a phenomenon that Koestler called *bissociation*: the immediate synthesis between two areas or matrices. The matrices are basically separated, either for their knowledge domain, or for their chronological background. [...] The dramatic passage of their reconciliation is the act of creativity [...] The metaphorical activity turns out to be the verbal side of inventive conceptualization." (our translation)

Wüster. Socioterminology (Gaudin 2002), the socio-cognitive theory (Temmerman 2000), the theory of communication in specialised languages (Cabré 2000) and cultural terminology (Diki-Kidiri 2007) deeply question the onomasiological, monoreferential paradigm that had so far characterized terminological studies. They promote a broader reflection on textual and discursive realizations of metaphor in technical-scientific contexts, contributing to identify a more complex role of metaphorical processes in LSP.

This important breakthrough is the result of the influence of other disciplines on terminology, following the development and evolution of related sciences such as text linguistics, pragmatics and cognitive linguistics. A fundamental contribution derives from the progress of cognitive studies on metaphor, which is by now to be considered as a complex interaction between different conceptual domains: from the forerunners such as Richards (1936) and Black (1954), to Lakoff and Johnson (1980), to the more recent *blend* theory by Fauconnier and Turner (2002). The concept of metaphor as a simple label – formerly the object of terminologists' interest – and the concept of metaphor as a creative instrument of scientific paradigms – formerly epistemologists and philosophers' interest – are completed by the vision of metaphor as a cognitive universal device, in which conceptual interaction can produce different linguistic (mainly lexical) realizations in texts and speeches. It is on the basis of Lakoff and Johnson's theory that Temmerman for example (2007) identifies the specific transfer from English into French of the metaphorical isotopy of the genetic code as a photographic film.

It is thus possible to identify different semiotic forms of metaphor in specialised languages. Far from being just episodic catachresis, based on a referential analogy, or strategies to legitimate epistemological paradigms in the history of scientific thought, or universal forms of knowledge informing our daily life, metaphors in specialised languages are to be considered as complex processes and phenomena, showing different semiotic natures and functions. Research on terminological metaphor rarely takes into account this complexity, or the plurality of functions that metaphor can assume in specialised texts and discourses. In particular, most of researches and studies focus on the communicative function of metaphor for popularization and dissemination of specialised knowledge – among these studies, we should mention Collombat (2003) whose analysis can be included in the field of discourse analysis and science popularization (Jacobi 1987, 1999). More recently, Oliveira's studies (2009) focus on this specific educational or informative purposes of metaphor in scientific domains – in the case of Oliveira, in cardiology.

During the last decades, the role of metaphor in terminology has been analysed in its various semiotic and functional aspects, and the field of study on this topic shows a certain autonomy within the broader research field on metaphor.

To name but a few, there have been numerous monographs and miscellaneous works dedicated to this subject in the last five years, such as in 2009, the book edited by Dury, Maniez, Arlin and Rougemont, reporting the proceedings of the CRTT symposium *La métaphore en langues de spécialité* (September 2008). The most recent essay by Oliveira (2009), which can be considered as a synthesis of preceding studies, finally highlights a range of expressive possibilities of metaphor in specialised languages.

Oliveira distinguishes different functions for metaphor in specialised languages:
- "nominative", when metaphor – normally a catachresis – is exploited to fill a lexical gap in the context of a specialised jargon. It is the case of the metaphorical term "geographic tongue" in the medical field, which is the only possible denomination for the disease in question;
- "heuristic", when metaphor has the role of a trigger for establishing new analogies and forms of understanding; according to Oliveira, this is the case of the application of the Dutch irrigation canals metaphor to the cardiovascular system, which allowed William Harvey to formulate his concise overview of this scientific discovery in the Seventeenth century;
- "hermeneutics", when metaphor offers a more immediate denomination or expression for a complex concept, easier to promote understanding if compared to the scientific name or technique. So, always in Oliveira (2009), the technical concept referring to the patent "Novacor" appears more accessible if designated by the competitor figurative term "*cœur de lion*";
- "popularization", when technical discourse makes use of metaphors for explanatory functions (see also the essays by Jacobi, 1986, 1999): in patient-doctor medical discourse, for instance, the term "*cœur en sabot*" will be more immediately comprehensible to the nonprofessional than the technical "*hypertrophie ventriculaire droite*";
- "teaching", when metaphor is used as a teaching tool, in order to lead the learner progressively from the level of a profane to that of a specialist.

2 A typology of terminological metaphors in scientific and technical domains

The most recent analysis by Prandi (2010) focuses on variety in terminological metaphor, identifying different semiotic natures of metaphor in specialised texts, from simple isolated catachresis, to consistent shared metaphorical concepts, to creative metaphors that challenge our ordinary conditions for consistency to generate a conceptual projection, and that are functional to the creation of new epistemological paradigms.

Metaphor is thus free from a traditional unified vision, and it can be considered in its various manifestations. This complexity finally puts into question the potential "career of metaphor" theory (Bowdle and Gentner 2005) or the conception of an inevitable cycle of life for metaphors (which would arise as conflicts and evolve then in catachresis) in favour of a more complex and articulated conception. The name of "terminological metaphors", far from designating a single concept, reveals a plurality of functions, for their textual and discursive behaviour as well as for their semiotic nature.

More specifically, according to Prandi and Rossi (2012), different semiotic manifestations can be identified for metaphors in special languages:

1. The first category of metaphors, more frequent in technical languages with a high concentration of concepts with a concrete referent, is realized as catachresis based on a formal analogy between referents. It is the case for example of "tears" or "legs" of wine, traces left by glycerol and alcohol on the glass in the phase of visual analysis:

Figure 1. Wine "legs" or "tears" (http://www.wineblogroll.com/2014/08/gli-archetti-del-vino-effetto-marangoni.html)

In this case, metaphor has a mainly denominative function and allows to fill in the gaps of a specific vocabulary, offering accessible denominations and ensuring a quick and effective cognitive anchor to the concept. However, its heuristic potential remains limited to isolated labels, crystallized in the formal analogy.

Similarly, in the vocabulary of fashion, there are many terms based on isolated metaphors: *batwing sleeve, egg dress, elephant leg pants*... Even in more scientific languages, related to engineering or hard sciences, formal catachresis is widely used, as evidenced by terms such as *squirrel cage* (see below) or the far more used *candles*...

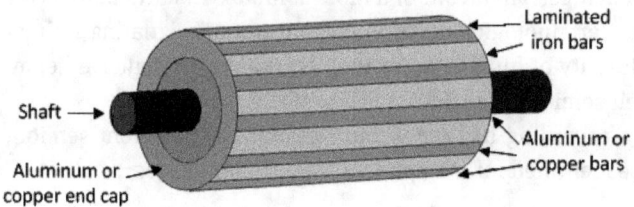

Induction Motor Squirrel Cage Rotor

Figure 2. Squirrel-cage rotor (http://nuclearpowertraining.tpub.com/h1011v4/css/Figure-5-Squirrel-Cage-Induction-Rotor-30.htm)

2. In a second category of metaphor, the metaphorical figure is used as a reference to a shared conceptual (often anthropomorphic) isotopy, which is functional to the creation of new terms. It is the case for example for the anthropomorphic metaphor in the terminology of wine tasting (Rossi 2009a, 2009b), in which various terms are created on the basis of the identification WINE IS A PERSON: the wine is therefore *noble, elegant, sincere, generous*, but also *old, young, mature, decrepit*, and so on.

Similarly, the UNIVERSE IS A PERSON isotopy generates within the terminology of astrophysics complex metaphorical series, such as *generation of stars, progenitor stars, stellar nursery* etc. (Giaufret and Rossi 2013).

To mention another interesting example, in the field of financial analysis, the FINANCIAL MARKET IS A ZOO isotopy is exploited to generate new technical terms for defining markets, investors and companies:

Table 1. Financial metaphorical isotopies

INVESTORS ARE ANIMALS	*lemming* [...] an investor that follows the crowd into an investment that will inevitably end unsuccessfully. *ostrich* [...] an investor who ignores important pieces of information, which have the ability to impact them or the market in which they operate. *pig* [...] an investor who is often seen as greedy, having forgotten [his] original investment strategy to focus on securing unrealistic future gains *sheep* [...] an investor who lacks a focused trading strategy and trades on the suggestions of others, including friends, family and financial advisors *shark* [...] an investor that is hostile to the target firm's management and that is interested in taking over the firm
MARKETS ARE ANIMALS	*deer market* [...] a flat market, characterised by low activity and investors' uncertaintly and unwilling-ness to buy or sell, as they are waiting for a sign of which way the market is going to end up moving *bull market* [...] characterised by an upward trend in the price of securities *bear market* [...]characterised by a downward trend – a market condition in which the prices of securities are falling
COMPANIES ARE ANIMALS	*gorilla* [...]a large company that dominates an industry *gazelle* a company [able to] to grow at an unusually high annual rate *lame duck* a company who has defaulted on its debts or has gone bankrupt due to the stock market *turkey* [...] a start-up company that may subsequently go bankrupt. *elephant* [...] an elephant is a large institution that has the funds to make high volume trades, thus having decisive influence on the price of the underlying financial asset

Adapted from Silaški 2009

The metaphorical isotopy in these cases is finally perceived as coherent, which allows the creation of new terms from the same (shared and accepted) source cognitive metaphor.

3. In the last possible case of metaphor terminologization, metaphor recovers all its conflictual potential force in the creation of new terms, challenging our ordinary conditions for consistency and forcing us to new mental projections, to new conceptualizations. We are thus in presence of founding metaphors of new epistemological paradigms, such as Darwin's *natural selection*, Maxwell's *wave theory* or the *theory of strings* in astrophysics – Gabriele Veneziano (1968) playing on the analogy between the elementary universe particles and musical

instruments strings. In this case, metaphor cannot be reduced to a simple formal analogy; neither can it be inserted into a series of expressions perceived as coherently acceptable and understandable: its function is rather to open up new perspectives on an extremely abstract, complex phenomenon, of which we have no sensory evidence. An important aspect as far as paradigmatic metaphors are concerned is finally related to the need for scientific legitimation, which is closely connected to the choice of terms for new scientific discoveries or theories. One of the differences with simple catachresis labels, or from coherent shared concepts, is that creative paradigmatic metaphors are usually the mark of a scientific trend or of an author, and their function is twofold: they are functional to a simple and accessible comprehension of the new concept, but above all they work as significant marks of intellectual property for scientists (see Rossi 2015). For this reason, scientists tend to impose their new point of view by creative, conflictual, stunning metaphors, which can often be compared to poetic metaphors (for example, Mermin's *boojum*, see Mermin 1981).

The choice of the source domain in this case is strongly dependent on specialised communities, called to accept, to validate and to approve the use of a certain term (see Gaudin 2002; Humbley 2012). This factor explains the motivation of many technical terms, which could seem incomprehensible if analysed superficially. To mention a few examples, the term *grey goo* in the field of nanotechnologies derive from Drexler's passion for science fiction, as we can read in the database *Grand Dictionnaire Terminologique*[3]:

---

[3] http://www.granddictionnaire.com (cons. 28/05/2015)

Table 2. Terminological entry *grey goo* in GDT

gelée grise n. f.		
Synonymes	**Terme anglais**	**Variante graphique**
matière visqueuse grise n. f. substance visqueuse grise n. f. masse grise n. f.	gray goo	grey goo
Définition		
Masse informe de matériaux, imaginée par certains spécialistes de la nanotechnologie, qui résulterait de l'autoreproduction incontrôlée de nanorobots accaparant, transformant et détruisant les ressources des écosystèmes.		
Notes linguistiques		
Le terme *gray goo* a été utilisé pour la première fois en 1986 par Eric Drexler *Engines of Creation*. Il provient de bandes dessinées de science-fiction. Robert A. Freitas *global ecophagy*, que l'on a traduit en français par *écophagie globale*. Date de la dernière mise à jour : 27 février 2013[4]		

Similarly, American financial specialists' shared interest for poker is the origin of a well-known financial metaphor, *blue chip*, easily comprehensible in the American context, more difficult to understand as a metaphor in other languages or cultures (for example in Italian or French).

Depending on their epistemological opportunity, paradigmatic metaphors may sometimes be found in different domains, passing from one scientific field to others, this phenomenon being considered as a form of "nomadism" (Rossi 2015), caused by a need to exploit successful and legitimate metaphors in order to achieve an easier validation from the scientific community. When François Jacob (Nobel prize for medicine in 1965) decides to exploit the cybernetic metaphor of the *code* in order to describe the structure of DNA (borrowing from Shannon and Weaver's communication theory terms such as *émetteur* (*transmitter*) or *récepteur* (*receiver*)), or when he decides to transfer into biology the terms *traduction* or *transcription* (borrowed from French linguistics), he exploits the legitimacy and

---

4 "Definition: Shapeless mass of materials, designed by some experts of nanotechnology, which results from the uncontrolled self-reproduction of nanorobots grabbing, transforming and destroying the ecosystem resources.
Notes: The term *gray goo* was used for the first time in 1986 by Eric Drexler in his book *The Engines of Creation*. It comes from science-fiction comics.
Jr. Robert Freitas, a specialist in molecular nanotechnology, later gave to the process the name of *global ecophagy*, which was translated into French by *écophagie globale*." (our translation)

prestige accorded to linguistics during the Sixties in order to find legitimacy for his newborn biological theory (for the conflict between *availability* and *opportunity* in this field, see Rossi 2015).

3 Are terminological metaphors cultural-bound?

An interesting aspect of the studies on metaphorical terminology is finally intended to enquire into the complex relations between figures of analogy and language/culture influence. The weight of a community's shared culture in the formation of terminological metaphors appears in studies as an obvious fact, beyond the alleged universality of the analogical process underlying the metaphor itself. Cortès (2006) establishes as a fundamental condition of the process of creating and decoding metaphorical expressions the fact of sharing a common conceptual area, called *interdiscours*:

> La construction du sens métaphorique présuppose une maîtrise totale de la construction du sens compositionnel. Le sens métaphorique est un construit énonciatif complexe qui mobilise de la part des interlocuteurs des connaissances sur le monde, sur le rapport du locuteur à ce qu'il entend transmettre et à ses interlocuteurs, ainsi que tout ce qu'il sait sur le plan linguistique, y compris sur le sens des unités lexicales dans tous leurs emplois, c'est-à-dire avec tous leurs effets de sens en fonction du contexte. Ces connaissances du matériau lexical et de ses emplois reposent sur la connaissance des textes que le locuteur a entendus et analysés et qui l'influencent dans ses choix d'expression. Nous appellerons ce type de compétence l'accès à l'interdiscours (Cortès 2006: 35).[5]

The relativistic nature of metaphor puts definitively into question Wüster's and TGT[6] terminological principle of a universally shared conceptual segmentation in specialised domains, as well as the common conception of scientific language as an objective, monosemic, purely denotative vocabulary. Actually, (see Montuschi 1993), the greatest terminological inventions in the history of scientific thought

---

[5] "The construction of the metaphorical sense requires a total control of the compositional construction of meaning. The metaphorical meaning is a complex construct that involves interlocutors' knowledge about the world, communication aims and the relation among interlocutors, and all a speaker knows linguistically, including the meaning of lexical units in all their acceptions, that is to say, with all their sense effects depending on the context. This knowledge of the lexical material and its meanings are based on knowledge of the texts that the speaker has heard and analyzed, and that influence his choice of expression. We call this kind of competence access to *interdiscourse*." (our translation)
[6] *Théorie générale de la Terminologie (General Theory of Terminology)*.

derive from individual acts of linguistic creation, involving the resources of collectively shared knowledge, inextricably linked to the culture they belong to:

> [...] même si les différents domaines du savoir et de la pratique sont souvent les mêmes d'un pays à l'autre, les façons de les découper et de les dénommer ne sont pas les mêmes, en vertu de la relative autonomie du langage. Dumarsais notait déjà que « chaque langue a des métaphores particulières, qui ne sont point en usage dans les autres langues ; par exemple, les Latins disaient d'une armée, *dextrum et sinistrum cornu* [la corne droite et la corne gauche], et nous disons *l'aile droite et l'aile gauche* (1998: 144–145, cited by Gardes-Tamine 2007: 15).[7]

To cite a well-known example (Humbley 2006), the computer language term *bootstrap* (referring to the English to *lift/hoist yourself up by your own bootstraps*) is linked to a metaphor which is deeply rooted in the source language, for which there is no isomorphic equivalent in other languages. This link makes conceptual interaction metaphor inseparable from its initial production context: adapted under abbreviated forms or transmitted as integral loan in other languages (*boot* in Italian and French), this term has rapidly lost all connection with its original analogical image, and it is completely opaque to non-English speakers. Similarly, the example of *splicing* in genetics biology (Humbley 2003) could be closely connected, according to Temmerman (2007), to the influence of American biologists' passion for cinema and home video:

> La prise en considération du système qui sous-tend le tout n'est pas sans conséquence pour les descriptions terminologiques (plurilingues) et la représentation des connaissances. Reconnaître la force créatrice du système de la langue compte tenu du caractère socialement et culturellement situé de cette dernière peut avoir un impact sur la gestion de ressources terminologiques dynamiques capables de rendre compte de l'évolution du sens (Temmerman 2007: 83).[8]

---

[7] "[...] Even if the different fields of knowledge and practice are often the same from one country to another, the way to cut them out and naming them is not the same, because of the relative autonomy of any language. Dumarsais already noted that "each language has special metaphors, which are not used in other languages; for example, the Latins said, about an army, *dextrum* and *sinistrum cornu* [the right horn and the left horn], and we say *the right wing* and *left wing*." (our translation)

[8] "The fact of taking into account the underlying system is not without consequences for (multilingual) terminological descriptions and knowledge representation. The acknowledgement of the creative power of language system (given the socially and culturally situated nature of the latter) can have a dynamic impact on terminology resources management, which can account for the evolution of meaning" (our translation).

More recent examples could be mentioned, such as Veneziano's *string theory* (1968) or the *crêpe stellaire* proposed by astrophysicist Jean-Pierre Luminet (Giaufret and Rossi 2013). A special issue of Cahiers du RIFAL (2007) devotes many essays to this kind of creation of terminology, later dealt with also in Dury et al. (2009).

Various studies in recent years focus on the problems of comparison or interlinguistic translation of metaphors in specialised terminology. In particular, the translation aspect seems to be a rapidly developing field since the beginning of the XXI century, in parallel with developments in variationist terminology and the ultimate failure of Wüster's ideal of interlinguistic terminologic matching 1:1. In his 2005 essay, Humbley pinpoints this as an important gap in translation studies:

> La question de la traduction des métaphores est un sujet très peu abordé dans le contexte des langues de spécialité. [...] On peut s'en étonner, car la place de la métaphore dans les discours et le lexique spécialisés fait l'objet de nombreuses études récentes, englobant des points de vue linguistique, terminologique et surtout cognitif. On sait par ailleurs que la métaphore tient une place importante en tant que technique de création terminologique dans l'aménagement linguistique, en particulier en français (Humbley 2005: 49).[9]

Studies by Vandaele (2001, 2007) mainly focus on issues related to cognitive and intercultural interlingual transposition of terminological metaphors in scientific languages.

Besides the specific translation issue, the analysis of the transfer of metaphorical terms from one source language to one or many target language(s) is linked to glottopolitical trends. The link of terminological metaphors with their culture of origin is indeed a mostly crucial factor, involving economic, socio-political, geo-political aspects and it is closely connected to the spread of specialised terminology and to the dynamics of creation and dissemination of terms (See Rossi 2017). As far as this aspect is concerned, Humbley's reflections (Humbley 2006), or Desmet's (2007), are of outmost interest:

---

[9] "The question of metaphors translation is a poorly discussed topic in the domain of specialised languages. [...] We may be surprised about this, because the place of metaphor in specialized lexicon and discourses has been at the basis of many recent studies, from a linguistic, terminological and above all cognitive point of view. We also know that metaphor is an important standpoint in technical terminology creation and language planning, especially in French." (our translation)

> Les mécanismes du succès ou de l'insuccès des néologismes terminologiques dans des cultures différentes, mais partageant une même langue restent encore mal connus et font appel à des études linguistiques orientées vers les habitudes culturelles de chaque société (Desmet 2007: 3).[10]

For metaphors that are directly transferred from one culture to another – "crossover metaphors" according to Humbley – translation is not in fact particularly difficult as a form of adaptation to the target language/culture (as in the example from Humbley 2005 showing the shared analogy in English, French and German between biological infections and computer viruses).

In other cases, however, such sharing is far from being true: an example among many others, based on the language of finance (Rossi 2015), presents different examples, from integral loan to direct translation, to adaptation:

Table 3. Terminological metaphors in the field of finance and their translations

	Source English term[11]	French	Italian
1. same metaphor L1–L2	One-shot	Coup unique	ABSENT
	Floating	Flottant	Floating (loan word) Flottante (translation loan)
	Burning cost	Taux de flambage	ABSENT

---

10 "The mechanisms of the success or failure of terminological neologisms in different cultures sharing the same language, are still poorly known and rely on language-oriented studies on cultural habits." (our translation)
11 Sources: the French database FRANCETERME and the Italian glossary from AIEBB: http://www.culture.fr/franceterme and http://www.bankpedia.org/index.php/it/home-page-it (cons. 26/05/2015)

Table 3. (continued)

	Source English term[11]	French	Italian
2. change in the metaphorical expression from L1 to L2 (adaptation)	Hit-and-run	Action éclair (loss of a part of the source metaphor, i.e. the baseball metaphor)	ABSENT
	Hot money	Capitaux flottants/capitaux fébriles	Hot money (loan word) syn. *Denaro caldo* (translation loan)
	Aggressive accounting	Comptabilité flatteuse (different point of view on the concept)	ABSENT
	Crawling-peg Peg	Cremaillère	ABSENT
	Window-dressing	Habillage de bilan	Window-dressing (loan word)
	Cherry picking	Picorage (la métaphore renvoie dans ce cas à l'action des oiseaux)	ABSENT
	Collar	Tunnel des taux	Collar (loan word)
	Tombstone	Faire-part de clôture	Tombstone (loan word)
	Walk-away clause	Clause de forfait	ABSENT
3. disappearance of the metaphor	Bear market	Marché baissier	Bear market (loan word)
	Bull market	Marché haussier	Bear market (loan word)
	Haircut	Marge de sécurité	ABSENT
	Straddle	Ordre lié	Straddle (loan word)
	Bullet	Remboursement in fine	Bullet (loan word)
	Flow-back	Retour de titres	ABSENT
	Credit crunch	Resserrement de crédit	ABSENT
	Blue chip	Valeur de premier ordre	Blue chip (syn. *Titoli guida*)
	Churning	Barattage financier (syn. *Moulinette*)	ABSENT

4 Conclusion

At the end of our brief overview on terminological metaphor, many possibilities of research are still open for further study. Among others, we will mention:
1. the various and different typologies of metaphors established to provide analysis tools for terminology work, especially as far as the study of lexicalization processes in specialised domains are concerned;
2. the vast and complex issues related to the influence of the source culture on the creation of metaphors in terminology, as well as on the transfer of metaphorical concepts from one language/culture to other languages/cultures.

Moreover, so far only a partial research has been done of the diachronic aspect of evolution of terminological metaphors in specialised domains, which is crucial for determining the discursive mechanisms underlying the acceptance of these metaphorical terms within the communities of professionals and communities of practice.
On these points, the debate is still widely open.

References

Assal, Allal. 1994. La métaphorisation terminologique. *Terminologie et traduction* 2. 235–242.
Black, Max. Metaphor. 1954. *Proceedings of the Aristotelian Society* 55: 273–294. 1954. Reprinted in Black, Max. 1962. *Models and metaphors*. Ithaca and New York: Cornell University Press.
Boyd, Richard. 1993 [1979]. Metaphor and theory change: What is 'metaphor' a metaphor for? In Andrew Ortony (ed.), *Metaphor and Thought*, 481–532. Cambridge: Cambridge University Press.
Boyd, Richard & Thomas S. Kuhn. 1983 [1979]. *La metafora nella scienza*. Milano: Feltrinelli.
Brown, Thomas L. 2003. *Making truth. Metaphor in science*. Champaign: University of Illinois Press.
Bowdle, Brian F. & Gentner Dedre. 2005. The Career of Metaphor. *Psychological Review* 112(1). 193–216.
Cabré, Maria Teresa. 2000. Terminologie et linguistique: La théorie des portes. *Terminologies Nouvelles* 21. 10–15.
Charbonnel, Nanine & Georges Kleiber (éds.). 1999. *La métaphore entre philosophie et rhétorique*. Paris: PUF.
Charteris-Black, Johnathan. 2004. *Corpus approaches to critical metaphor Analysis*. Basingstoke: Palgrave Macmillan.
Collombat, Isabelle. 2005. *Le discours imagé en vulgarisation scientifique: étude comparée du français et de l'anglais*. Université Laval, PhD thesis.

Cortès, Colette (ed). 2006. *La métaphore. Du discours général aux discours spécialisés*. Paris: Cahiers du C.I.E.L.

Dagut, Menachem B. 1987. More about the translatability of metaphor. *Babel* 33(2). 77–83.

Deignan, Alice. 2005. *Metaphor and corpus linguistics*. Amsterdam and Philadelphia: John Benjamins.

Desmet, Isabelle. 1995. *Variabilité et variation en terminologie et langues spécialisées: discours, textes et contextes*, in *Mots, termes et contextes, Septièmes journées scientifiques du réseau Lexicologie, terminologie, traduction (LTT) de l'Agence universitaire de la francophonie (AUF)*, 235–247. Paris: Éditions des archives contemporaines.

Détrie, Catherine. 2001. *Du sens dans le processus métaphorique*. Paris: Champion.

Diki-Kidiri, Marcel. Eléments de terminologie culturelle. *Cahiers du Rifal* 26. 14–25.

English, Katherine. 1998. Understanding science: when metaphors become terms. *ASp* 19–22. 151–163.

Dury, Pascaline, François Maniez, Nathalie Arlin & Claire Rougemont (eds.). 2009. *La métaphore dans les langues de spécialité*. Grenoble: Presses Universitaires de Grenoble.

Fauconnier Gilles & Mark Turner. 2002. *The way we think: Conceptual blending and the mind's hidden complexities*. Basic Books: New York.

Fox-Keller, Evelyn. 1995. *Refiguring life: Metaphors of twentieth-century biology*. New York: Columbia University Press.

Freixa, Judith. 2002. *La variació terminològica: anàlisi de la variació denominativa en textos de diferent grau d'especialització de l'àrea de medi ambient*. Barcelona: Institut Universitari de Lingüística Aplicada, Universitat Pompeu Fabra (Sèrie Tesis, 3).

Gardes-Tamine, Joëlle. 2012. *Au coeur du langage. La métaphore*. Paris: Champion.

Gaudin, François. 2002. *Socioterminologie. Une approche sociolinguistique de la terminologie*. Bruxelles: De Boeck.

Gentner, Dedre & Donald R. Gentner. 1983. *Flowing waters or teeming crowds: mental models of electricity*. In Dedre Gentner & Albert L. Stevens, *Mental Models*, 447–480. Hillsdale, NJ: Elrbaum.

Giaufret, Anna & Micaela Rossi. 2013. Métaphores terminologiques, circulation des savoirs et contact entre langues, *Signes* 10. http://www.revue-signes.info/document.php?id=3170&format=print

Gibbs, Raymond (ed.). 2008. *The Cambridge handbook of metaphor and thought*. Cambridge: Cambridge University Press.

Gibbs, Raymond & Gerard Steen. 1999. *Metaphor in cognitive linguistics*. Amsterdam and Philadelphia: John Benjamins.

Goatly, Andrew. 2007. *Washing the brain. Metaphor and hidden ideology*. Amsterdam and Philadelphia: John Benjamins.

Hallyn, Fernand (ed.). 2000. *Metaphor and analogy in the sciences*. Berlin: Springer.

Hesse, Mary. 1998. The cognitive claims of metaphor. *The Journal of Speculative Philosophy* 2(1). 1–16.

Holton, Gerald. 1998. *Thematic origins of scientific thought: Kepler to Einstein*. Harvard: Harvard University Press.

Humbley, John. 2006. Metaphor and secondary term formation. In Colette Cortès (ed.), *La métaphore. Du discours général aux discours spécialisés*, 197–210. Paris: Cahiers du C.I.E.L.

Humbley, John. 2005. La traduction des métaphores dans les langues de spécialité: le cas des virus informatiques. *Linx* 52.

Humbley, John. 2012. Retour aux origines de la terminologie: l'acte de dénomination. In G. Petit (ed.), *Langue française* 174. 111–129.
Jacobi, Daniel. 1986. *De la recherche à la vulgarisation; itinéraires du texte scientifique*. Paris: Annales de l'Université de Besançon et les Belles Lettres.
Jacobi, Daniel. 1999. *La communication scientifique; discours, figures, modèles*. Grenoble: Presses Universitaires de Grenoble.
Kövecses, Zoltan. 2005. *Metaphor in culture. Universality and variation*. Cambridge: Cambridge University Press.
Kövecses, Zoltan. 2010 [2002]. *Metaphor. A practical introduction*. Oxford: Oxford University Press.
Kocourek, Rotislav. 1991. *La langue française de la technique et de la science. Vers une linguistique de la langue savante*. Wiesbaden: Oscar Brandstetter.
Kuhn, Thomas S. 1962. *The structure of scientific revolutions*. Chicago and London: The University of Chicago Press.
Lakoff, George & Mark Johnson. 1980. *Metaphors we live by*. Chicago: University of Chicago Press.
Mermin, David. 1981. E pluribus boojum. *Physics Today*. 45–53.
Molino, Jean. 1979. Métaphores, modèles et analogies dans les sciences. *Langages* 54. 83–102.
Montuschi, Eleonora. 1993. *Le metafore scientifiche*. Milano: Franco Angeli.
Musolff, Andreas & Jörg Zinken (eds.). 2009. *Metaphor and discourse*. Basingstoke: Palgrave Macmillan.
Normand, Claudine. 1976. *Métaphore et concept*. Paris: Complexe.
Oliveira, Isabelle. 2009. *Nature et fonction de la métaphore en sciences. L'exemple de la cardiologie*. Paris: L'Harmattan.
Ortony, Andrew (ed.). 1993 [1979]. *Metaphor and thought*. Cambridge: Cambridge University Press.
Pragglejaz Group. 2007. MIP: A method for identifying metaphorically used words in discourse. *Metaphor and Symbol* 22(1). 1–39.
Prandi, Michele. 2010. Typology of Metaphors: Implications for Translation. *Mutatis Mutandis* 3(2). 304–332.
Prandi, Michele & Micaela Rossi. 2012. *Les métaphores dans la création de terminologie*. In *Terminologie: textes, discours et accès aux savoirs spécialisés*, 7–19. Brest: Ed. du GLAT.
Prandi, Michele, Anna Giaufret & Micaela Rossi (eds.). 2013. *Il ruolo della metafora nella creazione di terminologie*. Genova: Genova University Press.
Resche, Catherine. 2002. La métaphore en langue spécialisée, entre médiation et contradiction: étude d'une mutation métaphorique en anglais économique. *ASp* 35–36. 103–119.
Resche, Catherine. 2005. Réflexions à partir d'une métaphore banalisée en économie: la 'Main Invisible' d'Adam Smith. Leçons et perspectives. In Marie-Hélène Fries (ed.), *Travaux* 20.25, 57–76. Bordeaux: Université Victor-Ségalen.
Resche, Catherine. 2012. Towards a better understanding of metaphorical networks in the language of economics: The importance of theory-constitutive metaphors. In Honesto Herrera-Soler & Michael White (eds.), *Metaphor and Mills. Figurative Language in Business and Economics*, 77–102. Berlin: De Gruyter.
Richards, Ivor Armstrong. 1936. *The Philosophy of rhetoric*. New York and London: Oxford University Press.

Rossi, Micaela. 2009a. L'emploi de la métaphore comme ressource pour la néologie terminologique: le cas du langage de la dégustation du vin. In *La métaphore en langues de spécialité*, ed. by Pascaline Dury, *et al.*, 199–227. Grenoble: Presses Universitaires de Grenoble.

Rossi, Micaela. 2009b. Langue et culture dans un verre. Pour une étude multilingue du langage du vin. In Eva Lavric (éd.), *Food and Language. Sprache und Essen*, 161–170. Frankfurt: Peter Lang.

Rossi, Micaela. 2015. *In rure alieno. Métaphores et termes nomades dans les langues spécialisées*. Berne: Peter Lang.

Rossi, Micaela. 2017. Terminological metaphors and the nomadism of specialised terms. In Patrick Drouin, Aline Francœur, John Humbley and Aurélie Picton (éds.), *Multiple Perspectives on Terminological Variation*, 183–213. Amsterdam and Philadelphia: John Benjamins.

Samaniego Fernandez, Eva. 2013. Translation theory and the contemporary theory of metaphor. In Gonzálvez-García Francisco, Peña Cervel María Sandra & Lorena Pérez Hernández (eds.), *Metaphor and Metonymy revisited beyond the Contemporary Theory of Metaphor: Recent developments and applications*, 265–282. Amsterdam and Philadelphia: John Benjamins.

Schlanger, Judith. 1995. *Les Métaphores de l'organisme*. Paris: L'Harmattan.

Semino, Elena. 2008. *Metaphor in Discourse*. Cambridge: Cambridge University Press.

Silaški, Nadežda. 2011. Animal metaphors in some business-related terms in English. *Radovi Filozofskog fakulteta u Istočnom Sarajevu* 13(1). 565–576.

Stengers, Isabelle & Judith Schlanger. 1991. *Les Concepts scientifiques: Invention et pouvoir*. Paris: Folio.

Steen, Gerard J. 2007. *Finding metaphor in grammar and usage*. Amsterdam and Philadelphia: John Benjamins.

Schlanger, Judith. 1995. *Les métaphores de l'organisme*. Paris: L'Harmattan.

Taverniers, Miriam. 2002. *Metaphor and metaphorology: A selective genealogy of philosophical and linguistic conceptions of metaphor from Aristotle to the 1990s*. Gent: Academia Press.

Temmerman, Rita. 2000. *Towards new ways of terminology description: The sociocognitive approach*. Amsterdam and Philadelphia: John Benjamins.

Temmerman, Rita. 2007. Les métaphores dans les sciences de la vie et le situé socioculturel. *Cahiers du RIFAL* 26. 72–83.

Vandaele, Sylvie. 2001. Noyaux conceptuels et traduction médicale. *Meta* 46(1). 16–21.

Vandaele, Sylvie. 2007. Quelques repères épistémologiques pour une approche cognitive de la traduction spécialisée – Application à la biomédecine. *Meta* 52. 129–141.

Wüster, Eugen. 1968. *Dictionnaire multilingue de la machine-outil. Notions fondamentales, définies et illustrées, présentées dans l'ordre systématique et l'ordre alphabétique. Volume de base anglais-français. The Machine Tool. An Interlingual Dictionary of Basic Concepts comprising an Alphabetical Dictionary and a Classified Vocabulary with Definitions and Illustrations. English-French Master Volume*. London: Technical Press.

Part III: **Science**

Silvano Tagliagambe and Luca Guzzardi
Classical physics as a metaphorical tool for evoking quantum world

1 The boundary's twofold function

In the 1920s Vladimir Ivanovič Vernadskij, a Russian mineralogist and geochemist who was strongly influenced by D.I. Mendeleev and V.V. Dokučaev during his studying years at the University of St. Petersburg, pointed out the importance of a reflection on the idea of boundary in order to reconcile the autonomy of living beings (with their typical invariance of inner organization) with their openness to the environment. Some years before, Dokučaev had initiated a research tradition in Earth sciences centered on the interaction between soil, sea, lakes, rivers and the life they preserve, and treating living beings not as passive observers but as active participants within the process of evolution.

Vernadskij begins with observing that every outer variation, e.g. in temperature, is perceived by living beings through their physiological constitution as a change in their inner chemical structure. What is crucial in the process is not a signal proceeding unchanged from a sender (the environment) to a receiver (the organism living inside it), but a continuous transformation that can be more correctly described as a translation from one code (that of the outer world) to another one (that of a specific living being functioning within it).

Now, if we ask what the boundary between any living organism and its environment really is, one answer is certainly that it consists in a demarcation line preserving the organism as something separate from the environment and protecting its inner organization. But the boundary acts as an *interface* too: it is the place where two faces come to contact, the one looking at the interior (organism's inner organization), the other looking at the exterior (environment). The usual, standard contact of a living organism with "inert nature" presupposes therefore the presence of a bearing mechanism guaranteeing a preliminary translation of the elements of inert nature to be assimilated into the structural code of the biosphere. No living system could exist without such a bearing mechanism. It is in the light of this twofold function of the boundary line that Vernadskij frames in an original way the problem of the relation between living systems and natural environment. This gives rise to hybrid systems, made up both of living matter and

Silvano Tagliagambe, University of Sassari
Luca Guzzardi, University of Milan

inert substances penetrating each other and becoming inseparable – something that Vernadskij (1988: 8–9) describes as "bioinert natural bodies".

In this paper we propose that Vernadskij's bio-ecological view can be generalized by saying that boundaries are entities endowed with this twofold function: they do not only differentiate and separate but also act as "thin bridges", promoting communication between *domains that remain nevertheless separate in their specific characters*. They are both elements of separation (*demarcation line*) and a *trait d'union* between different spheres.

One of us has explored in full detail the consequences of this epistemological move (Tagliagambe 1997). In this context, though, we confine ourselves to observe that boundary epistemology, based upon this simple tenet, can serve to re-formulate Kant's doctrine of transcendental schematism, which rests on the difference between the real and the possible. For Kant, as far as *Realität* (a category of quality) is distinct from *Dasein* (a category of modality, also cognate of *Existenz* and *Wirklichkeit*), it does not refer to an actual existence in the external world but, more properly, to the possible determinations of this existence as *res*. Thus, reality designates the totality of the *res*'s possible determinations, i.e. the whole horizon of possibilities associated to a given concept. In this sense, Kant (1787: 273, A141=B180) epitomizes that:

> the concept of a dog signifies a rule in accordance with which my imagination can specify the shape of a four-footed animal in general, without being restricted to any single particular shape that experience offers me or any possible image that I can exhibit *in concreto*. This schematism of our understanding with regard to appearances and their m ere form is a hidden art in the depths of the human soul.

As pointed out by Heidegger (1929: 67), in grasping the reality of something "what we have perceived is the range of possible appearing as such, or, more precisely, we have perceived that which cultivates this range, that which regulates and marks out how something in general must appear in order to be able [...] to offer the appropriate look". Kant rejects the hypostatization of the totality of possible determinations, so the 'all of reality', into an *ens realissimum* that would contain all these determinations"; but he also does not mean "such a totality to be 'merely logical'. To the contrary, the logical space of all possible determinations has an ontological thrust, which is why Kant asserts that the concept of such a completely determined object is "transcendent" [...] and serves as transcendental Ideal" (Schulting 2011: 187).

In the following sections, footing on this dynamical distinction between the real and the possible which characterizes what one of us has termed an "intermediate space" (see Tagliagambe 1997, 2008), we develop a boundary-epistemologic approach to quantum mechanics in its relationship with classical physics. In particular we attempt:

- to account for the ideal 'boundary' between quantum and classical world insisting on differences between these two domains (§ 2);
- to show, through a case study, how physicists put them together without erasing the boundaries in order to get better insights (§§ 3–4);
- to advocate a boundary-based concept of metaphors in science (§§ 5–6).

2 Quantum world as an "intermediate space"

As we mentioned, Kant's sphere of *Realität* is described as the category of quality governing the *totality of possible determinations* of a given thing. To us, Kant's dynamicization of the boundary between the real and the possible has an important *pendant*. Something can be assumed in its *Realität* as an object of our knowledge only after abandoning a rigid notion of boundary between the phenomenal world and the system of concepts employed to grasp it. What emerges is the notion of a boundary as an interface: a bearing area connecting distinct domains – *Realität* and *Existenz*, or the actuality of a particular aspect (see the quotation of Heidegger above).

This sheds new light on the way physicists usually contrast classical physics with quantum mechanics. Following Reichenbach (1944: 20–21), in the quantum realm we have to do not merely with *phenomena* – which are, in the wake of Kant's terminology, entities endowed with exact positions in space-time and subject to the ordering and structuring action of categories – but with *interphenomena*, something in the middle between the real and the purely possible. Phenomena are "observable", Reichenbach insists, and in a certain sense they are characterized in terms of classical entities: "All those occurrences which consist in coincidences, such as coincidences between electrons, or electrons and protons, etc. [...], connected with macrocosmic occurrences by rather short causal chains". By contrast, interphenomena are in a certain sense "unobservable", because they "happen between the coincidences, such as the movement of an electron, or of a light ray from its source to a collision with matter [...]. Occurrences of this kind are introduced by inferential chains of a much more complicated sort; they are constructed in the form of an interpolation within the world of phenomena". In other words, they lie "between" reality as understood by classical physics and the domain of the possible – a domain that classical physics would recognize as having its own right just in the realm of thought, considering it as a *presence* with an intrinsic indetermination as far as possible observations upon it are concerned.

The world of classical mechanics is – to pick up a phrase by Alexandre Koyré (1967) – an entire "universe of exactness", that is a well-ordered world where theories refer to *universes of discourse* made up of objects (or individuals) enjoying *properties* and *relations*. These theories employ a language that processes information (especially that from the reality around) according to established procedures, conceived for the purpose of reaching, through a sequence of reproducible and logically analyzable arguments, results not contained in the initial information. Such results are expressed in a formal, symbolic language, which exploits self-consistent logical manipulation rules from a repertoire of symbols shared by everybody both in their meaning and use, so it makes evident a verifiable consequence of the initial assumptions. Its prevailing content is mostly equivalent to an unstated proposition of the form "if...then", whose dots it fills out. Its semantical rules behave in a *compositional* way, following Frege's principle of compositionality that "the meaning of a composite expression is a function of the meaning of its component expressions"[1]: in other terms, the meanings of the parts determine the meaning of the whole. Ambiguity is completely excluded, since meanings conveyed by language are exact, so all fuzzy or indeterminate semantics is in principle excluded. Contradictions are *a fortiori* ruled out in a twofold sense: a proposition A and its denial *Not A* cannot both be true because of the *semantical* principle of non-contradiction, and every sentence of the form *A and not A* is false because of the *logical* principle of non-contradiction. Lastly, every problem stated in the language of a theory is *semantically decided* because of the semantical principle of the excluded middle, according to which every proposition is either true or false.

On the other hand, the world of quantum mechanics challenges every claim for an "omniscient mind" able to give a positive or negative answer to each question making sense[2]. An example of the inherent quantum indetermination is the so-called Schrödinger's cat, named after Schrödinger (1935): a cat has been trapped into a box geared to a devilish device that would have either poisoned and killed him or guaranteed his survival depending on two equally probable events, the decaying or non-decaying of a radioactive atom inside a Geiger counter. If the atom decayed, the Geiger counter would trigger a hammer that in turn would break a tube containing, say, hydrogen cyanide. In quantum terms the *closed* box and its

---

[1] Although it was never stated in this form, the principle is usually extracted from § 32 of Frege's *Grundgesetze der Arithmetik*: see Pelletier, 2001.

[2] This is the claim of the classical, deterministic mechanics raised by Galilei (1632, p. 130): "Ma pigliando l'intendere intensive, in quanto cotal termine importa intensivamente, cioè perfettamente, alcuna proposizione, di che l'intelletto umano ne intende alcune così perfettamente, e ne ha così assoluta certezza, quanto se n'abbia l'istessa natura; e tali sono le scienze matematiche pure, cioè la geometria e l'aritmetica, delle quali *l'intelletto divino ne sa bene infinite proposizioni di più, perché le sa tutte*, ma di quelle poche intese dall'intelletto umano credo che la cognizione agguagli la divina nella certezza obiettiva, poiché arriva a comprenderne la necessità, sopra la quale non par che possa esser sicurezza maggiore". In other words, if human knowledge equals God's *intensive* in mathematics, extensively ("*extensive*") God's knowledge is obviously incomparable.

content, i.e. the system as a whole, is described by Schrödinger's equation. This determines – without taking into account observers and their act of measurement or observation – how the states of the objects in that world spontaneously evolve. Notice that such world includes the cat, whose fate is entangled with the behavior of the radioactive atom. On the one hand, the cat is a macroscopic object, for which quantum laws average to the same results as classical mechanics, so they are usually left aside; on the other hand, the radioactive decay of an atom is a typical microscopic event whose description in classical terms is practically impossible – it is appropriately described only in quantum terms. And since Schrödinger's quantum mechanical equation is a *wave* equation, the states cat alive/cat dead are merely two "extreme cases" in a continuum. So what Schrödinger's equation describes is a system whose temporal evolution is *continuous* and *linear*; its mathematically admissible solutions are not just those exactly determining the state of the object (cat alive/cat dead), but also those predicting the cat in a superposition of life and death. When an observer opens the box and looks inside, she causes it *precipitating* into the state of life (or death) and eliminates superposition.

In more technical terms, Schrödinger's equation does not admit solutions belonging to a special class K^0 with the following properties:
1. If both $\varphi_1(x)$ and $\varphi_2(x)$ belong to K^0, but with very different average positions, their superposition $C_1\varphi_1(x)+C_2\varphi_2(x) = \varphi(x) = (A)$ does not belong to K^0 anymore;
2. If $\varphi_1(xt_0)$ belongs to K^0 at an instant t_0, $\varphi_1(xt)$ does not belong to K^0 when the time interval $[t-t_0]$ is long enough.

This simply means that in quantum world also superpositions of type A (not included in the special class K^0) *must* be taken into account.

Once the system has been defined and the initial instant has been chosen ("prepared"), Schrödinger's equation provides predictions on its behavior *in a perfectly deterministic way* by calculating the *probability* of any state. Let us imagine to have a beam of particles having gone through a slit in a screen, it is possible to predict the position of diffraction patterns they cause on a wall beyond the screen, but not the exact point of the wall hit by a specific particle. This makes quantum mechanics a statistical theory: it describes physical processes by *calculating the average value* a physical quantity can have when measured upon a set of identical physical systems, giving up any prediction of the exact value this quantity takes in a given system. And this violates a fundamental tenet of classical mechanics, that is the possibility of *maximal non-contradictory knowledge* characterizing Galileo's omniscient mind: a knowledge which is impossible to consistently extend to a more precise information and is capable of *semantically deciding* all relevant physical properties an object whatever can have.

To sum up, and for the sake of shortness, we limit ourselves to remind that in the semantics suggested by quantum theory the following conclusions hold, which openly contradict any semantics stemming from classical physics:
1) *Global meanings* are inherently *vague* in so far they leave many relevant properties of the objects under study semantically undecided.
2) Every meaning determines some *partial* meanings that are usually vaguer than the global one.
3) Meanings can be represented as *superpositions* of other meanings, possibly associated with probability values.
4) Observation and measurement sweep this superposition of meanings away, reducing the former range of alternative possibilities to the one found through these acts.

3 Classical entities contrasted with Quanta: The double-slit experiment

From the tension between classical and quantum mechanics we pointed out in the previous section, it turns out that by no means we could ever account for quantum behavior by using any classical tool. Not only it would be overwhelmingly difficult; rather, any attempt is bound to contradiction. The world of classical mechanics is intrinsically exact, in principle governed by sort of Laplacian determinism; quantum mechanics predicts a world intrinsically vague.

Nevertheless, the observation of physicists' behavior tells us that they openly contradict this conclusion. They do use of classical tools in order to illustrate quantum mechanics. Let us take another example of a typical quantum experimental set-up we have already evoked, that is the double slit experiment. In Feynman's (1967: 130) words, it is so important because it "has been designed to contain all of the mystery of quantum mechanics". But it was first performed in a classical context, long before the quantum revolution. The story traces back to the beginning of the 19th century, as Thomas Young, a 29-years-old polymath, advanced a new interpretation of some experiences described in the Third Book of Newton's *Opticks*, concerning shadows and fringes around small objects (like knives or even hairs) in a beam of light. In a first experiment, Young (1802) observed that, by splitting a beam of light into two portions (e.g. by making two thin slits in a card at a certain distance one from another) and projecting it onto the wall of his room a pattern of alternating dark and bright fringes appeared.

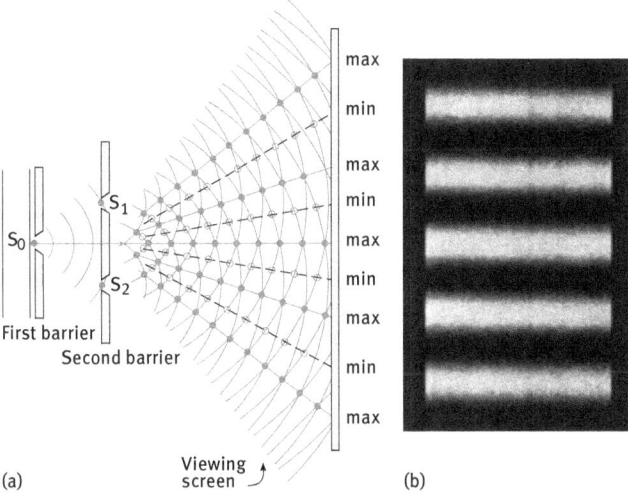

Figure 1. Schematic diagram of Young's double-slit experiment. Slits S1 and S2 behave as coherent sources of light waves that produce an interference pattern on the viewing screen (drawing not to scale). (b) An enlargement of the center of a fringe pattern formed on the viewing screen with many slits could look like this. (Figure and caption from: D. Halliday, R. Resnick, J. Walker, Fundamentals of Physics, Hoboken: Wiley § Sons, 2010, p. 1187).

For Young, his experiments, more accurately repeated during the following year (Young 1804), were the proof of the wavelike behavior of light versus Newton's corpuscular theory. At least they proved that light was subject to interference, a phenomenon which is horribly complicated to explain in corpuscular terms, but very simple if light is conceived as a wave. Let us imagine a dark room with a light source, a viewing screen (e.g., a photographic plate recording the light radiation), and – between the source and the screen – a wall with two tiny horizontal slits. A single wave of homogeneous light coming from the light source runs into the wall with the double slit and it splits into two individual waves. Given that the size of the holes is small, if compared with the wave-length of the light, and that the holes are far from the plate, both of them can be regarded as two different point-like sources transmitting coherent light. So the waves have the same "shape" (they have the same crests and troughs; more precisely, they have the same wave-length and frequency). In a superposition of two or more individual waves, crests and troughs of each wave sum together in a resulting wave. In Young's experiment, due to the distance between the holes the two individual but equal waves follow a slightly different path towards the plate, so when they meet their crests and troughs do not match exactly. "Positive" contributions of each wave (say the crests) partially sum with "negative" contributions (say the troughs). Bright fringes appear at any location of the plate where the individual waves interfere "constructively"; dark fringes appear where they combine "destructively" (Figure 1).

During the 19th century the wave theory of light became firmly established. However, in the 1890s physicists became progressively aware of some phenomena which were not easily explicable in terms of continuous radiation. For example, the discovery that metal plates emit electrons when they are illuminated with light had dramatic consequences on the theory of light itself. The problem with this phenomenon – the so-called photoelectric effect – was that it occurs only if the incident light reaches or exceeds a threshold frequency. This is an unexplicable behavior if light is conceived as a wave, which is a continuous radiation. In 1905 Einstein overcame the difficulty in the simplest manner: in agreement with Max Planck's theory of blackbody radiation, he hypothesized that light was constituted by discrete packages of radiant energy or *light quanta* (named *photons* in 1926 by Frithiof Wolfers).

So at the beginning of the 20th century physical optics was thrown into a deep identity crisis. To sum up with Feynman's (1970: III, 1–1):

> Newton thought that light was made up of particles, but then it was discovered that it behaves like a wave *[Young's experiment]*. Later, however (in the beginning of the twentieth century), it was found that light did indeed sometimes behave like a particle *[Einstein's theory of the photoelectric effect]*. Historically, the electron, for example, was thought to behave like a particle, and then it was found that in many respects it behaved like a wave. So it really behaves like neither. Now we have given up. We say: "It is like *neither*" *[i.e., nor particle neither wave]*.

Nevertheless, according to Feynman we are basically lucky, because quantum behavior is common to all atomic objects (electrons, protons, neutrons, photons, and so on). Though some technicalities would be needed, they are all "particle waves". So he argues, "what we learn about the properties of electrons will apply also to all 'particles', including photons of light". On the other hand, given what we have discussed in the previous section of this paper, we have also some bad news: atomic behavior is "so unlike ordinary experience" that we need "a sort of abstract or imaginative fashion" (Feynman 1970) – in fact, some very artificial analogies Feynman constructs in the subsequent passages.

4 Feynman's experimental setups

To begin with, Feynman "choose[s] to examine a phenomenon, which is impossible, *absolutely* impossible, to explain in any classical way, and which has in it the heart of quantum mechanics" (Feynman 1970: III, 1–1). What he is referring to is a version of the double-slit experiment, which according to him "in reality (…) contains the only mystery. We cannot make the mystery go away by 'explaining' how it works. We will just tell you how it works. In telling you how it works, we will have told you about the basic peculiarities of all quantum mechanics".

He initiates the experiment by using a gun – a classical device – in order to explain light as composed by photons – quantum particles. In other terms, he contrasts *classical behavior* on the one hand with *quantum behavior* on the other; or rather, the more familiar classical physics is *instrumentally* used to describe the unknown quantum physics. He is performing what scientists and philosophers of science usually call a "thought experiment" or a *Gedankenexperiment*. The key-idea is that not always you have to do a real experiment, which might not be possible for some technical reasons; in some cases we can offer convincing arguments by imagining an experience and logically developing the consequences. There is plenty of examples of such thought experiences of many different kind overall in science (see e.g., Kühne 2005, Sorensen 1992), so Feynman is doing something very usual for a scientist. Let us consider his "mental experimental setup":

> We have a machine gun that shoots a stream of bullets. It is not a very good gun, in that it sprays the bullets (randomly) over a fairly large angular spread (…). In front of the gun we have a wall (made of armor plate) that has in it two holes just about big enough to let a bullet through. Beyond the wall is a backstop (say a thick wall of wood) which will "absorb" the bullets when they hit it. In front of the wall we have an object which we shall call a "detector" of bullets. It might be a box containing sand. Any bullet that enters the detector will be stopped and accumulated (…). For our present purposes we would like to imagine a somewhat idealized experiment in which the bullets are not real bullets, but are *indestructible* bullets – they cannot break in half. In our experiment we find that bullets always arrive in lumps [*that is as discrete blocks of matter, which are all the same: bullets are indistinguishable from one another*], and when we find something in the detector, it is always one whole bullet. If the rate at which the machine gun fires is made very low, we find that at any given moment either nothing arrives, or one and only one – exactly one – bullet arrives at the backstop. Also, the size of the lump certainly does not depend on the rate of firing of the gun. (Feynman 1970: III, 1–1, 1–2)

With this experimental apparatus you can ask, for example: "What is the probability that a bullet which passes through the holes in the wall will arrive at the backstop at the distance x from the center?" More technically, you are asking the probability of arrival of a lump measured as a function of x. If you try to cover a hole, say 2, you may expect the maximum probability occurring at the value of x which is on a straight line with the gun and hole 1; then probabilities of arrivals diminish as the distance x from such straight line – such axis – grows. So you can draw a curve like P_1 in the part *b* of the Figure 2. Let's cover the hole 1, and we obtain the symmetric curve P_2. Note that at the center, where $x = 0$, you find many bullets, because the holes are not so distant and each bullet can easily contribute to the amount found in the center; but the bullets will be not as many as on the straight line with the gun and each hole.

What does happen now if none of the holes is covered? Looking at each curve, you may expect that few bullets passed through hole 1 contribute to what you find on the backstop position corresponding the axis between the gun and hole 2, and few bullets passed through hole 2 contribute to what you find on the backstop position corresponding the axis between the gun and hole 1. However, at the center, where you found many bullets in the 1-hole-covered situation, but not as many as on the straight line with the gun and an individual hole, you now find most bullets – twice the amount you found with the hole 1 or the hole 2 covered. That is, to use Feynman's own words, "probabilities just add together. The effect with both holes open is the sum of the effects with each hole open alone".

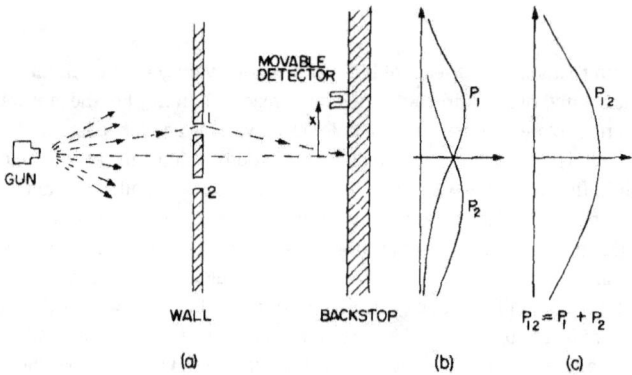

Figure 2. From Feynman 1970: III

This is substantially different from the interference pattern Young observed and explained in terms of a sign of a wavelike behavior. Following Feynman, let us employ another classical *analogon* and repeat the experiment with water waves. If we cover a hole in turn, we find a similar result for the part *b* of the Figure 3, except that we shall not measure how many lumps arrive at the backstop, because waves do not arrive in discrete blocks; but we shall measure the intensity of each wave.

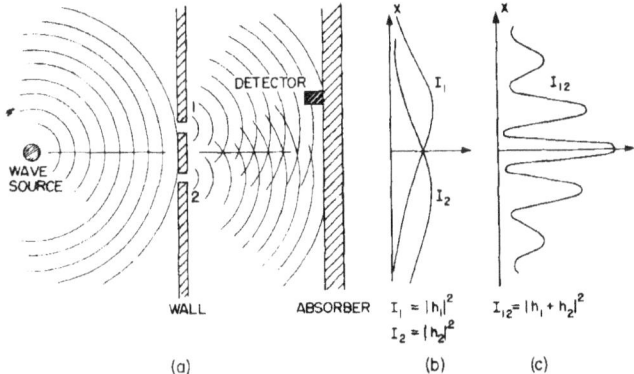

Figure 3. From Feynman 1970: III

However, if the holes are free, we have to take into account both the positive and the negative contributions of the waves. So we obtain a graph like in part *c* of the Figure 3, that resembles an interference pattern like in Young's experiment.

Now we imagine to use a similar apparatus – but with light 'waves' instead of water waves. In a certain sense, our third *Gendankenexperiment* is midway between the first and the second one, for we have seen that light is a wave (Young's interference); but, since it is electromagnetic radiation, it is quantized, so you can conceive it arriving in discrete blocks, or "lumps" in Feynman's own words, like the bullets of our first example. Except for the fact that photons or electrons and such things are not visible and you cannot simply count them. But you can imagine using detectors which are sensible to light and click at any arrive. So you hear a sharp 'click' as soon as a photon arrives: all clicks are the same and there are no "half-clicks".

To stick to our analogy with gun & bullets, what we use is a "photon gun", very similar to the "electron gun" imagined by Feynman in the following Figure 4[3].

---

[3] For technical reasons, which are not relevant here, Feynman employs electrons rather than photons and describes his 'weapon' as an "electron gun". However, for more clarity we assume that quantum behavior of electrons and photons is the same in the case of the double-slit experiment. But in general this equivalence does not hold: in the Standard Model of particle physics electrons and photons are two different elementary particles having distinct properties and associated with different interactions.

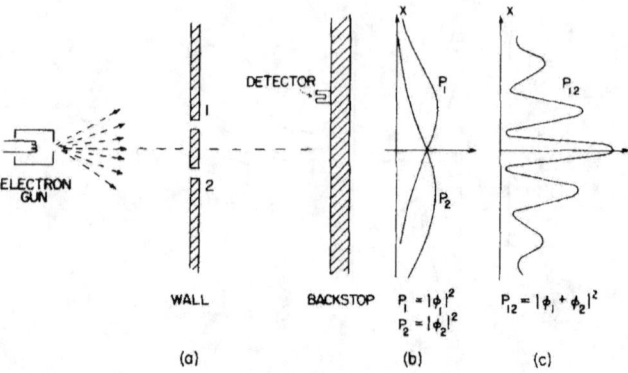

Figure 4. From Feynman 1970: III

Now we can study the behavior of the individual photon-bullets. Let us try to cover one hole in turn: we clearly expect to obtain the probability curves P_1 and P_2, like in our first experiment. We perform our single-slit experiment by closing in turn hole 1 and hole 2, and find out that our expectation was correct.

What does happen if both holes are left free? Under our assumption that we are using indestructible photon-*bullets*, i.e. in a certain sense 'tiny particles' – an assumption strongly confirmed by our best physical knowledge –, we could consistently infer that we will find a result like in our first experiment with bullets. However, after Young's original experiment we already know that this expectation is incorrect: if both holes are left free, photons do not behave like bullets. In more technical terms, the probability curve of arrivals is not $P_{1,2} = P_1 + P_2$ but forms an interference pattern, which results in a probability curve like that in the part *c* of Figure 3 for the water waves.

This is surprising, because it signals a flaw somewhere in our analogies. On the one hand, from Young we know that light is a wave and classical electromagnetic theory has explained what kind of a wave it is; so a *classical* analogy with water waves holds and we can easily explain the pattern of interference observed in terms of a certain undulatory theory of light. By contrast, interference cannot be (easily) explained by means of any classical corpuscular theory. On the other hand, from Einstein we know that light is formed by quanta (photons): this is an experimentally, firmly established knowledge. So our expectation is that a *classical* analogy with bullets holds; but we don't know how to explain the interference pattern if we assume that photons are classical entities like our supposed indestructible bullets.

For that reason Feynman says that the double-slit experiment "has in it the heart of quantum mechanics" and that "it is impossible, *absolutely* impossible, to explain in any classical way". As we saw in Part I of this paper, in classical physics we have always to do with entities for which we can specify, in any given time, where they are. This holds true both for particles and waves, *classically considered*. But the quantum version (with photons) of Young's experiment shows that things are different in quantum context. Here emerges what we called "superposition": the contemporary occurrence of two (in classical terms) contradictory states.

It is not our aim – and it would take a lot of space – to expound how Feynman goes on introducing Heisenberg's principle of uncertainty and explaining the 'tricks' of the double-slit experiment. We only aim at exploring how physicists can and do use of some classical tools in the quantum context.

5 Metaphor and description

Let us give a closer look to Feynman's way of describing the double-slit experiment. Though he announces that it is impossible to give any classical *explanation* of this phenomenon, he does employ classical means to *expose* what's going on, to *describe* the situation: "To try to understand the quantum behavior of electrons, we shall *compare* and *contrast* their behavior, in a particular experimental setup, with the *more familiar behavior* of particles like bullets, and with the behavior of waves like water waves" [emphasis added]. So Feynman proposes an *analogical* way. That analogy should be constructed – to a certain extent, *arbitrarily* constructed.

First of all, we have a *machine gun* which is arbitrarily, intentionally chosen (imagined) as a very bad one, spreading bullets randomly "over a fairly large angular spread". Moreover, Feynman admits that holes are designed on purpose, so that only *one bullet* may pass through each time; and bullets are incredibly *indestructible*, so that they "arrive in lumps", which are indivisible blocks. In the second part of his idealized experiment series, Feynman explains that also individual electrons or individual photons arrive "in lumps". But it is clear that he forces the reader to bear in mind the analogy with the bullets of his first experiment: we now *know* that electromagnetic radiation is quantized, and quanta of radiation are photons, so we know that photons come in lumps. And *in order to describe* their behavior Feynman deliberately creates an artificial analogy with bullets, exaggerating their hardness so that they're now indestructible; similarly, in the second experiment Feynman replaces the gun with a water wave source and notices that interference is produced. What he obtains is a complex analogy in which some pieces of a vocabulary go into another, some classical tools are adopted as *metaphors* for quantum theoretical descriptions. They don't provide an explanation but do illustrate a situation.

We want to point out that we are not using the concept of metaphor in a somewhat weak sense, like a *simile* or the mere expression of a likeness. The concept of metaphor we are adopting has been explored by Davidson (1978). He refers some stanzas of T.S. Eliot's poetry *The Hippopotamus,* which was intended as a harsh caricature of the Church:

> The broad-backed hippopotamus
> Rests on his belly in the mud;
> Although he seems so firm to us
> He is merely flesh and blood.
>
> Flesh-and-blood is weak and frail,
> Susceptible to nervous shock;
> While the True Church can never fail
> For it is based upon a rock.
>
> The hippo's feeble steps may err
> In compassing material ends,
> While the True Church need never stir
> To gather in its dividends.
>
> The 'potamus can never reach
> The mango on the mango-tree;
> But fruits of pomegranate and peach
> Refresh the Church from over sea.

One could complain that the text does not contain either a simile ("the Church is *like* a hippopotamus") or a metaphor ("The Church *is* a hippopotamus"). Davidson (1978: 256) comments that nevertheless "the words are being used to direct our attention to similarities between the two". Eliot describes a hippopotamus as resting "on his belly in the mud" and suggests by means of an ironical juxtaposition that the Church is doing the same. Therefore, we have no metaphor properly but do have a metaphorical effect – one that can do its job, directing our attention to a similarity, because of its *literal meaning*. "The hippopotamus really does rest on his belly in the mud", Davidson argues; "the True Church, the poet says literally, never can fail. The poem does, of course, intimate much that goes beyond the literal meaning of the words. But intimation is not meaning." In the end, Davidson's thesis is that "metaphors mean what the words, in their most literal interpretation, mean, and nothing more".

To us, Feynman's not less ironical juxtaposition between the classical and the quantum experiments resembles very much Eliot's irony on the Hippo-Church.

Also in Feynman's case we are neither told that "bullets are like photons" or "photons are like a wave" (simile), nor that "bullets are photons", "photons are a wave" (metaphor). Rather, Feynman let us understand something like the literal (i.e. phenomenological) behavior of bullets and the literal behavior of waves, and finally the literal behavior of electrons. Paraphrasing Davidson, the accounts of the thought experiments do, "of course, intimate much that goes beyond the literal meaning of the words. But intimation is not meaning". Only if we understand *literally* the behavior of bullets, wave, and electrons/photons, we can also grasp the metaphoric effect conveying the relevant information Feynman gives at the end of his account:

> *We would like to emphasize a very important difference between classical and quantum mechanics.* We have been talking about the probability that an electron will arrive in a given circumstance. We have implied that in our experimental arrangement (or even in the best possible one) it would be impossible to predict exactly what would happen. We can only predict the odds! This would mean, if it were true, that physics has given up on the problem of trying to predict exactly what will happen in a definite circumstance. Yes! Physics *has* given up. *We do not know how to predict what would happen in a given circumstance*, and we believe now that it is impossible – that the only thing that can be predicted is the probability of different events. It must be recognized that this is a retrenchment in our earlier ideal of understanding nature (Feynman 1970: III, 1–10).

If we look at Feynman's account in the broader context of the history of modern physics, this is the approach most physicists took at least since the second half of the 19th century (see Guzzardi, 2010: 129–136). They worked out the idea that the search for analogies is essential in science and ended up in developing the notion of physical model. A distinguishing feature of this approach is that *giving descriptions* (re-tell something "in other words") is more important than *saying why something happens* (i.e. *explaining*). Could we really say *why* photons and electrons behave this way, while bullets do not behave in the same fashion? To find an explanation would mean to find what Feynman calls "a machinery behind the law" – a machinery which "no one has found". If explanation is reduction to "a more basic mechanism from which these results can be deduced", then "no one can 'explain' any more than we have just 'explained'. No one will give you any deeper representation of the situation". (Feynman 1970, III, 1–10).

We can compare Feynman's approach to that of James Clark Maxwell as described by Mach (1905: 168–169):

> Maxwell consciously developed the use of analogy into a very perspicuous physical method (...). To him, the phenomena of electrostatics, magnetism, electric currents and so on reveal common traits reminiscent of the flow of a fluid. To complete the analogy, he idealizes the fluid: it has no inertia (no mass) and is incompressible and taken to flow through a resistive medium whose resistance is proportional to the speed of the current. The picture is imaginary and based on analogy but nevertheless intuitive: we do not take it as real and we know precisely how it coincides *conceptually* with the facts to be represented (...). His picture is such that its mental consequences are pictures of the consequences of facts.

Even if we give up explication in strong, causal sense, this particular kind of metaphors, which are properly analogy-based models and conserve structures (i.e. mutual relations within each "picture", reflected in the equations)[4], are nevertheless powerful. In Mach's words, "incomplete analogies too can promote enquiry, by revealing differences in the fields being compared". Back to Feynman again, after reading his lecture on the 'metaphoric' double-slit experiments with bullets, waves, and photons/electrons we did learn a lot of things we didn't know; it has also revealed, in agreement with Mach's statement, "differences in the fields being compared" – and by doing so it can (and it did) open new directions to research.

6 Conclusion

I) Let us come back to the boundary epistemology that served us as a starting point and a framework. From boundary epistemology we learned essentially two things:
   1) First of all, boundaries may have a twofold function:
      a) They provide demarcation lines
      b) However, demarcation lines as such also suggest exchange possibilities (that is, they signal the need to go *beyond* the boundaries, they demand *crossover capabilities*).
   2) Moreover, and for what we expressed in 1b), boundary epistemology says that we are allowed to "dynamicize" boundaries between real and possible phenomena.
II) So we may look at the quantum phenomena as *interphenomena* in Reichenbach's sense, that is something *in the middle* between the real and the purely possible. This challenges our understanding of phenomena themselves and

---

[4] This is a kind of what many philosophers of science nowadays call "structural realism" (see Worrall 1989, Ladyman 1998 and 2002), insisting on its novelty. A 'novelty' that in its fundamental features traces back to Maxwell, though.

the way we picture them, because the semantics we have to adopt in quantum descriptions is completely different from the usual: meanings are intrinsically vague, represented as superpositions of possibly conflicting meanings (e.g. the oxymoronic "particle-wavelike" behavior of point-like particles like electrons and photons).

III) Boundary epistemology suggests that, in order to cope with this challenge, one should adopt a typical *in-between strategy* by inventing metaphorical tools. These must be understood as an expression of the crossover capabilities mentioned in point 1b); in this sense, Feynman's approach is a boundary epistemology-approach. More importantly, metaphorical tools are non-reductive tools. They do not erase boundaries; on the contrary, they recognize demarcation lines accounting for differences. They let differences exist. They take care of differences among things and let them be. And in doing this, they open new possible worlds to a variety of possible understandings. That is to say, they make both the world and our understanding richer and colorful.

References

Davidson, Donald. 1984 [1978]. What metaphors mean. In *Inquiries into Truth and Interpretation*, 245–264. Oxford: Clarendon Press.
Feynman, Richard P. 1967. *The character of physical law*. Cambridge: MIT Press.
Feynman, Richard P., Leighton Robert B. & Sands Matthew (eds.). 1970. *The Feynman lectures on physics*. London: Addison Wesley Longman.
Frege, Gottlob. 1893. *Grundgesätze der Arithmetik*. Jena: Hermann Pohle.
Galilei, Galileo. 1988 [1632]. *Dialogo sopra i due massimi sistemi del mondo*. Pordenone: Edizioni Studio Tesi.
Guzzardi, Luca. 2010. *Lo sguardo muto delle cose: Oggettività e scienza nell'età della crisi*. Milano: Raffaello Cortina.
Heidegger, Martin. 1929. *Kant and the problem of metaphysics*. Bloomington and Indianapolis: Indiana University Press.
Kant, Immanuel. 1787. *Critique of pure reason*. New York: Cambridge University Press.
Koyrè, Alexandre. 1967. *Dal mondo del pressapoco all'universo della precisione*. Torino: Einaudi.
Kühne, Ulrich. 2005. *Die Methode des Gedankenexperiments*. Frankfurt: Suhrkamp.
Ladyman, James. 1998. What is structural realism? *Studies in History and Philosophy of Science* 29. 409–424.
Ladyman, James. 2002. Science, metaphysics and structural realism. *Philosophica* 67. 57–76.
Mach, Ernst. 1905. *Knowledge and error*. Dordrecht-Boston: Reidel.
Pelletier, Francis J. 2001. Did Frege believe Frege's principle? *Journal of Logic, Language, and Information* 10. 87–114.
Reichenbach, Hans. 1944. *Philosophic foundations of quantum mechanics*. Berkeley and Los Angeles: University of California Press.

Schrödinger, Erwin. 1935. Die gegenwärtige Situation in der Quantenmechanik. *Die Naturwissenschaften* 23. 807–812, 823–828, 844–849.
Schulting, Dennis. 2011. Limitation and idealism: Kant's 'long' argument from the categories. In Dennis Schulting & Jacco Verburgt (eds.), *Kant's Idealism: New Interpretations of a Controversial Doctrine*, 159–191. Dordrecht: Springer.
Sorensen, Roy A. 1992. *Thought experiments*. Oxford: Oxford University Press.
Tagliagambe, Silvano. 1997. *Epistemologia del confine*. Milano: Il Saggiatore.
Tagliagambe, Silvano. 2008. *Lo spazio intermedio*. Milano: Università Bocconi Editore.
Vernadskij, Vladimir I. 1988. *Filosofskie mysli naturalista* [Moskva Nauka], Italian partial translation: *Pensieri filosofici di un naturalista*, by Silvano Tagliagambe. Roma: Teknos, 1994.
Worrall, John. 1989. Structural realism: The best of both worlds? *Dialectica* 43. 99–124.
Young, Thomas. 1802. An account of some cases of the production of colours, not hitherto described. *Philosophical Transactions of the Royal Society of London* 92. 387–397.
Young, Thomas. 1804. Experiments and calculations relative to physical optics. *Philosophical Transactions of the Royal Society of London* 94. 1–16.

Carmela Morabito
Integration and differentiation at the basis of metaphor: dexterity in behaviour and degeneracy in the nervous system

1 Integration and differentiation in the mind and brain

Cognitive neurosciences indicate that integration and differentiation are two fundamental properties of conscious experience as well as of the nervous system. Among the fundamental properties of conscious experience are the following two: first, consciousness is highly integrated or unified – every conscious state constitutes a unified whole that cannot effectively be subdivided into independent components – and second, at the same time, it is highly differentiated or informative – there is an enormous number of different conscious states, each of which can lead to different behavioural consequences.

The distributed neural processes underlying conscious experience also share these properties: they are highly integrated and, at the same time, highly differentiated. We believe that this convergence between neurobiology and phenomenology is not mere coincidence (Edelman and Tononi 2000: 111).

In trying to explain the neurobiological basis of mind, contemporary neurosciences clearly state the social and cultural nature of our cognitive functions, in that their emergence is a product of specific neural processes and interactions between our brain, body and environment. Mental capacities are a complex system that is grounded in the brain; and interaction between the organism and its environment (also in a social and cultural sense) is essential for cerebral function.

The cognitive system has two main features: it is a complex of unique cerebral processes which are at the same time extremely integrated (unitary) and differentiated: states of consciousness cannot be divided into single parts and are extraordinarily variable. Therefore, we need to understand the neural mechanisms of integration and differentiation. And these mechanisms – in the mind as well as in the nervous system – form the basis of metaphor.

By analysing the correlation between subjective experience and the brain, with its "open" architecture and dynamical functioning, we can establish meta-

---
Carmela Morabito, University of Roma 'Tor Vergata'

DOI 10.1515/9783110549928-011

phor as a fundamental form of thought and language in the complex dynamical structure of action – *dexterity* in the organism's interaction with its environment – and in the unique functional architecture of the brain – the *degeneracy* of the nervous system.

As we know, the neural basis of consciousness is not in single neurons or in single cerebral areas, but in complex systemic processes, changes in activity patterns occurring simultaneously in many regions of the brain. Plasticity and variability are essential to the brain's capacities to copy innumerable and unpredictable situations. Therefore, it is worthwhile to study the structure and dynamic functioning of the brain, also in the case of neuropsychological diseases which elucidate the impressive plasticity and individuality of each single brain at many levels of its organisation simultaneously, from biochemistry to morphology.

Evidence from neuropsychology clearly illustrates the many different ways in which, after a ictus or a chirurgical resection, the organism can rapidly "re-unite" itself (i.e., in anosognosia or emi-inattention) within an ever-changing, uninterrupted network. Dynamic integration makes it possible to eliminate any visible space, even in cases in which there is actually an enormous gap. Hence, neuropsychology demonstrates how powerful brain plasticity and recovery of function are.

How can the brain maintain its multiplicity without losing its unity and coherence?

How does it integrate, assimilate, generalise, substitute and overlap different kinds of information, goal-directed actions, problem-solving strategies, synaptic pathways and neural circuits?

In studying the intimate mechanisms of intelligent behaviour, and at the same time the cerebral basis of the mind, we come upon two basic concepts which are at the core of our metaphorical ability: dexterity on the behavioural level and degeneracy on the neurobiological level.

2 Bernstein's idea of "Dexterity"

Starting in the 1940s, Nikolaj Bernstein studied the dynamic and adaptive aspects of brain and behaviour, which are essentially characterised by plasticity and individual variability. His aim was to understand how the brain controls movement: in athletes, work-related movements (he founded and directed the Biomechanical Laboratory at the Central Institute of Labour in Moscow for many years) and veterans wounded in war, i.e., people suffering from different motor pathologies and copying their motor deficits in different ways.

In Lurija's (1987: 805) brief biography of Bernstein for the *Oxford Companion to the Mind*, he describes him as "A rare case of a scientist who practically devoted his whole life to one problem: the physiological mechanisms of human movements and motor action". While these words amplify Bernstein's studies on movement from a physiological and neuroscientific standpoint, in my opinion, they do not at any rate acknowledge the neuropsychological dimension of his studies of movement and the brain and their great relevance for a neurologically plausible model of mind.

Bernstein studied movement to understand the brain, and the brain to understand the mind. The deeply heuristic value of his interdisciplinary approach and the relevance of his thought for cognitive neurosciences lie in this connection. By integrating the theoretical frameworks of evolutionary theory and clinical neuropsychology, Bernstein ([1961] 1967: 144–147) studied the integrated and dynamic aspects of movement, based on the assumption that adaptive action cannot be partitioned into single motor acts.

Movements are the means by which the organism does not simply passively interact with the environment, but actively *acts upon it* in whatever way is necessary. (…) The remarkable structurality and completeness of a motor act makes it impossible to treat it as an arbitrary collection of successive reflex elements (…) [We need] to find a bridge between the *physiology of reactions*, with which psychophysiologists have been exclusively concerned for some time, and the *physiology of activity*[1].

The core concept of his analysis is that of dexterity, a concept arrived at through in-depth study of the origins and mechanisms of the production of adaptive action (which – as aforementioned – cannot be partitioned into single motor acts), voluntary movement, the nature of movement coordination, motor skill and exercise.

---

1 Starting with the study of motor coordination, Bernstein delineates a new conceptual framework: Physiology of Activity (not of simply reactions to stimuli), and in doing so makes it truly possible to link neurophysiology, psychology and cybernetics by merging and synthesising clinical and experimental data. To understand action, we need to integrate physiology and psychology, biomechanics and the Information Theory. Had Bernstein's *Dexterity* been published right when it was written, between 1946 and 1949, it would have offered powerful theoretical support to Gibson's emerging ecological analysis.

Dexterity is the ability to find a motor solution to any external situation, that is, to adequately solve any emerging motor problem
- correctly (i.e., adequately and accurately),
- quickly (with respect to both decision-making and achieving a correct result),
- rationally (i.e., expediently and economically), and
- resourcefully (i.e., quick-wittedly and initiatively) (Bernstein [1946] 1996: 228).

With these words Bernstein summarises his detailed analysis of dexterity and its features. Assuming that to act dexterously is to adapt flexibly to many new circumstances, dexterity is a special level of neuropsychological functioning (i.e., the process of solving motor problems, not of producing particular movement patterns). In this process, three elements are of fundamental importance: the nervous system, the mind and behaviour in the environment.

Dexterity refers to our body's quickness, agility, flexibility and skilfulness. It is exercisable and it builds – in Bernstein's words (1996: 3–19) – "a bridge to the area of genuine intellect" because it is seeking a motor solution to any situation and under any condition, in order to solve the problem correctly, or rather adequately and accurately, quickly and successfully.

The basic feature of dexterity is *extravertedness* (the intrinsic relationship of dexterity to the external world): this is the very psycho-physiological core of dexterity. It always refers to the environment and it always has an element of extemporaneousness. Demand for dexterity does not lie in the movements themselves but in the surrounding conditions (Bernstein 1996: 210).

Development leads to an increased need to be able to adjust quickly to new, changing environments; to solve unexpected, nonstandard motor tasks; and to successfully overcome unforeseen circumstances.

3 Dexterity, movement and the nervous system

This is Bernstein's global – we could even say – 'ecological' action-based theory of mind and behaviour. The fundamental characteristic of behaviour is variability because the organism always faces unpredictable situations and rearranges its adaptive strategies on the basis of experience and expectations. In every situation, multiple connections are possible between external needs, endogenous chemical activity and action patterns. The features of the brain underlying the organism's capacity to cope with any different and unexpected situation are precisely plasticity, adaptability and flexibility.

In *On Dexterity*, Bernstein challenged the very foundations of traditional neuroscientific theories with an *ecological*, action-based theory of development. Dexterity – as we have seen – is not a characteristic of movement as such, but of movement in situations. One cannot move dexterously; one can only solve a motor problem dexterously. Therefore, Bernstein's thought is in contrast with the leading physiological and psychological (behaviourism) theories of his time,[2] asserting itself as a real behavioural science, independent from behaviourism and based on embodied action: in intelligent behaviour, actions are primary.

The primacy of action implies a radical shift in thinking regarding the acquisition of skill and – in general – in physiology as well as in psychology. Functional actions are primary and the control of movements and postures is secondary. Movement is not the building block of action, but rather control of movement is one of the results of the development of action. And movement is a real cognitive factor, in that it is grounded in the core of our cognitive functions from a genetic point of view.

Bernstein summarised his theory of motor learning with the phrase "repetition without repetition". This represents a whole new way of thinking about behaviour. Absolute repetition of a movement pattern is not possible due to the inherent variability and complexity of the environment. Based on the principles of self-organising dynamics, "repetition without repetition" will tend to lead to the production of stable, smooth and efficient solutions to motor problems; these solutions can be considered intelligent.

Variability[3] is not "noise" for the nervous system, but rather a fundamental environmental fact that exerts selection pressure on the evolution of nervous system, which is strongly characterised by "functional non-univocality between impulses and effects: (...) one and the same sequence of changes in forces may produce different movements on successive repetitions" (Bernstein 1967: 62).

The nervous system is not mechanical (as an input-output mechanism, i.e., a reactive system), it is an active, self-organising, dynamic system in which alterations in the activities of a single part may cause the radical reorganisation of the whole. The features of the brain underlying the organism's capacity to cope with

---

[2] He contrasts his "physiology of activity" with the classic Pavlovian "physiology of reaction". What he proposes is a complex synthesis of neurophysiology and psychology. "Is the brain or the muscle the ruling Czar when you jump, walk, or run?" (cit. from Feigenberg and Latash 1996: 255). Cf. also Reed and Bril (1996).

[3] Variability in behaviour is a central topic within the evolutionary and selectionistic theoretical framework. To adaptively cope with an ever-changing and unpredictable environment, the organism has to reorganise its adaptive strategies on the basis of its experiences and expectations.

every different and unexpected situation are precicesly plasticity, adaptability and flexibility.

> Switchability and plasticity were born together with the brain cortex [...] Motor dexterity is very closely related to the functioning of the brain cortex. These brain areas are the youngest in the history of brain development, and they are, so to speak, soaked with the ability to absorb one's individual life experience (Bernstein 1967: 231).

Since intelligent movements have a structure, and they are never the same, what is central is the goal-directed "schema". This requires a new theoretical approach that is interdisciplinary and integrated, a new conception of movement and behaviour, of brain and mind. It implies a deep conceptual inversion: in the words of Bernstein, "the biomechanics of the environment sculpts the brain". What is needed is a dynamic systems theory of the nervous system to understand the complex interactions among perception, action and cognition. A theory which could explain – at the same time – the dynamic and integrative functions of our mind. Environment, culture and individual experience sculpt our cognitive system as well, which is clear in language and the way we use it.

4 Edelman, Degeneracy

Over the last four decades, Gerald Edelman has developed a selectionistic theory of the brain which can be applied as a general theoretical framework to the new cognitive neurosciences. It is a theory based on the redundancy, complexity and plasticity of the nervous system and on the historical and individual dimension of the brain with regard to its epigenetic development and functioning. Every brain has a unique anatomical and dynamical structure, since synaptic connections and maps are continuously modified by what we perceive, by the way we move, by our experience.

> We emphatically do not identify consciousness in its full range as arising solely in the brain, since we believe that higher brain functions require interactions both with the world and with other persons (Edelman and Tononi 2000: XII).

> The brain is not organised like a computer, its functioning rests instead on such properties as variability, differential amplification, degeneracy and value (Edelman and Tononi 2000: 93).

Degeneracy is "the ability of structurally different elements of a system to perform the same function or the same output. It is a ubiquitous biological property [...] it is both necessary for, and an inevitable outcome of, natural selection" (Edelman and Gally 2001: 13763). It is a characteristic of all selective systems in which different elements and structures can carry out the same function or reach the same goal (Park and Friston 2013).[4]

Various examples of degeneracy may be found at different levels of biological organisation: the genetic code, the protein folding process, metabolism, immune responses, connectivity in neural networks and neural dynamics. Moreover, degeneracy is not redundancy: "unlike redundant elements, degenerate elements can produce new and different outputs under different constraints. A degenerate system, which has many ways to generate the same output in a given context, is thus extremely adaptable in response to unpredictable changes in context and output requirements. The relevance to natural selection is obvious" (Edelman and Gally 2001: 13767).

Hence, different populations of neurons in response to identical external stimuli can produce similar behavioural responses. Cerebral networks are extraordinarily complex and degenerate; epigenetically they are embodied in the anatomical structures and in the neuronal connections in a way that is different for each individual.

> As neural currents develop, variant individual experiences leave imprints on the brain. [...] As intricate as the microstructure of neuronal connections may be, this intricacy is magnified by the number of different interactions, in space and time, interactions that can affect synaptic transmission. [...] The brain contains a variety of chemicals called neurotransmitters and neuromodulators that bind to a variety of receptors and act on various biochemical pathways. The chemical identity of these neurotransmitters and of their receptors, the statistic of their release, and the time and place of electrical and biochemical interactions all govern the thresholds of response of neurons in an extraordinarily intricate and variable manner. [...] This molecular intricacy and the resulting dynamics superimpose several more layers of variability on that of the neuroanatomical picture, contributing to what may be called the historical uniqueness of each brain. Metaphorically, we can say that we house a jungle in our heads (Edelman and Tononi 2000: 41–42).

---

4 The concept of 'degeneration' was already present in the 18th century: In 1754, Boscovich (*De continuitatis lege*, para. 69) used it to express the idea that a phenomenon – in certain conditions – could possibly shift toward a different organisation. In Boscovich' geomometry, a degenerate quantity – for example – is a quantity stressed to its limit until it changes in kind.

Edelman (2006a: 33–35) clearly states the psychological relevance of degeneracy in neuroanatomical functional organisation[5]: "Degeneracy is seen at many levels of biological organization, ranging from the properties of cells up to those of language. [...] Degeneracy in brain circuits leads almost inevitably to association, a key property required for memory and learning. This associative property occurs due to the overlap of different degenerate circuits leading to a similar output". Metaphorical capacity is the first link between brain organisation and cognitive functioning:

> The metaphorical capacity of linking disparate entities derives from the associative properties of a re-entrant degenerate system. [...] Being selectional systems, brains operate prima facie not by logic but rather by pattern recognition. This process is not precise, as is logic and mathematics. Instead, it trades off specificity and precision, if necessary, to increase its range.[6] [...] It is likely, for example, that early human thought was proceeded by metaphor, which, even with the late acquisition of precise means such as logic and mathematical thought, continues to be a major source of imagination and creativity in adult life (Bruner 1973: 58).

Since human brains essentially operate in terms of pattern recognition rather than of logic, they are highly constructive in settling on given patterns while, at the same time, constantly open to error. In my opinion, this is extremely useful to explain the neurobiological mechanisms of metaphor: to explain the "openness" of nervous circuits and of cognitive functions, as well as the "dexterity" of intelligent behaviour. The dynamical and associative nature of pattern recognition demonstrates its heuristic value with respect to metaphoric thinking: "A fundamental early mode of thinking that is highly dependent on pattern recogni-

---

[5] This is true even in relation to neuropsychological data on the robustness of the brain and recovery of function. A partial functional overlap of elements with flexible functionality can explain vicarious functionality: the redundancy of functions confers robustness, i.e., the ability to cope with variations in an operating environment with minimal damage, alteration or loss of functionality; the recovery of function and functional substitution require the degeneracy of a complex system. Degenerate networks allow for widespread, compensatory adjustment: many neurological lesions that appear to have little effect upon behaviour within familiar contexts reveal the presence of degeneracy in the brain. Robustness makes the non-catastrophic response of the system to a perturbation or damage possible.

[6] Jerome Bruner (1973) deeply analyses the brain's ability to generate an adaptive perception of the individual environment (as *Umwelt*) that goes well beyond the perceptive data received. Gestalt Psychology – in the 1920s – experimentally demonstrated the so-called Gestalt Laws of visual perception. They show how the functional organisation of the mind is deeply grounded in the intertwining of inside and outside, internal and external. On the neurobiological level of organisation, the "openess" of mind has important roots in the associative power of our degenerated cerebral circuits.

tion involves metaphor. Metaphor is a reflection of the range and associativity of enormously complex and degenerate brain networks. [...] Language itself reflects the constructive yet inherently ambiguous and indeterminate aspect of this mode of thought" (Bruner 1973: 58).

Therefore, openness is a fundamental principle in the architecture of the functional organisation of the mind, i.e., the openness of intelligent behaviour and the nervous system as illustrated in the aforementioned reflections on dexterity and degeneracy. The term "dexterity" is clearly metaphorical in and of itself, in that it defines a skill and a complex system of relationships between the individual and his/her environment under an adaptive profile. A "dexterous" action is a goal-directed action that reaches its target in an ever-changing world. The term recalls right-hand/left hand differentiation in motor ability and presupposes hemispheric functional specialisation and the related development of our cognitive system.

Degeneracy as a term points instead to a "shift", a sort of "deviation" from a definite pathway. A degenerated system is a complex network in which many different pathways can be activated to reach the same goal, or – inversely – different goals can be reached through the activation of the same nervous pathway (or circuit). Both terms form the basis of our specie-specific openness (to the environment, cultural and social context and individual experience), which can be seen as a sort of "Kantian condition of possibility" – a necessary framework – for our metaphoric capacity. We are intrinsically metaphoric, in our brains as well as in our behaviour.

References

Bernstein, Nikolaj A. 1967 [1961]. *The coordination and regulation of movement.* Oxford: Pergamon Press.
Bernstein, Nikolaj A. 1996 [1946], On dexterity and its development. In Mark L. Latash & Michael T. Turvey (eds.), *Dexterity and its development*, 1–244. Mahwah, NJ: Erlbaum.
Bruner, Jerome. 1973. Beyond the information given: Studies in the psychology of knowing. New York: W.W. Norton & Company.
Edelman, Gerald M. 2006a. *Second nature. Brain science and human knowledge.* New Haven and London: Yale University Press.
Edelman, Gerald M. & Joseph A. Gally. 2001. Degeneracy and complexity in biological systems. *Proceedings of the National Academy of Sciences* 98. 13763–13768.
Edelman, Gerald M. & Giulio Tononi. 2000. *A universe of consciousness. How matter becomes imagination.* New York: Basic Books.

Feigenberg, Iosif M. & Latash Lev P. 1996. N.A. Bernstein: the reformer of neuroscience. In Mark L. Latash & Michael T. Turvey (eds.), *Dexterity and its development*, 247–275. Mahwah, NJ: Erlbaum.

Lurija, Aleksandr Romanovich. 1987. Bernstein Nicholas In. Richard R. Gregory (ed.), *The Oxford companion to the mind*, 805–806. Oxford: Oxford University Press.

Park, Hae-Jeong & Karl J. Friston. 2013. Structural and functional brain networks: From connections to cognition *Science* 342(6158). 1238411.

Reed Edward S. & Blandine Bril. 1996. The primacy of action in development. In Mark L. Latash & Michael T. Turvey (eds.), *Dexterity and its development*, 431–451. Mahwah, NJ: Erlbaum.

Giulia Frezza and Elena Gagliasso
Building metaphors: Constitutive narratives in science

1 Introduction

"Science does not have anything in common with metaphor!". When confronting with scientific metaphors many, and scientists themselves, often do not recognize metaphors or they even consider the two incongruous terms (science and metaphor) as an oxymoron. On the contrary, we stress that metaphors are so much part of the scientific discourse, being both heuristically relevant and even privileged objects of study[1] that they became almost invisible. The principal aim of this paper is to clarifying the ambiguous relation between the spread of metaphors in science and their invisibility.

We propose that what counts as "science" and as "metaphor" through times makes the relation between science and metaphor alternatively swinging from opposition to dialogue. Indeed the process is inversely proportional: the more science is considered only a rational and axiomatic system, the more metaphor undertakes qualitative and ambiguous features and is dubbed as irrational. Therefore scientific metaphor turns out to be a chimera.

The building of scientific-metaphorical thought has been studied in depth by the literature (e.g., Hesse 1993). We more plainly, and synthetically, will refer to it here as "scientific metaphoring". Along with the analysis of scientific common metaphors, their crystallization in influent concepts and the raising of new metaphorical terminology we will review three main conceptual oppositions which oppose science to metaphor, namely: at the epistemological level "rational vs. irrational", at the methodological level "axiomatic vs. ambiguous" and at the cognitive level "counter-intuitive vs. intuitive".

Our inquiry does not intend to be an indepth historical-epistemological work, but rather wishes to offer a brief outline and insight into scientific metaphoring.

---

[1] An interdisciplinary field of study dedicated to metaphor is well-documented: in books see e.g., Gibbs 2008; Ritchie 2013; reviews such those in the journals *Metaphor and Symbol* (Routledge), and *Metaphor and the Social World*. As the international RaAm conferences show the issue of metaphoric language in science is becoming more and more multi and inter disciplinary.

Giulia Frezza, Sapienza University of Rome
Elena Gagliasso, Sapienza University of Rome

DOI 10.1515/9783110549928-012

It combines epistemological and conceptual analysis focusing on life sciences, especially biology, biomedicine, cognitive and neuroscientific researches.

The considerations provoked by the three conceptual oppositions will allow not only to better clarifying the role of metaphor in science, but at the same time they will provide also a deeper epistemological insight into scientific practice itself. In the end scientific metaphor will be revealed as a legitimate as well as a very fertile field of study. Especially, the entanglement of metaphoring at the crossroad of embodiment and environment would be profitably outlined with regards to the context of lab scientific metaphoring where prosthesic practices extend the actual mindbody.

2 Every science must start from metaphor to end with algebra?

We recall attention to Black's assertion within his "interaction" view of metaphor: "Perhaps every science must start from metaphor to end with algebra; and perhaps without metaphor there would never have been any algebra" (Black 1962: 242). We would try to clarify yet again this controversial issue.

The rational character of science is a *topos* in epistemology and in every argument about scientific research from Galilei to Popper. The opposed alleged irrational nature of metaphor can be traced back to an old debate begun in modern times with the beginning of the scientific enterprise.

The roots of metaphor in the Renaissance are immersed in analogic thought at the crossroad of metaphysical, rhetorical, logical, hermeneutical and artistic styles of reasoning[2]. The crucial feature of analogical and metaphorical thinking, which would be a signpost of modern times and also criticized for this very same reason, is that metaphor plunged *ontologically* and not only *lexically* the description of phenomena into reality. Things were seen as metaphors themselves, nature was metaphoric (e.g., Rossi 1997).

Analogies and metaphors were secretly written in the mirroring of things in an infinite coil, from micro to macrocosms: everything mirrored something else through sympathies that connected every phenomenon to the whole universe. Language, bursting metaphors, by means of words was direct representation of reality pervaded by significant resemblances. Savants and natural philosophers exploited analogical and metaphorical language as a semantic morass for pre-

---

[2] The topic is vast and deeply studied by the literature e.g. Foucault 1966; Metzger 1975; Webster 1984; Rossi 1997.

serving science an élite domain. Therefore truth should be understood not *by means* of the language but rather *notwithstanding* the language (Rossi 1997). The esoteric core of metaphor in the *episteme* between XV and XVI centuries upheld knowledges detaching them from common sense and ordinary world. At the root of modern times magic and scientific knowledges were entangled in this ambiguous and allusive language.

Eventually scientific reasoning departed from this metaphorical world. Ontological qualitative metaphors were conflicting with the possibility of scientific method, value free and based on reproducibility, quantification and falsifiability. The slow establishment of a rigorous scientific enterprise, built on cognitive and practical features such as calculus, modelling, experimenting, and theorizing as well as searching for funding, instituting academic credibility, diffusing knowledge through books, and so on (MacLean 2002) made science diverging from metaphor. Therefore the irrational, esoteric, character of thought inherent to the observation of reality became something to be fought by scientists and by the epistemological tradition, turning metaphor into an ambiguous linguistic tool to be suspicious of.

This is the main reason why the epistemological "rational vs. irrational" opposition between science and metaphor easily couples with the second, methodological, opposition "axiomatic vs. ambiguous". Bacon, Hobbes and Leibniz and other natural philosophers strove for a regulative ideal of a universal scientific language protected from the "innumeris aequivocationibus" of ordinary languages (Leibniz 1875–1890, VII: 205). They searched and proposed a linguistic template endowed as much as possible with the functionality of calculus[3]. Nonetheless, metaphoric language was indeed a controverted issue (Formigari 2010). Hobbes in the Leviathan in the fifth chapter dedicated to reason and science in opposition to reason ("reason is the pace; increase of science, the way; and the benefit of mankind, the end") defined metaphors "ignes fatui" (5.13) and underlined their misleading nature despite their tempting ineludible presence. Bacon stressed their ambiguous essence ("faciunt enim lumen et velum"), while Leibniz, attempting to build "the alphabet of human thoughts", a universal, perfect, language equipped of incontrovertible and exact structure, described it in a letter to the Duke of Brunswick in the fall of 1969 as the following:

---

[3] Between XVII and XVIII centuries, theories on the trope of metaphors and analogies were typical of discussions about the relation between rhetoric and logics, and allow to acknowledging their continuity rather than their discontinuity (Capozzi 2010). See especially Capozzi's analysis of the establishment of a "visual standard" feature of logic ("geometrisations") and her critical discussion of Leibniz's idea of calculus as "cogitatio caeca".

> My invention encompasses every use of reason: it is a judge of controversies, an interpreter of notions, a scale for weighing probabilities, a compass to guide us through the ocean of experiences, an inventory of things, a table of thoughts, a microscope to inspect near things, a telescope to discover things far away, a general calculus, an innocent magic, a non-chimerical Cabbala (Leibniz 1969: 261).

Quite interestingly from our viewpoint stressing the coagulum of metaphor in scientific reasoning, Leibniz in the effort of depurating language from any trope, on the contrary, made a champion of the use of metaphoric speech in philosophical literature (Formigari 2010).

In the beginning of XX century, with the development of modern philosophy of science, axiomatization would become the core of scientific enterprise from a methodological viewpoint. Due to analyticity and exactitude which paralleled it to mechanicistic calculus, the axiomatic method was considered providing the most eminent form of scientific lexicology. Science and rationality are coupled being tautological, self-justifying and mutual guarantees. This double-bind reinforced also with the projection of logic and ontological antagonism to one common enemy (fictitious): anti-rationality or "irrationality". Inasmuch as the epistemological framework of scientific "rationality" is linked with the methodological tool of "axiomatization", consequently, the practice of scientific reasoning exploiting non axiomatic connections and insights does not have citizenship in this bottleneck, becoming irrational.

In this kind of scientific framework metaphors are on the opposite side of the coin, the most ambiguous lexical forms: a tension carves and polarizes the opposition between the hermetic ambiguousness of metaphor and the total axiomatic language of calculus. Making science and making metaphor are two opposed, alien, practices, disavowing all preconditions for developing their dialogue.

Since the linguistic turn and with the developments of contemporary trends historically oriented in philosophy of science the emphasis given especially to rationality and axiomatic/logic scientific features has been reviewed. All criteria claimed by any scientific method should necessarily be understood historically, being "ideals of knowledge" (Amsterdamsky 1983), "styles of reasoning" (Hacking 2012), or "matrices of thought" (Lakatos 1978). Style-lab, style of statistical probability, style of virtualization, style of deep time sciences all work with different methodological criteria. Every style is self-justifying and it determines its own criteria of truth and the set of rules of scientific procedure (Ziman 2002). Along these lines, rational science vs. irrational metaphor becomes a fallacious opposition because "irrationality" is a term intended only in privative sense. This antinomy impoverishes the complexity of reasoning: it is useful, rhetorically, as a criterion for defining science in a strict sense (analytic demonstration) and in opposition to everything that escapes this specific category (e.g., Popper).

The third opposition between science and metaphor that we underline here is "counterintuitive" vs. "intuitive". A typical definition of science is counterintuitive (Rossi 1997). In Wolpert's account: "Both the ideas that science generates and the way in which science is carried out are entirely counter-intuitive and against common sense [...]. Science does not fit with our natural expectation" Wolpert (1993: 1). Along with the classic distinction between experience and experimentation made by Koyré, many studies emphasize also the non-rationality of human cognition as opposed to rationality of scientific knowledge by means of structural biases in the selection and measure of phenomena (Gigerenzer and Gaissmaier 2015).

Underlining three counterintuitive features of science – against common sense, heuristically built as well as product of intentional activity – we stress that in many cases metaphor might turn out to be inasmuch counterintuitive as science.

A classic description of intuition is "ineffable insight", which in the last thirty years cognitive science researches have more finely detailed as "unconscious cognition" (Kihlstrom 1987) or "automatic cognition": a form of processing "without intent, awareness and deliberate encoding" which is essential for "structuring our skills, perceptions and behavior" (Kaufman 2011: 443; Epstein 1991). In this sense intuition is a fundamental, cognitive activity which recognise at glance, condensing together multiple and heterogeneous, also subliminal, perceptions in a procedural, "fast" thinking (Kahneman 2011) and also "smart" processing (Gigerenzer 2007). Intuition is intended not as ineffable insight, but rather as "synesthesic intelligence", not only sensorial, and poetical but more properly embodied synesthesia, which preconsciously learns patterns also for hypothesizing projectively future patterns (heuristics).

This form of intuition is akin to metaphoring. Metaphor is typically defined as a bridge connecting different domains, creating new connections, operating as a form of synesthesia, though not being it.

At another level, intuitive knowledge is outlined as what derives from, and is adherent to common sense, or ordinary observation. The champion is *Gestalt* perceptive illusions the "sensata experientia" of our misleading representation of reality contrasting with the scientific one.

Maintaining the "intuitive" character of metaphoring only as "adherent" to common-sense experience would undermine centuries of creative metaphoring: literature, poetry and drama invented and exploited powerful metaphoric expressions precisely to emphasizing rather than following common experience. Metaphor informs reality boosting it rather than simply describing it – and even revealing entirely new patterns of reality previously opaque. In this sense, metaphor is counterintuitive, it does not adhere to reality; it goes against common sense establishing a peculiar relationship between reality, its observation and description.

Moreover, metaphorical activity described as unconscious and automatic (Gibbs 2008) is also outlined by means of opposed counterintuitive features. Recent cognitive studies on metaphor highlight its deliberative character, twofold intentional (Steen 2013, 2015). At the same time recent neuroscientific advances are searching for the keys accessing the very mental process underpinning the activity of metaphoring, sketching the preconditions necessary for metaphoric cognition. Recent neuroscientific studies split into two main trends facing "the strength of sensorimotor engagement in metaphor" (Jamrozik et al. 2015). Aside to strong embodied theory (i.e. "metaphor comprehension relies on automatic and obligatory sensorimotor simulation" such as in studies by e.g., Wilson and Gibbs 2007) soft embodied idea of metaphor (Chatterjee 2010) endorses the decreasing of sensorimotor grounding in the brain with the familiarization of metaphors and their use for abstract thinking. Soft-embodiment metaphoring would be a bridge for abstract thought elaboration so that the strength of sensorimotor engagement in metaphor "may reflect the degree of experience people has deriving a metaphoric abstraction" (Jamrozik et al. 2015).

Other neurophysiological works support this idea of "counterintuitive metaphoring" emphasizing how metaphoring is bound to discourse goals (Utsumi and Sakamoto 2015). They highlight a radical difference: for "explanatory goal" metaphoring activity produces more apt and conventional metaphor whereas for "literary goal" metaphors bear more familiar and imageable features. This should be further investigated; nonetheless we can suggest that in the case of scientific metaphoring targeting explanatory goals metaphors should probably combine conventional with specific features, while metaphors directed towards heuristic goals would require to have more familiar and imageable traits.

From this outline scientific metaphor rather than only unconscious and automatic emerges also as deliberate, intentional, and as a possible cognitive route to abstraction. In conclusion we may propose a parallelism to be further developed. According to recent cognitive researches, creative cognition is distinguished in two main phases, "generative" and "explorative", the first being a sort of preinventive and redundantly productive phase, the second a more refined examination (Kaufman 2011). The two natures of metaphoring, automatic and deliberate, may somehow correspond to this distinction within creative cognition outlining two different form of scientific metaphoring: the first extemporaneous and unconscious while the second would be more intentional and deliberate.

3 Looking back into invisible scientific metaphors

Since the 1970s, in a broad conception of science, metaphors received a considerable attention also in their epistemological nature, especially in theory building and in heuristics (cfr. Black 1962; Blumenberg 1997 [1960]; Boyd 1993 [1979]; Hesse 1966, 1993). The field addresses especially to all creative productions in the interaction between mind and environment, and, we underline, does not mean passing from rational and axiomatization into a domain of oblivion and ambiguousness[4]. Thought indeed works as well with metaphors and analogies, heuristically generating constitutive metaphors.

Life sciences are extremely rich in metaphorical language. In this domain, axiomatization though increasingly used also for its application as a controlling and provisional-probabilistic device, is not always enhancing life sciences explicative power or extending their connections with other domains. On the contrary, the cognitive activity of metaphoring is constantly at work.

We define here metaphoring by means of a double standpoint: the product of lexical activity (linguistic metaphor), and the process of cognitive activity (a way of processing through metaphorical production)[5]. Moreover, metaphoring should be addressed to specific contexts, extending the double (linguistic and cognitive) standpoint also to the broader issue of communication (i.e., "linguistic expression in context", Steen 2015, "communicative context" Ritchie 2007). This three-level perspective (linguistic, cognitive and contextual) would seem suitable also for targeting the specific context of life sciences metaphoric communication/rhetoric.

Life sciences' metaphoring produces constitutive metaphors, influent concept (as "organism" or "environment", "modularity", "network"), synthesizes or dubs theories (e.g. "evolution", or "natural selection"), opens new research domains (as "artificial intelligence", "artificial life", "genetic engineering", "biomechatronics"), or enhances the spreading of new theoretical terms ("scaffolding", "constraint", "esposome").

Philosophical, epistemological and semiotics reflections, especially confronting with biomedicine and neuroscience are intertwining their questioning

---

[4] As Mary Hesse (1993: 53) stressed in terms of moderate scientific realism knowledge is "particular rather than general, local rather than universal, approximate rather than exact, immediately describable and verifiable rather than theoretically deep and reductive".
[5] The meaning and functioning of metaphoring is studied at the crossroads of various disciplines and levels: from Lakoff's and Johnson's Contemporary theory of metaphors (Lakoff and Johnson 1980); Conceptual Metaphors Theory (CMT), for a recent review see *Journal of cognitive semiotics* 5(1–2), 2013; Career theory of metaphor (Bowdle and Gentner 2005) and discourse analysis, genre perspective (Deignan, Littlemore and Semino 2013).

in the field of metaphors. Constructing metaphors, answering to metaphors or to metonymical assertions are all object of neurophysiological researches (cfr. Weiland, Bambini and Schumacher, 2014; Bohrn, Altmann, and Jacobs 2012); they have been tested also on patients affected by autism (cfr. Rundblad and Annaz 2010), as well as for potential therapeutic strategies in the case of brain damages (cfr. Choudhury and Slaby 2012)[6]. As mentioned above recently neuroscientific analyses are focusing also on the use of metaphors for developing abstract thoughts bridging embodiment with abstraction through metaphoring (Jamrozik et al. 2015).

We should go back, then, to the issue suggested above: why scientific metaphors are still almost invisible?[7] First of all metaphors in science are not in the usual "nominal" form "A is B" such as the common and extensively studied metaphors "life is a trip", or "science is an adventure". Moreover in life sciences metaphors are of the most different kinds. Despite delineating a real taxonomy we would outline a sort of family resemblance à la Wittgenstein. Multidisciplinary and multifold approaches towards metaphoring underline that reciprocal inbreeding often happen between terms, disciplines and fields of study. The terminological transfer yet introduces a new metaphor which can be recursively used and sometimes conceals its original meaning too. For instance "broad-metaphors" are those which go beyond a precise epoch or environment denoting a specific socio-cultural context. As underlined by the literature, the longlasting metaphor of "heredity" was originally born in the field of law asserting the passing on of properties through generations (Sabean 2007). Only around the 1830s the metaphor of heredity was transferred from law to biology affirming the notion of biological inheritance; and only after the rediscovery of Mendelian works it has been established as a pillar concept of classical genetics (Müller-Wille and Rheinberger 2007, 2012).

Transfers of this kind, hence, are creating "bridges" or new "cognitive routes", which might later turn metaphors into new theoretical terms. For instance, the notion of "constraint", architectural and phyletic bonds, and ontogenetic "pathways of development", themselves were referring to the classic notion of "*Bauplane*" (plan of development) in the anti-adaptationist programme proposed by Gould and Lewontin in 1979. Scientific metaphors are also frequently resulting from the contraction between two terms as mythical "chimeras", animals that

---

[6] Potential therapeutic strategies for patients with lesions to sensory motor brain areas could be developed by means of their innate capacity of expressing themselves with metaphors. The metaphorical expression eliciting somatosensory feedbacks canalizes cognitive recognition (cfr. Choudhury and Slaby 2012).

[7] For instance, in Ritchie (2013)'s book "*Metaphor*" there is no reference to scientific metaphor.

were made up of two different beasts ("genotype", "genome", "epigenome", "esposome", "microbiome").

These are all projective metaphors which being either chimeric terminologies or connecting bridges, anyhow, they are useful for opening new routes and ways of thinking. This metaphoring can be paralleled to the well-known serendipity process: often scientists discover by chance and often with the help of new techniques or technologies such as computer simulation, big data, which eventually make the scientific enterprise advancing.

Metaphors work in the same way. There is a vital link between unpredictability and metaphor. Thus it is not surprising that heuristic is the most significant moment of scientific practice where metaphors are found. New data and evidences raise the production of metaphors such as mixed concepts, transferred from ordinary language or merging different, distant, fields of study. For instance, in the domain of epigenetics the main underpinning metaphor is the electric metaphor of switch (Stelmach and Nerlich 2015).

On the other hand, another kind of metaphoring is due to the stratification of existent metaphoric matrices. Once a metaphoric term is established as theoretical term, it often tends to generating entire families of terminologies. In this case naming derives from the old metaphoring which is being triggered again but canalized into a new concept. For example "biology" is an ancient crasis of the Greek *bios* (life) and *logos* (discourse)[8], then "biome" from *bios* has been used to dub the totality of living beings in ecological terms and recently "microbiome" baptized the microbes' populations inhabiting organic apparatuses.

After this first heuristic phase of scientific metaphor another phase opens. When metaphoric attempts of naming, of baptizing new notions are acknowledged by the scientific community they can furtherly evolve into "theoretical terms", in a process known as conventional crystallization (Gagliasso 2010). Only rarely theoretical terms spread also in the use and extend through times becoming "influent concepts". In many cases this terminology refers to a specific domain, provides lexical access and is confined to designate a shortcut code such as bow-tie for evolutionary theories, or microbiome in symbiontology.

Many different circumstances impinge on these pre-paradigmatic times, what can be dubbed "the narrative of metaphors": standard circulation/spreading of terms within scientific community, trends, styles of thinking, funding, rhetoric, and communication strategies. In a sort of scientific propagation and propaganda through metaphors elsewhere discussed more in detail (Frezza and

---

[8] This was introduced in the same year, 1802, by the German physician and naturalist Gottfried Treviranus and the French naturalist Jean-Baptiste Lamark who both refers to biology as the domain of life and living bodies, respectively.

Gagliasso 2014) or such as in the well-known case of mirror neurons (Frezza 2012). Scientific metaphors are always built in a specific context of values and to a determined *Weltanschaaung*[9]. Some heuristic metaphors which seem useful in a specific time, due to new discoveries and changings in styles of thinking may later disappear. This is the case of the opposite destinies of two metaphors both invented by Ernst Haeckel: "ecology" that should have been dedicated to the relations between living beings and their habitats, which is effectively established as a structured discipline and "essology" that should have addressed to the inanimate part of the world, and which has never entered current scientific vocabulary.

Terms that originally were metaphors lay at the basis of ordinary scientific language: they become foundational and entangled within language to the point that they become transparent or invisible.

"Organism" is a perfect example. It has an ancient metaphorical origin. "Organum" and "organa" of the body were conceived in analogy to mechanical or musical instruments: each organ, in analogy with a tool, is in accord with the function it performs in the whole instrument, but the whole body is also instrument "as an ax" (Aristotele 1993 [1937] I,1, 642a10). Between the philological, metaphorical ancient derivation of "organon" as a tool, and the biological meaning of "organism" as influent crystallized anti-mechanistic concept (Lenoir 2000) lays a gap and an inversion of meaning. First of all conceiving a living being as something that contains a coherent organizing principle apt to maintain order in itself (Gagliasso 2008) was crucial: firstly as an internal organization (organized body), then as relational organization in interaction with living environments (the link organism-environment). Similarly to most metaphorical systemic concepts related to living beings, "organism" generated metaphorical archipelagos with an explicative power that went beyond the field of biology. So this constitutive metaphor turned into a comprehensive notion extended from biological explanations to human contexts (organicist sociology, psychology and so on)[10].

---

9 Andrea Grignolio's talk at the 10th RaAm conference underlined the evolution of the information metaphor. In the 1950s Quastler & Co. studied if cybernetics and information were to be applied to living beings. Since molecular biology to genome project the informatics metaphor maintained its fortune especially in philosophical and science communication field (see e.g. Evelyn Fox-Keller's and Lily Kay's work) emphasizing "noise" and "fuzzy" features. In recent post-omics era, "information" is again a core issue, functionally and practically, underlining both its overwhelming complexity and that it is no more something *to be applied to* living beings but rather *extracted* (big data) and then interpreted informing about biological phenomena.

10 It may also include ideological contents. We find examples of this reasoning in the philosophies of populism at the beginning of XX century (Merker 2013). Organic state exposure reveals the implications of the concept of totality to fill it with political content (Schlanger 1995): from

In this way, the common gaze (often of scientists themselves) does not easily recognize metaphors in its own language. "Environment", "individual", "organism", became so much part of current terminology that nobody would guess that there was a metaphor underneath. These are old and spread conceptual metaphors covering whole scientific theoretical domains. For instance, the metaphors of organism and environment had an explicative power that has been extended even beyond the domain of biology.

Figure 1. The spread of life science into theoretical terms

4 Techno-scientific embodiment and the "environment" in life sciences metaphoring

In the domain of life sciences, which offers a champion of the heuristic production of metaphors, a loop between ontological and epistemic issues can be underlined. The hermeneutic circle between observer and observed typical of many reflection here becomes epitomized or embodied. The observer is both subject

---

"organismic" philosophy in XX century applied to building States and politics, eventually to a misleading conceptual vehicle in the organicist conception of German Nazism in the 1920s–1940s.

and object of study. A part of metaphors of living beings is therefore intrinsic to this specific issue. This requires the analysis of two layers impinging on each other but which are not isomorphic. On the one hand metaphoring is explored as part of our embodied experience, projected, extended and abstracted too. Scientific metaphors of the kind often refer and express our internal "cinestesic" and "somestesic" dimension, our co-constitution and co-evolution with the environment and with other animals[11]. Moreover they reveal how the nature-nurture relation carves us in our second nature underlining by means of relational metaphors our relational nature. On the other hand, these descriptions are part of determined historical pathways and in continuous feedback loops: stratifications of metaphors that change with new paradigm shifts and that handling embodied human perspective are especially subject to ideological biases, as in the case of "organism" mentioned above.

In the last decades semiotic cognitive studies have treated in depth these topics centering the core issue of linguistic embodiment (Lakoff and Johnson 1980) with different albeit conflicting perspectives opening also to many neuroscientific studies of the kind (Gallese and Lakoff 2005; Wilson and Gibbs 2007).

Scientific reasoning itself is a highly subtle product of the mind, which cognitive neuroscience describes as an "embodied" mind. The embodied mind, or mindbody in science since the last thirty years is no longer represented and thinkable only as an isolate machinery, a black-box, a box full with representations, or a system of abstract calculation. Our cognitive predisposition or "posture" (Berthoz and Petit 2006) derives from being both part of the biological world and constituted by it; it is embedded in our physical structure with its material organic underpinning[12].

We can underline an extension of this embodied reasoning in the same metaphor of "environment", that is a meaningful and relational space within and outside the body to which the mindbody is always connected. At the same time the very concept of environment is metaphorical. The influent concept of environment develops within the metaphor of organic embodiment: "circum-stante", "milieu", "environ-ment", and "Umgebung" are not simple spatial indicators. They have all relational meanings. Environment or *milieu* are related to living beings, are enfolding them, as well as their projection continuously relates with feedbacks loops to organic individual constitution and shared intersubjectivity.

---

[11] These metaphorical terms are classic in phenomenological studies: from Husserl's intersubjectivity and *Lebenswelt* to Merleau-Ponty's "croisement", and Von Uexkull's *Umwelt*.
[12] The embodied underpinning of thought has been underlined also by recent researches in logic (Cellucci 2015).

Individuals moreover inhabit the environment and living in it they change it along times: producing, reproducing, exploiting and depredating it too. Since Darwinian evolutionary and ecological perspective this local definition (place) was replaced with a more productive feature: every environment is result of organic trophism that determines and transforms it by living in it. The metaphor of the environment is itself in motion: from a locus (physical, geographical and topological space) to a relational dimension which emphasizes the environment that enacts on living beings (selective environment) and is transformed by them (niche construction) (Odling-Smee, Laland and Feldman 2003), therefore "environment" is both a locus and a product (Canguilhem 1965; Gagliasso 2013).

From a lexical perspective "environment" is the product of explanations with metaphorical origin, at the same time, as index of its relational dimension it involves the position of the subject and of the individual embodiment too. In the same way as "organism" is rooted in a remote term with ancient metaphorical origins, the organism cannot exist without the environment and the environment has descriptive properties only if it is connected to the body.

In this way, the interactive corpus of the metaphor of environment emphasizes its link with the classic metaphor of organism. Organism and environment can be considered an ancestral couple of metaphors: axes of longlasting biological dynamics and *preconditions* of thought. They express how we think ourselves as living beings and offer core scientific explanations of living beings themselves: from *Naturalis Historiae*, to classic evolutionary and recent eco-evolutionary theories.

If the embodied brain works as a complex and integrated projector (Berthoz and Petit, 2006) the whole process of metaphoring, and not only its lexical outputs, is a complex and powerful system: a dynamic system embedded in its environment and actively and continuously interconnected and interacting with it.

The mindbody is embedded in the environment as well as in specific social and technological contextual environments in a mutual foundational relation[13]. Different lived environments are actively stimulating metaphoring activity. As mentioned, recent theories on metaphor indeed stress the dependence of metaphoring from specific contexts (Steen 2015) and goals (Utsumi and Sakamoto 2015).

---

[13] Recently the debate has been opened again in psycology adressing the perspective of the naturalization of the mind as a necessity of the mind: which would be granted not only by biological underpinnings but also by the condivision of the implicit assumptions fundament of the social world (Emiliani and Mazzara 2015).

As in every other activity where mindbody is in action, thus, also in the process of scientific production there is a *loop between acting and thinking* from the very first step of the experiment: putting it up, ad-hoc, with a combined use of technologies and simulation models, connecting vision and practical-haptical abilities, relying senses with abstraction and high-technology devices.

The whole mindbody system is operating. It collects and recognizes perceptions coming from different senses, which are a peculiar set of perceptions. Within techno-scientific practice, perceived phenomena are focused and magnified by technologies and subtle prosthetic products and they are combined in a unique spectrum. Usually starting from a general, theoretical, question, all these data are collected thanks to the extended use of technology, transforming the question in a very specific and practical one. In this activity mental *imaginerie* à la Bachelard[14] elaborates new issues processing and intertwining ideas and empiric data as well as moving between heterogeneous fields.

This is a second level of metaphoring in which mindbody operating through prosthetic technologies for expansion is exploited and enhanced: from microscopes and telescopes, fMRI, quantum scanner, sequenome, robotics[15]. We can dub this a subtler and more specific "experimental" kind of metaphoring, with metaphors such as "trigger", "scan", "map", "scaffolding", "loop", which is highly prosthetic and processing via cybernetic *Erlebnis*.

Moreover, recently iconic models increasingly extended practical into virtual activities especially, but not only, through simulation techniques. At the same time these very practices enhance semiotic-abstract cognitive capacities underlining that modelling and metaphoring share common patterns. We may suggest and further study the hypothesis that broad metaphors or influent concepts are becoming abstract modelling, eventually overlapping with models[16]. In technoscience metaphoring overlaps with models from a cognitive as well as from an epistemological standpoint, alternatively to what often hypothesized (Cordeschi 2010).

---

[14] Bachelard defines *imagerie* the activity combining observations, data, theorethical structures and ideological sedimented archetypes.

[15] See the studies about human enhancement and robotics and the works about embodied technoscience such as e.g., Ihde 1999.

[16] For an interesting review of the relation between models and metaphor see Bailer-Jones (2009), *Scientific Models in Philosophy of Science*, especially the fifth chapter.

5 Conclusion

Three conceptual oppositions between science and metaphor, "rational vs. irrational" (epistemological), "axiomatic vs. ambiguous" (methodological) and "counter-intuitive vs. intuitive" (cognitive) allowed us to clarifying and deconstructing common places about metaphor in science, conversely underlining the constitutive dialogue of science and metaphor. The leitmotiv expressed through these oppositions should be dismissed although it is well rooted in common sense. Epistemologically its origin can be traced back to modern times with the birth of experimental scientific thinking when metaphor, however, had a completely different meaning and value.

Indeed we stress that in the last decades science has revealed how much it has in common with metaphor; especially life sciences, and namely theory building and heuristic. Recently metaphoring, intended as cognitive, lexical and contextual practice, is outlined also by means of its deliberate and abstract features belonging to scientific discourse as much as logic, calculus and axiomatization.

In this sense we claim that Max Black's insightful statement «Perhaps every science must start from metaphor to end with algebra» (Black 1962: 242) should be twisted a bit: metaphors lay at the beginning, at the core and in the future of scientific researches.

Acknowledgements: We wish to thank Elisabetta Gola and Francesca Ervas for inviting us to organize the workshop metaphor in science at the 10th RaAm conference. Giulia Frezza, especially, thanks Gerard Steen and Anjan Chatterjee for sharing early versions of their works and for their insightful comments. We thank also Lia Formigari for her valuable suggestions.

References

Amsterdamsky, Stefan. 2013 [1992]. *Between history and method: disputes about the rationality of science* (Boston Studies in the Philosophy and History of Science). New York: Springer.
Aristotele 1993 [1937]. *Parts of animals*. Edinburgh: LOEB.
Bailer-Jones, Daniela M. 2009. *Scientific models in philosophy of science*. Pittsburgh: University of Pittsburgh Press.
Berthoz, Alain, & Jean-Luc Petit. 2006. *Phénoménologie et physiologie de l'action*. Paris: Odile Jacob.
Black, Max. 1962. *Models and metaphors*. Ithaca, NY: Cornell University Press.
Blumenberg, Hans. 1997 [1960]. *Paradigmen zu einer Metaphorologie*. Frankfurt am Main: Suhrkamp.

Bohrn, Isabel C., Ulrike, Altmann, Jacobs & Arthur, M. Jacobs. 2012. Looking at the brains behind figurative language-A quantitative meta-analysis of neuroimaging studies on metaphor, idiom, and irony processing. *Neuropsychologia* 50. 2669–2683.

Boyd, Richard. 1993 [1979]. Metaphor and theory change: What is 'metaphor' a metaphor for? In Andrew Ortony (ed.), *Metaphor and thought*, 533–542. Cambridge: Cambridge University Press.

Bowdle, Brian F. & Dedre Gentner. 2005. The career of metaphor. *Psychological Review*. 112(1). 193–216.

Canguilhem, Georges. 1965. *La connaissance de la vie*. Paris: Vrin.

Capozzi, Mirella. 2010. Logica e retorica. Separazione di campi e motivi di continuità fra Seicento e Settecento. In Elena Gagliasso & Giulia Frezza (eds.), *Metafore del vivente*, 51–60. Milano: Franco Angeli.

Cellucci, Carlo. 2015. Naturalizing the applicability of mathematics. *Paradigmi. Rivista di critica filosofica* 2. 25–44.

Cordeschi, Roberto. 2010. Fare a meno delle metafore: il metodo sintetico e la scienza cognitiva. In Elena Gagliasso & Giulia Frezza (eds.), *Metafore del vivente*, 113–122. Milano: Franco Angeli.

Chatterjee, Anjan. 2010. Disembodying cognition. *Language and Cognition* 2. 79–116.

Choudhury, Suparna & Jan Slaby (eds.). 2012. *Critical neuroscience: A handbook of the social and cultural contexts of neuroscience*. Chichester and Oxford: Wiley, Blackwell.

Deignan, Alice, Jeannette Littlemore & Elena Semino. 2013. *Metaphor, genre and register*. Cambridge: Cambridge University Press.

Emiliani, Francesca & Bruno Maria Mazzara. 2015. Dalla naturalizzazione delle scienze umane alla naturalità dell'ovvio. Le ragioni sociali per le quali la mente non è il cervello. *Giornale italiano di psicologia* 42(1–2). 31–56.

Epstein, Seymour. 1991, Cognitive experiential self-theory: an integrative theory of personality. In Rebecca C. Curtis (ed.), *The relational self: theoretical convergences in psychoanalysis and social psychology*, 111–137. New York: Guilford Press.

Formigari, Lia. 2010. Prefazione. In Elena Gagliasso & Giulia Frezza (eds.), *Metafore del vivente*, 9–13. Milano: Franco Angeli.

Foucault, Michel. 1966. *Les mots et les choses. Une archéologie des sciences humaines*. Paris: Gallimard.

Frezza, Giulia. 2012. Lo specchio della trasparenza. La metafora come strumento concettuale tra scienza e cultura e il caso dei neuroni specchio. *Rivista sperimentale di Freniatria, Il senso delle neuroscienze per la salute mentale* 1. 129–138.

Frezza, Giulia & Elena Gagliasso. 2014. Fare metafore e fare scienza. *Aisthesis, Formare per metafore. Arte, scienza, natura* 7(2). 25–42.

Fusaroli, Riccardo & Simone Morgagni. 2013. Conceptual metaphor theory: Thirty years after. *Journal of cognitive semiotics* 5(1–2). 1–13.

Gagliasso, Elena. 2008. "Organismo" e "individuo" come arcipelaghi di metafore. In Lorenzo Calabi (ed.), *Il futuro di Darwin. L'individuo*, 81–104. Torino: Utet.

Gagliasso, Elena. 2010. Tra epistemologia e vissuto: il ruolo delle metafore del vivente. In Elena Gagliasso & Giulia Frezza (eds.), *Metafore del vivente*, 17–25. Milano: Franco Angeli.

Gallese, Vittorio & George Lakoff. 2005. The brain's concepts: The role of the sensory-motor system in reason and language. *Cognitive Neuropsychology* 22. 455–479.

Gibbs, Raymond W. 2008. *The Cambridge handbook of metaphor and thought*. New York: Cambridge University Press.

Gigerenzer, Gerd. 2007. *Gut feelings: The intelligence of the unconscious*. New York: Viking.
Gigerenzer, Gerd & Wolfgang Gaissmaier. 2015. Decision making: Nonrational theories. In James D. Wright (ed.), *International encyclopaedia of the social & behavioral sciences*, 911–916. Oxford: Elsevier.
Hacking, Ian. 2012. 'Language, truth and reason' 30 years later. *Studies in History and Philosophy of Science* 43(4). 599–609.
Hesse, Mary B. 1966. *Models and analogies in science*. Indiana: University Notre Dame Press.
Hesse, Mary B. 1993. Models, Metaphors and truth. In Frank R. Ankersmit & Jan J. Mooij (eds.), *Knowledge and Language, Vol. 3: Metaphor and Knowledge*, 49–66. Dordrecht and Boston: Kluwer.
Ihde, Don. 1999. *Expanding hermeneutics: visualism in science*. Evanston, IL: Northwestern University Press.
Jamrozik, Anja, Meredith McQuire, Eileen R. Cardillo & Anjan Chatterjee. 2015. Metaphor: bridging embodiment to abstraction. *Psychonomic Bulletin & Review* 23(4).1080–1089.
Kahneman, Daniel. 2011. *Thinking, fast and slow*. New York: Farrar, Straus, and Giroux.
Kaufman, Scott B. 2011. Intelligence and the cognitive unconscious. In Robert J. Sternberg & Scott B. Kaufman (eds.), *The Cambridge handbook of intelligence*, 442–467. New York: Cambridge University Press.
Kihlstrom, John F. 1987. The cognitive unconscious. *Science* 237(4821). 1445–1452.
Lakatos, Imre. 1978. *The methodology of scientific research programmes: Philosophical papers*, volume 1. Cambridge: Cambridge University Press.
Lakoff, George & Mark Johnson. 1980. *Metaphors we live by*. Chicago: University of Chicago Press.
Leibniz, Gottfried. W. 1969. *Philosophical papers and letters*. Dordrecht and Boston: D. Reidel Publishing.
Leibniz, Gottfried W. 1875–1890. *Die philosophischen Schriften*, Gerhardt C. I. (hrsg.), 7 voll. Berlin: Weidmann.
Lenoir, Timothy. 1982. *The strategy of life. Teleology and mechanics in Nineteenth century German Biology*. Dordrecht: Reidel Publishing Company.
MacLean, Ian. 2002, *Logic, signs and nature in the Renaissance*. Cambridge: Cambridge University Press.
Merker, Nicolao. 2013. *Il Nazionalsocialismo. Storia di un'ideologia*. Roma: Carocci.
Müller-Wille, Staffan & Hans-Jörg Rheinberger (eds.). 2007. *Heredity produced: At the crossroad of biology, politics, and culture, 1500–1870*. Cambridge, MA: MIT Press.
Müller-Wille, Staffan & Hans-Jörg Rheinberger. 2012. *A cultural history of heredity*. Chicago: University of Chicago Press.
Odling-Smee, F. John, Kevin N. Laland & Marcus W. Feldman. 2003. *Niche construction*. Princeton: Princeton University Press.
Ritchie, L. David. 2007. Gateshead revisited: Perceptual simulators and fields of meaning in the analysis of metaphors. *Metaphor and Symbol* 23(1). 24–49.
Ritchie, L. David. 2013. *Metaphor*. New York: Cambridge University Press.
Rossi, Paolo. 1997. *La nascita della scienza moderna in Europa*. Roma and Bari: Laterza.
Rundblad, Gabriella & Dagmara Annaz. 2010. The atypical development of metaphor and metonymy comprehension in children with autism. *Autism* 14. 29–46.
Schlanger, Judith. 1995. *Les métaphores de l'organisme*. Paris: L'Harmattan.
Sabean, David W. 2007. *From clan to kindred: Kinship and the circulation of property in premodern and modern Europe*. Müller-Wille, Staffan & Hans-Jörg Rheinberger (eds.).

2007. *Heredity produced: At the crossroad of biology, politics, and culture, 1500–1870*, 37–59. Cambridge, MA: MIT Press.

Steen, Gerard J. 2013. Deliberate metaphor affords conscious metaphorical cognition. *Journal of Cognitive Semiotics* 5(1–2). 179–197.

Steen Gerard J. 2015. Developing, testing and interpreting Deliberate Metaphor Theory. *Journal of Pragmatics* 90. 67–72.

Stelmach, Aleksandra & Brigitte Nerlich. 2015. Metaphors in search of a target: the curious case of epigenetics. *New Genetics and Society* 34(2). 196–218.

Utsumi, Akira & Maki Sakamoto. 2015. Discourse goals affect the process and product of nominal metaphor production. *Journal of Psycholinguist Researches* 44(5). 555–569.

Webster, Charles. 1984. *From Paracelsus to Newton. Magic and making of modern science*. Cambridge: Cambridge University Press.

Weiland, Hanna, Valentina Bambini & Petra B. Schumacher. 2014. The role of literal meaning in figurative language comprehension: evidence from masked priming ERP. *Frontiers of Human Neuroscience* 8. 583.

Wilson, Nicole L. & Raymond W. Gibbs. 2007. Real and imagined body movement primes metaphor comprehension. *Cognitive Science* 31. 721–731.

Wolpert, Lewis. 1993. *The unnatural nature of science*. Cambridge: Harvard University Press.

Ziman, John. 2002. *Real science. What it is and what it means*. Cambridge: Cambridge University Press.

Clara Inés López-Rodríguez and Maribel Tercedor-Sánchez
Identification and understanding of medical metaphors by non-experts

1 Introduction

The role of metaphor in Medicine has been widely explored in literature (Diekema 1989; Salager-Meyer 1990; Van Rinjn 1997; Arroliga et al. 2002; Méndez 2004; Tercedor 2004; Periyakoil 2008), and its relevance in the field of Translation and Terminology has been acknowledged (Faber and López 2012; Tercedor et al. 2012; Prieto and Tercedor 2014). Metaphor is an essential tool for comprehension, an instrument that can facilitate the understanding of medical concepts by lay people and enables improved communication between health care providers and patients. However, metaphors can also invent non existing similarities between the conceptual source domain and the conceptual target domain. In fact, there are some critical approaches to the role of metaphor in science, since metaphor can distort the picture (Sontag 1989; Ball 2011). In this sense, Cameron (2003: 196) states that there is "an interesting paradox or conflict between the needs of science texts to inform accurately, and the inaccuracy prompted by the use of metaphors employed to inform effectively".

Medicine is based on understanding between patients and medical personnel (Hadlow and Pitts 1991). In the process of communication, metaphor is used by doctors and patients alike with the aim of bridging communicative gaps. In this regard, metaphorical processes have been studied as facilitators in the understanding of cryptic concepts, as for example those contained in research articles (Knight 2003), which through resources such as metaphor are made accessible in dissemination to lay audiences. But patients use metaphor too as a creative resource to express their symptoms (Teodoro Ricci 2010). Thus, metaphoric conceptualization is a cognitive operation with a key role in creativity and knowledge representation and dissemination in specialized fields (Temmerman 2000; Tercedor and López 2012; Vandaele and Lubin 2005).

Therefore, it can be said that metaphors in Medicine are used with 3 functions:
a) As a neology mechanism. Some metaphors were created in the history of Medicine to name new concepts and phenomena. These metaphors are lexi-

---
Clara Inés López-Rodríguez, University of Granada
Maribel Tercedor-Sánchez, University of Granada

DOI 10.1515/9783110549928-013

calized in language, and can be opaque both for experts and lay people. Some etymology research can be illustrative of the way our predecessors perceived some medical concepts[1]. For example, in Spanish, the upper cavities of the heart are called *aurículas* (from Latin *auricular*, little ear) from a perceived similarity in shape to a pair of ears. This resemblance was already noted by Hippocrates in 5th century BC (Figures 1 and 2).

b) As a means to disseminate science in medical texts for the general public such as popular science articles, websites with information for patients, blogs, etc.
c) As a potential facilitator in doctor-patient communication. Doctors use metaphors so that patients can understand them, and patients use metaphors to explain their symptoms to their doctor.

Even so, some of these metaphors are culturally motivated (Kövecses 2005, 2006) and can lead to misconceptions and misunderstandings in science dissemination and doctor-patient communication.

aurícula [auricle]
1. f. (Anat.) Cada una de las dos cavidades, derecha e izquierda, situadas en la parte superior del corazón, que reciben la sangre de las venas y comunican con los ventrículos.
Wikipedia
2. f. (Anat.) Pabellón de la oreja.
3. f. (Bot.) Prolongación de la parte inferior del limbo de las hojas.
lat. *auricula(m)* [*aure(m)* lat. 'oreja' + *-cula(m)* lat. 'pequeña']
　　Leng. base: lat. Antigua, significado antiguo y nuevo. Docum. en 1225 en esp. En el sentido de 'pabellón auditivo'; en 1450 en el sentido de 'cavidad del corazón'. La metáfora subyacente en la 1ª acep. está en gr. desde Hipócrates, s. V a.C., que llama a las aurículas del corazón *ôta* ὦτα, es decir, 'orejas'; se documenta incluso de forma aislada (en Pseudo Galeno, s. IV d.C.) el diminutivo *ôtíon* ὠτίον para ese valor. En lat. mediev., en Constantino el Africano, s. XI,
tenemos *auricula* significando 'cavidad del corazón'; se sigue documentando en ss. posteriores en lat. y en esp. español del s. XV encontramos *oreja* con ese significado. El árabe actuó como lengua intermediaria entre latín y griego. El ingl. documenta la 1ª acep. en 1664 y la 3ª en 1665.

Figure 1. Entry for the Spanish term "aurícula" in the *Diccionario médico-biológico, histórico y etimológico (University of Salamanca)* http://dicciomed.eusal.es/

---

[1] The following lexicographical resources can be useful for searching the etymology of medical words: *Diccionario médico-biológico, histórico y etimológico (Universidad de Salamanca)*: http://dicciomed.eusal.es/; *Diccionario de Términos Médicos de la Real Academia Nacional de Medicina*; *American Heritage Dictionary*; Marcovecchio, Enrico. 1993. *Dizionario etimologico storico dei termini medici*. Firenze; *Online etymology dictionary*: http://www.etymonline.com/

Studies looking into the real effectiveness of metaphor in the access to knowledge by non-specialists are still scarce, with some exceptions, like Semino et al. (2015) who investigate the significant use of violence and journey metaphors by patients with cancer. Research on how metaphors are the basis for conceptualization and term formation processes within the field of Medicine is needed in order to understand the potential role of figurative thinking in facilitating doctor-patient communication and improving understanding on the part of patients. For this reason, in this paper we concentrate on metaphors underlying the subdomain of *cardiology* and *cardiovascular diseases*[2] and describe empirical research to elicit the use of metaphors in Cardiology. We presume that laypersons are familiar with those metaphors because: a) the heart has been a key concept in many civilizations as the seat for feelings, thoughts and good and bad deeds, and b) cardiovascular diseases are the number one cause of death globally (WHO 2015), and therefore governments and mass media are currently raising concern about them in lay people.[3]

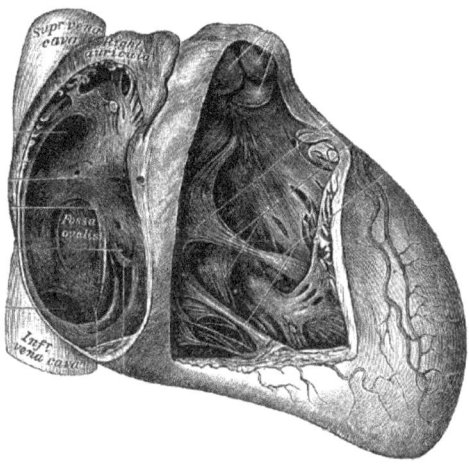

Figure 2. Interior of right side of heart [Source: Gray, Henry. 1918: *Anatomy of the Human Body*: http://www.bartleby.com/107]

To this end, following usage-based paradigms, we set out to analyze metaphor presence in a textual corpus and study the identification and understanding of meta-

---

2 In Medicine, cardiovascular disorders are classified as Diseases of the circulatory system (I00–I99) following the International Classification of Diseases (version 10).
3 http://www.who.int/mediacentre/factsheets/fs317/en/

phorical terms experimentally, since analyses and experiments of actual language use are needed (e.g. Cruse 2000). The theoretical foundations of our study are Frame-Based Terminology (Faber 2012) and metaphor studies in Cognitive Linguistics.

1.1 Frame-Based Terminology

Frame-Based Terminology (FBT) (Faber 2012) is a cognitive approach to terminology that uses frame-like representations of knowledge in a cognitive approach to the description of specialized knowledge. In FBT, frames are situated knowledge structures reflected in the lexical relations codified in terminographic definitions (Faber 2014: 14), and in the lexicalizations of concepts through different variants, as it happens in the case of metaphorical terminological units. More specifically, frames reveal particular culturally embedded scenes, situations or events (Evans 2007: 85). It is through the conceptual lexicalizations that we can access frames. Lexicalizations are often culture-based (Kerremans, Temmerman, and Tummers 2003), following three types of motivations (Levinson 2008: 257–258):
1. Categories driven by perceptual or cognitive salience;
2. Categories driven by affordances or constraints on human activities;
3. Categories driven by conceptual templates.

These categories are quite related to the metaphorical motivations proposed in section 2.1.

1.2 Metaphors and image schemas in terminological variation

Metaphoric conceptualization is a cognitive operation with a key role in creativity, knowledge representation and dissemination in specialized fields (e.g. Temmerman 2000; Tercedor and López 2012; Vandaele and Lubin 2005). Metaphoric conceptualization gives rise to alternative names in Medicine as it does in other domains. Such alternative names or terminological variants are a reflection of the different frames activated for a particular phenomenon (Langacker 1987: 164–165). It is therefore commonplace that a concept receives various lexicalizations, and among these we find metaphorical terms (e.g. "aortic arch syndrome" for "subclavian artery occlusive syndrome"). One of the issues in the understanding of the motivations for different lexicalizations is the identification of the underlying image schemas giving rise to the metaphorical terms.

As far as image schemas are concerned, there is agreement that they are "a recurring dynamic pattern of our perceptual interactions and motor programs that gives coherence and structure to our experience" (Johnson 1987: xiv). Knox (2003: 55) points to the preconceptual nature of image schemas. One key aspect in the understanding of image schemas is embodiment. Images schemas are indeed recurrent patterns of perception and bodily movement (Johnson 2005: 29), deriving from our sensory-perceptual experience with our body (Johnson 1987: xix). Image schemas can be deconstructed into different elements. For example, the metaphor *the heart is a container* is based on the image schema *in-out* and *up-down*. In cardiology, force dynamics (Talmy 1988) form the basis of many image schemas, since parameters such as flow of movement and rhythm define the functions of the circulatory system. Image schemas are ubiquitous both in everyday experience and in specialized domains, and both in humans and animals, as in the case of the mimic octopus (Ureña Gómez-Moreno 2014). A simplified visual representation of image schema was created to be distributed amongst the students participating in the study (Appendix 1).

1.3 Hypothesis, objectives and research questions

Hypothesis
The identification and understanding of metaphorical processes in Medicine is a result of embodied cognition and can be elicited in spontaneous production of metaphors.

The objectives of the present study are the following:
a. To propose a typology of metaphors in Cardiology based on previous literature and knowledge.
b. To experimentally study how trainee translators understand and produce metaphors in spontaneous production and translation tasks based on data from the CombiMed corpus.
c. To shed some light on the comprehension of widely used metaphors in Medicine by non-experts.

These objectives are related to the following research questions:
1. What medical metaphors are elicited in spontaneous production tasks by students of translation?
2. What are the recurrent source domains mapped by non-experts in Cardiology?
3. What are the most prevalent image schemas in the domain of Cardiology?
4. Can spontaneous translation tasks shed light onto the cognitive basis of metaphor?

2 Methods

We followed a combined top-down and bottom-up approach. For the first, we proposed a preliminary classification of medical metaphors according to perceptual criteria, i.e. morphology and resemblance, their function-based motivation and cultural specificity.

The bottom-up methodology followed the usage-based approach proposed in usage-based cognitive linguistics (Tummers et al. 2005: 226). More specifically, we combined the study of metaphorical expressions in a specialized corpus of texts on the function of the heart and main heart dysfunctions (see details in section 2.2.1.) with the spontaneous elicitation of metaphors in experimental settings (section 2.2.2.). The close study of text to see behavior of specialized language and to extract knowledge for terminographical databases and definition construction is also one of the main methods in Frame-Based Terminology (Faber 2014). Spontaneous production offers valuable data as there is usage information revealed in experimental tasks that contradicts or confirms corpus data (Tercedor 2010; Tercedor, López, and Alarcon 2013). This might particularly be so in cognitive operations involving comprehension and production, such as metaphorical conceptualization.

2.1 Top-down approach: Preliminary classification of metaphors

Based on previous studies on metaphor, we propose a preliminary classification of metaphors that combine image schemas (Johnson 1987, Lakoff 1990), and the classification of metaphors made by Salager-Meyer (1990) and Méndez Cendón (2004). This taxonomy (Table 1) has been useful in the selection of stimuli for the experiment.

The categories under the column *Source domains* have been illustrated with data from the CombiMed corpus, which includes medical texts aimed at experts, semi-experts and laypeople. Although we have combined a top-down and a bottom-up methodology to come to this proposal, more source domains can be found to be relevant.

Table 1. Preliminary classification of metaphors in cardiology

Image schemas	Motivation of metaphor	Source domains
Containment		Geomorphical
In-out		Phytomorphical (Plants)
Path		Anatomical
Up-down/scale	Metaphors based on perceptual motivations	Zoomorphical
Circularity	(shapes, structures and sound)[1]	Geometrical
Force		Sounding
Center-periphery		Alpha-numerical
Part-whole		*Architectural
Linking		
	Function-based metaphors[2]	Processes
		Functions
		*Architectural
		Food
	Culture motivated metaphors[3]	Man-made artifacts
		Beliefs
		Professions
		Musical instruments

[1] Morphological metaphors in Salager-Meyer (1990)
[2] Physiological metaphors in Salager-Meyer (1990)
[3] Material culture metaphors in Méndez Cendón (2004)
* Metaphors with both a perceptual and cultural motivation

For example, the source domains *architecture* and *anatomy* can be further developed (Table 2) to include metaphorical terms, their etymology (which reveals source-domain concepts) and some relevant multi-word lexical units in English and Spanish. Considering that the focus of this paper is on the identification of metaphors by non-experts, we will not dwell on this issue any longer.[4]

---

[4] The authors are presently working on a classification of metaphors based on corpus evidence. The preliminary results were presented in the conference *III Jornadas Ciencia y Traducción: Puentes interdisciplinares y transmisión del conocimiento científico* held in Cordoba (Spain) in April 2014 with the title "Ritmos, máquinas y otras analogías: la metáfora en textos sobre cardiología en inglés y español".

Table 2. Source-domain concepts and lexicalizations of architectural and anatomical metaphors in English and Spanish

Architectural metaphors	
[Source-domain concept] **English/Spanish lexicalizations**	**Examples** **from the CombiMed corpus**
[*wall*] wall, septum/tabique, septo	ventricular wall/pared ventricular arterial walls/paredes arteriales interatrial septum, atrial septum/tabique interauricular, septo interatrial
[*door*] valve/válvula	heart valves/válvulas cardiacas
[*beam*] trabecula/trabécula	septomarginal trabecula/trabécula septomarginal
[*hall*] atrium	atrial fibrillation
[*arch*] arch/arco	aortic arch
[*window, opening*] window/luz	aortopulmonary window luz proximal, luz distal
[*room*] chamber/cámara	chambers of the heart/compartimentos
Anatomical metaphors	
[Source-domain concept] **English/Spanish lexicalizations**	**Examples** **from the CombiMed corpus**
[*hair*] capillary/capilar	blood capilaries/capilares sanguíneos
[*breast*] sinus	coronary sinus/nódulo sinoauricular sinus of Vasalva / seno de Vasalva
[*ear*] aurícula, auricular	aurícula derecha
[*throat*] regurgitation/regurgitación	aortic regurgitation/regurgitación aórtica heart valve regurgitation/regurgitación valvular cardíaca mitral regurgitation/regurgitación mitral
[*belly*] ventricle, ventricular/ventrículo, ventricular	ventricular tachyarrhythmia/taquiarritmia ventricular ventricular tachycardia/taquicardia ventricular ventricular fibrillation/fibrilación ventricular

2.2 Bottom-up approach: Corpus data analysis and experimental tasks with students of translation

2.2.1 Corpus analysis to extract stimuli

The stimuli for the spontaneous production and translation tasks were selected on April 2014 from the corpus compiled within the VariMed and CombiMed projects. This corpus follows a combined *web for corpus* and *web as corpus* methodology (Buendía and López Rodríguez 2013). Specifically, we compiled:

(a) A comparable (non-translated) corpus in English and Spanish

The English comparable corpus includes the EnTenTen12 corpus (12,968,375,937 tokens), and the English section of the Oncoterm Corpus on oncology (28,771,714 tokens).

The Spanish comparable corpus includes the Spanish EsTenTen11 corpus (12,103,770,763 tokens), the Oncoterm corpus (13,645,317 tokens), and a cardiology corpus for non-experts (1,113,053 tokens).

The 'TenTen' corpora for English and Spanish were compiled and accessed by means of the Sketch Engine corpus query system (Lexical computing Ltd., n.d.).

(b) A parallel (translated) Spanish corpus

This corpus is composed of the MedlinePlus site in Spanish (7.709.764 tokens) and the *Translational Web Corpus of Medical Spanish* (TWCoMS)[5] with 29.861.260 tokens, composed by texts from US health organizations (CDC, cancer.gov, Women´s Health, the State Departments of Health of New York, New Jersey, Texas, California and Arizona, hospital and health providers websites and NGOs).

We extracted English textual segments (Appendix 2) from the comparable English corpus on cardiology. Texts on the function of the heart and the main heart dysfunctions were selected, and a pool of widely used metaphorical expressions was collected. Wide usage of metaphors was determined by their recurrent presence in non-medical textbooks which include sections on the heart and the circulatory system. Metaphorical expressions were extracted together with the textual fragments where they appeared.

---

[5] This corpus has been compiled by Miguel Ángel Jiménez Crespo from Rutgers, The State University of New Jersey (Jiménez Crespo and Tercedor 2014).

2.2.2 Spontaneous production and translation tasks with students: Materials, participants and procedure

Spontaneous use of language is a gateway to the situated representation constituting the scenario where previous experience, contextual information, and knowledge of the world all converge. For this reason, our main methodological tenet is the spontaneous production of metaphorical terms.

Participants were given both written and oral instructions prior to the task. Instructions included a short explanation of the concepts METAPHOR, METONYMY and IMAGE-SCHEMA. Despite being different phenomena, no distinction was made between metaphor and metonymy in the experiment for the sake of simplicity. Additionally, similes were also part of the stimuli. The tasks involved (a) eliciting spontaneous intuitions about metaphorical mappings in cardiology; (b) identifying metaphorical expressions in sentences, their underlying image schema and explaining the metaphor; (c) translating the metaphorical expression from English into Spanish within a textual context.

An online experiment was designed to elicit students' intuitions about the use of metaphor in cardiology in English and Spanish. The experiment was carried out in a course on Multimedia Translation, and consisted of two tests that took place within a period of 10 days.

The tests were hosted in the online platform LimeSurvey® to facilitate data gathering and analysis[6]. Prior to the test, the concepts *metaphor* and *image schema* were explained, and a table with different image schema (Appendix 1) was provided. Both tests included three tasks to elicit:
(a) Students' spontaneous intuitions about metaphorical mappings in cardiology.
(b) Their identification of metaphorical expressions (MEs), their underlying image schema and an explanation of metaphors.
(c) English into Spanish translation of MEs in context.

The stimuli were open-ended questions on metaphor and sentences extracted from the CombiMed corpus containing at least 1 metaphorical expression (ME).

The tests were distributed to 74 final year Translation students from the University of Granada (Spain), all of them enrolled in a course on Multimedia Translation (English-Spanish) in three different class groups. We ruled out the tests that were incomplete, as well as those of students who were not native speakers of Spanish since languages can lexicalize metaphors differently. According to Alexiev (2005: 36) the choice of a target language conceptualization strategy

---

[6] We had used the platform in previous experiments (López, Buendía, and García-Aragón 2012, López Rodríguez and García Aragón 2014).

and a subsequent translation technique are determined not only by cognitive, but also by language- and culture-specific factors.

As a result, our study population whose responses we analyzed consisted of 58 final year students of the Degree in Translation and Interpreting of the University of Granada. Their first language was Spanish, and English was their first foreign language. Their ages ranged from 20 to 29, and the mean age was 21.5. Standard deviation was 1.56.

First test (18th May 2014)

The first test included 26 questions in 3 sections: 1) personal information; 2) intuitions on metaphor/metonymy in cardiology, and 3) metaphor in context: identification, translation, comprehension and image schemas. Students had 15 minutes for section 1 and 2, and 25 for section 3. The test served as pilot study, and as a means to elicit students' previous knowledge and intuitions about metaphors in cardiology.

Students had to answer questions such as the following: "When translating a text on cardiology, what metaphors or metonymies describing the shape or function of the heart would you find in texts in English or Spanish? *The heart is/ functions /works like a...*". The same question was formulated in relation to the circulatory system.

> Si tradujera un texto sobre Cardiología, ¿qué metáforas o metonimias para describir la forma o la función del corazón se podría encontrar en inglés o español?
>
> El corazón es / funciona / hace (como...)
>
> Metáfora
> Metáfora
> Metáfora
> Otras metáforas (separadas por barras /)

There was also a task in which students had to read 20 sentences in English (extracted from the CombiMed corpus), and from these stimuli, they had to identify metaphorical expressions, and to translate the selected items into Spanish. They were also asked to provide an explanation of the metaphorical basis of the word. Finally, they had to match each metaphor with at least one of the image schemas represented in Appendix 1.

The chambers of the heart are separated by a wall of tissue called the septum.

	Metáfora 1	Metáfora 2	Metáfora 3	Metáfora 4
Palabra(s)				
Traducción				
Explicación de la metáfora				
Esquema(s) de imagen (A, B…)				

Second test (28th May 2014)

The second test was distributed 10 days later, after the students had translated a webpage entitled Heart Valve Surgery[7]. We wanted to test whether reading and translating real texts on cardiology would change their initial perceptions.

The second test was a simplified version of the first one, and included 13 questions to be completed in 20 minutes. This time the translation task involved translating into Spanish 10 full sentences in English, all of which contained metaphors. The sentences were also extracted from the CombiMed corpus.

- A small amount of leak (insufficiency or regurgitation) is usually not symptomatic and may be detected with a physical exam.

- A trabecula is a tissue element in the form of a small beam, strut or rod.

---

7 http://www.cts.usc.edu/hpg-heartvalvesurgery.html

3 Results and discussion

3.1 Research question 1: Spontaneous production of medical metaphors by students of translation

The answers in which students wrote their intuitions on the use of metaphors in texts on cardiology indicated that 94.83% of students were able to metaphorically describe the form and function of the heart, and 84.48% used metaphors to describe the circulatory system.

Their answers confirmed the idea that metaphor is a term creation device and a means for lexical variation, as seen in the definition of the heart as a MACHINE (*pump/*"bomba", *engine/*"motor", *clock/*"reloj", *battery/*"pilas"/"batería", *filter/*"filtro", *spark plug/*"bujía"...), the CENTER OF LIFE (*centre/*"centro", *nucleus/*"núcleo", *essence/*"esencia"... *of life/*"de la vida"), a SOUNDING OBJECT (*a ticking bomb, a metronome/*"metrónomo", *the heart roars/*"el corazón ruge"...), an object resembling a *fruit* (*a peach/*"un melocolón", *an apple/*"una manzana"), and an element moved by ENERGY. These metaphors were produced under different lexicalizations such as the following (Table 3):

Table 3. Selected responses to the cue *The heart is/functions /works like a...*

una bomba	el motor del cuerpo	
Bomb	Bomba	
El corazón es el motor del cuerpo humano	El corazón es el núcleo de la vida	El corazón es la pieza clave del puzzle del cuerpo humano
El corazón es como una batería de la que dependen el resto de órganos.	Bomba que impulsa la sangre por nuestro sistema circulatorio.	
Motor	Centro	
funciona como una bomba	tiene el tamaño de una manzana	tiene forma triangular
es el motor del cuerpo humano	es la esencia de la vida	
es el motor de la vida.	es el núcleo de la vida.	
una bomba	a ticking bomb	
motor de nuestro cuerpo	El corazón es el director del cuerpo humano	
El núcleo de la vida	el músculo de la vida	el motor de la vida

Table 3. (continued)

El corazón es el motor de nuestro cuerpo	El corazón funciona como unas pilas que se van desgastando poco a poco.	El corazón es como un melocotón.
el núcleo de la vida	el motor de la vida	
el motor del coche		
motor y bujías	una bomba de agua	un filtro
el centro	como un reloj	bombear
Bomba	Centro	fuente
un motor	una bomba	
El corazón funciona como un reloj	El corazón es el entrenador del cuerpo	
Impulse	motor	
El corazón es el motor..	Funciona como una válvula	El corazón bombea...
El corazón es el motor del organismo	El corazón funciona como una bomba, con la que llega a todo el cuerpo la sangre	
es el músculo de la vida	es la bomba de la sangre	fuerza
Bomba	puño	motor
una bomba de agua	un reloj	un engranaje
Motor	puño	bombeo
es el motor del cuerpo humano	funciona como un reloj	hace de metrónomo para nuestra vida
El motor	Nuestro motor ruge	Una batería
El corazón es el motor del cuerpo humano	El corazón funciona como un reloj	El corazón es como un metrónomo

It is interesting to note that many students drew similarities between the heart and human features. For example, some students compared it with a fist ("puño") and said that the heart was like the *conductor* ("director del cuerpo humano") or *coach* ("entrenador") of the body. These anthropomorphic references in metaphorical expressions are a natural consequence of embodiment (Tercedor, Faber, and D'Angiulli 2011).

Table 4. Selected responses to the cue *The circulatory system is/functions /works like a...*

la autopista del cuerpo		
Tube	Metro	
El sistema circulatorio es el sistema de riego de la vida	El sistema circulatorio es un circuito	Distribuye el la vida por el cuerpo
Es como un conjunto de autopistas que deben estar descongestionadas para que funcione bien.	Funciona como un sistema de regadío interior que tiene que alcanzar cada parte de nuestro cuerpo.	
cadena	Rio	
es como un sistema de transporte	es una red con forma radial	
funciona como una red de túneles por la que nunca deja de fluir nuestra sangre	es como un sistema de regadío	
funciona como el camino de la vida.	es el empuje constante de la vida.	
Mapa	es como un tren que transporta los alimentos	
un repartidor que lleva todo lo que necesitamos a las diferentes partes de nuestro cuerpo.		
la carretera de la vida	los afluentes del corazón	el río de la vida
Está compuesto por diferentes ríos que abastecen todo nuestro cuerpo.	Árbol	
como transporte en la vida	el transmisor de la vida	
las tuberías de una casa		
el motor de un coche	un sistema de refrigeración de líquidos	
una manguera	un sistema de riego	
Riego	Carretera	Vía
un circuito	una carretera	
ríos y afluentes		
máquina	ramificaciones	conjunto de cables
Es el río en el que fluye la sangre	El sistema circulatorio está formado por tuberías	

When describing the form and function of the circulatory system, students highlighted the idea of MOVEMENT/TRANSPORTATION (*road/*"carretera", *highway/*"autopista", *tube/*"metro", *tunnel/*"túnel", etc.), NETWORK (*cobweb/*"red", *circuit/*"circuito", *the branches of a tree/*"ramificaciones", etc.), and FLOW (*river of life/*"río de la vida", *tributaries/*"afluentes", *pipes/*"tuberías", *hose/*"manguera", etc.) as can be seen in Table 4.

Moreover, the metaphors identified in the first test were almost the same as those identified in the second test, with the exception of those relating to houses (*a house with different rooms/*"una casa con diferentes habitaciones"), which were only used in the second test. The fact that there is not a significant change after exposure to texts on cardiology might be indicative of the existence of some metaphors that are widely-used to explain Medicine. In our opinion, Western scientific and medical models have been somehow internalized by laypeople of Western societies as a result of education and science dissemination. Furthermore, some metaphors have become conventionalized in language as technical terms in medical fields and science in general (Cameron 2003: 200). For instance, the word *muscle* was created because of the resemblance between a muscle and a little mouse (in Latin *musculus*), although nowadays no one would identify a metaphor in this word.

Further research on the different metaphorical terms could shed some light on the study of metaphor variation as a pointer to instability of terms (Pecman 2014: 8). Meanwhile, we grouped the different instances of metaphor in order to notice the source domains that pervade the field of cardiology.

3.2 Research question 2: Recurrent source domains

The metaphors used by students to describe the heart (N=109) fell into one of the following categories: MACHINERY, CENTRE OF LIFE, BODY PARTS, SOUNDING OBJECT, ENERGY, FRUITS AND OTHER. The conversion of data into percentages indicates the proportions of different metaphors used in this particular dataset although it could point to a wider use in cardiology.

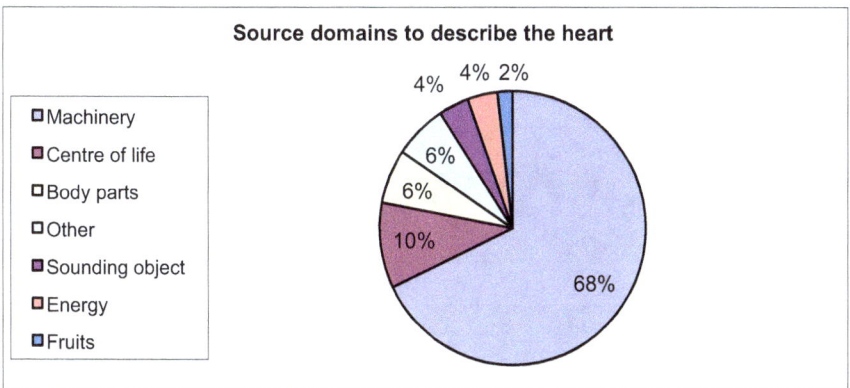

Figure 3. Describing the heart with metaphors: source domains

Regarding the metaphors used to describe the circulatory system (N=91), they concerned TRANSPORTATION, different types of systems (WATER SYSTEM, ELECTRICAL SYSTEM, FUEL SYSTEM), NATURE ELEMENTS and OTHER.

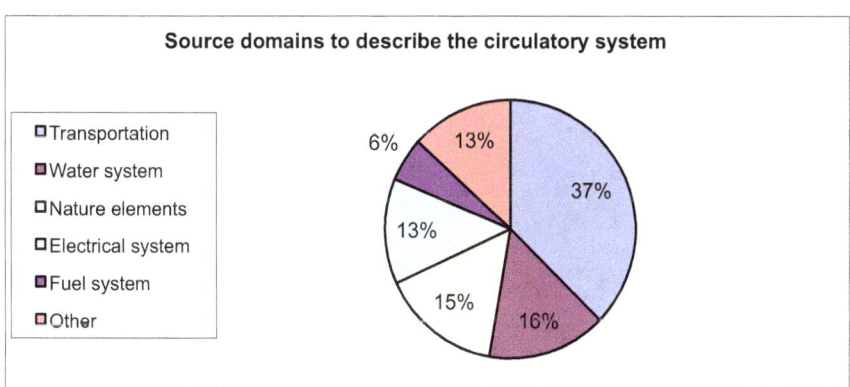

Figure 4. Describing the circulatory system with metaphors: source domains

From tests results and the classification of metaphors proposed in section 2.1., we represent recurrent source domains in cardiology in relation to their perceptual (yellow), functional (green) and cultural (blue) motivation in Table 5.

Table 5. Recurrent source domains in cardiology and its motivations.

	Perceptual, Functional, Cultural motivation **SOURCE DOMAIN**	Absolute frequency (N=109)
The heart is a...	MACHINERY (engine, pump, clock, battery...)	74
	CENTRE OF LIFE (nucleus, essence, core, center...)	11
	BODY PARTS (fist, muscle...)	7
	OTHER	7
	SOUNDING OBJECT (rhythm, metronome, pum-pum, drum)	4
	ENERGY (force, impulse, fight...)	4
	FRUITS (apple, peach)	2
	SOURCE DOMAIN	**Absolute frequency (N=91)**
The circulatory system is a...	TRANSPORTATION (tunnel, road, map, highway, roadway, underground, train, way...)	34
	WATER SYSTEM (tube, hoses, irrigation, watering system...)	14
	ELECTRICAL SYSTEM (circuit, circuitry, wires...)	12
	FUEL SYSTEM (oil, gasoline, machine, car, engine)	5
	NATURE ELEMENTS (river, tributary, tree, cobweb, tsunami...)	14
	OTHER (chain, net, maze...)	12

Data indicate that students were able to metaphorically identify perceptual and functional features of the heart. They mainly used metaphors related to the function *(the heart is a machine/energy)* of the heart, followed by metaphors based on how it is perceived by the senses *(the heart is a body part/a sounding object/a red apple)*. They also identified the key role of the heart in cultural models, with expressions such as: "el corazón es el núcleo/la esencia de la vida".

The functional role of the circulatory system was also highlighted in most metaphors (TRANSPORTATION, WATER/ELECTRICAL/FUEL SYSTEM). Morphological metaphors were less frequent (NATURE ELEMENTS). Culture-motivated metaphors related to the circulatory system were not produced by students.

We can conclude that non-experts deemed that the most salient features of the heart are mainly based on its vital function for life. Perceptual features were also relevant in their mental representation of the heart. In any case, function and form were intertwined in the metaphors provided. For example, the comparison with a network of highways that should be decongested for proper functioning indicates that the perceptual representation as web is related to the function of the circulatory system, as revealed in the response "un conjunto de autopistas que deben estar descongestionadas para que funcione bien". We are aware that function is associated to cultural models derived from education in Western societies. The role of functional metaphors in non-Western societies deserves further research.

3.3 Research question 3: prevalent image schemas in the domain of cardiology

The test included one question in which students had to associate the metaphors they had identified with at least one of the image schemas represented in Appendix 1. The wealth of data obtained (with some metaphors associated to up to 8 image schemas) was an obstacle for analysis, and we decided to analyze only a sample of 14 stimuli (Figure 5) which were collected at random.

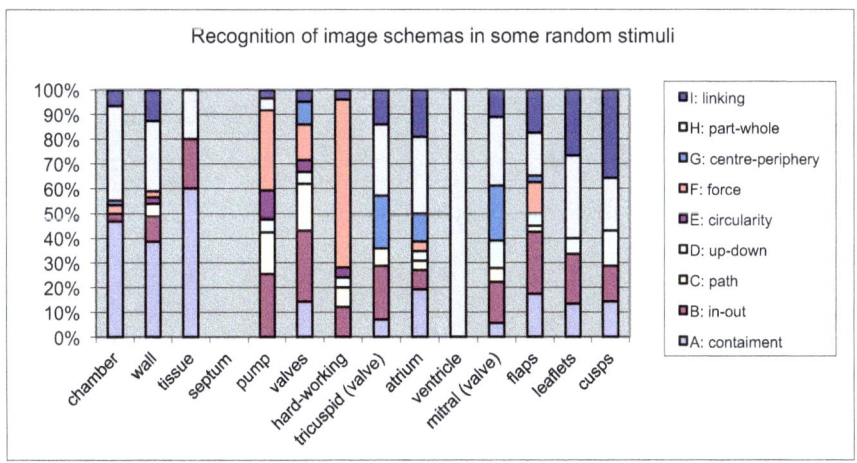

Figure 5. Image schemas recognized by students

Experimental data showed overlapping in some categories: the CONTAINMENT image schema tends to co-occur with the PART-WHOLE and LINKING schemas, whereas the IN-OUT schema co-occurs with FORCE. More experimental data are needed to elaborate a data-driven taxonomy of image schemas, and to check whether this overlapping is just exclusive of the domain of cardiology. In any case, it seems that our perception of metaphors is multidimensional in line with theories of situated cognition.

We grouped the results for the above stimuli in order to figure out if some of these image schemas where prevalent in cardiology. Despite the scarcity of data, we found that the most activated image schema was the PART-WHOLE schema, followed by CONTAINMENT, IN-OUT, FORCE and LINKING, a result that is in line with the metaphors MACHINERY, BODY-PARTS, ENERGY and SYSTEMS. For instance, machines and bodies are made up of linking parts, some of which are containers, and they need energy to move and function.

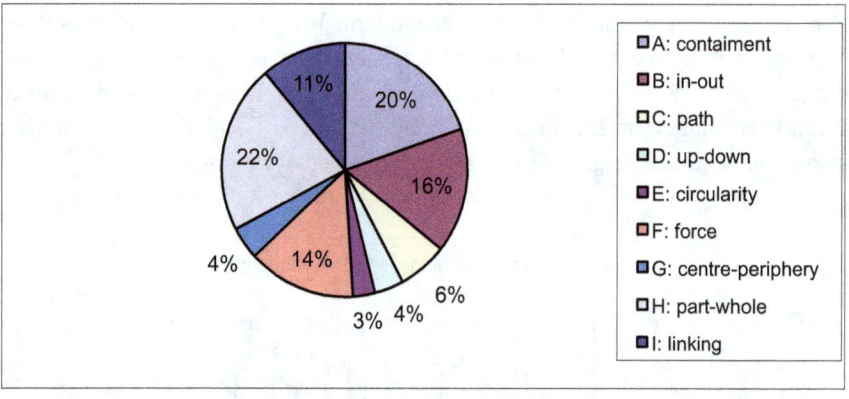

Figure 6. Prevalent image schemas in cardiology

3.4 Research question 4: cognitive basis of metaphor as revealed in translation tasks

Our study included tasks in which students had to identify the metaphoric expressions contained in full sentences, and then, to translate these expressions from English into Spanish. The identification of metaphors also implied associating them to their underlying image schema. We assumed that spontaneous translation tasks could shed some light on the cognitive and cultural basis of metaphor, and on the cognitive operations performed by translators. Under time pressure, students recall conceptual and lexical information from their internalized cultural models. As opposed to thinking-aloud protocols, which have been shown to only point to consciously processed information and not to automated cognitive processes (O'Brien 2011: 3; Muñoz Martín 2010), we propose that spontaneous translation tasks can be an alternative innovative data-eliciting method. Translation also provides a good opportunity to explore the extent to which the basis of metaphor is culturally motivated since translation tasks imply comparing two languages and cultures.

Table 6 summarizes the results of translation tasks. The first column includes the metaphorical expressions contained in the stimuli which were presented to students (see Appendix 2). Some of these metaphors are non-transparent because they are based on a resemblance that has been lexicalized in Greek or Latin, and has passed on to other languages. This opaqueness of metaphors is indicated with the symbol #. The second column indicates with a percentage to what extent students recognized those metaphors. Metaphors have been arranged according to this percentage so as to highlight the most salient metaphors to the eyes of our students. The third column indicates image schema, and the fourth column includes the Spanish translations of the English metaphorical expressions offered by students. Translation mistakes involving meaning and spelling are marked with an asterisk (*). We also highlight those instances in which translation has caused a shift of source domain.

Results indicate that metaphors on cardiology have primarily a cognitive universal basis although they also have a cultural basis. Students' translations pointed to the same source domains (ENGINES, HOUSES, RECIPIENTS, SOUND, etc.) in the majority of cases, and to different source domains in other cases (those in yellow). Despite shifts in source domains as revealed by translation options, there is a consistency in the image-schema structure of the source and target domains (invariance principle) ensuring the consistency of the metaphors at work. The image schemas recognized in this translation task are coherent with those recognized in the identification of metaphors task (see section 3.3).

Since our subjects were speakers of a romance language, they were able to recognize some opaque metaphors (marked with #) coined in Greek or Latin such as coronary (CROWN) artery, septum (WALL), chorhdae (ROPE) tendinae, regurgitation (THROAT) or ventricle (BELLY). However, their low frequencies indicate that these metaphors are non-transparent for laypeople.

Table 6. Recognition and translation of metaphors in the translation task

Recognition of metaphoric expressions	%	Recognition of image schema	Lexicalizations in translation task
Shift of source domain/* Translation mistakes /# Non-transparent metaphors			
chamber	93.1	containm, part-wh., linking	cámara, cavidades, habitaciones, aurículas, ventrículos, canales*, partes, cuartos, compartimentos
heart murmur	87.9	force, up-down	soplo, murmullo*, rumor*, susurro*
branch off	86.2	center-periph., part-wh, linking	bifurcarse, ramificarse, dividirse
pick up the trash	84.5	circularity, linking, in-out	recoger desechos/residuos / restos/ sobras/ desperdicios / basura
Wall	81	containment, part-wh., linking	pared(es), tabique, muro, capa*, válvulas*, membrana,
deliver lunch	75.9	linking, circularity, in-out	comida, alimento, almuerzo, nutrients
travel	74.1	path, circularity	viaja, recorrer, circular, transporter
Flaps	72.4	in-out, containment, part-wh	solapas, tapadera, tapas, aleta, alas, puerta, cúspide*, pestaña, cierre, colgajos, membrana, cubierta
pump	67.2	force, in-out, path	bomba, bombear, transportarse, circula
beam	63.7	force, part-whole, linking	viga, rayo*, puntal, haba*, haz*, habichuela*, travesaño
aortic arch	65.5	linking, part-whole	arco aórtico, cayado, bóveda
semilunar valves	56.9	linking, part-whole, circularity	válvula semilunar, válvula con forma de media luna
cardiac arrest	62.1	Force	paro, parada, ataque, arresto*
racing	62.1	force, linking, path	acelerar, competir, corer
pounding	50	force, linking, path	palpitar, aporrear, golpear, martillear

Table 6. (continued)

Recognition of metaphoric expressions	%	Recognition of image schema	Lexicalizations in translation task
hard-working	48.2	force, in-out	trabajadora, eficiente, funcionamiento continuo, que trabaja muy duro/mucho,
Leak	48.2	in-out, containment	fuga, escape, reflujo, filtración
valves	43.1	in-out, path, containment	Válvulas
strut	41.4	Force	puntal, barra
cusps	36.2	linking, part-whole	cúspide, umbral*, corona, pico, valva*, membrana*
vessel	36.2	containment, path	vaso
atrium	32.7	part-wh, containment, linking	aurícula, atrio*, atria*, patio interior*, patio*, cavidad
mitral (valve)	32.7	part-wh, center-periph., in-out	válvula mitral, v. biscúspide
leaflets	32.7	part-whole, linking	folleto*, hojas, aletas, solapa, membrana
tricuspid (valve)	29.3	part-wh, in-out, center-periph.	válvula tricúspide, de tres segmentos triangulares
atrial flutter	25.9	force, linking	palpitación, aleteo, fibrilación*, ritmo*
tissue	25.8	containment	tejido, seda*, pañuelo*
Flow	24.1	Circularity	fluir, circular
(#) coronary artery	12.1	circularity, linking, path	coronaria
(#) septum	8.6		septo, tabique
(#) chordae tendinae	6.9	Linking	cuerdas
(#) regurgitation	3.4	in-out, containment	regurgitación
(#) ventricle	1.7	part-whole	ventrículo

4 Conclusion

Metaphors are commonplace in cardiology and can facilitate doctor-patient communication and dissemination of scientific findings. In this article, we have described how a population of non-experts made up of 58 Translation students identified, understood and produced medical metaphors related to cardiology in the context of an experiment which included spontaneous production and translation tasks. The stimuli were chosen on the basis of a preliminary typology of cardiology metaphors, and on data from the CombiMed corpus.

After evaluating the experimental tasks, we concluded that non-experts spontaneously produced metaphors through a myriad of forms, and that many of these forms fall under the same source domains (MACHINERY, SYSTEMS, ENERGY, TRANSPORTATION, NATURE ELEMENTS, SOUNDING OBJECTS, CENTRE OF LIFE). Students mainly produced metaphors related to the function of the heart/circulatory system, followed by metaphors based on perceptual features, although the boundary between these two categories is fuzzy. In a certain way, these metaphors are culturally-motivated, since they are based on the biomedical model of illness and healing, which is still dominant in Western Medicine (Bennett Johnson 2012). To our mind, the different lexicalizations of metaphors instantiated in lexical and terminological variation might point to different cognitive and communicative motivations, as well as cultural models and personal experience (Tercedor and López 2012, Alarcon, López, and Tercedor 2016). Further experimental and corpus studies are needed to test this intuition.

We also found that metaphorical expressions were unevenly identified by trainee translators. Nevertheless, we found some patterns in the identification of image schemas by students, the most salient being PART-WHOLE, CONTAINMENT, IN-OUT, FORCE and LINKING. Moreover, the most opaque metaphors were those lexicalized through words of Greek and Latin basis. In this regard, interesting insights might be derived from the study of the connection between etymology and the transparency of metaphors for laypeople.

The analysis of the translation tasks also showed that source domains were mostly the same in English and Spanish. Metaphoric production in translation tasks tended to reproduce the metaphors used in the source text. We assume that this reproduction of metaphors in the translation is not the result of interference between the source and target language but rather it derives from what Lakoff (1987: 267) calls "collective biological capacities". Besides, the experiment yielded an extensive body of English-Spanish term pairs whose constituents have the same metaphorical motivation. However, we found many shifts in target domains which point to the cultural dimension of metaphor.

To conclude, this study has shed some light on the identification and comprehension of widely used metaphors in Medicine by non-experts based on ecological experimental tasks and corpus data analysis.

Acknowledgement: This research has been carried out within the framework of the research projects *CombiMed: Lexical combinations in Medicine: Cognition, Text, and Context* (FFI2014-51899R) and *VariMed: Denominative variation in Medicine: Multilingual multimodal tool for research and knowledge dissemination* (FFI2011-23120), funded by the Spanish Ministry of Economy and Competitiveness [http://varimed.ugr.es/]. It is also part of the innovative teaching project *Tradusaluda: audiovisual resources for the promotion of Health in Europe: accessible subtitling and translation,* funded by the University of Granada [https://tradusaluda.wordpress.com/]

References

Alarcon-Navío, Esperanza, Clara Inés López-Rodríguez & Maribel Tercedor-Sánchez (2016). Variation dénominative et familiarité en tant que source d'incertitude en traduction médicale. Meta 61(1). 117–144 (Special issue Zones d'incertitude en traduction. Guest editor: N. FROELIGER)
Alexiev, Boyan. 2005. *Contrastive aspects of terminological metaphor*. Sofia: University of Sofia PhD Thesis.
Arroliga, Alejandro C., Sara Newman, David Longworth & James K. Stoller 2002. Metaphorical medicine: Using metaphors to enhance communication with patients who have pulmonary disease. *Annals of Internal Medicine* 137(5). 376–379.
Ball, Philip. 2011. A metaphor too far. *Nature.* 1–8.
Bennett Jonhson, Suzanne. 2012. Medicine's paradigm shift: An opportunity for psychology. *Monitor on Psychology* 43(8). 5.
Buendía Castro, Miriam & Clara Inés López Rodríguez. 2013. The web for corpus and the web as corpus in translator training. *New Voices in Translation Studies* 10. 54–71.
Cameron, Lynne. 2003. *Metaphors in educational discourse*. London and New York: Bloomsbury Publishing.
Diekema, Douglas S. 1989. Metaphors, medicine and morals. *Soundings: An Interdisciplinary Journal* 72(1). 17–24.
Evans, Vyvyan. 2007. *A glossary of cognitive linguistics*. Salt Lake City: University of Utah Press.
Faber Benítez, Pamela (ed.). 2012. *A cognitive linguistics view of terminology and specialized language.* Berlin: De Gruyter.
Faber, Pamela. 2014. Frames as a framework for terminology. In Hendrick J. Kockaert & Frieda Steurs (eds.), *Handbook of terminology*. 14–33. Amsterdam and Philadelphia: John Benjamins.

Faber, Pamela & Clara Inés López-Rodríguez. 2012. Terminology and specialized language. In Pamela Faber (ed.), *A cognitive linguistics view of terminology and specialized language*, 9–31. Berlin and Boston: De Gruyter.
Hadlow, Jan & Marian Pitts. 1991. The understanding of common health terms by doctors, nurses and patients. *Soc Sci Med* 32. 193–196.
Jiménez, Crespo, Miguel Ángel & Maribel Tercedor Sánchez. 2014. La traducción médica del inglés al español: variación terminológica en el corpus comparable. Paper presented at TWCoMS. XI Congreso Internacional Traducción, Texto e Interferencias, Baeza (Spain), 22–24 July.
Johnson, Mark. 1987. *The body in the mind: the bodily basis of meaning, imagination, and reason.* Chicago: University of Chicago Press.
Johnson, Mark .2005. The philosophical significance of image schemas. In Beate Hampe & Joseph E. Grady (eds.), *From perception to meaning: image schemas in cognitive linguistics*, 15–33. Berlin and New York: De Gruyter.
Kerremans, Koen, Rita Temmerman & Jose Tummers. 2003. Representing multilingual and culture-specific knowledge in a VAT regulatory ontology: Support from the termontography method. In Robert Meersman & Zahir Tari (eds.), *On the Move to Meaningful Internet Systems 2003: OTM 2003 Workshops*, 662–674. Berlin Heidelberg: Springer.
Knight, Jonathan. 2003. Scientific literacy: clear as mud. *Nature* 423. 376–378.
Knox, Jean. 2003. *Archetype, attachment, analysis. Jungian psychology and the emergent mind.* Hove and New York: Brunner-Routledge.
Kövecses, Zoltán. 2005. *Metaphor in culture. Universality and variation.* New York: Cambridge University Press.
Kövecses, Zoltán. 2006. *Language, mind, and culture. A practical introduction.* New York: Oxford University Press.
Lakoff, George. 1990. The invariance hypothesis: is abstract reason based on image-schemas? *Cognitive Linguistics* 1(1). 39–74.
Langacker, Ronald. 1987. *Foundations of cognitive grammar.* Volume I. Stanford: Stanford University.
Levinson, Stephen C. 2008. Landscape, seascape and the ontology of places on Rossel Island, Papua New Guinea. *Language Sciences* 30. 256–290.
Lexical Computing Ltd. (n.d.). Sketch engine. Available at: http://www.sketchengine.co.uk/
López-Rodríguez, Clara Inés, Miriam Buendía-Castro & Alejandro García-Aragón. 2012. User needs to the test: Evaluating a terminological knowledge base on the environment by trainee translators. *The Journal of Specialised Translation* 18. 57–76.
López-Rodríguez, Clara Inés & Alejandro García Aragón. 2014. Recursos multimodales para traducir y divulgar contenidos medioambientales. *Trans-Kom* 7(2). 222–243.
Méndez Cendón, Beatriz. 2004. Estudio descriptivo inglés-español de las metáforas en el lenguaje del radiodiagnóstico médico. *Panace@* 5(17–18). 229–231.
Muñoz Martín, Ricardo. 2010. On paradigms and cognitive translatology. In Gregory M. Shreve & Erik Angelone (eds.), *Translation and Cognition*, 169–187. Amsterdam and Philadelphia: John Benjamins.
O'Brien, Sharon. 2011. *Cognitive explorations of translation.* Continuum studies in translation. London and New York: Bloomsbury Publishing.
Pecman, Mojca. 2014. Variation as a cognitive device: How scientists construct knowledge through term formation. *Terminology* 20(1). 1–24.

Periyakoil, Vyjeyanthi S. 2008. Using metaphors in medicine. *Journal of Palliative Medicine* 11(6). 842–844.

Prieto Velasco, Juan Antonio & Maribel Tercedor Sanchez. 2014. The embodied nature of medical concepts: image schemas and language for PAIN. *Cognitive Processing* 15(3). 293–296.

Salager-Meyer, Françoise. (1990). Metaphors in medical English prose: a comparative study with French and Spanish. *English for Specific Purposes* 9(2). 145–159.

Semino, Elena, Zsòfia Demjen, Jane Demmen, Veronika Koller, V., Sheila Payne, S. Andrew Hardie & Paul Rayson. 2015. The online use of violence and journey metaphors by patients with cancer, as compared with health professionals: a mixed methods study. *BMJ Supportive and Palliative Care*. 10.1136/bmjspcare-2014-000785

Sontag, Susan. 1978. *Illness as metaphor*. New York: Farrar, Straus & Giroux.

Sontag, Susan.1989. *Illness as metaphor and AIDS and its metaphors*. New York: Farrar, Straus & Giroux.

Talmy, Leonard. 1988. Force dynamics in language and cognition. *Cognitive Science* 12. 49–100.

Temmerman, Rita. 2000. *Towards new ways of terminology description: The sociocognitive-approach*. Amsterdam and Philadelphia: John Benjamins.

Teodoro Ricci, Ricardo. 2010. La índole metafórica de la relación medico-paciente. *Medicina y cultura*. 4(38).

Tercedor Sánchez, Maribel. 2004. Esquemas metafóricos en el español de la ciencia y la tecnología. In Pamela Faber, Catalina Jiménez & Gerd Wotjak (eds.), *Léxico especializado y comunicación interlingüística. VI Congreso Internacional de Lingüística Hispánica*, 233–242. Granada: Granada Lingvistica.

Tercedor, Maribel, Pamela Faber & Amedeo D'Angiulli. 2011. The depiction of wheels by blind children: Preliminary studies on pictorial metaphors, language, and embodied imagery. *Imagination, Cognition and Personality* 31(1). 113–128.

Tercedor, Maribel & Clara Inés López-Rodríguez. 2012. Access to health in an intercultural setting: The role of corpora and images in grasping term variation. *Linguistica Antverpiensia* 11. 153–174.

Tercedor Sánchez, Maribel, Clara Inés López-Rodríguez, Carlos Márquez Linares & Pamela Faber. 2012. Metaphor and metonymy in specialized language. In Pamela Faber (ed.), *A Cognitive Linguistics View of Terminology and Specialized Language* 33–72. Berlin, Boston: De Gruyter Mouton.

Tercedor Sánchez, Maribel, Clara Inés López-Rodríguez and Esperanza Alarcón Navío. 2013. Identifying translation features in multiword lexical units. *Belgian Journal of Linguistics* 27. 87–109.

Tummers, Jose, Kris Heylen & Dirk Geeraerts. 2005. Usage-based approaches in Cognitive Linguistics: A technical state of the art. *Corpus Linguistics and Linguistic Theory* 1(2). 225–261.

Ureña Gómez-Moreno, José Manuel. 2014. The role of image schemas and superior psychic faculties in zoosemiosis. *Biosemiotics* 7(3). 405–427.

Van Rinjn-Van Tongeren, Geraldine W. 1997. *Metaphors in medical texts*. Amsterdam: Rodopi.

Vandaele, Sylvie & Leslie Lubin. 2005. Approche cognitive de la traduction dans les langues de spécialité: vers une systématisation de la description de la conceptualisation métaphorique. *Meta* 50(2). 415–431.

Appendix 1

List of image schema provided

A				CONTAINMENT
B				IN-OUT
C				PATH
D				UP-DOWN/ SCALE
E				CIRCULARITY

Identification and understanding of medical metaphors by non-experts — 245

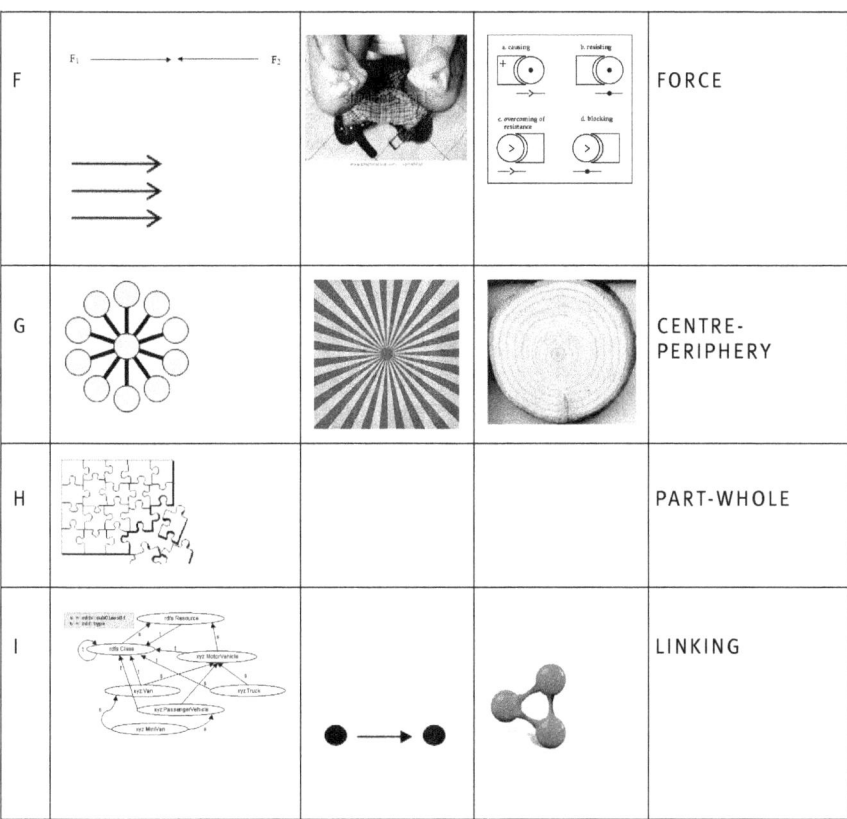

F				FORCE
G				CENTRE-PERIPHERY
H				PART-WHOLE
I				LINKING

Appendix 2

Stimuli in the translation task
- The chambers of the heart are separated by a wall of tissue called the septum.
- Blood is pumped through the chambers, aided by four heart valves.
- The normal heart is a strong, hard-working pump.
- The tricuspid valve is located between the right atrium and the right ventricle.
- The mitral valve is between the left atrium and left ventricle.
- Each valve has a set of "flaps" (also called leaflets or cusps).
- Blood returns to the heart through veins and enters the right atrium.
- Blood gets oxygen from the lungs and travels to your heart through the coronary arteries.

- A large vessel called the aorta carries blood from your heart to the rest of your body.
- The coronary arteries branch off from the aorta. Smaller arteries branch off from the coronary arteries.
- A small amount of leak (insufficiency or regurgitation) is usually not symptomatic and may be detected with a physical exam.
- A trabecula is a tissue element in the form of a small beam, strut or rod.
- Chordae tendineae are structures that close the valves of the heart and help to keep the blood flowing.
- Cardiac arrest is a serious cardiac event that is often confused with heart attack, but there is a difference.
- A heart murmur isn't a disease, and most murmurs are harmless.
- Interrupted aortic arch is a rare and usually lethal malformation, representing approximately 1% of congenital heart disease.
- The semilunar valves are flaps of endocardium and connective tissue reinforced by fibers which prevent the valves from turning inside out.
- The blood delivers lunch to the cells and then has to pick up the trash!
- Others do experience symptoms, which may include: heart palpitations (feeling like your heart is racing, pounding, or fluttering), fast, steady pulse, shortness of breath, trouble with everyday exercises or activities.
- Atrial flutter (AFL) is a common abnormal heart rhythm, similar to atrial fibrillation, the most common abnormal heart rhythm.

Part IV: **Education**

Graham Low
Eliciting metaphor in education research: Is it really worth the effort?

1 Introduction

In the last ten to fifteen years there has been a series of psycholinguistic experiments, strongly suggesting that, when presented with a text/story or a visual display consistent with a particular underlying conceptual metaphor (or metaphoric "frame"), participants orient their opinions or beliefs towards that metaphor. Exposure to the metaphor thus results, even if just temporarily, in a related mindset (see overview in Geary 2010; Gibbs and Colston 2012; Thibodeau et al. 2016). The psycholinguistic experiments rarely deal with educational scenarios, but one might expect the same results to apply.

The psycholinguistic experiments tend to be concerned with the impact of metaphor of which the participant is unaware. In this chapter I deal with elicited metaphor (henceforth EM) research in education, in much of which the metaphors are presented directly to the participants or direct metaphors are explicitly requested, so the situation is not quite the same as with the psycholinguistic studies. There have been a considerable number of EM studies over the last twenty or so years, with the focus ranging from science education to literacy and academic writing; overviews can be found in Wan and Low (2015).

Elicited metaphor can cover two rather different situations: firstly, where a participant is asked explicitly for an "A is B" statement about the topic in question (resulting, it is hoped, in explicit, direct and deliberate metaphor) and secondly where written or spoken discourse about the topic is elicited in order to see what metaphors arise spontaneously. The present paper focuses primarily on the former, with just tangential references to the latter.

The aim of EM studies is generally a practical one: to change a counter-productive belief or attitude (which might include a feeling of stress, or the impossibility of mastering a particular task), to improve a skill, or to help the participant (and/or an administrator) make a choice of some sort. EM is thus a tool, like any other, and it is reasonable to ask whether it 'works' and whether it might have been preferable to use another tool instead.

EM research procedures frequently involve some sort of intervention plus a measurement of change (which may well include "before and after" interviews

Graham Low, University of York

asking about/looking for topic-related metaphors), or else they stop after the initial elicitation phase and the researcher evaluates the result and recommends a treatment (or intervention).

I took a fairly sceptical position about the validity of many EM studies in my 2003 and 2008 papers, being unhappy about things like the assumption that the use of conventional figurative language (such as that involving the conduit metaphor) necessarily reflected underlying states of mind about the educational topic, or the view that if a metaphor *could* conceivably be taken to reflect adherence to a particular educational theory, then it *should necessarily* be so construed. In short, I took the view that EM in an educational context often tended to produce studies that were methodologically unsound, unnecessarily indirect and unlikely to generate viable real-world solutions. I have to some degree, since then been eating my words, and this chapter explains why I have, in part, changed my mind. I have been influenced in this change of heart by the series of reflective critical analyses in Wan and Low (2015) and in particular by a study where I taught and talked to the participants (Wan, 2012). The latter tracked the progress of Chinese applied language MA students at the University of York, who agreed in a rash moment to sign up for a three-term research project on improving their academic writing via regular discussions about the metaphors they used.

2 A simple participant-researcher model

I would like to begin by establishing a very simple research design/procedure model and then ask questions about the various steps involved. But before doing this, however, I need to address the general question of randomised controlled trials.

It is generally agreed by many social science researchers that a series of randomised controlled trials, plus a systematic review comparing the results and checking for publication bias, is the best way to establish if a treatment, intervention or procedure "works" (Torgerson 2003). The argument is that a large enough sample will allow the researcher not only to establish if an outcome can be believed (being reliable and valid), but also to establish the likely source of that outcome. To date I have come across no educational EM study using an RCT. RCT purists would thus argue that to date we have no proof that EM techniques are effective at solving real-world educational problems, let alone what might account for the effectiveness, or what might be done to make them more effective.

It has to be said that, in the field of education and classroom-based research, not all researchers or practitioners are convinced of the superiority of RCTs and

RCT-based systematic reviews, arguing that they are too narrowly focussed intellectually. And indeed RCTs are notoriously hard to set up in education, if only because of the difficulty of avoiding using intact classes (= non randomised) as samples. Also, the need to work intensively with participants in many EM studies has meant that it would in practice be hard to have a sample large enough for a valid RCT. A third point is that an EM study on skills like writing might well take a long time to generate a change that was large enough to be statistically significant (or lead to a large enough effect size), and long-term EM studies are few and far between.

The model I propose to use here is set out in Figure 1, where P is the participant and R is the researcher:

P ACTS, BELIEVES, OR EXPERIENCES	→	P FORMULATES AS METAPHOR	→	R INTERVENES OR R RECOMMENDS	→	P ALTERS METAPHOR AND/OR P ALTERS BEHAVIOUR

Figure 1. Typical four-step EM design model in education research

3 Comments on the model

I shall take each pair of stages in turn.

3.1 Steps 1–2

P ACTS, ETC	→	P FORMULATES AS METAPHOR

Q1. Do we really need metaphors to study "improving my job", "writing a paragraph" or "answering a multiple choice question"?

One may reasonably ask, "why not simply investigate the topic directly"? From personal discussion with "mainline" second language acquisition researchers, I am aware that EM research is the source of much scepticism. So the question, why involve direct metaphor is a key one.

Is it simply a question of increasing the "fun" level of the research? Or hoping the participant will commit a Freudian slip, and the unconscious will out (assuming we can interpret it accurately)? Fisher (2013a: 205, 2013b), whose primary interest was in UK 12 to 13 year olds' beliefs concerning studying a foreign language (German), argued that there were three good reasons for working indirectly: (1) metaphors give access to thoughts that are hard to describe literally, or in detail, (2) metaphors allow easy links to images and (3) metaphors are a common device for expressing emotion, so allow participants to generate responses which include emotion or affect. She does not consider "fun" as a central feature, and indeed, observing Wan's (2012) group of Chinese MA students, there seemed little mention of fun in the early interview responses.

While Fisher's three reasons seem potentially valid, it should be pointed out that not all EM datasets are quite as metaphoric as they are sometimes claimed to be (see Low 2003, 2015); metaphors cited would appear to be metonymic or literal rather than (or as much as) metaphoric. Thus THE TEACHER IS A FRIEND can be interpreted as a teacher demonstrating what would seem to be a basic aspect of the job of being a professional teacher.

Q2. Is it reasonable to expect all participants to be able to formulate anything at all as a metaphor?

At an overall level, there is little summary information available about the range of topics across which learners, administrators or teachers can metaphorise. Topics frequently used in EM studies involve both generic labels ("teaching", "a class", "a/the teacher", "a textbook") and specific terms ("my textbook" etc). There is sporadic evidence of difficulty: Zapata, for example, reports that her adult participants found "the classroom" harder than "teaching" or "learning" (Zapata 2015; Zapata and Lacorte 2007), but beyond this little is known.

One of Wan's Chinese MA students, on finding it hard to invent an appropriate metaphor for her views on academic writing, borrowed one from another research study. In some circumstances this recycling might be seen as somehow "cheating", but in this case the student claimed that the re-used metaphor reflected what she felt, so one needs to query how far originality and creativity are really needed in EA studies.

Indeed, in addition to querying creativity, one needs to query how far one should expect learners or teachers to actually possess pre-constructed symbolic worlds for everything in life, large or small, concrete or abstract, hypothetical or experienced. Very few researchers discuss whether they need to know whether a metaphor was somehow pre-constructed or whether it was put together "on the fly", maybe as an artefact of the elicitation procedure. The "Clean Language" group of researchers, who work in the area of management training (e.g., Tosey 2014; Tosey, Lawley, and Meese 2014), would argue that such artefacts are important and need to be minimised: for them the solution is to avoid cueing metaphor(s) directly and even not to mention words like 'metaphor' at all in the instructions. The Clean Language stance thus argues against all EM research in the sense being discussed here (Sense 1, in Sec 1). The CL, position, however, leaves open the question of how, or even whether, to proceed if the participant produces no metaphors that are clearly related to the topic at hand.

Just as difficulty level can relate to topic formulation and personal creativity, so it may well relate to age and experience. There are so few EA studies on children under ten years old or on old-age/retired learners that it is hard to draw any conclusions, beyond obvious ones such as the hypothesis that learners (or indeed beginning teachers) might find it hard to find metaphors for generic labels – which assume participants have undergone a range of experiences, as well as have the ability to find similarities between them.

A further point is that the verb in the prompt in an EA study may well affect the responses. How far one can expect participants to be able to differentiate metaphorically between "X is like ...", "X was like ...", "X should be like ..." and the corresponding negatives remains unclear and, to the best of my knowledge, untested.

Lastly, one cannot assume that the same person will create consistent, or at least convergent, metaphors for similar topics. Zapata and Lacorte (2007) for example found repeated differences between participants' metaphors for "teacher(s)" and "learner(s)". And Strugielska (2008) found her Polish adult learners sometimes created very different metaphors across five related EFL topics. Table 1 (cited from Low 2015: 29, Table 1) illustrates two such cases:

Table 1. Two examples of EM response non-convergence

Participant	Teacher	Teaching	Learner	Learning	Classroom
P16	a guide	driving a car	a long-term investment	flying a plane	a parliament
P5	a corporal	leading a dog	–	being on a diet	a cage

Source: Strugielska (2008)

The question here is whether these results suggest that the EM eliciting technique is unreliable and thus invalid. If the researcher starts from the assumption that each participant is ultimately, deep down, motivated by one particular set of attitudes towards foreign language learning (or towards a particular teaching-learning philosophy), non-convergent results represent unwanted "noise" in the system. However, if the researcher takes the seemingly quite reasonable view that learners can have very different reactions to their teachers, their learning and their classrooms, then non-convergent EM data seem to be hinting at what those differences might be and which participants seem to have particularly diverse reactions. The elicitation does not itself provide the pedagogical answers wanted by the end of the study, but it would seem to flag points and participants that/ who can be followed up, say by face-to-face interviews at a later stage. In short, within-participant metaphor non-convergence does not invalidate the EM elicitation technique.

Q3. Would participants do better if they were trained in advance (or during the procedure)?

The first question for a researcher to answer as regards training is how many participants can fail to provide valid metaphors without endangering the study. The topic is rarely discussed in print, but is clearly related to the sample size. In a small-scale qualitative study (as most EM studies tend to be), the inability of, say, two out of six participants to find metaphors, can be catastrophic; whereas in a study with 2000+ participants, a failure rate of two would be negligible (Wan, 2011).

For a small-scale study, some training seems essential[1], but there is little consensus in the literature on how to go about establishing and designing appropriate training activities. Indeed, apart from Wan (2011) and Low (2015), there is minimal discussion on the topic. A hint of what "works" can, however, be gained from Wan's 2012 MA group, who were asked to report retrospectively on what they found useful (for the elicitation sessions, the one-to-one interviews and the group discussions) from the four two-hour MA sessions on metaphor (taught by me) that they had undergone in the first term of the three-term study. Table 2 summarises those activities reported as being helpful:

---

[1] I am grateful to Linda Fisher for pointing out (p.c.) that *checking* whether training is needed is important; in her case, the precheck showed that her UK teenagers knew what similes were and were able to create them (possibly as a result of teaching in their English classes): thus no further training was deemed necessary (2013a: 75, 2013b: 379).

Table 2. Training tasks reported as helpful by Wan's (2012) participants.

---

1. A set of short invented sentences in the form of an 11-question Socratic dialogue: a naïve observer addresses questions or comments to a teacher.
   Task: Ps listen and discuss with T. Some group discussion.
   Aims: Ps realise problems of defining and characterising metaphor & non-metaphor.

2. Linguistic sentences and phrases in 6 small sets (from various sources, inc. me).
   Task: Ps complete source-target A IS B labels: Topic/source is given at first ('Ideas are ….?'), then omitted ('What is What?').
   The task becomes progressively more challenging.
   Ps discuss in pairs. Then whole group discuss own and T's answers.
   Aim: Ps recognise the creation of an A IS B as a "best generalisation", given the data available: there is no necessary single right answer.

3. A set of anger-related expressions (from various sources, inc. me).
   Task: Ps match with set of source terms (like "steam engine"). Group discussion.
   Aim: Ps discover the notion of elaboration: similar logic, but different images.

4. Given TEACHING IS COOKING (from Cortazzi and Jin 1999).
   Task: Ps work out "because….." reasoning. Then compare with originals. Group discuss.
   Aims: Ps get used to evaluating reasons/solutions.
   Ps discover that their own solution could be "better" than the originals.
   To appreciate the need for "because …" data.

5. Three short texts (in English) by Chinese undergraduates (in China) explaining their choice of "Writing is (like)…" metaphors. I selected "writing is driving"; "writing is weaving" and "writing is painting" (Source: Wan 2007).
   Task: Ps establish correspondences and grounds (create a list).
   Ps look for 'gaps': what the metaphors do not cover.
   Ps evaluate educational usefulness of metaphors.
   Aims: To practice critiquing via group discussion.

The above activities have in common (1) an interplay between individual thought and group discussion, (2) an emphasis on critiquing the appropriateness of, and grounds for metaphors, (3) a focus on concrete rather than abstract tasks, and (4) a focus on the difficulties of defining and labelling metaphors.

Q4. Can/should we believe the metaphors that participants produce?
The answer is most clearly "No", or not without further checking. Participants are in no way on oath to be accurate or honest and may well say anything out of boredom, frustration or to shut the researcher up. Strugielska (2015) stresses the importance of initially requesting the grounds of the metaphor by prompt-

ing "*X is like ..., because ...*". Firstly, "*because...*" data can establish whether a metaphor is involved. Thus Strugielska rejects "Teaching is like flying because it's fun and I like it" as metaphoric. Secondly, without *because* data, examples like Fisher's (2013b: 380) "Learning German is like man-eating pink celery in Austria wearing Jeremy Clarkson clothes... because it's just that random" are unclassifiable, as well as unclear with respect to their credibility.

The value of *because* data illustrates the importance of gathering additional detail and contextual information. Fisher and Cortazzi (2002) have both recommended looking for gestures in accompanying interviews. Fisher also included checking behaviour observed in class and choices made by participants, as well as asking participants to create short stories about their teaching and learning.

Q5. What does a good prompt look like?

Many EM studies involve giving an explicit metaphor prompt to the participant; there is, however, little published research evidence of what characterises an effective (versus a less effective) prompt. I raise here five questions that need further work.

(a) Should the participant be prompted for single or multiple analogies?

It is clearly statistically easier to process a dataset where everyone reports the same number of metaphors for a given topic. However, there is some research evidence (Spiro et al. 1989) that thinking using more than one metaphor can aid learning. Wan (2012) also reported that one of her seven participants was frustrated by not being allowed more than one answer.

One solution to this problem is what I have called the "Pop/Saban" task, in that it was used by Pop (2008) who adapted it from Saban (2003). The task involves presenting participants with a series of pre-constructed metaphor correspondences (see the examples in Figure 2, below), and asking them how far they agree with each. Agreement is measured on a Likert-type scale ranging from "strongly agree" (SA) to "strongly disagree" (SD). While this format has the four big advantages of requiring a degree of reflection by the participant, allowing for overlap between metaphors, being contextually precise, and focusing on systemic aspects of metaphor (= relational structure), there remain a number of potential problems (Low 2015: 24–26).

"Think of yourself as a future teacher and your preferred conception of schooling"

Schooling metaphor for *Student – School – Teacher*	SA	A	D	SD
Raw material – Factory – Manufacturer (e.g., Student is *raw material* – School is *factory* – T is *manufacturer*)				
Criminal – Prison – Guard (e.g., Student is *criminal* – School is *prison* – T is *guard*)				
Passenger – Bus – Driver (e.g., Student is *passenger* – School is *bus* – T is *driver*)				
Customer – Restaurant – Chef (e.g., Student is *customer* – School is *restaurant* – T is *chef*)				

NOTE: A=*agree*, D=*disagree*, S=*strongly*
Source: Pop (2008: App. F), adapted from Saban (2003)

Figure 2. The Pop/Saban elicitation task (cited from Low 2015: 23)

The main difficulties are as follows. First, the scaled agreement is substituting for the degrees of preference given in the instructions at the top (see Low 1988 for a discussion of substitute scales), and there is no guarantee that the participant will map one scale accurately onto the other. For example, does "I agree" (or "I disagree") substitute accurately for "metaphor X reflects to some degree what I would like"?). Secondly, the participant is likely to be influenced by the researcher's choice of labels/correspondences (like making the teacher a chef, rather than a waiter or proprietor, in the restaurant metaphor). Thirdly, the lack of *because* data means that the researcher cannot be sure whether the teacher is a chef because s/he is clever, creative, productive, controlling, client-centred, dressed differently, over-emotional, or what (see Strugielska's results above). Fourthly, if the participant agrees that the school is a restaurant, but not that the teacher is a chef, what does s/he do? Presumably tick "disagree" (or should it be "agree", as one level below "strongly agree")? The addition of the "*e.g.*" between the metaphor and the correspondences only serves to increase the confusion. In short, even where a participant selects a particular agreement value, we cannot be sure (a) that a metaphor is involved, (b) if it is, how far it is involved, or (c) what the participant's reasoning is; follow-up interviews or explanations are needed in all cases.

(b) Should the prompt take the form (linguistically) of a metaphor or a simile?

The problem here is that, although Lakoff and Johnson (1988) treated simile as hedged metaphor, it is not difficult to find pairs of sentences where the metaphor has a different meaning from the corresponding simile, or at least where the difference is more than a weakening or hedging. To give but one example: in Littlemore and Low (2006) we cited: "life is a joke" (not funny) and "life is like a joke" (could well be funny).

In practice, however, in a typical education research study, analogies like "school is a restaurant" and "school is like a restaurant" are not likely to involve words or phrases which differ in this way. So a prompt with *like* would seem to have several advantages: "*A is like* ..." formulation:
- focuses on the need for an analogy more than "*A is....*";
- allows fairly easily for partial analogies (*a bit like...*);
- does not discourage multiple analogies (if enough space for multiple responses if provided);
- allows for hybrid prompts, such as "*School is/is like ....*".

(c) Does the prompt address over- or under-specification of the topic?
The appropriate degree of specification is not always discussed in much detail in EM research studies. While it may be the case that teenagers exposed to one foreign language taught in one school by one teacher may conflate their views on learning a foreign language in general with their view on the particular experience they have undergone (with the result that the specificity of the prompt may not matter), in other cases the researcher needs to make it abundantly clear what opinions they do and do not want. To be fair to Pop (2008), the Figure 2 prompt makes it explicit that the task is a hypothetical and generalised one, whose results might well differ from a prompt asking about participants' past experience of (say) the last two years of EFL teaching at their school.

(d) Should prompts (and responses) be in the participants' own language (L1)?
Where the participants are overseas and of mixed languages, and the researcher speaks none or just some of the latter, having prompts and answers in the participants' L1 (or one of their L1s) is not a practical possibility. However, thinking and responding in an L2 inevitably limits the quality of the responses, for all but the most advanced learners.

In the case of Wan's and Fisher's studies, both were undertaken in the UK and both involved the participants' L1 (Chinese in the former and English in the latter). As a final point, it should be noted that some smaller studies (like Zapata 2015: 173) have prompted participants in one language, but asked them to reply in whichever of two languages they are more comfortable with. Where the researcher then acts as translator, a validity check, using a third party, or where possible the participants themselves, is needed.

(e) Are pictures good prompts?

The Clean Language paradigm uses pictures as one check on the validity of metaphors expressed by participants, but they can just as easily be used as the prompts. In a survey of EM prompt formats in educational research, Seung et al. (2015: 51) found only one study which used drawings for prompts (Ben-Peretz, Mendelson, and Kron 2003). Sixty Israeli high-school teachers were given drawings of professional roles, like shopkeeper, judge, or animal keeper in a zoo, and asked to pick the drawing that represented their current vision of themselves and explain their choices. The researchers argued that pictures would encourage teachers "to voice their feelings, emotions and thoughts" (Seung et al.: 51); whether they do so more effectively than verbal prompts needs further research.

Q6. Is EM looking for old analogies, new analogies or either?

This question seems rarely posed in EM studies, or at least rarely discussed in the reports. Indeed, in many cases it may not matter, but if the study is longitudinal and involves either group discussion, or exposure to published EM reports, the question of the reuse of one's own or of other people's metaphors becomes quite important. Not only should the researcher establish if metaphors are expected to change as views or skills develop across the study, but they should decide whether the participant should try and indicate when a metaphor is borrowed. Thus in Wan's (2012) study, one participant (as stated above) admitted reusing a metaphor which her EFL support teacher had used (or found in an earlier study), because (1) she herself found creating metaphors difficult and (2) the metaphor encapsulated what she felt at that point in her studies. The reasons for or against accepting borrowed metaphor are not clear cut. One might reject them on the grounds that personal reflection is not demonstrated, or accept them if they are slightly adapted, as this seems to indicate a degree of commitment. The question of inferring commitment on the part of the participant will be revisited below.

Q7. Must the experience being requested have been lived?

Several EM studies, especially those involving trainee teachers (see de Guerrero and Villamil 2015) have researched opinions about future or hypothetical situations, and some have compared them with opinions once teaching has been experienced. Perhaps the only danger to avoid is the same one that can be raised in connection with attitude questionnaires (e.g., Low 1988), namely to avoid mixing (or at least conflating responses to) questions about actual and hypothetical scenarios: "How do you feel?", "How would you feel?", "How might you feel?".

3.2 Steps 2 and 3

P FORMULATES AS METAPHOR → T/R INTERPRETS, EVALUATES AND INTERVENES

As the study moves from steps two to three, the researcher begins to categorise the data, evaluate responses, establish connections with educational practice, or theory, and then recommend what should happen next, like changing the administration, or undergoing further training. Each phase of the above is fraught with problems.

Q8. How should Ps' metaphors be classified and evaluated?
If there is no direct-metaphor (or simile) prompt, then the researcher will need to employ one of the several available techniques for identifying metaphor in discourse, like those in Cameron and Maslen (2010) or a version of MIP/MIPVU (Pragglejaz group 2007; Steen et al. 2010). If a prompt is used, then the researcher will probably move straight to grouping metaphors into "similar" piles, where similarity may involve similar topics, but commonly relates to similar educational implications.

The first question is to decide if the A is B formulation is indeed metaphoric. I have already noted Strugielska's (2008) concerns in this connection, and would simply reiterate here that formulations such as TEACHING IS HARD WORK, TEACHING IS BEING HELPFUL or THE TEACHER IS A CONTRACTED PROFESSIONAL (the last from Block 1992) would seem metonymic or literal, rather than metaphoric: just parts of the job of being a teacher.

Having established the set of acceptable metaphors in the dataset, the researcher needs to group them and label each group. The same problem can occur here as with formulating individual metaphors: the label may cover a group of metaphors but may not itself be metaphorical. Now different theories of metaphor accept different degrees of A:B difference as representing metaphoricity, with Conceptual Metaphor theory accepting much smaller differences than, say, Cameron and Maslen's Discourse Dynamics. It thus makes sense to flag either that seemingly metonymic or literal labels come within the theory being used (like e.g. Williams 2015: 251), or else to indicate that with the higher-level grouping, one is leaving the field of metaphor.

I have listed elsewhere the difficulties of matching metaphors and metaphor groupings reliably to pre-determined educational theories (Low 2003, 2008, 2015); the matching is inevitably rough and overlaps will often occur. To take an example at random from Shaw and Mahlios's (2015: 196–197) literacy Study 3, "writing is baking a cake", baking a cake clearly comprises a set of component sub-activities, and this fragmentation is consistent with a behaviourist view of learning tasks. However, if the cake is to be edible, the baker must think hard about the final product, and if the cake is to excite the consumer, the baker needs to be creative and to exercise artistic judgement (and possibly constraint): processes consistent with more exploratory and/or holistic theories of education.

If free conversation is used at the follow-up stages, to triangulate the EM metaphors, a decision needs to be made whether only what Steen (2011a, 2011b and elsewhere) calls "deliberate metaphor" is retained and analysed, or whether the researcher is also looking for Freudian slips or metaphoric phrases of whose attitudinal significance the participant is unaware. The danger is obvious: holding a coherent informal conversation requires one to use conventional metaphors such as conduit and journey metaphors. Indeed, avoiding them and still sounding "natural" or fluent is remarkably hard. However, using a phrase such as "they finally *got it*, I think" hardly necessarily reflects a dictatorial, teacher-centred approach, such that professional retraining is needed. It remains, though very difficult to establish in many cases whether a metaphor was genuinely deliberate or not.

Q9. What form should the intervention take?

This question is unanswerable in a general context, and might simply involve more foreign language, science (for learners), or pedagogy (for teachers) training. I wish to address here interventions where participants present, discuss, or at least evaluate, their own metaphors. We simply do not know what formats are the most effective, nor whether the task is easier, and generates more critical reflection and learning, if certain types of metaphor are used.

The Wan (2012) study exposed all seven learners to a session involving a simple model, involving three criteria for evaluating an educational metaphor, and gave practice in applying it in small groups of three to four persons (Activity 5, Table 2, above). The model comprised:

A pedagogically appropriate metaphor of writing should do at least three things:

1. It should contain all the *stages* involved in the writing process.
2. It should be able to describe *problems* and not just successful writing.
3. It should indicate *ways to resolve* the problems.

A metaphor might be relatively *unsuccessful* because it lacks (1)–(3) above, but it could also be inappropriate because, like WRITING IS LIKE KILLING SOMEONE, it shows a highly undesirable way of treating writing (and the reader!).

Extract from workshop handout

The logic behind it was similar to that developed and tested recently by Thibodeau et al. (2016), namely that exposure to systemic metaphor should facilitate critique at a relational level. Unfortunately, it was not possible to evaluate how far each of the seven MA students took the model on board and actively used it in their classroom discussions. So the question of how to get participants to critique their metaphors remains open. As does the question of whether participants should be asked to critique their metaphors at the initial elicitation/prompt stage, or whether this would seriously inhibit metaphor construction and reporting.

3.3 Steps 3 to 4

R INTERVENES	→	P ALTERS METAPHOR AND/OR BEHAVIOUR

There would seem to be two key questions to ask, neither of which have clear-cut answers.

Q10. Just how much evidence do we need to draw inferences about change?
Seung et al. (2015) argue that multiple sources of data are needed, especially in small-scale qualitative studies. Such are not always in evidence. In the case of the Wan (2012) study, change could not be measured in terms of writing produced during or after the study, as it was not possible to separate the different factors involved in writing MA assignments or dissertations. Fisher (2013a), however, represents an unusually broad set of tasks and data types, in that she gathered and compared after-intervention data , as well as before-, and during-intervention information:
- Three pre-intervention expanded metaphors on learning German (e.g. "(Learning German is like) having salt rubbed into your eyes with a razor blade covered in lemon and onion juice it is so painful". p.120);
- A written opinion sentence about learning German ('When I'm learning German, I…');
- A written story about a boy or girl who is learning German (+ optional picture);
- Pre-intervention one-to-one interviews with participants and teachers;
- Class observations (both videos and researcher's notes);
- Three post-intervention metaphors;
- A post-intervention affect item ("When I'm learning German, I…");
- Post-intervention one-to-one interviews with 13 participants and their teachers;
- Post-intervention administrative data about exam (GCSE) choices.

Q11. How do we know if participants alter their attitudes, beliefs or behaviour as a direct result of the EM study?

The lack of an RCT format means that EM researchers frequently cannot be precise about the impact of EMs. Even Fisher's use of a concrete list of post-intervention choices is at best a guide in the triangulation of sources, since exam choices about whether or not to take German are likely to depend in some cases on more than one's view of one's own ability as critiqued via EMs. Wan's (2012) MA-level participants began by expressing quite cynical views on the usefulness of EMs in improving their ability to construct written assignments, but most expressed much more positive views by the end, arguing that they believed the EM critiquing to have helped.

There are singularly few models in the EM literature of the relative strength with which we can infer change of belief from post-intervention (or Stage 2) data, but Fisher's list (2013a: Section 8.1) suggests the beginnings of one. Essentially, it consists of six likely participant data states, and argues that, other things being equal, the construction of a new metaphor, with a new rationale, is stronger evidence of a change in belief than the appropriation of someone else's metaphor, and that the least reliable evidence is that of no change in metaphor or rationale. This is not to say that the participant who changes neither metaphor nor rationale is not committed to that view of the topic, or indeed that nothing attitudinal or behavioural has changed: just that the likelihood of validly inferring change is lowest. The fact that Table 3 is probabilistic not definite does not, however, invalidate EM research; it simply reinforces the need for triangulation follow-up interviews and, where possible, observation.

Table 3. Strength of evidence of internalised change

Stage 2 metaphor	Affect data/*because* data	Evidence of internalised change
1. Same as Stage 1 metaphor	Same as Stage 1	Very weak
2. Same as Stage 1 metaphor	New	Weak
3. New but appropriated met'r	Same as Stage 1	Weak
4. New but appropriated met'r	New	Stronger
5. Newly constructed metaphor	Same as Stage 1	Stronger
6. Newly constructed metaphor	New	Strongest

Source: Fisher (2013a: 169–170)

4 Conclusion

I have tried in this chapter to go beyond the account in Wan and Low (2015) and to explain why EM studies rarely adopt the experimental paradigm used by cognitive psycholinguistic studies, being frequently practically-oriented, small-scale, class-oriented and largely qualitative. The result is that while several have been closely adapted to the participants involved (a "good thing"), it has rarely been possible to infer the precise impact of eliciting or discussing EMs (not such a "good thing"). A second result is that we often don't really know "what works" best, as regards pre-training participants, eliciting EMs, classifying them, and designing interventions involving EMs. There are, however, several hints and suggestions as to what has seemed to work on particular occasions, but the numerous dangers and 'open questions' remain. Despite the latter, I was convinced by the very positive personal reactions of the seven MA students at the end of their study, and by the largely convergent evidence from multiple data sources in Fisher (2013a, 2013b), that EM studies can really be worth the effort.

Acknowledgement: My thanks to Linda Fisher for reading the first draft of this chapter and commenting so helpfully on it.

References

Ben-Peretz, Miriam, Nili Mendelson & Friedrich W. Kron. 2003. How teachers in different educational contexts view their roles. *Teaching and Teacher Education* 19. 277–290.
Block, David. 1992. Metaphors we teach and learn by. *Prospect* 7(3). 42–55.
Cameron, Lynne & Robert Maslen (eds.). 2010. *Metaphor analysis: Research practice in applied linguistics, social sciences and the humanities*. London: Equinox.
Cortazzi, Martin. 1993/2002. *Narrative analysis*. London: Falmer Press.
Cortazzi, Martin & Lixian Jin. 1999. Bridges to learning: Metaphors of teaching, learning and language. In Lynne Cameron & Graham D. Low (eds.), *Researching and applying metaphor*, 149–176. Cambridge, UK: Cambridge University Press.
de Guerrero, Maria & Olga Villamil. 2015. Metaphor analysis in L2 education: Insights from data-based research. In Wan Wan & Graham D. Low (eds.), *Elicited metaphor analysis in educational discourse*, 93–115. Amsterdam: John Benjamins.
Geary, James. 2010. *I is another: The secret life of metaphor and how it shapes the way we see the world*. New York: Harper.
Gibbs, Raymond W. Jr. & Herbert L. Colston. 2012. *Interpreting figurative meaning*. Cambridge, UK: Cambridge University Press.
Low, Graham D. 1988. The semantics of questionnaire rating scales. *Evaluation and Research in Education* 2(2). 69–79.

Low, Graham D. 2003. Validating metaphoric models in applied linguistics. *Metaphor and Symbol* 18(4). 239–254.
Low, Graham D. 2008. Metaphor in education. In Raymond Gibbs (ed.), *The Cambridge handbook of metaphor and thought*, 212–231. Cambridge, UK: Cambridge University Press.
Low, Graham D. 2015. A practical validation model for researching elicited metaphor. In Wan Wan & Graham D. Low (eds.), *Elicited metaphor analysis in educational discourse*, 15–37. Amsterdam: John Benjamins.
Fisher, Linda. 2013a. *Constructing beliefs in the foreign language classroom using metaphor as a sociocultural tool*. Unpublished doctoral dissertation, University of Cambridge.
Fisher, Linda. 2013b. Discerning change in young students' beliefs about their language learning through the use of metaphor elicitation in the classroom. *Research Papers in Education* 28(3). 373–392.
Pop, Margareta M. 2008. "Teaching in the eyes of beholders". Preservice teachers' reasons for teaching and their beliefs about teaching. Unpublished doctoral dissertation, Florida State University.
Pragglejaz group. 2007. MIP: A method for identifying metaphorically used words in discourse. *Metaphor and Symbol* 22(1). 1–40.
Saban, Ahmet. 2003. A Turkish profile of prospective elementary school teachers and their views of teaching. *Teaching and Teacher Education* 19. 829–846.
Seung, Eulsun, Soonhye Park & Jinhong Jung. 2015. Methodological approaches and strategies for elicited metaphor-based research: A critical review. In Wan Wan & Graham D. Low (eds.), *Elicited metaphor analysis in educational discourse*, 39–64. Amsterdam: John Benjamins.
Spiro, Rand J., Paul J. Feltovitch, Richard L. Coulson & Daniel K. Anderson. 1989. Multiple analogies for complex concepts: antidotes for analogy-induced misconceptions in advanced knowledge acquisition. In S. Vosniadou & A. Ortony (eds.), *Similarity and analogical reasoning*, 498–531. Cambridge, UK: Cambridge University Press.
Steen, Gerard J. 2011a. When is metaphor deliberate? In Nils-Lennart Johannesson & David C. Minugh (eds.), *Selected papers from the 2008 Metaphor Festival, Stockholm*, 43–63. Stockholm: Acta Universitatis Stockholmiensis.
Steen, Gerard J. 2011b. What does 'really deliberate' really mean? More thoughts on metaphor and consciousness. *Metaphor and the Social World* 1(1). 53–56.
Steen, Gerard J., Aletta G. Dorst, J. Berenike Herrmann, Anna Kaal, Tina Krennmayr & Trijntje Pasma. 2010. *A method for linguistic metaphor identification: From MIP to MIPVU*. Amsterdam: John Benjamins.
Strugielska, Ariadna. 2008. Coherence relations and concept dynamic in learners' personal theories. *Vigo International Journal of Applied Linguistics* 5. 107–129.
Thibodeau, Paul. H., Anna Winneg, Cynthia Frantz & Stephen J. Flusberg. 2016. The Mind is an Ecosystem: Systemic metaphors promote systems thinking. *Metaphor and the Social World* 6(2). 225–242
Torgerson, Carole. 2003. *Systematic reviews*. London: Continuum.
Tosey, Paul. 2014. Clean language in research interviews. *Rapport* 40. 44–46.
Tosey, Paul, James Lawley & Rupert Meese. 2014. Eliciting metaphor through clean language: An innovation in qualitative research. *British Journal of Management* 25(3). 629–646.
Wan, Wan. 2007. *An examination of metaphorical accounts L2 writers tell about their writing processes*. Unpublished MA dissertation. Dept of Educational Studies, University of York.

Wan, Wan. 2011. An examination of the validity of metaphor analysis studies: Problems with metaphor elicitation techniques. *Metaphor and the Social World* 1(2). 261–288.

Wan, Wan. 2012. *Using metaphorical conceptualisation to construct and develop ESL students' writing: An exploratory study*. Unpublished doctoral dissertation, Dept. of Education, University of York.

Wan, Wan, & Low, Graham D. (eds.). 2015. *Elicited metaphor analysis in educational discourse*. Amsterdam: John Benjamins.

Williams, Jeanine. 2015. Metaphorical conceptualizations and classroom practices of instructors teaching an accelerated postsecondary developmental literacy course. In Wan Wan & Graham D. Low (eds.), *Elicited metaphor analysis in educational discourse*, 239–264. Amsterdam: John Benjamins.

Zapata, Gabriela C. 2015. The role of metaphors in novice and experienced L2 instructors' classroom practice. In Wan Wan & Graham D. Low (eds.), *Elicited metaphor analysis in educational discourse*, 167–186. Amsterdam: John Benjamins.

Zapata, Gabriela C. & Manel Lacorte. 2007. Preservice and inservice instructors' metaphorical constructions of second language teachers. *Foreign Language Annals* 40(3). 521–534.

Susanne Niemeier
Teaching (in) metaphors

1 Introduction

Over the last few decades, starting with the publication of Lakoff and Johnson's seminal book *Metaphors We Live By* (1980), metaphor has come to be acknowledged as a major cognitive and linguistic strategy for facilitating the comprehension of mostly abstract concepts. Metaphor is generally seen as ubiquitous and pervasive in language and thought and is most of the time produced and understood subconsciously, at least by native speakers of a language. However, when it comes to second/foreign language learners, the situation is somewhat more complicated in a couple of respects. First of all, L2 speakers normally do not share a native speaker's world view, culture and socialization and may therefore not be able to understand certain expressions subconsciously as metaphors but may instead try and process the meaning of a metaphor literally, which may not infrequently result in incomprehension. Furthermore, a non-advanced L2 speaker may not have access to the conceptual metaphors of the target language in question but instead rely on L1 concepts, a fact which may result in comprehension problems as well, for the speaker himself/herself as well as for native speaker interlocutors or for interlocutors from other linguistic backgrounds.

Making learners aware of figurative expressions can therefore be seen as equipping them with tools for producing and understanding the target language in a more native-like and thus more successful way. The current paper presents a practical example of how this can be achieved for the field of figurative colour expressions. The learners that this paper takes into account are pre-intermediate German learners of English at a Common European Framework of Reference (in the following abbreviated as CEFR) level between A2 and B1. The paper argues that, although the relevant German curricula and textbooks do not deal with metaphors at all, current L2 teaching methods may profit from focusing on raising metaphor awareness in these (and potentially other) L2 learners. After a brief evaluation of the role of metaphor in current German L2 teaching the perspective is widened and the role of metaphor in second/foreign language education is discussed in general, i.e., research results are scrutinized for their usefulness in the German context. The paper ends with the presentation and analysis of a lesson series for pre-intermediate learners of English which was held in an 8th grade of a German secondary school, focusing on non-literal colour expressions.

Susanne Niemeier, University of Koblenz

DOI 10.1515/9783110549928-015

As mentioned above, none of the English textbooks used in Germany mentions metaphor explicitly. The term itself normally only appears in the classroom when the first literary analyses are introduced, which only begins during the intermediate stage. However, metaphor is then usually presented as a stylistic device, a traditional view that especially Cognitive Linguistics (in the following abbreviated as CL) has long since helped to overcome. Very frequently, neither the textbooks nor the L2 teachers know about the role that everyday metaphors play in language and thought, and therefore the learners are not told about their importance either. When it comes to figurative language, textbooks sometimes mention idioms, but usually treat them as unanalyzed chunks to be learnt by heart. However, it is not only the textbooks that omit to deal with metaphors, as the curricula for English at the pre-intermediate level do not even once mention metaphors either. In Germany, every federal state has its own curricula (one for each level per school type), which can be confusing because general statements about the German curricula for English as a second language are often impossible – however, in relation to metaphor, all current curricula unanimously agree not to mention this topic.

From a CL perspective, this situation might be amended by raising the learners' awareness of metaphor and it may be hypothesized that introducing L2 learners to metaphor is beneficial and contributes to an increase of the size of their vocabulary as well as to an enhanced intercultural communicative competence (in the following abbreviated as ICC), which the CEFR sees as the most important competence to be developed in L2 teaching.

2 Metaphor in the classroom

Although metaphor is not officially a topic in German L2 teaching at the pre-intermediate and intermediate levels, with a bit of interpretative liberty the curricula can be seen as leaving some room for integrating metaphor into L2 teaching. This chapter briefly presents the potential role that metaphor can play in the curriculum for English in secondary schools for the grades 5–10 in the Rhineland-Palatinate[1]. In the Rhineland-Palatinate, English teaching starts in the first grade of primary school (if the schools did not opt for French as a foreign language). When the pupils enter secondary school (from grade 5 onwards), many of them have already had four years of experience with the English language, although

---

[1] This curriculum was chosen because the author works in the federal state of the Rhineland-Palatinate.

this experience is limited to about one English lesson per week in which English is usually taught without a textbook. From grade 5 onwards, learners have 3–4 English lessons per week and textbooks are introduced.

The curriculum for the grades 5–10 does not mention metaphors directly, although at some points metaphors could be alluded to if the statements[2] in question are interpreted in a slightly more liberal way. The curriculum claims, for example, that learners are to acquire communicative competence, which entails to correctly decipher information and to react accordingly. As metaphors are pervasive in language, they certainly need to be deciphered correctly and reacted to correctly as well. The curriculum further states that translation exercises should aim at what is called "communicative translation", focusing on equivalence and not on correctness, i.e., what is asked for is a simulation of what a native speaker would say if s/he were in a similar situation to the person in the original text. The expression "correct translation", still present in former curricula, has disappeared a while ago.

The only multi-word units that the curriculum mentions are idioms, and – interestingly enough – it is clearly stated that teachers have to make their learners aware that these have to devote a lot of time to learning idiomatic expressions in order to adequately express their thoughts in the target language. The term "idiom" is obviously used as an umbrella term for all kinds of figurative language and may therefore be interpreted as also referring to metaphorical expressions. Some idioms are even dealt with explicitly in certain textbooks, although this happens without exception in an unstructured way, entailing the implicit command "learn them by heart". However, the time-consuming task of learning idioms by heart is presumably not the best way of tackling them. Sometimes the textbooks add humorous illustrations (as for example real dogs and real cats that fall from the sky as an illustration for "it is raining cats and dogs"), which may amuse the learners but frequently do not provide them with a single clue as to the idioms' meanings. If learners are instead shown how to access the underlying meaning of an idiom/metaphor, the curricular warning that learning idioms can be very time-consuming may lose some of its threatening undertones.

As the following classroom example refers to colour expressions, it should be mentioned that when an idiom such as "to be caught red-handed" is typed into a search engine a lot of explanations and visualizations are offered. Although visualizations are generally seen as advantageous for learning (cf. Paivio's Dual

---

2 The statements from the curriculum have been translated from German into English by the author, see also http://lehrplaene.bildung-rp.de/lehrplaene-nach-faechern.html?tx_abdownloads_pi1[action]=getviewcatalog&tx_abdownloads_pi1[category_uid]=88&tx_abdownloads_pi1[cid]=5786&cHash=b85201556b835e435cca6d356df20b02.

Coding Theory, e.g., Paivio 1986), many of the visualizations of colour expressions do not explain the expressions' meanings very well. As one of many possible examples, when searching for "to be caught red-handed", a picture of a woman (head and torso) whose inner hands are painted red can be found (https://thehuffmanpost.files.wordpress.com/2014/05/caught-red-handed.jpg). The woman is frowning, her eyes are opened widely and her mouth is open as if she was crying out aloud – altogether, she looks scared and aghast rather than guilty and as if she has just committed a (major or minor) crime and has been caught in the act. Furthermore, her red hands may also lead to the assumption that she is a painter having used finger-paint. Such a visualization of the idiom's meaning does not contribute in the least to a language learner's understanding of this idiom, but on the contrary will presumably rather confuse the learner. Many of the colour idiom illustrations that the internet offers are comparable, i.e., they are just nice and sometimes even funny pictures that are not able to establish any mental link between the idioms and their meanings for the learners.

If some examples without visualizations are taken into consideration, their value from an educational and psychological angle is not exactly higher. Several L2 publishers offer extra training material on idioms, independent from the use of a specific textbook. Cambridge University Press, for example, offers publications for two different learning levels (intermediate and advanced), allegedly suitable for self-study and classroom use. However, these materials might – for various reasons – not be entirely suitable for the intended target audience.

To illustrate this claim with an example, McCarthy's and O'Dell's (2002) "English Idioms in Use – Intermediate" claims to aim at CEFR levels B1 to B2 and is at the same time recommended for the third year of English, where normally the learners are still quite far away from the levels B1 to B2. In this publication, the idioms are grouped quite haphazardly. The first and longest part of the book with 30 chapters deals with idioms concerning specific topics such as health, happiness/sadness, anger, problems, knowing/understanding, success/failure, power/authority and so on. The second part with 14 chapters presents idioms from the topic areas time, elements, colours, games, animals etc., and the third part with 15 chapters focuses on idioms with certain key words – mostly referring to body parts – such as thumb, finger or hand. The colour chapter (chapter 34) has only two pages: the first page mentions 3–4 idioms for each of the colours red, blue, green and black/white/grey, explains their meanings and provides example sentences such as "be in the red = have a negative amount in your bank account". The second page presents four exercises in which the correct colour has to be inserted or in which parts of sentences have to rewritten using one of the idioms. The presentation of the idioms and the exercises can be seen as quite useless insofar as an understanding on the learners' part is involved, as the idioms' motivations remain unexplained and where therefore, once again, learning them by heart seems the only feasible solution.

In the follow-up book for advanced learners, O'Dell and McCarthy briefly mention metaphors, saying that they involve "a comparison" (2010: 12)[3] and that many idioms are based on metaphors. No further explanations are provided, although the authors claim that the metaphors underlying idioms are "much less thought-provoking and original than those used in literary contexts" (2010: 12), disregarding the fact that conventional metaphors may also prove to be thought-provoking for learners, as these frequently do not understand them. It is obvious that for learners all metaphors that they encounter for the first time will be novel, and thus "original" and "thought-provoking". Furthermore, everyday metaphors and metaphors in literature after all both depend on the same conceptual metaphors (see Lakoff and Turner 1989). Not informing the learners about the metaphors'/idioms' motivation does not help them to understand the meanings of the figurative expressions and not making the learners aware of the underlying conceptual metaphors foregoes the possibility for them to develop a mental representation of their meanings. Overall, also in this follow-up book an utter lack of systematicity is to be observed.

3 Potential benefits of including (conceptual) metaphor

This sub-chapter briefly presents arguments for including the notion of (conceptual) metaphor in the foreign language classroom, the main argument being that conceptual metaphors provide reasons for the use of certain expressions and thus facilitate communication and understanding. If learners know a conceptual metaphor, they are better able to understand its linguistic instantiations even if they have never encountered these before. "Creative" metaphors learners may come up with on the basis of a conceptual metaphor and that are not part of the target language are nevertheless understandable for native speakers (cf. Juchem-Grundmann 2009: 179, see also Boers 2004).

Furthermore, conceptual metaphors enable insightful learning due to their experiential basis. Learners can deduce meanings from bodily actions, for example, *to grasp a problem* can be related to "holding sth in one's hands and looking at it in detail".

---

[3] The term *comparison* can be seen as somewhat misleading in this context, as it can also refer to similes, i.e., direct comparisons including the term "like".

Conceptual metaphors help learners to retain vocabulary more easily, as learners are enabled to systematically expand on their prior knowledge and use already known words in extended senses. Vocabulary can be introduced in a more organized way, which facilitates retrieval (see also Boers 2004: 214) because expressions are stored as meaningful units and not as isolated words. This also means that learners can employ the words they already know in more ways than just the basic ones. In this way, their communicative competence gets enhanced and a more critical view on texts can be instilled (cf. Holme 2004: 130).

Research has shown that it is beneficial to draw the learners' attention to the literal senses of figurative expressions in order to "enhance indepth comprehension" (Boers 2001: 1). Furthermore, Boers (2004) and Boers et al. (2004) provide empirical evidence for the use of etymological elaboration as one of the most important forms of semantic elaboration. The mnemonic effect of naming the origin of an expression as explanation is equally strong both for transparent and for opaque idioms. Learners are more likely to recall an idiom when they know about its origin than when they only know its meaning (see Boers et al. 2004).

Furthermore, knowledge about source domains can help learners to increase their understanding of the foreign language, for example, Boers et al. (2007) show that learners are more likely to choose the correct definition for an idiom when they already know about its source domain. A basic awareness of the source domain can facilitate vocabulary retention as well (Boers 2004). However, restricting this finding somewhat, Beréndi (2005) claims that an awareness of the source domain and the metaphorical framework indeed facilitates understanding, but only if the teaching is explicit and not implicit (e.g., via pictures). In the same vein, Boers (2004) argues that explicit teaching of linguistic metaphors may result in productive vocabulary acquisition, however, continuous explicit awareness raising seems to be necessary to actually reach a long-term effect. It also has to kept in mind that learners' guessing activities concerning idiomatic meanings seem to be immensely useful but need to be guided (see Skoufaki 2008).

To conclude with two more general findings which are of importance for the current paper, teaching metaphors seems to work best with intermediate learners, as beginners do not yet have enough vocabulary and more advanced learners are afraid of taking risks (cf. Boers 2004), which is why the teaching example presented in the next sub-chapter focuses on intermediate learners of English as a foreign language. Last but not least, colour expressions such as *green with envy* are called "extraordinary equivalences" by Roche (2012), who claims that they are more easily retained by learners than "ordinary equivalences".

4 Teaching example: Colour expressions

Before starting on the example, the question needs to be raised whether the topic "colour expressions" is indeed dealing with metaphors or whether the expressions in question may not rather be seen as metonymies. The current paper suggests a functional view on the metaphor-metonymy dichotomy, in which the difference is seen as a matter of degree: if the etymology of an expression and thus the common domain of the vehicle and the target or, frequently, the enchainment of domains in further metonymizations is/are known to a language user, the expression in question is seen as a metonymy. If the etymology and/or the metonymization(s) is/are unknown to the language user, it is a metaphor. As intermediate learners' vocabulary knowledge is not yet that far advanced, most of the colour expressions will therefore be metaphors for them. Even if native speakers may see these expressions as conventional, for language learners encountering them for the first time they are novel.

The lesson series in question was conducted in an 8th grade of a German "Realschule" (lower secondary school), i.e., the pupils had been learning English for 4–8 years at the time of the intervention[4]. The learners' level of English was intermediate and corresponded to a CEFR level between A2 and B1. The group was composed of 26 pupils, aged between 13 and 15. The experiment followed a one-week school project called "Mach mein Leben bunt" ("Colour my Life"), in which names of colours and colour symbolicity were discussed in the German and English lessons[5]. The experiment comprised three English lessons of 45 minutes each within one week and focused on colour metaphors/metonymies, i.e., English multi-word expressions which contain a colour term. The researcher developed the materials, instructed the regular English teacher and took on the role of an observer during the lessons.

The learning targets of the lesson series were for the learners to develop an awareness for the figurative use of English colour expressions, to extend their use of already known vocabulary, to store the expressions as meaningful units, to acquire intercultural competence and to acquire "conceptual competence" (Danesi 2003: 72f.). In order to reach these aims, the underlying meanings of the colour expressions were to be elaborated semantically and etymologically and the explanations for those expressions that the learners were unable to find on

---

[4] Primary schools in the Rhineland-Palatinate are free to choose to teach either English or French from grade 1 onwards, and as not all learners had English in primary school, it is difficult to say precisely for how many years they had been learning English.
[5] Other subjects were involved in the project as well, such as physics, art, handicraft or physical education.

their own were to be made explicit. The teaching method used was a task-based approach (cf. Willis and Willis 2007, Nunan 2005) split up over the three lessons, of which the second and the third lesson are described in detail further down after a brief overview of the lesson series.

The first lesson focused on the pre-task and was meant to prepare the upcoming task. The learners were first asked to recall what they had learnt about colour symbolicity during the project week, after which they collected English colour expressions (from their memories and from dictionaries, online access was not allowed) in a competitive game. They ordered the expressions by colour and tried to find German equivalents, which of course was not always possible. The second lesson focused on the actual task, which was to get together in groups and construct a radial network of the colour expressions found. The range of analysed colours was restricted to only four colours, namely the primary colours red, blue, green and yellow. The third lesson was devoted to the learners' reports, contained a language focus and a transfer task for the previously gained knowledge. The learners were supposed to discuss the meanings of the colour expressions, to speculate on the origins of the expressions and to try to find contexts in which to use the expressions.

For the second lesson, the learners split up into four groups. Each group was allotted one colour and received a list with seven colour expressions, chosen by the teacher from the pool of expressions gathered during the first lesson. The expressions for *red* were *to catch somebody red-handed*, *red-hot news*, *to see red*, *to be in the red*, *red-letter day*, *red herring* and *redneck*. The expressions for *blue* were *to scream blue murder*, *to feel blue*, *out of the blue*, *a bolt from the blue*, *once in a blue moon*, *blue blood* and *blue movie*. The expressions for *green* were *green thumb*, *green politics*, *to give somebody the green light*, *green card*, *greenhorn*, *greenhouse* and *to be green*. The expressions for *yellow* were *yellow-bellied*, *yellow pages*, *yellow fever*, *yellow press*, *to be yellow*, *yellow card* and *yellow line*.

Furthermore, each group received a hand-out with three concentric circles. The innermost circle contained the colour term (i.e., red, blue, green, or yellow) and was labelled "basic meaning/s", the middle circle was labelled "Western meaning/s" and the outer circle was labelled "Anglo meaning/s". The learners were instructed to first discuss which real-world entities are related to the colour in question in a non-figurative way and then write these entities into the inner circle. For *red*, the learners agreed on *blood* and *fire*; for *blue*, they chose *sky*, *ocean* and *eyes*; for *green*, they used *grass*, *plants* and *trees*; for *yellow*, they entered *sun*, *ripe corn* and *gold*.

In a second step, they put those expressions for which they had been able to find German equivalents into the middle circle. For *red*, these expressions were *to see red* (German = "rot sehen"), *to be in the red* (German = "in den roten Zahlen sein", literally: *to be in the red numbers*) and *red-hot news* (German = "brandheiße

Nachrichten", literally: *fire-hot news*). For *blue*, the learners entered *blue blood* (German = "blaues Blut"), *out of the blue* (German = "aus heiterem Himmel", literally: *out of a cloudless sky*) and *a bolt from the blue* (German = "wie ein Blitz aus heiterem Himmel", literally: *like a lightning from a cloudless sky*). For *green*, the learners agreed on *green thumb* (German = "grüner Daumen"), *green politics* (German = "grüne Politik"), *to be green* (German = "grün hinter den Ohren sein", literally: *to be green behind one's ears*) and *to give somebody the green light* (German = "jemandem grünes Licht geben"). For *yellow*, the expressions found were *yellow fever* (German = "Gelbfieber"), *yellow pages* (German = "gelbe Seiten") and *yellow card* (German = "gelbe Karte").

All the remaining expressions were placed into the outer circle ("Anglo meaning/s"). For *red*, these were *red herring*, *redneck*, *red-letter day* and *to catch somebody red-handed* (see Figure 1):

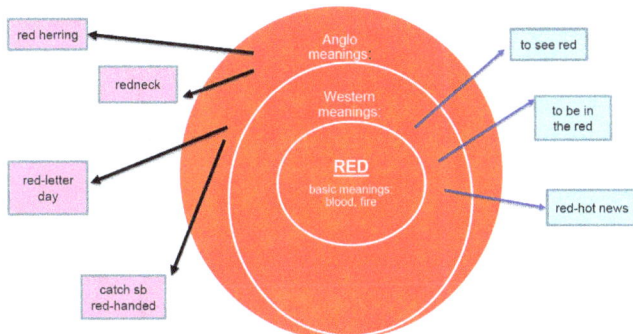

Figure 1. Colour circles for *red* expressions

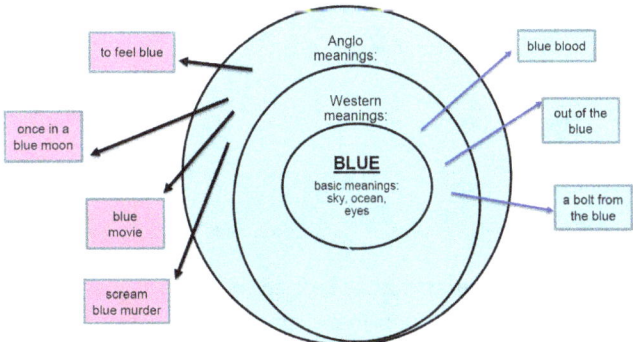

Figure 2. Colour circles of *blue* expressions

For *blue*, the expressions for the outer circle were *to feel blue*, *once in a blue moon*, *blue movie* and *to scream blue murder* (see Figure 2).

For *green*, the expressions in question were *greenhouse*, *green card* and *greenhorn* (see Figure 3).

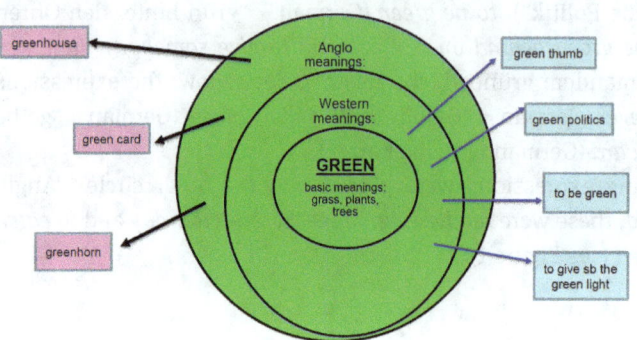

Figure 3. Colour circles of *green* expressions

For *yellow*, the remaining expressions were *yellow press*, *yellow line*, *yellow line* and *yellow-bellied* (see Figure 4).

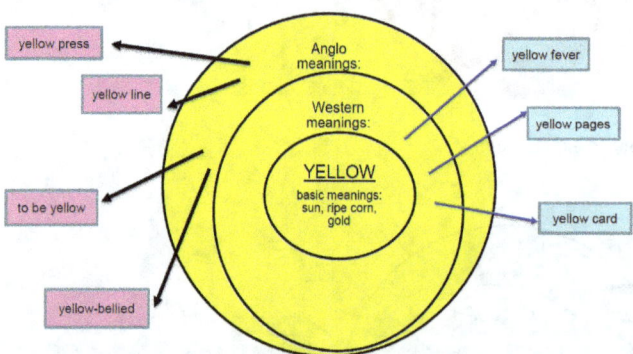

Figure 4. Colour circles of yellow expressions

During the third lesson, the learner groups first reported on the outcomes of their task, followed by a discussion about the non-literal meanings of the expressions in question with the guiding question what the relation between the meanings of the expressions in the middle and the outer circles to the concepts listed in the inner circle might be. During the discussion, the learners presented their ideas and speculated on the origins of the expressions. This was done with some minor help from the teacher's side, thus, the procedure might be seen as "guided guessing" (cf. Skoufaki 2008). The discussion yielded a multitude of results and the learners were to a certain degree able to deduct the meanings of the middle and outer circle expressions from the inner circle concepts. As to be expected, this procedure worked better for the middle circles, as these were expressions with a (near-) equivalent in the German language.

Concerning the "red" expressions, the learners realized that the expression *red-hot news* is related to the concept "fire/heat", because such news are brand-new and therefore getting people's attention, similar to a fire which immediately gets people's attention. One learner suggested that the newspaper might still be warm as it only just left the printing press[6]. The learners furthermore found out that the expressions *to catch somebody red-handed* and *to see red* are related to the concept "blood". In the first case, somebody did something bad, such as committing a crime, and was caught with his/her hands still full of blood or – in a metaphorical reading – evidence. In the second expression, blood vessels in the eye burst due to an increase in heart pressure, which may happen when someone is insanely angry.

All the three "blue" expressions that the learners could relate to one of the basic concepts of "blue" were related to the basic concept "sky". They identified *out of the blue*, *a bolt from the blue* and *once in a blue moon* as referring to sky-related phenomena, namely the suddenness of something that is happening unexpectedly, as if something had dropped from the sky, or the suddenness of a lightning when none is to be expected because the sky is blue. The third expression was interpreted as relating to something very infrequent, as the moon does not normally look bluish.

For "green", nature was the domain to which the learners could relate some of the expressions in question, namely *green thumb*, *green politics* and *greenhouse*. They argued that "green" has to do with plants, with growth and the preservation of nature in ecologically oriented politics.

---

[6] This suggestion was wrong, but this was not pointed out to the learners as it was important that they speculated on potential meanings and thus formed mental pathways – even idiosyncratic ones – connecting the expressions to their everyday knowledge, which they had to use in order to make sense of the expressions. Such mental pathways will presumably help them in the future to remember the expressions in question.

Concerning the expressions with "yellow", the learners felt unable to relate any of the given expressions to the basic concepts. This left the class with a couple of expressions for which no meaning could be deducted, most of these expressions stemming from the outer "Anglo" circle. As the German learners were not immensely familiar with English-speaking cultures, this came as no surprise. Therefore, the last step in the third lesson was to render these more opaque colour expressions transparent, which could be achieved by explicitly imparting some cultural knowledge.

For "red", it was explained that *red-letter day* refers to the days which are written in red in a calendar, usually Sundays or public holidays, which is a cultural convention that English-speaking cultures and the German one share. A similar explanation accounts for *to be in the red*, as the red print on a bank account is on the debit side[7]. The expression *redneck* refers to another meaning of "red", namely to the colour of burnt skin. It originated in the Carolinas, where farm workers worked in the sun in a bent-down position and thus burnt their necks. Today, this expression refers to a close-minded, uneducated person, which is a characteristic that common belief links to farm workers. *Red herring* was the most difficult expression for the learners, as they would have needed specific cultural knowledge from Great Britain about fox hunting in order to be able to decipher it. A *red herring* is something misleading, a distractor, and the expression originates from the fact that a smoked (= red) herring was used to cover the traces of the fox so that it could not be smelt so easily by the hunting dogs.

Some of the "blue" expressions were not immediately interpretable by the inner circle concepts either. Thus, *blue blood* refers to nobility and has its origin in Southern Spain, where the Moors' darker skin was contrasted with the noble people's paler skin, which lets their bluish veins shine through. *To scream blue murder* necessitated more explanation as well, as it allegedly stems from the French exclamation "morbleu" as a euphemism for "mort de Dieu" and today means "to make an unnecessary fuss". As such, it has actually nothing to do with the colour "blue" itself. *To feel blue*, on the other hand, has again a physiological origin and is relatable to the bluish skin colour which hints at illness, in this case mental illness, and the expression is used for sad, melancholic and depressed persons. Finally, *blue movie* again presupposes cultural knowledge in order to be interpretable, as it comes from Puritan America, where laws against sinful behaviour, such as prostitution, consummation of alcohol etc. happened to be written down on blue paper and later on became known as "blue laws". Today,

---

[7] This is something the learners presumably had no experience with, which is why this expression was probably not a good choice, although it is quite popular.

the meaning has narrowed down to pornography and the expression refers to pornographic movies.

Concerning the "green" expressions, *to give somebody the green light* can be connected to traffic lights, as the green light gives people permission to go ahead, in this case with a plan or with a project. *Greenhorn* and *to be green* were used as descriptions for cowboys who were new to the job and this "newness" can be related to freshly grown leaves or saplings. *Green card*, on the other hand, again presupposes cultural knowledge. Some of the learners had heard the expression before, but did not manage to relate it to the colour "green", as green cards (permanent US residence documents) today are no longer green, although they used to be at some point.

For "yellow", most expressions needed further explanation. *Yellow fever*, *yellow pages* and *yellow card* turned out to be easily understandable, as these expressions are used in German as well and as the colour yellow is actually present in the concept. Yellow fever is a viral disease that turns the patients skin yellowish due to liver damage. The yellow pages are a telephone directory of businesses used since 1883, when due to mere coincidence yellow paper was used because a printer had run out of white paper. The yellow card in soccer is a warning and can also be connected to the concept of traffic lights where the yellow light serves as a warning that the red light is about to appear. *Yellow line* needed more explanation, as it refers to a roadmarking prohibiting parking in Great Britain. *Yellowbellied* and *to be yellow* are 19th century American expressions with an unknown origin and both relate to the concept of cowardice. A possible explanation is the fact that yellow is the colour of sickness, which means that a person lacks strength and stamina (and "guts"). Another possible explanation is that an overproduction of yellow bile in the Galenic theory of the four humours stood for peevishness and jealousy. A third possible explanation is that the expression is connected to the yellow-belly lizard, a reptile not known for its intestinal fortitude ("guts"). Equally difficult to explain was y*ellow press*, which refers to sensationalistic journalism and has its origin in the expression "yellow kid journalism" in early 1897, which was named after a popular comic strip and was soon shortened to "yellow journalism".

After this exploration into the underlying meanings of the colour terms the learners tried to find suitable contexts in which to use the expressions and even came up with word plays and puns. Finally, the homework consisted of a creative writing task in which at least four of the expressions in question had to be used.

5 Conclusion

Apart from the fact that most of the learners seemed to have enjoyed the exercise in language analysis, their range of vocabulary and their analytic skills improved noticeably. The learners went from the source (colour) to the target (idiom meanings) and by detecting the motivation of the expressions they were able to make sense of the colour expressions in question and thus proceeded from seeing them as metaphors to seeing them as metonymies, as the link between the source and the target no longer seemed unmotivated and subjective but became objective, could be explained and traced back to the underlying concepts.

The learners were given a post-test, which consisted of gap-filling, three weeks after the lesson series had taken place. The text in question was a story which described different emotions a character went through (the character was green, felt blue, saw red, was yellow etc.). The post-test generally yielded good results. However, it was noticeable that the concepts that the learners had found on their own were better retrievable for them than the concepts for which they had needed the teacher's help or explanations. The results can of course be criticized as there was no control group (which would have had to learn the colour expressions by heart), and thus no statistic validity can be claimed. It can also be criticized that "yellow" was the most difficult colour and therefore presumably not a good candidate for analysis, as the expressions used did not refer to naturally occurring yellow entities.

Concerning the learning targets, the learners indeed developed an awareness for the figurative use of English colour expressions and extended their use of already known vocabulary. They succeeded in storing the expressions as meaningful units and acquired intercultural as well as "conceptual" competence. Although current textbook and teaching materials do not offer any explanations of colour expressions that would allow deep processing and the teachers therefore have to create and develop the materials and the lesson sequences on their own, it is definitely worth it. The usefulness may even go beyond the actual expressions that were discussed, as some of the learners might see vocabulary items and figurative expressions differently in the future and may feel motivated to find out the underlying meanings. Such reflections are valid in themselves, even if they may not always lead the learners to the desired results, but thinking about language and using language in a ludic way is beneficial in its own right and helps to develop the learners' language awareness.

References

Beréndi, Marta. 2005. *Metaphor in vocabulary teaching. A cognitive linguistic approach.* Pécs: University of Pécs.
Boers, Frank. 2000. Metaphor awareness and vocabulary retention. *Applied Linguistics* 21(4). 553–571.
Boers, Frank. 2004. Expanding learners' vocabulary through metaphor awareness: what expansion, what learners, what vocabulary? In Michel Achard & Susanne Niemeier (eds.), *Cognitive Linguistics, Second Language Acquisition, and Foreign Language Teaching*, 211–232. Berlin: Mouton de Gruyter.
Boers, Frank, Murielle Demecheleer & June Eyckmans. 2004. Etymological elaboration as a strategy for learning idioms. In Paul Bongaards & Batia Laufer (eds.), *Vocabulary in a Second Language*, 53–78. Amsterdam: John Benjamins Publishing.
Boers, Frank, June Eyckmans & Hélène Stengers. 2007. Presenting figurative idioms with a touch of etymology: More than mere mnemonics. *Language Teaching Research* 11(1). 43–62.
Danesi, Marcel. 2003. *Second language teaching - A view from the right side of the brain.* Dordrecht: Kluwer Academic Publishers.
Ellis, Rod. 2003. *Task-based language learning and teaching.* Oxford: Oxford University Press.
Holme, Randall. 2004. *Mind, metaphor and language teaching.* Basingstoke: Palgrave Macmillan.
Juchem-Grundmann, Constanze. 2009. *"Dip into your savings!" Applying cognitive metaphor theory in business English classroom. An Empirical Study.* University Koblenz-Landau: Doctoral Dissertation.
Lakoff, George & Mark Johnson. 1980. *Metaphors we live by.* Chicago: Chicago University Press.
Lakoff, George & Mark Turner. 1989. *More than cool reason.* Chicago: University of Chicago Press.
Littlemore, Jeannette & Graham Low. 2006. Metaphoric competence, second language learning, and communicative language ability. *Applied Linguistics* 27(2). 268–294.
Littlemore, Jeannette. 2011. *Applying cognitive linguistics to second language learning and teaching.* Basingstoke: Palgrave Macmillan.
MacArthur, Fiona. 2010. Metaphorical competence in EFL. In Jeannette Littlemore & Constanze Juchem-Grundmann (eds.), *Applying cognitive linguistics to second language learning and teaching. AILA Review* 23, 155–173. Amsterdam: John Benjamins Publishing.
McCarthy, Michael & Felicity O'Dell. 2002. *English idioms in use. Intermediate.* Cambridge: Cambridge University Press.
Niemeier, Susanne. 1998. Colourless green ideas metonymise furiously. In Friedrich Ungerer (ed.), *Kognitive Syntax und Semantik*, 119–146. Rostock: Universität Rostock.
Niemeier, Susanne. 2003. The concept of metaphor in cognitive linguistics and its didactic potential. In Dagmar Abendroth-Timmer, Britta Viebrock & Michael Wendt (eds.), *Text, Kontext und Fremdsprachenunterricht*, 263–271. Frankfurt: Lang.
Niemeier, Susanne. 2007. From blue stockings to blue movies – colour metonymies in English. In Martina Plümacher & Peter Holz (eds.), *Speaking of Colors and Odors*, 141–154. Amsterdam: Benjamins.
Nunan, David. 2005. *Task-based language teaching.* Cambridge: Cambridge University Press.

O'Dell, Felicity & Michael McCarthy. 2010. *English idioms in use. Advanced*. Cambridge: Cambridge University Press.
Paivio, Allan. 1986. *Mental Representations – A Dual Coding Approach*. Oxford: Oxford University Press.
Roche, Jörg. 2012. Zum überfälligen Paradigmenwechsel in der Fremdsprachendidaktik. In Andrea M. Birk & Claudia Buffagni (eds.), *Linguistik und Sprachdidaktik im universitären DaF-Unterricht*, 33–52. Münster: Waxmann.
Skoufaki, Sofia. 2008. Conceptual metaphoric meaning clues in two L2 idiom presentation methods. In Frank Boers & Seth Lindstromberg (eds.), *Cognitive Linguistic Approaches to Teaching Vocabulary*, 101–132. Berlin: Mouton de Gruyter.
Willis, Dave & Jane Willis. 2007. *Doing Task-Based Teaching*. Oxford: Oxford University Press.

Curriculum

http://lehrplaene.bildung-rp.de/lehrplaene-nachfaechern.html?tx_abdownloads_pi1%5bactio n%5d=getviewcatalog&tx_abdownloads_pi1%5bcategory_uid%5d=88&tx_abdownloads_ pi1%5bcid%5d=5786&cHash=b85201556b835e43ca6d356df20b02 – last access: June 23, 2015

Susan Nacey and Bård Uri Jensen
Metaphoricity in English L2 learners' prepositions

1 Introduction

English prepositions are traditionally considered to be challenging for foreign language learners: "an area of almost universal difficulty among second language learners of English" (Low 1988: 137), "a traditional and recurring nightmare for all learners of English" (Littlemore and Low 2006: 284), and "the *bête noire* of both teachers and learners, being impossible to teach and impossible to learn" (Gilquin and Granger 2011: 60). A number of reasons have been advanced to explain why prepositions might be difficult to acquire. First, most prepositions are highly polysemous, making it challenging for learners to intuitively grasp a particular preposition's meaning(s); definitions of "at" in various online English advanced learners' dictionaries, for instance, range from 7 to 19 main sense entries.[1]

Second, learners may sometimes find it difficult to tease apart the nuances of various prepositions which encode slightly varied aspects of a single domain, as might be the case with prepositions encoding a time relationship (e.g. *in* the morning, *on* Monday morning, *at* night). Third, there may be a mismatch between English prepositions and those in a learner's L1 (assuming that language has prepositions), resulting in potential negative L1 transfer. Finally, textbooks and other reference works frequently treat preposition choice as arbitrary and unpredictable as a result; rote memorization is often recommended as a solution, along with a healthy dose of cramming and the development of good dictionary habits (see e.g. Lindstromberg 1998: 227; Parrott 2010: 94; Taylor 1988: 299, all of whom either discuss or suggest one or more of these options).

---

[1] Number of main sense entries for the preposition 'at' among various online English dictionaries:
Cambridge Advanced Learner's Dictionary (http://dictionary.cambridge.org/dictionary/british/at) = 7;
Macmillan Dictionary http://www.macmillandictionary.com/dictionary/british/at) = 10;
Oxford Advanced Learner's Dictionary (http://www.oxfordlearnersdictionaries.com/definition/english/at?q=at) = 15;
Longman Dictionary of Contemporary English (http://www.ldoceonline.com/dictionary/at) = 18;
Collins English Dictionary (http://www.collinsdictionary.com/dictionary/english/at = 19.

Susan Nacey, Inland Norway University of Applied Sciences
Bård Uri Jensen, Inland Norway University of Applied Sciences

This paper presents empirical evidence into the use of prepositions in learner English, to shed additional light upon the challenge prepositions present. In doing so, this paper looks into one particular variety of L2 learner English, building upon previous work into prepositions in written and spoken Norwegian L2 English: Nacey (2013) and Nacey and Graedler (2015). Nacey (2013: 205–239) examined all prepositions in a selection of written Norwegian L2 English, identifying all metaphorical prepositions and all divergent prepositions, before focusing on case studies of *to* and *on*. Nacey and Graedler (2015) examined preposition use in spoken Norwegian L2 English and compared preposition use across the spoken and written modes. Conclusions from these two pieces of earlier work indicate that the most likely source for production of divergent prepositions is negative L1 transfer, i.e. learners may choose a particular English preposition because it is the nearest equivalent to the Norwegian preposition that would have been appropriate had the text been in Norwegian. Despite being the single most likely motivation for divergent prepositions, however, L1 transfer was found to be able to account for less than half of the observed instances in either mode. The present study turns toward the same data, but with a focus on metaphor. The main aim is to discover whether the degree of metaphoricity of a preposition plays a role with respect to divergent choice by language learners. "Divergence" in this context refers to choices of prepositions that may be regarded as non-standard, in the sense that the contextual senses are not listed in general dictionaries of English.

Immediately following this introduction, section 2 provides the theoretical background underlying the hypothesis concerning a possible link between metaphor and preposition divergence in L2 learner language. Section 3 then outlines the material used as data for the present study (section 3.1), as well as the methods employed for data extraction (section 3.2), identification of metaphor (section 3.3) and identification of divergence (section 3.4). The paper continues by providing a general overview indicating the true magnitude of the challenge prepositions pose for these learners, first with an outline of the overall preposition frequency in the data (section 4) and then with an overview concerning the frequency of divergent prepositions and metaphorical prepositing in the data (section 5 and section 6 respectively). Sections 7 and 8 then turn to metaphor, addressing two related research questions which are the focus of the present paper:
1. Is there a significant difference between metaphorical use of prepositions in the spoken and written modes in Norwegian L2 learner English (section 7)? and
2. Is there a correlation between divergent use and metaphorical use (section 8)?

Section 9 closes the paper with concluding remarks.

2 Why metaphor?

Both Norwegian and English are Germanic languages which encode spatial relationships in much the same ways, often using prepositions.² Although many English language textbooks in Norway do not tackle the topic of preposition use at all, lists of L1/L2 preposition equivalents are not uncommon in those textbooks that do attempt to guide learners in this area (see e.g. Lysvåg and Johansson 1995: 125–129). Such correspondence tends to be based upon the spatial senses of the prepositions in the two languages, senses which may be considered "basic". Thus, English *in* is presented as the translation correspondent for Norwegian *i* because they share the same basic spatial sense of being within a physical container or area (see section 3.3 for more information about basic senses). The two prepositions, however, are not one-to-one equivalents in every context, especially as meaning diverges away from the prototypical spatial sense towards more peripheral – and often metaphorical – senses. If learners perceive metaphorical extensions as less central meanings (either consciously or subconsciously), then they might also perceive metaphorical extensions as abnormal. Such items may be more difficult for learners to acquire and more prone to learner anomaly as a consequence. This hypothesis then provides the foundation for testing whether there is any correlation between metaphoricity and divergence in the production of prepositions by English language learners.

3 Material and methods

3.1 Corpus data: LINDSEI and ICLE

This study is corpus-driven, with the primary data having been harvested from two corpora of L2 learner English, the Norwegian components of the International Corpus of Learner English (NICLE) and the Louvain International Database of Spoken English Interlanguage (LINDSEI-NO). Both belong to the Louvain family of corpora, developed to facilitate comparison across learner varieties, between learner varieties and a reference corpus, and/or across the written and spoken modes (as in the present study). NICLE is a collection of written Norwegian L2 English in the form of untimed, argumentative essays, where the prompts

---

2 Some languages rely on other grammatical constructions as an alternative to prepositions, e.g. Estonian that uses case endings or Korean that employs special combinations of nouns and verbs (see Tyler and Evans 2003: 164–169).

were provided in advance. The data for this study was taken from 29 of the total 317 NICLE essays, originally gathered as part of a wider study into metaphoricity in Norwegian learner language that is reported in detail in Nacey (2013). The 29 texts contain a total of 20,466 words.[3] LINDSEI-NO is a collection of spoken Norwegian L2 English, consisting of transcriptions of 50 informal conversations between an English native speaker and a Norwegian informant, all lasting for approximately 15 minutes. The interview structure follows a tri-fold structure, with a warm-up task, then a freer conversation, and finally a brief picture-task description. The learner turns in LINDSEI-NO equal 83,674 words of text, meaning that approximately four times more spoken text was analyzed for preposition use in this study. The average spoken text is thus longer than the average written text. The minimum text length in LINDSEI-NO is 1128 words and the maximum text length 2738 words (mean = 1674, median = 1598, sd = 349). In NICLE, by contrast, the minimum text length is 497 words and the maximum text length is 1179 words (mean = 706, median = 626, sd = 268). The informants for both corpora were students taking a year-long tertiary level course in English at a Norwegian institution, with upper intermediate to advanced proficiency in English. Although the production of these informants is thus comparable, it is important to note that the written and spoken language of the same students has not been compared: NICLE was collected between 1999 and 2002, whereas LINDSEI-NO was collected between 2010 and 2012.[4] There are 79 individual informants in total, as no informant contributed more than one text to either corpus.

3.2 Extraction of the data

The NICLE texts were submitted to the CLAWS part of speech (PoS) tagger, and all lexemes tagged as PRP or PRF (for "prepositions" and "of", respectively) were transferred to a spreadsheet and analyzed for metaphoricity and divergence.[5] The LINDSEI-NO texts, by contrast, were manually combed for prepositions rather than being annotated with CLAWS, because it was feared that the abundant number of disfluencies recorded in the transcribed texts (overlaps, truncated words, silent and filled pauses) would make the annotation results unreliable.

---

[3] Note that in all subsequent sections of this paper, 'NICLE' is used to only refer to the 29 texts investigated here, rather than the entire corpus. Also note that the term 'word' refers to word forms rather than lexemes, such that multiword lexemes are here considered as two or more words.
[4] LINDSEI-NO will form part of the second edition of LINDSEI, the first edition having been published in 2010 (Gilquin, Cock, and Granger 2010).
[5] The CLAWS tagger is located here: http://ucrel.lancs.ac.uk/claws/.

Instead, a concordancer was used to search the corpus for all occurrences of 92 different prepositions, following a list compiled from a variety of sources that included grammar books and school textbooks. This search served to narrow the list to 50 prepositions that had been uttered at least once by one or more learners during the course of the interviews. Concordance lines for each such occurrence were then transferred to a spreadsheet, where each entry was coded for metaphorical status and divergence.[6] While the NICLE data was analyzed by a single researcher (Nacey), the LINDSEI-NO data was analyzed by one of two researchers who discussed any unclear cases to reach a joint decision (see Nacey and Graedler 2015).

Excluded from consideration in this study are all prepositions in cited movie titles, book titles etc., since they do not necessarily provide evidence about the learners' preposition use per se. Moreover, prepositions occurring in "polywords" have been excluded, polywords being short, fixed expressions such as *of course* and *on top of* that are perceived as single lexical units even though they consist of two or more orthographic words (Becker 1975; Nattinger and DeCarrico 1992: 38–39). In such expressions, the individual components have "lost their semantic identity" (Sinclair 1991: 110–111), and should therefore not be separated when it comes to semantic analysis. In other words, all prepositions included in the present analysis consist of a single word only. Particles in phrasal verbs and prepositions in prepositional verbs, illustrated in (1) and (2) respectively, were also differentiated, by excluding the former for analysis but including the latter.

(1) they're all *handed **in*** at roughly the same time (NO026)[7]

(2) I think I'll *talk **about*** Germany (NO047)

Differentiation was carried out following Quirk *et al.*'s criteria (1985: 1156–1157, 1167), the most helpful criterion with respect to transitive constructions being the inability of the particle to be moved to a position after the linked noun phrase.

---

[6] The "WordSmith Tools" software package (Scott 2013) was employed to create lists of concordance lines for each preposition.
[7] In these and all other examples, the preposition in focus is marked with bold italics, and any immediate relevant co-text with italics. The tags from examples from both corpora first identify the learners' L1 (NO = Norwegian). LINDSEI-NO tags then include a number indicating the individual learner, while NICLE tags include a two-letter code identifying the institution where the text was collected followed by a number for the individual text.

Finally, the dividing line between prepositions and some other word classes (especially conjunctions) is sometimes blurry, something particularly true of the lexemes *as*, *like*, and *than* (Quirk et al. 1985: 658–661). For this reason, all occurrences of these three words have been discarded from the data. All told, these exclusions account for 1,264 occurrences in LINDSEI-NO (37 titles, 385 phrasal verbs, 477 polywords, 67 cases of *as*, 244 cases of *like*, and 54 cases of *than*) and 588 occurrences in NICLE (3 titles, 112 phrasal verbs, 129 polywords, 236 cases of *as*, 56 cases of *like*, and 52 cases of *than*).

3.3 Identification of metaphor

The metaphorical status of each preposition was established through the application of the Metaphor Identification Procedure Vrije Universiteit (MIPVU; see Steen et al. 2010), a procedure developed to allow for reliable and valid identification of metaphorical words in discourse (that is, not just for prepositions). MIPVU first calls for comparison of the contextual and basic senses of each word in a text. If those two senses are sufficiently distinct from one another and if the relationship between the two differing senses may be attributed to some form of similarity, the word is marked as metaphorical in use. Otherwise, the word is marked as non-metaphorical. The relative coarseness of such a nominal scale with a yes/no decision by which a word is judged as metaphorical is less than ideal, since metaphor is a graded phenomenon. But as Steen argues (2007: 92–93), any more fine-grained scale – such as rank scales or interval scales – would have to be universally and reliably applicable; moreover, even gross orderings of an admittedly complex reality may prove useful.

The basic sense is defined as the most concrete, specific and human-oriented sense within the same word class and grammatical category, and is determined through dictionary consultation, in this case using the online version of the corpus-based *Macmillan English Dictionary for Advanced Learners* (MED) as the primary resource.[8] MIPVU stipulates that the basic sense must be codified in such a standard dictionary of the contemporary language, because that sense could otherwise not possibly be basic for present-day users – that is, historical dictionaries are not consulted because the diachronic perspective is largely irrelevant for the average language user. That aside, English is spoiled for choice when it comes to selection of an appropriate contemporary dictionary (as indicated in footnote 1), so MED is but one of many possible alternatives.

---

[8] The online version of MED is found here: http://www.macmillandictionary.com/.

The main consideration is avoidance of reliance purely on intuition in determining basic senses, as these meanings may not be the first that come to mind and risk being overlooked.

As an example of MIPVU in practice, consider the italicized preposition in (3), taken from the NICLE material.

(3) We will still be here *in* a thousand years... (NOAC1001)

When it comes to prepositions, the basic sense is nearly always spatial, as is the case with *in* where the basic sense corresponds to the first sense entry in MED: "used for showing where someone or something is". This sense may also be effectively depicted with the help of an icon, which illustrates the basic senses pictorially; see Figure 1 portraying the basic sense of *in* (adapted from Lindstromberg 2010: 72).

Figure 1. Icon representing the basic sense of *in*

By contrast, the contextual sense of *in* in (3) is MED's fourth sense entry for the preposition: "used for showing when something happens". The senses clearly contrast in this case, an example of the linguistic manifestation of the TIME IS SPACE conceptual metaphor, not uncommon for prepositions. That said, it should be emphasized that MIPVU only identifies metaphors on the level of language – i.e. linguistic metaphors – rather than metaphors on the level of thought – i.e. the underlying conceptual metaphors. Even though the procedure relies on a cognitive linguistic model of cross-domain mappings underlying linguistic metaphors, these mappings are not identified. Further, MIPVU is as agnostic to whether the particular metaphors are perceived as metaphor by the recipients or intended as such by the language producers. Indeed, the function of metaphor on the level of communication with regard to prepositions is generally insignificant, meaning that producers rarely deliberately play with the metaphoricity of prepositions in order to achieve a particular effect.

3.4 Identification of divergence

The prepositions in the material were categorized for divergence based on whether their contextual senses and/or collocations are lexicalized in contemporary dictionaries of English. Procedures for determination of divergence followed MIPVU precedence, by relying upon corpus-based dictionaries intended for advanced learners of English, such as MED. Because such dictionaries are intended to help users to both decode and encode words, they include carefully selected illustrative sentences of the word in context. These sentences are often the most effective means of providing information in a user-friendly way, especially about very frequent words such as prepositions. They serve to clarify points regarding common collocations, syntax, variety of usage, and meaning (Landau 2001: 208; van der Meer 1997: 566), thereby functioning as a complement to reliance on informed intuition.

The term "divergence" rather than "error" is deliberately employed here, in recognition of the variable preposition use that may occur in different varieties of world Englishes, as well as acknowledgement of the ongoing discussions over English as a lingua franca, where successful communication is prioritized over strict adherence to the rules of any particular L1 English variety. English language teaching in Norway, however, has traditionally been characterized by a native speaker bias, with the target being British English or, less frequently, American English (Rindal 2010: 241–242). It thus makes sense to use one or both of these varieties as the benchmark by which to measure the learners' preposition production, and to define divergence with respect to dictionary classification: preposition use is deemed standard only if the contextual meaning for the preposition in question matches one of its sense entries in standard dictionaries of English.

In this way, prepositions such as both occurrences of *in* in (4) were classified as "standard", a usage corresponding to the first MED entry for the preposition (previously cited in section 3.3). By contrast, the use of *in* in (5) was classified as "divergent" because there is no corresponding entry for the preposition with this particular collocation in the dictionary (although there is for *at*, the conventionally standard preposition and presumably the target item).

(4) I got some relatives (em) **in** *New Jersey* and **in** *Salt Lake City* as well (NO046)

(5) we're going to Tallinn **in** *the end of March* (NO017)

While these two decisions tallied with the analysts' intuition, such was not always the case. In any clashes between the analysts' intuitive understanding and dictionary evidence of what might be considered standard, the latter was allowed to trump the former.

When it comes to spoken data, however, divergence was sometimes impossible to determine due to the online processing factor inherent in the nature of oral language. Specifically, it was impossible to determine the divergence status of 148 occurrences of prepositions because the speaker suddenly broke off and either restructured the utterance or began to express a new (usually related) thought, or because the learner's utterance was interrupted by the interviewer as part of the natural flow of conversation. In (6), for example, it is not possible to definitively categorize *after* for appropriateness, as the learner never completed the prepositional phrase (the "=" symbol indicates a truncated word). Such usages have therefore been coded as "Don't Know" (DK). Although included in the data for preposition frequency outlined in section 4, they have not been further analyzed for either divergence or metaphoricity.

(6) so I went there and: . I really liked it so **after** *the=* and it was only for three months a half semester (NO014)[9]

There were no parallel cases in the NICLE material, not unexpected in argumentative university essays.

4 Overview of preposition frequency

There are a total of 6839 preposition tokens in the combined data, representing 6.6% of the total 104,140 words in the analyzed data. This means that one of every 15 words is a preposition. Although there are 53 types in the data, the "top 10" most frequent prepositions represent 92.3% of the total number of preposition tokens. Thus, a relatively small handful of prepositions account for most of the data. These 10 prepositions are, in order from most to least frequent, *in, of, to, for, with, on, at, from, about,* and *by*.

A look at preposition frequency per mode reveals 5170 preposition tokens in the spoken material, equaling 6.2% of the total number of words in the LINDSEI-NO corpus. These tokens are divided into 49 different types, with the

---

[9] Note that colons in transcribed LINDSEI texts mark drawn-out words, while periods mark unfilled pauses.

top 10 prepositions accounting for 93.4 % of the total number of prepositions. The written data, by contrast, contains 1669 preposition tokens – 8.1% of the NICLE words – divided into 38 types. The top 10 most frequent prepositions amount to 82.9 % of the total number of prepositions in that corpus. An overview of the most frequent prepositions in the two corpora is presented in Figure 2, listing all prepositions in LINDSEI-NO and NICLE with fifteen or more occurrences. While the vertical axis in both panels presents frequencies to allow for easier comparison between the two corpora, the numbers above the bars provide the figures for observed occurrences of each preposition.[10]

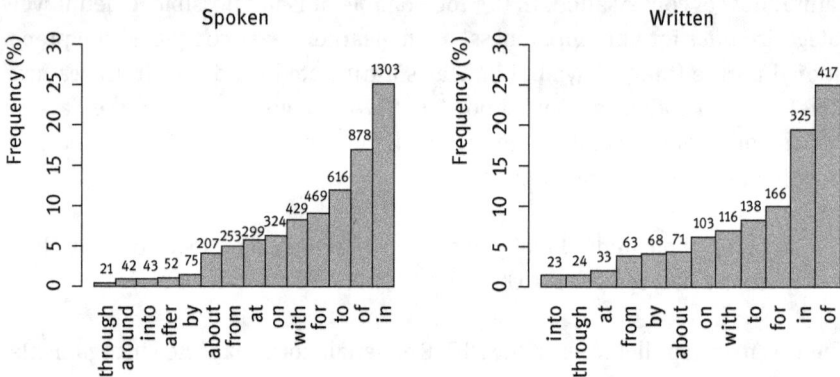

Figure 2. Preposition frequency in LINDSEI-NO and NICLE (≥ 15 occurrences)

The learners have thus produced fewer different prepositions in the written texts, but vary more in their preposition use; the most frequent prepositions account for a lesser proportion of the whole. In the spoken material, a more limited number of prepositions have been re-used more often. The NICLE data, however, is much smaller than the LINDSEI-NO data, something that might account for the smaller number of preposition types in that corpus. Table 1, presenting a complete overview of the observed occurrences of prepositions in the two corpora, sheds further light on this matter. In this table, the prepositions are arranged in order from the most to least frequent in the two corpora combined. Those prepositions written in bold script letter are only found in the spoken material, whereas italicized prepositions occur only in the written data.

---

[10] All graphical visualizations and statistical tests were carried out using R (R Foundation for Statistical Computing 2010).

Table 1. Observed occurrences of prepositions in LINDSEI-NO and NICLE

	Preposition	Total	**Spoken**	*Written*
1	in	1628	1303	325
2	of	1295	878	417
3	to	754	616	138
4	for	635	469	166
5	with	545	429	116
6	on	427	324	103
7	at	332	299	33
8	from	316	253	63
9	about	278	207	71
10	by	143	75	68
11	into	66	43	23
12	after	56	52	4
13	through	45	21	24
14	around	45	42	3
15	without	23	10	13
16	during	22	13	9
17	over	19	14	5
18	between	15	10	5
19	among	15	8	7
20	within	13	2	11
21	*upon*	12	0	12
22	under	12	7	5
23	behind	12	7	5
24	towards	11	4	7
25	down	11	10	1
26	*but*	11	0	11
27	until	9	8	1
28	**till**	9	9	0
29	before	8	2	6
30	across	7	6	1
31	**past**	6	6	0
32	**outside**	5	5	0
33	**out**	5	5	0
34	against	5	4	1
35	*up*	4	4	0
36	throughout	4	1	3
37	near	4	3	1
38	beyond	4	1	3
39	**beside**	4	4	0
40	*via*	3	0	3
41	**since**	3	3	0
42	off	3	2	1
43	inside	3	1	2

Table 1. (continued)

	Preposition	Total	Spoken	Written
44	except	2	2	0
45	despite	2	1	1
46	versus	1	1	0
47	per	1	1	0
48	including	1	1	0
49	concerning	1	1	0
50	besides	1	1	0
51	below	1	1	0
52	alongside	1	1	0
53	alike	1	0	1

From Table 1, we see that seven prepositions that are not found in NICLE occur only once in LINDSEI-NO: numbers 46–52. Each such single occurrence necessarily contributes to increasing the number of separate types of prepositions in the spoken data. When it comes to single occurrences in NICLE only, there is only one such word: *alike* (number 53). Although this lexeme does not function as a preposition in standard English, it was used as one by a NICLE writer and has therefore been included in the present analysis; that it was not used as a preposition by any LINDSEI-NO informant is unsurprising.

An interesting question related to preposition frequency is whether there might be certain prepositions that belong primarily to either a spoken or written mode. Table 1 shows, for example, that *upon* and *but* (illustrated in (7) and (8) respectively) both occur more than ten times each in the written texts but not a single time in the spoken interviews, indicating that these two prepositions might seem to be more characteristic of written language.

(7)   They balance **upon** the very border of reality, as we know it. NOAG1017

(8)   Never mind that the moon is **but** a lump of earth. NOAG1017

While this may indeed be the case, closer investigation reveals that 5 of the 12 instances of *upon* as well as 10 of the 11 instances of *but* (when used as a preposition) were produced by a single author. Apart from being topic-dependent, preposition use may therefore sometimes be a matter of personal preference rather than utility only.

5 How often do Norwegian learners of English produce a divergent preposition?

The (in)frequency with which Norwegian learners produce a divergent preposition has been previously addressed in Nacey (2013) with respect to the written mode and in Nacey and Graedler (2015) with respect to the spoken mode. The empirical evidence from both LINDSEI-NO and NICLE indicates that preposition usage does not present much of an obstacle for these L2 English learners. The rate of divergence in the 79 total texts ranges from a minimum of zero to a maximum of 15.9% of all prepositions produced, averaging less than 5% per text when considering the two combined corpora (mean = 4.0, median = 3.2, sd = 3.5). Therefore, most preposition use constitutes contextually standard choices. This type of evidence raises doubt with respect to the prevailing view of prepositions posing a formidable challenge for L2 learners, and serves to highlight the necessity for additional empirical investigation of preposition use among learners with differing L1s and/or differing proficiency levels.

One question related to that of the divergence rate in L2 learner English is whether there is any difference between divergent preposition use in the spoken and written modes. A higher divergence rate in the spoken mode might have been expected because of the online nature of oral production where there is little chance of editing – even of those divergent prepositions resulting from inadvertent mistakes (rather than errors indicative of a gap in knowledge). In addition, the number of registered divergent prepositions in the spoken material is somewhat inflated by having included all uttered prepositions in the analysis, even in cases where the speaker initially uttered a divergent preposition and then corrected him/herself (a rare occurrence). Writers, by contrast, stand a better chance at weeding out divergent prepositions during an editing process, except when that divergent choice resulted from not knowing what the standard preposition might be. This cross-mode comparison is illustrated in the boxplots in Figure 3, showing the overall divergence frequency per text, in the spoken and written modes respectively.

Here we note that there is more overall variation in the divergence rate in the written texts, indicated by the bigger box size and longer upper whisker. This difference in variation is significant, as shown by an F test (N_s = 50, N_w = 29, F = 0.337, $p < 0.001$). The maximum value for the spoken data is 10.6% while that for the written material is 15.9%. The minimum value for both corpora is zero: 8 of the 29 NICLE texts have no divergent prepositions at all, while only 2 of the LINDSEI-NO texts have none. A Fisher's Exact test reports this difference as significant ($p < 0.01$, odds ratio ≈ 8.87, 95% CI [1.59, 92.7]); Cramér's $V ≈ 0.34$, indicating a medium effect sized. However, the difference in text length between the two text types probably accounts for this apparent difference. The median values for each mode, indicated by the bold horizontal lines within each box, are 3.2% for the spoken texts and 2.6% for the written texts (LINDSEI-NO sd = 3.2, NICLE sd = 4.7). A Wilcoxon rank sum test indicates that this difference is not statistically significant ($N = 79$, $W = 754$, $p \approx 0.77$) – that is, the data analyzed for the present study shows no significant difference in divergence frequency between the spoken and written modes. This result is in concordance with the findings in Nacey and Graedler (2015), even though that earlier study had not considered inter-learner variation within the two corpora.

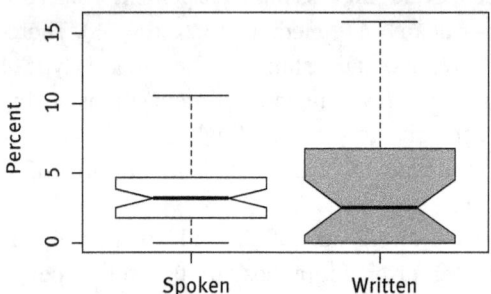

Figure 3. Divergence frequency per mode

6 Overall metaphor frequency

In the material analyzed for the present study, the average overall metaphor frequency of prepositions in the texts is slightly more than 70% (mean = 70.4, median = 71.9, sd = 12.7); see Figure 4, where the median is indicated by a vertical dashed line. There are far more metaphorical prepositions than non-metaphorical ones in the data, the difference in the numbers of observed occurrences of metaphorical and non-metaphorical prepositions per text being highly significant (W = 5426.5, $p < 0.001$). Prepositions are without a doubt the most metaphorical word class.

This particular observation, in and of itself, is not new. The developers of MIPVU, who systematically analyzed roughly 50,000 words of text in four separate registers from the BNC Baby for metaphorical status, were among the first to provide empirical support for this contention. They report metaphorical preposition frequencies of 42.5% for academic texts, 38% for news, 33.4% for fiction and 33.8% for conversation – more than for any other word class. These frequencies were calculated without taking *of* and *for* into consideration due to difficulties in ascertaining the basic senses of these prepositions, even though these two words account for about 1/3 of all preposition occurrences (Steen et al. 2010: 201–208). Nacey too reports that no other word class comes close to matching the tendency of prepositions towards metaphoricity, in either NICLE or in the English L1 learner texts also investigated (Nacey 2013: 144–148).

Yet although prepositions are the most metaphorical word class, not all prepositions are equally metaphorical – something that has not been empirically shown before, as far as we know. Any sort of aggregate figure masks the fact that not all prepositions contribute equally to the overall degree of metaphoricity. This fact is neatly illustrated in Figure 5, which shows the metaphor frequency of all 53 prepositions in the spoken and written corpora analyzed for the present study. Some prepositions have a greater tendency towards metaphoricity – including several that were *only* used metaphorically; others were never used metaphorically.

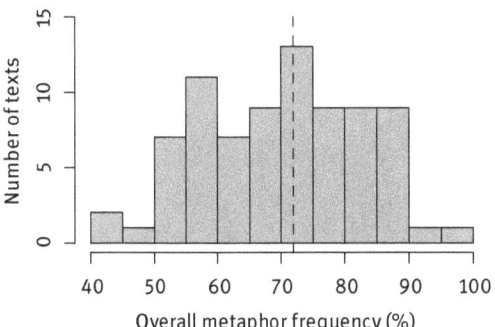

Figure 4. Overall metaphor frequency

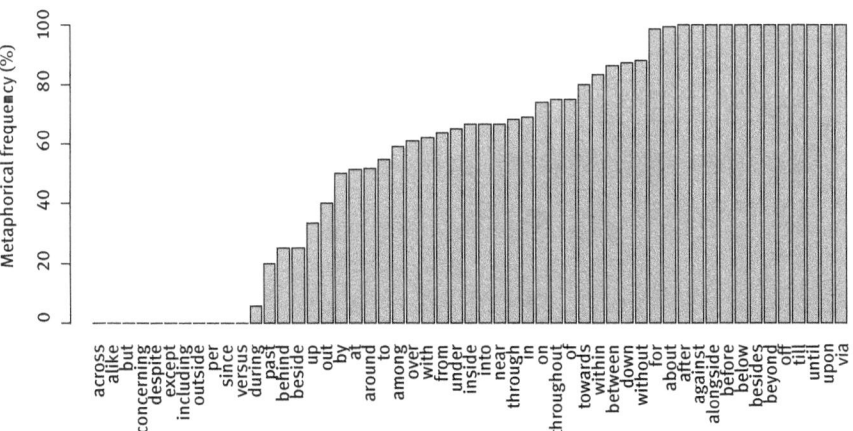

Figure 5. Metaphoricity per preposition

Figure 5 may be somewhat deceptive, however, as there are very few occurrences of some of the 53 prepositions listed along the horizontal axis; as previously noted, one word – "alike" – is not even a standard preposition, although it is used as such in NICLE. We nevertheless see the same type of pattern among the prepositions listed in Figure 6, which includes only those prepositions that occur fifteen times or more in the combined corpora. Note that *during* is one of the few prepositions whose basic sense lies in the domain of time rather than space, and as a result is rarely metaphorically used. The one exception in the present material occurs (9) in from LINDSEI-NO.

(9) the words lost . *during* translation (em) . NO030

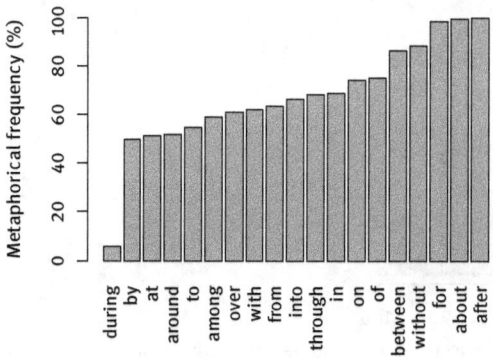

Figure 6. Metaphoricity per preposition (≥ 15 occurrences)

7 Is there a significant difference between metaphorical use of prepositions across the spoken and written modes in Norwegian L2 learner English?

Figure 7 presents the metaphor frequency for texts in the spoken and written mode, respectively. The difference between the two modes is clearly statistically significant (W = 130, $p < 0.0001$) and quite substantial (Cohen's $d \approx 2.1$, as calculated on the difference in medians), with there being far more metaphor in the written texts (median 83.3%) than in the spoken texts (median 63.8%).

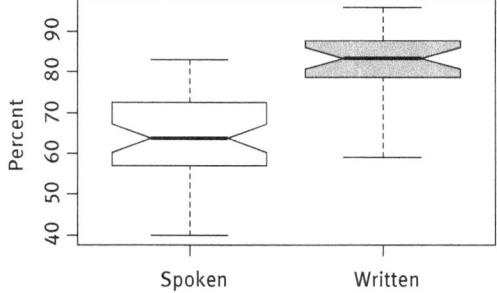

Figure 7. Metaphor frequency by mode

This difference between the two modes may be attributed to topic. The vast majority of LINDSEI-NO interviews contain a good deal of discussion about topics that naturally trigger use of non-metaphorical prepositions. One typical such example is presented in (10), where the preposition *to* is employed in its basic spatial sense, rather than any metaphorical extension.

(10) I went to Italy when I was (eh) seventeen NO033

Steen et al. (2010: 201–208) also found that conversation was, in general, the least metaphorical of the registers they investigated. Such findings indicate that a lesser degree of metaphorical language may be a distinguishing characteristic of many informal conversations, perhaps because we often discuss very "concrete" subjects.

8 Is there a correlation between divergent use and metaphorical use?

The scatter plot in Figure 8 shows the correlation between metaphoricity and divergence for all prepositions per text. Each dot represents the scores of two variables – the rate of metaphoricity and the rate of divergence – for one text. The 29 triangles represent the scores in the NICLE (written) texts, while the 50 dots represent the scores in the LINDSEI-NO (spoken) texts. A Spearman's test of correlation does not indicate any relationship between metaphoricity and divergence on the text level ($N = 79$, $r_s = -0.06$, 95% CI [−0.28, 0.16], $p \approx 0.58$). The only discernible pattern is a clustering of NICLE prepositions as metaphoricity increases – that is, the NICLE prepositions are generally more metaphorical in use, as was established in section 7.

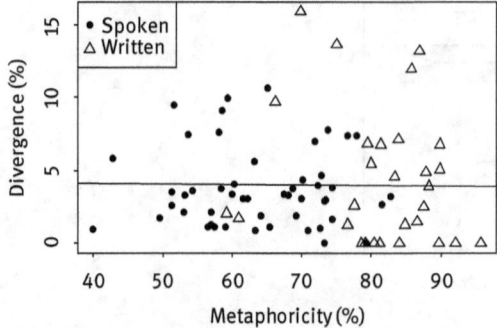

Figure 8. Text correlation: Metaphoricity and divergence

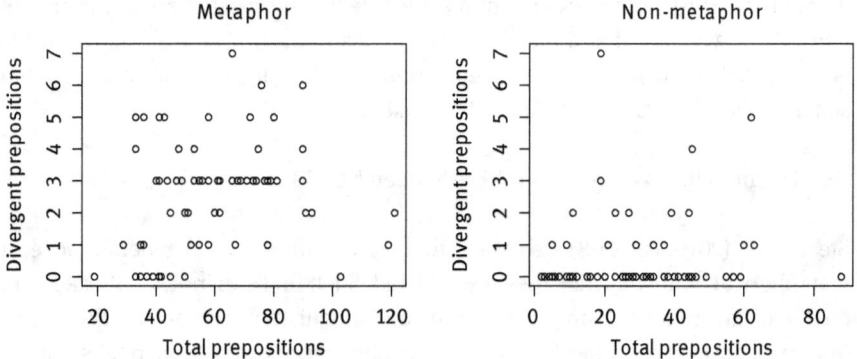

Figure 9. Divergent prepositions by Total prepositions (observed occurrences)

A further means of investigating the relation between metaphor and divergence, if any, is to compare the number of observed occurrences of divergent metaphorical and non-metaphorical prepositions per text, to determine whether either the former or the latter are produced more frequently. One potential problem with such a comparison, however, lies in the "zero" observations, i.e. with those texts where the number of divergent prepositions – metaphorical and/or non-metaphorical – is zero. Figure 9 shows the number of observed occurrences of divergent prepositions in relation to the total numbers of prepositions produced per text, for all metaphorically-used prepositions (left panel) and non-metaphorical prepositions (right panel). All texts contain instances of both metaphorical and non-metaphorical prepositions: the numbers of metaphorical prepositions range from 19 to 121 per text (mean = 58.6, median = 44, sd = 20.5), while the numbers of non-metaphorical prepositions range from 2 to 88 per text (mean = 27.9, median = 26, sd = 18.5). But Figure 9 shows that divergent prepositions begin to be more common in cases where learners have produced roughly 40 or more prepositions, at least when it comes to these Norwegian learners at the B2/C1 proficiency levels. The production of zero divergent prepositions may therefore possibly be due to a low overall production of prepositions, rather than to any other factor.

The preponderance of zero observations of divergent non-metaphorical prepositions, indicated in the right panel, results from there being far fewer non-metaphorical prepositions overall; as discussed in section 6, prepositions are a highly metaphorical word class, such that there are far more observations of metaphorical prepositions than there are of non-metaphorical prepositions. The fewer instances of a particular item learners produce, the less chance they have of producing unconventional language. In short, many of the texts analyzed for the present study were simply too short to contain a sufficient number of prepositions that would make for a reliable comparison of metaphorical and non-metaphorical divergent prepositions. This is particularly true for the non-metaphorical prepositions, which are less frequently produced, even in spoken texts where the topic of conversation more often triggered reference to concrete places (co-occurring with prepositions used non-metaphorically). Note, however, that all texts contained instances of both metaphorical and non-metaphorical prepositions.

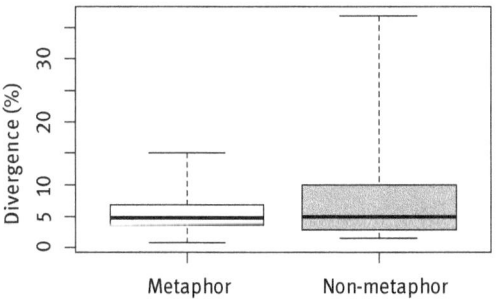

Figure 10. Observation correlation: Metaphor and divergence

The boxplots in Figure 10 present a comparison of the observed frequencies of those prepositions that are metaphorical and divergent with those that are non-metaphorical and divergent, per text, but excluding all texts with no divergent prepositions. While a total of 10 texts (8 in NICLE and 2 in LINDSEI-NO) have no divergent prepositions at all (as stated in section 5), 12 of the 79 total texts analyzed for this study contained no divergent *metaphorical* prepositions; 59 of the 79 total texts contained no divergent *non-metaphorical* prepositions. Hence, the boxplot on the left in Figure 10 illustrates data from 67 texts while that on the right illustrates data from 20 texts – that is, here we see only those cases where learners actually *did* produce a divergent preposition. Clearly, it is far from ideal to discard so many texts from a comparison; any corresponding future study should preferably include much longer texts per informant to increase validity. Given this weakness, however, Figure 10 shows that without the zero observations, the median figures for both the combined spoken and written data become almost identical, with medians 4.8% divergence for metaphor and 4.9% for non-metaphor. A Wilcoxon rank sum test does not indicate a difference between the two ($N = (67, 20)$, $W = 592$, difference in location ≈ -0.0075, 95% CI [−0.033, 0.011], $p \approx 0.44$).[11] The overall conclusion, therefore, is that there would seem to be no correlation between preposition divergence and metaphor, no matter how one looks at the data – whether by text correlation (Figure 9) or by observation correlation (Figure 10).

9 Conclusion

This study has contributed to two distinct, albeit related, areas: metaphor and L2 learner language. With regard to the field of metaphor in and of itself, the unique contribution of the present study has been the graphic illustration of the variability of metaphoricity among prepositions – that is, while prepositions as a word class are highly metaphorical in general, some prepositions tend to be more (or less) metaphorical than others (section 6). As far as we know, this is the first study to present this type of data, adding to the empirical, corpus-based knowledge concerning the interaction between metaphor and word classes.

With respect to preposition divergence in L2 learner language, it should first be noted that there are relatively few divergent metaphors overall in the two corpora. The vast majority of prepositions chosen by these learners, in both spoken and written production, adhere to the standardized norms of English codified in dictionaries. In other words, prepositions may not be as tricky to acquire as is traditionally thought. Further, this study has not been able to show any difference in preposition divergence between spoken and written texts (section 5), despite the nature of online processing in oral language, where one is more prone to mistakes.

---

[11] Note that 17 texts appear in both samples, such that the observations are not completely independent.

When it comes to metaphorical use of prepositions in L2 learner language, this study has shown that there are more metaphorical prepositions in the written data investigated, which may be attributed to topic (section 7). Metaphorical use is necessarily context-dependent, and conversations about concrete topics trigger non-metaphorical language. Finally, this study has failed to support the hypothesis of a possible link between divergent prepositions and metaphoricity, indicating that there seems to be no link between them; analysis of longer texts is called for, however, to produce more conclusive evidence (section 8). Nevertheless, it strongly appears that the search for motivating factors for the production of divergent metaphors (in addition to the factor of negative L1 transfer) must look elsewhere than metaphor.

References

Becker, Joseph D. 1975. The phrasal lexicon. In Bonnie L. Nash-Webber & Roger C. Schank (eds.), *Theoretical issues in natural language processing*, 60–63. Cambridge, MA: Bolt, Beranek and Newman.

Gilquin, Gaetanelle, Sylvie D. Cock & Sylviane Granger (eds.). 2010. *LINDSEI: Louvain international database of spoken English interlanguage*. Louvain-la-Neuve, Belgium: Presses universitaires de Louvain.

Gilquin, Gaetanelle & Sylviane Granger. 2011. From EFL to ESL: Evidence from the International Corpus of Learner English. In Joybrato Mukherjee & Marianne Hundt (eds.), *Exploring second-language varieties of English and learner Englishes: Bridging a paradigm gap*, 55–78. Amsterdam: John Benjamins.

Lindstromberg, Seth. 2010. *English prepositions explained*. Amsterdam: John Benjamins.

Littlemore, Jeannette & Graham Low. 2006. *Figurative thinking and foreign language learning*. Basingstoke: Palgrave Macmillan.

Low, Graham. 1988. On teaching metaphor. *Applied Linguistics* 9(2). 125–147.

Lysvåg, Per & Stig Johansson. 1995. *Going for grammar*. Oslo: Aschehoug.

Nacey, Susan. 2013. *Metaphors in learner English*. Amsterdam: John Benjamins.

Nacey, Susan & Anne-Line Graedler. 2015. Preposition use in oral and written learner language. *Bergen Language and Linguistics Studies* 6. 45–62.

Nattinger, James R. & Jeannette DeCarrico. 1992. *Lexical phrases and language teaching*. Oxford: Oxford University Press.

Parrott, Martin. 2010. *Grammar for English language teachers*. Cambridge: Cambridge University Press.

Quirk, Randolph, Sidney Greenbaum, Geoffrey Leech & Jan Svartvik. 1985. *A comprehensive grammar of the English language*. London: Longman.

R Foundation for Statistical Computing. 2010. *R: A language and environment for statistical computing*. http://www.r-project.org/

Rindal, Ulrikke. 2010. Constructing identity with L2: Pronunciation and attitudes among Norwegian learners of English. *Journal of Sociolinguistics* 14(2). 240–261.

Scott, Mike. 2013. *WordSmith Tools*. Liverpool: Lexical Analysis Software.
Sinclair, John. 1991. *Corpus, concordance, collocation*. Oxford: Oxford University Press.
Steen, Gerard J. (2007). *Finding metaphor in grammar and usage*. Amsterdam: John Benjamins.
Steen, Gerard J., Aletta G. Dorst, Berenike J. Herrmann, Anna A. Kaal, Tina Krennmayr & Trijntje Pasma. 2010. *A method for linguistic metaphor identification: From MIP to MIPVU*. Amsterdam: John Benjamins.
Taylor, John R. 1988. Contrasting prepositional categories: English and Italian. In Brygida Rudzka-Ostyn (ed.), *Topics in cognitive linguistics*, 299–326. Amsterdam: John Benjamins.
Tyler, Andrea & Vyvyan Evans. 2003. *The semantics of English prepositions: Spatial scenes, embodied meaning and cognition*. Cambridge: Cambridge University Press.

John C. Wade
Metaphor and the shaping of educational thinking

Education is not the filling of a pail, but the lighting of a fire.
(W. B. Yeats 1865–1939)

1 Introduction

It is the purpose of this paper to illustrate a small part of a wider ongoing study into educational discourse, examining, in particular, how the focus has moved from generally applicable principles of educational practice towards a greater attention paid to the needs of the individual. The first section of the paper examines some aspects of how metaphor is used, from the more overt, creative metaphor through to the conceptual metaphor which some argue underpins our thinking and the way in which we view the world around us. In the second section the analysis moves on to the specific field of education and the possible influence of metaphor on educational thinking, both from the perspective of educational policy, in theory and practice, and from the perspective of central role-players, i.e. teachers and, in particular, learners.

2 Metaphor in context

> Metaphor as central to the task of accounting for our perspectives on the world: how we think about things, make sense of reality, and set problems we later try to solve. In this second sense "metaphor" refers both to a certain kind of product – a perspective or frame, a way of looking at things – and to a certain kind of process by which new perspectives on the world come into existence (Schön 1979: 254, cited in Block 1999: 135).

Cameron and Low (1999: 78) argue that there is a need to examine metaphor from different perspectives which include the analysis of the surface structure of metaphorical expressions and a deeper level analysis of how language is more widely imbued with metaphorical reference at a cognitive level. In this section we shall attempt to trace a path from the former through to the latter.

John C. Wade, University of Cagliari

From a literary point of view metaphor can be seen as a form of "enhanced content", as Humboldt (1836/1999: 87) defines an aspect of language which is more or less overt with the aim of creating a marked poetic effect. This is reflected, for instance, in the Elizabethan and Metaphysical concept of "conceit" in the poetry of the time, that is to say a figurative use of language "which depended on wit or ingenuity of idea for its effect" (Wales 1989: 86). Metaphor is collocated within this range of figurative language uses which we might see as "enhancing" the content of the message. From a structural point of view, a metaphor is conventionally accepted as consisting of three elements: *tenor* (the underlying theme), *vehicle* (analogy) and *ground* (the characteristics that the former have in common). The metaphor, however, extends beyond a mere analogy between *tenor* and *vehicle*. It is a way of saying that one thing is not only similar, but the same as another (Low 1988: 126), unlike the simile, which is a comparison between two distinct elements:

(1) She smokes like a chimney.

Here, we are not stating that she *is* a chimney, but that she shares only some of the same "smoky" characteristics as the chimney. Metaphor, on the other hand, is considered as uniting, rather than simply comparing, two distinct and, apparently, incompatible elements in such a way that they represent a single concept (Cameron and Low 1999: 77). This is illustrated by the literary examples below, in which the emotion LOVE (abstract – tenor) is represented as a source of heat or FIRE (concrete – vehicle), i.e. LOVE IS FIRE:

(2) Are you so *hot*? marry, come up, I trow (William Shakespeare *Romeo and Juliet* Act II-Scene IV, 1596)

(3) But when an even *flame* two hearts did touch (John Donne *Loves Deitie*, 1669)

(4) The *flame* she felt, and ill could she conceal (Samuel Taylor Coleridge *Julia*, 1789)

(5) Time to drown our *lit fire* (Nick Cave *Wings off flies*, 1983)

In these cases LOVE possesses all of the characteristics of FIRE: heat, flame, burning, igniting. This metaphor is, in fact, extremely common (the examples above range from the sixteenth through to the twentieth century) and easily recognised, to the extent that it might be considered almost banal if it were not for an adroit and original use of language which represents a marked extension or linguistic embellishment of the basic concept, an extension which is aimed at capturing the attention of the reader in a "poetic context", that is to say that the strategy of the writer is to have an effect or to influence the reader emotively.

Schön (see the opening quote above) views metaphor from a different perspective which extends beyond a merely rhetorical artifice. Instead metaphor is likened to a tool employed in identifying the salient characteristics of a given phenomenon. In particular the active use of metaphor is examined in his case studies of what could be defined as 'creative professional contexts', which include architecture, art and sport among others. In these contexts there is a marked use of abstract concepts which can only be expressed linguistically through metaphor, since they are more *sensations* or *intuitions* rather than concrete, tangible $A^1 = A^2$ constructs, as in dictionary entries: FIRE = "the hot, bright flames produced by things that are burning" (*Collins Cobuild English Dictionary*, 1995). In practical terms, a sensation or novel concept A is explained in terms of B, i.e. A = B (Pinker 2008: 262). The metaphorical tool may be used in describing, for example, how an architect explains spatial relationships or the brush technique of an artist (cf. Schön 1983: 96, 184):

(6)   a general pass-through

(7)   a paintbrush is a kind of pump

Example 6 refers to a project for an open-plan classroom, in which the concepts of "space", "accessibility" and "free movement" underlie the fundamental principles of the plan, while Example 7 describes how different effects can be created by increasing or decreasing the pressure on the bristles of the paintbrush in order to regulate the flow of paint. This unconventional use of metaphor arises from the need to describe or explain aspects of professional practice which may be in part ascribed to an innate talent and, perhaps to a greater extent, perfected through practice or experience. These skills are difficult to define in a quantifiable or "scientific" approach and the use of metaphor serves to fill this gap. Its function is to explain what is unfamiliar and difficult to codify in conventional terms. Schön (1983: 184) defines this type of metaphor as "generative". The generative metaphor is characterised by a process which may start from the general idea that similarities exist between two given elements and which then moves on to identifying what the relationships might be between these elements. This process provides a new perspective on the problem under examination, which in turn "generates" new solutions. While the poetic metaphor may be based on well-established concepts and relies on a clever use of language to bring it alive, the generative metaphor allows the exploration of new ground.

So far we have dealt only with metaphors which could be defined as "active" or "conscious". The addresser has a specific aim, here we have examined poetic and professional domains, in influencing the addressee's reaction (emotive) or in solving a particular problem (directed). A further perspective views metaphor as underlying the way in which we think and act (Lakoff and Johnson 1980: 3). The conceptual metaphor permeates the language we use every day, firmly collocated in the context of culture and experience. It starts from a deep level and is expressed at a surface level by extension. At a deep level we might hypothesise the following metaphor (Lakoff and Johnson 1980: 47):

(8) IDEAS ARE PRODUCTS

At a surface level the base-metaphor is elaborated into its linguistic manifestation:

(9) We've *generated* a lot of ideas this week.

(10) He *produces* ideas at an astounding rate.

(11) His *intellectual productivity* has decreased over the years.

(12) It's a rough idea; it needs to be *refined*.

While this perspective has stimulated great interest in the last few decades, certain limitations to the approach have been identified (Cameron and Low 1999: 88), for example, the tendency to use a limited selection of samples based on intuitive introspection, and more work needs to be carried out in this field.

Before moving on to metaphor use in the field of education, some basic principles which come out of this brief overview are outlined below:
- Metaphor may be used consciously or subconsciously
- Metaphor may be manipulated in order to influence the reaction of the addressee
- Metaphor may be a useful tool in problem-framing and problem-solving
- Metaphor underlies our thinking at a deep level

3 Education: From product to process

He has to *see* on his own behalf and in his own way the relations between means and methods employed and results achieved. Nobody else can see for him, and he can't see just by being "told", although the right kind of telling may guide his seeing and thus help him see what he needs to see (Dewey 1974: 151, cited in Schön 1987: 17).

Etymologically the word "education" derives from the Latin verb *educere* (*The New Shorter Oxford English Dictionary*, 1993) meaning "draw out" or "lead out" ("e" (out) and "ducere" (lead). This concept is close to the thinking of the philosopher Socrates (469–399 BC) who envisaged an educational approach based on stimulating inner reflection and intellectual self-realisation, metaphorically "drawing out what is within" or, in W. B. Yeats' words, "the lighting of a fire".

From a historical point of view, education has passed through different phases which are at times contradictory, swinging from Socratic inner reflection (internal/thinking) to the acquisition of knowledge (external/provision). The metaphorical foundations for these approaches may be expressed as follows:

(13) EDUCATION IS A CATALYST

(14) EDUCATION IS THE FILLING OF AN EMPTY VESSEL

For example, in medieval times the focus was on acquiring knowledge and, not necessarily, the practical applications of that knowledge, in Victorian Britain it was on moulding the individual into an upright, morally irreprehensible citizen, in post-modern society the realisation and inner growth of the individual. All of these approaches have their implications in the implementation of educational policy underpinned by a metaphorical perception (Examples 8 and 9) of what the educational process should be.

Carr (1995: 94) also reflects on the historical implications of educational thinking on a metaphorical plane, illustrated in Table 1 below.

Table 1. (Adapted from Carr 1995)

Empirical analytic	Historical hermeneutic	Critical
Neo-classical	Liberal progressive	Socially critical
MOULDING	GROWTH	EMPOWERMENT
Reaching pre-set objectives	Interpretative	Self-realisation

The neo-classical approach is based on the assumption that our knowledge of the world is quantifiable, it can be classified and categorised and successively transmitted to those who do not possess that knowledge. This knowledge represents an absolute truth which the learner is constrained to accept and success is judged on the basis of the ability to acquire a set of fixed principles, regardless of his or her innate propensities. It is a markedly product-oriented approach.

With the liberal-progressive philosophy of education the focus moves more towards the intellectual development of the individual and in which knowledge acquired in the learning process is employed in bringing about an understanding of the workings of the world in which we live and viewing this understanding from different perspectives.

Finally, the social critical perspective sees the individual as central to the educational process. It is directed towards fostering reflection on the world around us and the learner acquires the capacity to analyse problems critically in order to bring about change. The approach is based on an ongoing dialogue which may not have a specific goal since it is more a form of exploration leading to the discovery of new perspectives which in turn feed into further exploration and reflection. It is a process-oriented approach.

If we examine education policy at a governmental level, we discover that there is often no clear-cut boundary among these three perspectives in that they move along a kind of continuum which sways between traditional and innovative. At its highest level the semantics of ministerial denominations can be quite revealing with regard to the philosophy underpinning institutional perspectives on education. In England and Wales, for example, the 1944 Education Act instituted the "Ministry of Education", which has since undergone a series of reforms leading to its present denomination "Department for Education". It is interesting to note the change of preposition from "of" to "for", since this transformation has a certain significance from a semantic point of view. In the former case the preposition means "responsible for" expressing the idea of AUTHORITY (highly structured focusing on universal fixed goals), while in the latter it moves more towards promoting or FOSTERING (flexible focusing on the individual's learning needs) education. Of course, the name does not necessarily reflect the practical applications of educational policies, as we shall see later in this paper.

If our aim, then, is FOSTERING education, i.e. establishing a process, it is clearly also necessary to identify what our objectives are. In formal education objectives are usually set out in curricula, an overarching philosophical perspective, and syllabi, which lay out the specific content of an educational programme. For Dewey (see the quote at the beginning of this section) a key element is that of "bringing about understanding". This process cannot be brought about simply by "telling" or "explaining", but the learner needs to be guided towards "seeing" or internal realisation. Therefore, the underlying metaphor in Example 10 might be hypothesised as:

(13) UNDERSTANDING IS SEEING

If this is the case, we need to ask how the SEEING process comes about. In Locke's *An Essay Concerning Human Understanding* (1690, cited in Wade 2006: 11) understanding is likened to a light penetrating into a dark and untidy room. In fact, we observe the stark contrast between LIGHT and DARKNESS:

(14) UNDERSTANDING IS LIGHT

(15) DARKNESS IS IGNORANCE

Federici and Wade (2007) carried out a corpus-based study of educational texts into how this might be interpreted on different levels ranging from external to internal. The findings reveal that LIGHT may be a form of "heightened visibility" (ibid.: 15):

(16) [...] casts LIGHT on dark childhoods [...]

(17) [...] seen in this LIGHT [...]

(18) [...] considers him in a new LIGHT [...]

(19) [...] viewed in a whole different LIGHT [...]

In these examples, all commonly used set expressions which have lost their innovative metaphorical force, the underlying meaning is that of providing a new perspective or focusing on a given problem. A second aspect is that of inspiring or influencing:

(20) [...] can be our guiding LIGHT [...]

Here the LIGHT represents a model or a "guide" in the sense intended by Dewey above. Finally, LIGHT might also represent a form of "revelation" or internally activated realisation:

(21) [...] good teachers LIGHT candles in dark places [...]

Underlying the concept of LIGHT, therefore, we might hypothesise that they are encapsulated in the metaphor:

(22) UNDERSTANDING IS ILLUMINATION

It is not sufficient, however, to conceive of education in terms of the rather vague and abstract goal of achieving enlightenment. Bassey (1999), for example, observes that education consists firstly of "the experience and nurture of personal and social development" and secondly "acquisition, development, transmission, conservation, discovery and renewal" (Bassey 1999: 38).

The question is raised as to whether is possible to establish goals at all in a perspective which encompasses the way in which we live, our view(s) of the world and the culture on which our thinking and our very existence is founded. In reality, educational objectives are largely based on prescriptive institutional principles to be found, for example, in the National Curriculum of England and Wales, introduced by the Education Reform Act in 1988. In principle, the learner starts from the status of *tabula rasa*, in terms of what the institutions have established in the curriculum, and follows a path towards the reaching of pre-established goals, which in the National Curriculum are divided into a series of steps or Key stages from five to sixteen years of age. In a metaphorical sense this path represents a JOURNEY from A to B with a number of Key stage interludes along the way. That is to say that it is perceived as a horizontal movement from DEPARTURE to DESTINATION. In a corpus-based study of academic papers[1] Wade (2013) examines the ways in which the learning JOURNEY may be defined. It appears that there is a marked divergence between theory and practice and that the A to B path is a gross oversimplification of what the educational process represents with respect to the whole learner as an individual with his or her own inclinations and talents (Wade 2006: 45). The data collected in the corpus study is illustrated in Table 2 below (adapted from Wade 2013: 120):

---

[1] The data was acquired from 101 academic papers, available online at the University of Leeds *British Education Index* (approximately 600,000 words of text), dealing with a wide range of educational issues. The corpus was analysed using the KWIC concordancer.

Table 2. Corpus data

Keyword (High↓Low frequency)	Context
way	offer a way forward
course	vocational course
pathway	learning pathways
path	go down a path
track	stay on track
route	work-based route
road	on the road to
journey	reflective journey
lane	a special lane
highway	rough highway

It is immediately apparent that these examples are deeply embedded in everyday language use. While the metaphorical meaning may be identified in forward movement, in the most frequently used examples they have lost their prototypical metaphorical force. Both *way* and *course* are used in expressing the idea of "purpose" or "means" and "flow of time" respectively:

(23) find ways to

(24) during the course of

In a strictly educational context *course* refers above all to a pre-established programme of studies based on a syllabus which outlines the content.

Related to this, the idea of a planned itinerary with specific goals is reflected in the terms *track, route* and *lane*. They are often associated with planning for the solution of problems arising outside the set objectives of an educational programme:

(25) fast-track

(26) alternative routes to

In this way the educational process might be envisaged as having a central or core itinerary which can be reinforced with alternative options which serve the needs of the learner in specific contexts.

While the above itineraries are implemented within strict boundaries, i.e. movement towards a goal, the terms *path, road* and *highway* refer more to aspects of EXPERIENCE in the learning process. This process might be perceived either as a smooth transferral from DEPARTURE to DESTINATION or an itinerary which is conditioned by problems and impediments:

(27) winding path

(28) take a wrong turn in the road

(29) to be at a professional crossroads

Thus, the itinerary may be tortuous and complex (Example 24), erroneous judgements need to be taken into account (Example 25) and decisions need to be made (Example 26).

The term *journey* offers further connotations. It is not merely a pre-destined route, but a journey of EXPLORATION and DISCOVERY:

(30) learning journey

Of particular interest is the term *pathways*. It has become common is speaking about the modular organisation of courses, especially at university level. It is generally used in its plural form and opens the way for learners to choose what to study according to their personal inclinations and interests. It is a concept central to modern thinking about curriculum design. As Hamilton (1990: 41) asserts: "The introduction of curriculum options (or electives) has recast the notion of a curriculum, not as a course but as a branching tree. By selecting options, each student takes a different learning route".

This perspective fits in with current European Union educational policy in a much wider context which goes beyond formal schooling and sees education as a lifelong process within a complex and changing society. This process not only includes compulsory and higher education, but also professional development (cf. Eraut 1994: 10–12, 25) and post-retirement opportunities.

There are, however, dangers with viewing education as a JOURNEY, whatever form it takes, whether it be directly from A to B or whether it be with multiple options. There is the risk that it becomes a fragmented itinerary or a series of sporadic episodes in the learning experience. And here the focus must move towards the main players in the educational process: teachers and learners.

The teacher's role in the education process is complex since he or she has a number of responsibilities which might be summarised as follows: "[...] the teacher gives space to students, is able to manage interpersonal relationships, has a good knowledge of his (sic) subject, understands his students' needs and is capable of managing the classroom in such a way that the learning process is facilitated" (Wade 2000: 345). This is generally reflected in the way teachers are trained and in the way the multi-faceted role of the teacher is defined in current educational thinking (Corpus data – high to low frequency):

(31) in *supporting* trainee teachers

(32) emphasises facilitation, *mentoring* and tutoring

(33) not only being his *tutor*, but also his mentor

(34) Special Needs *Co-ordinator*

(35) to *guide* young learners through a series of stepping stones

(36) including the roles of *facilitator*, manager, explicit teacher, coach and councellor

(37) teachers act as *mediators* between the academic world of teacher education and the local context

(38) undertake different functions: *moderator*, facilitator, supervisor

Thus, in training at least, a teacher is seen as a GUIDE and ORGANISER.

At an institutional level, however, the role is very different and often comes into conflict with the theoretical principles of teacher training. In England and Wales the introduction of the National Curriculum brought about significant changes in the role of the teacher within the school system. Increased "bureaucratization" (Trowler 2003: 158) and teaching to inflexible, institutionally imposed goals in the Key stage system have lead to a "loss of control over the work process" (ibid.). In addition, this has led to the fragmentation of the system into a series of steps where the teacher's role is more that of manager or ORGANISER rather than guide.

To be taken into consideration is also the deeply-rooted influence of well-established traditions, for example in Italy (my own personal experience), where teaching from secondary school to university and beyond is still largely based on the *lectio magistralis* or formal lecture format. Here the role of the teacher is that of SOURCE OF KNOWLEDGE and the learner's role is largely passive, i.e. the EMPTY VESSEL metaphor.

This runs contrary to modern theories of the learning process centred on the student rather than the system. This idea may be exemplified in the thinking of Kolb (1984: 1) who claims that:

> Human beings are unique among all living organisms in that their primary adaptive specialisation lies not in some particular form or skill or fit in an ecological niche, but rather in identification with the process of adaptation itself – in the process of learning. We are thus the learning species, and our survival depends on our ability to adapt not only in the reactive sense of fitting into the psychological and social worlds, but in the proactive sense of creating and shaping those worlds.

In this perspective the learner is an active participant in the educational process and within this framework needs to be guided towards an independent and critical view of the world which not only takes into consideration established values, but also provides the intellectual tools for bringing about change. This radically changes our view on the educational process, which rather than a linear series of episodes, becomes a cyclical process which serves to "enable students to become controllers rather than victims of their learning experiences" (Zimmerman 1998: 1). In this model three essential elements are identified: the ability to plan, the ability to make informed decisions and the ability to analyse the outcome of that action in order to feed into a new cycle. As Kenny (1993: 436) asserts: "[...] the real goal of education, is to unlock the inner self, permitting the generation of knowledge [...]". Therefore, education is seen as "generating knowledge" rather than "providing knowledge". Taking the different metaphorical perspectives on education discussed up to now we can attempt to build an overall model which places the learner at the centre of the process EDUCATION AS CYCLE illustrated in Figure 1.

In the context of lifelong learning the learner integrates each new experience with his or her understanding and interpretation of the world. The metaphors underlying this perspective can be found in the works of Dewy (1938) and Kolb (1984) where the process is activated through EXPERIENCE, and Schön (1983, 1987) where the JOURNEY is carried through by ACTION and reflection bringing about UNDERSTANDING.

It would appear from the brief overview in this section that educational theory, from one perspective or another, is constructed from a combination of metaphorical ideas, which range from a top-down position (AUTHORITY – product-oriented) to a bottom-up approach (SELF-REALISATION – process-oriented). These combinations change according to the particular position taken, which may be more or less biased towards either process or product within a multi-layered framework rather than a single underlying concept of education.

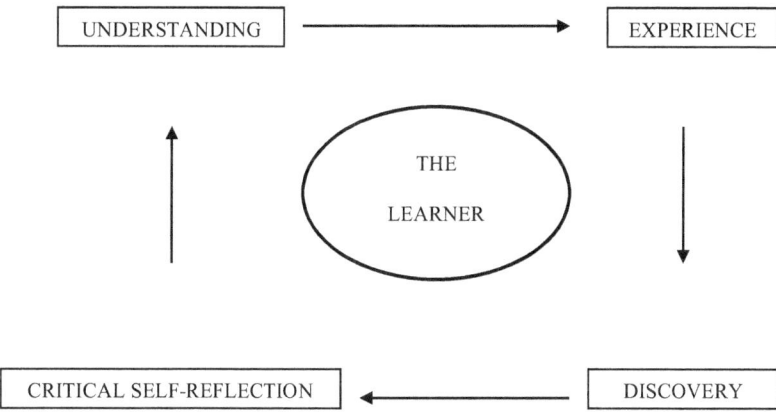

Figure 1. A model for the cyclical educational process

4 Conclusion

In the first section of this paper four general aspects of metaphor were identified. In the corpus data analysed here, the metaphors used are largely conventional and commonly found in the literature regarding education in general. In this sense they might be considered as underlying our thinking about education and used in a largely subconscious way, coming to the surface only when extended, as in talking about "*rough* highways" or "*winding* paths", for example. More creative metaphors are rare in the corpus data examined, but this aspect could be misleading in that the range of data is restricted due to the relatively small size of the corpus examined. This would be an interesting area of study itself with a larger corpus base and focusing on the "linguistic embellishment" of conventional metaphors or the use of metaphor as a tool in understanding the world around us.

In this study most of the samples are based on nouns and it would be interesting in further studies to look, for instance, at how prepositions, adjectives and verbs are used in metaphorical expressions, e.g. "to" for horizontal movement towards a destination, "up" and "down" where a "journey" might be more or less difficult or with different verbs of movement, such as "walk", "tread", "run" and so forth, which describe how the journey is undertaken.

References

Bassey, Michael. 1999. *Case Study Research in Educational Settings*. Buckingham, PA: Open University Press.

Block, David. 1999. Who framed SLA research? Problem framing and metaphoric accounts of the SLA research process. In Lynne Cameron & Graham Low (eds.), *Researching and applying metaphor*, 135–148. Cambridge: Cambridge University Press.

Cameron, Lynne & Graham Low. 1999. Metaphor. *Language Teaching* 32(2). 77–96.

Carr, Wilfred. 1995. *For education: Towards critical educational inquiry*. Buckingham: Open University Press.

Dewey, John. 1938. *Experience and education*. Indianapolis: Kappa Delta Pi.

Dewey, John. 1974. *John Dewey on education: Selected writings*. Chicago: University of Chicago Press.

Eraut, Michael. 1994. *Developing professional knowledge and competence*. London: Falmer.

Federici, Stefano & John C. Wade. 2007. Letting in the light and working with the WEB: A dynamic corpus development approach to interpreting metaphor. In Matthew Davis, Paul Rayson, Susan Hunston & Pernilla Danielsson (eds.), *Proceedings Corpus Linguistics Conference 2007*, Article #207. University of Birmingham.

Hamilton, David. 1990. *Learning about education: An unfinished curriculum*. Buckingham: Open University Press.

Humboldt, Wilhelm von. 1836/1999. *On language: On the diversity of human language construction and its influence on the mental development of the human species*. Cambridge: Cambridge University Press.

Kenny, Brian. 1993. For more autonomy. *System* 21(4). 431–442.

Kolb, David A. 1984. *Experiential learning: Experience as the source of learning and development*. Englewood Cliffs, NJ: Prentice Hall.

Lakoff, George & Mark Johnson. 1980. *Metaphors we live by*. Chicago: University of Chicago Press.

Low, Graham. 1988. On teaching metaphor. *Applied Linguistics* 9(2). 125–147.

Pinker, Steven. 2008. *The Stuff of Thought: Language as a window into human nature*. London: Penguin.

Schön, Donald A. 1979. Generative metaphor: A perspective on problem-setting in social policy. In Andrew Ortony (ed.) *Metaphor and thought*, 154–283. New York: Cambridge University Press.

Schön, Donald A. 1983. *The reflective practitioner: How professionals think in action*. New York: Basic Books.

Schön, Donald A. 1987. *Educating the reflective practitioner*. San Francisco: Jossey-Bass.

Trowler, Paul. 2003. *Education policy*, 2nd edn. London: Routledge.

Wade, John C. 2000. Some considerations concerning in-service training for teachers of English as a foreign language. in *Annali della Facoltà di Scienze della Formazione dell'Università di Cagliari* 23. 345–365.

Wade, John C. 2006. The whole learner: Exploiting the language learner's potential to the full. In H. Bowles, J. Douthwaite & D.F. Virdis (eds.) *Ricerca e didattica nei Centri linguistici di Ateneo*. Cagliari: CUEC.

Wade, John C. 2006. *English for education*. Venice: Cafoscarina.

Wade, John C. 2013. Metaphor use in education: A corpus-based approach to investigating language use in a specific field of study. In Elisabetta Gola & Francesca Ervas (eds.) *Metaphor in Focus: Philosophical perspectives on metaphor use*, 113–134. Newcastle upon Tyne: Cambridge Scholars Publishing.

Wales, Katie. 1989. *A Dictionary of Stylistics*. Harlow: Longman.

Zimmerman, Barry J. 1998. Developing self-fulfilling cycles of academic regulation: An analysis of exemplary instructional models. In Dale H. Schunk & Barry J. Zimmerman (eds.), *Self-regulated learning: From teaching to self-regulated practice*, 1–19. New York: Guilford Press.

Index

abstract thinking 204
alignable differences 50, 51
ambiguity 112, 140, 174
analogy 12, 44, 51, 137, 145, 151, 153, 155, 157, 158, 160, 163, 181–183, 186, 208, 258, 306
anomalous juxtaposition 70
argument/argumentation 21, 79, 121, 174, 179, 200, 250, 271, 285, 291
artificial intelligence 2, 20, 205
association
– metaphorical 137
– hidden 140
audiovisual
– metaphors 9, 95–98, 100, 103, 105–107, 108, 109, 112, 113,
– metonymies 95, 97, 98, 100, 102, 108, 114

background 11, 16, 65, 68, 104, 105, 109, 113, 267, 284
– knowledge 140, 146
behavioural
– goals 13
– reactions/responses 98, 195
– consequences 189
– change 263
Bernstein 13, 14, 190–194
Biological/cerebral basis of mind 189, 190
blended 50, 51
blending 5, 6, 44
– conceptual 46, 50
boundary 12, 13, 80, 171–173, 186, 240
brain 189
– activation 7, 63, 67, 68, 75, 78, 79, 82
– imaging 6, 62, 64
– 'open architecture' of 189

categorization 64, 138,
character arcs 44, 49, 57
classical mechanics 174–176
climate change
– metaphors 9, 10, 119, 122, 123–125
– war 119, 121, 125, 127–130
– race 121, 125, 127–130
co-speech gestures 8, 77, 80, 82, 85, 86, 91

cognitive model 7, 11, 70, 136, 138
cognitive neurosciences 14, 189, 191, 194
colour expressions 16, 18, 267, 269, 270, 272–274, 278, 280
communication 1, 3, 4, 8, 10, 12, 14, 15, 19, 29, 68, 79, 80, 93, 114, 120, 121, 125, 135, 137, 139, 141, 153, 159, 160, 172, 205, 207, 208, 217–219, 240, 271, 289, 290
comprehension 1, 3, 6–8, 16, 18, 61–63, 68, 70, 77–79, 81, 82, 91, 158, 204, 214, 217, 221, 222, 227, 267, 272
conceptual blending 5, 44, 46, 50; see also *blended*
conceptualization 31, 39, 120, 130, 152, 157, 217, 219, 220, 226
connotation 110, 140, 314; see also *symbolic connotation*
corpus 5, 15, 17, 44, 46, 48–50, 55, 100–102, 124, 211, 219, 221–228, 240, 287, 286, 287, 291, 292, 312, 317
– corpus analysis 54, 225, 241
– corpus-based approach 55, 165, 287, 288, 290, 302, 311, 312, 319
– corpus data analysis 222, 225, 241, 313, 315, 317
– corpus evidence 223
corpus linguistics 17, 166
creative thought 39
creativity 53, 152, 196, 217, 220, 252, 253
culture 16, 38, 79, 84, 85, 97, 100, 106, 111, 113, 135, 136, 140, 142, 152, 159–163, 194, 220, 223, 224, 227, 234, 237, 267, 278, 308, 312
curriculum 268, 269, 312, 314, 315

depression 9, 95, 99–113
describing/description 7, 9, 13, 18, 78, 85, 102, 128, 151, 152, 161, 175, 183–185, 200, 203, 204, 210, 220, 227, 232, 233, 279, 286, 307
dexterity 13, 189, 190–194, 196
discourse dynamics approach to metaphor 124
domain 8, 13–15, 49, 79, 81, 84, 98, 108, 109, 120, 121, 135, 142, 145, 152–154,

159–162, 172, 173, 201, 203, 205, 207, 209, 217, 220, 221, 235, 273, 283, 289, 298, 308
– conceptual domain 10, 13, 96, 121, 139, 140, 152, 153
– source domain 4, 5, 31, 32, 38, 78, 79, 84, 96, 101–103, 105, 106, 109–113, 121, 130, 136, 138, 141, 142, 151, 152, 158, 221–224, 232–234, 237, 238, 240, 272
– emotional domain 4, 30
– target domain 78, 84, 96–98, 101, 107, 114, 121, 138, 151, 152, 217, 237

Edelman 14, 21, 189, 194
education 3, 4, 8, 15–19, 29, 64, 120, 153, 232, 235, 249–251, 253, 255, 258–261, 267–270, 273, 305, 306, 308–317
efference copies 83
elicited metaphor 15, 18, 249
embodied 4, 5, 16–18, 77, 95, 96, 105, 109, 111–114, 193, 195, 203, 204, 209–211, 221
– cognition 1–3, 6, 8, 9, 12, 18, 19, 25, 38, 90
– mind 23, 210
– simulation 7, 8, 20, 21, 77, 78, 82–84, 86–88, 90
embodiment 1, 2, 8, 77, 86, 148, 200, 204, 206, 209–211, 221, 230
emotion 4, 5, 9, 16, 21, 29–41, 67, 70, 78, 83, 95–103, 106, 108–116, 252, 257, 259, 280, 306
– language 30
– metaphors 30, 34, 39, 97–101, 111, 113
– expert theories of 4, 5, 29, 32, 34, 37, 39
– folk theories of 4, 29, 30, 37–39
epistemology 12, 13, 172, 186, 200
etymology 218, 223, 240, 273

features 2, 10, 16, 62, 67, 70, 79, 102, 142, 145, 186, 189, 192, 193, 199, 201–204, 208, 230, 234, 235, 240
figurative language 22, 122, 142, 250, 268, 269
Flux Capacitor 5, 6, 44, 46–57
fMRI 7, 65–67, 70, 212
foreign language 16, 17, 227, 252, 253, 258, 261, 267, 268, 271, 272, 283

framework 1, 3, 8, 9, 12, 13, 50, 61, 80, 85, 124, 135, 138, 141, 151, 186, 191, 193, 194, 202, 267, 272, 315, 316
framing 9, 24, 101, 112, 114, 122, 123, 128, 130, 308

gender 55
gesture 7, 8, 61, 77–86, 91, 95, 97, 256
ground/grounding 36, 86, 204, 254, 259, 306, 307
Google n-grams 48, 49, 51, 53

hearing and deaf children 79, 91
heuristics 204, 205
hidden ideology 165
higher-level grouping 260
history of
– science/scientific thought 12, 153, 160
– modern physics 185
– medicine 217
idiom 88, 268–272, 280
image/images 9, 16, 62, 63, 64, 66, 68, 70, 80, 96, 109, 111, 113, 136, 138, 172, 252, 255
– analogical image 161
– literal 7, 62, 63, 64, 66
– mental 6, 61, 62, 109
– metaphors/metaphorical 7, 62, 63, 64, 66
– moving 95, 96, 97, 98, 100, 114
– schema/schemata 15, 95, 96, 97, 102, 111–113, 220–223, 226, 227, 235–238, 240, 244
– visual images 136
imagery 6, 61, 62, 69, 70, 72, 81
inference 32, 137, 141
interface 12, 83, 171, 173
intermediate space 172, 173
invariance principle 237

judgement 261, 314

Keats heuristic 52

learning 1, 15, 17–19, 54, 67, 69, 193, 196, 252, 253, 256, 261, 262, 269–273, 281, 310, 313, 314, 316
left superior temporal gyrus 68

Likert-type scale 256
literal 7, 16, 38, 45, 54, 62–69, 75, 76, 79, 91, 137, 184, 185, 217, 252, 260, 267, 272, 274–276
– meaning 64, 72, 184, 185, 276

meaning
– evolution 135, 139, 140, 142, 147, 161
– extension 10, 135, 145, 147, 306–308
metaphor
– in science 3, 4, 12–15, 152, 173, 199–203, 206, 213, 217, 218, 223, 232
– prompts 258, 259, 285
– in Cardiology 15, 153, 219–240
– translation 12, 15, 162–164, 217, 221, 225–229, 236–245, 269, 285, 298
metaphors, audiovisual 9, 95–114
– bodily 2–4, 7, 8, 15, 17, 31, 35, 36, 77–86, 106, 109, 112–114, 221, 271
– constitutive 205, 213
– deliberate 79, 130, 183, 204, 213, 249, 261
– direct 249, 251, 260
– scientific 3, 10–12, 14, 15, 29, 34, 38, 122, 123, 135, 136, 139, 151–154, 158–160, 162, 199–201, 204–209, 213
– technical 10, 11, 135, 136, 139, 140, 151–156, 212, 232
– terminological 11, 12, 151–155, 160–165, 220, 240
– visual 3, 6, 7, 61–70, 79, 102, 106, 108, 136–139, 146, 147
metaphoric meaning transfer 137, 142–145
– polysemy 10, 139, 140, 147
– production 14, 15, 205, 207, 221, 222, 225, 226, 229, 240
– term 11, 125, 135, 138–143, 147, 154, 158–161, 211, 219, 229, 240, 268, 314
metaphorical competence 11, 16, 146, 268–273, 280
– paradigms 11, 77, 137, 152–157, 219
– vehicles clean/dirty energy 119, 126
MetaphorMagnet 5, 53–58
Metonymy/metonymic 4, 5, 9, 32, 38, 39, 98, 101, 109, 110, 114, 206, 226, 227, 252, 260, 273
mirror neurons 83, 208
modality/ies 6, 7, 61–63, 70

– visual-gestural 7, 70, 79, 80
– vocal 79, 80
model 1, 3, 5, 7, 11, 13, 18, 43–46, 58, 69, 70, 83, 135, 136, 147, 181, 185, 191, 240, 250, 251, 261, 262, 289, 311, 316, 317
motivation 35, 136, 222, 223, 233, 234, 240, 271, 280, 284
moving images 95–100, 114

native speakers 16, 17, 226, 267–273, 286, 290
narrative transformations 43
neology 217
neuropsychology 190
non-verbal 6, 68

Obama's speech 120–127
Occurrences 81, 173, 287–300
Online 123, 226, 283, 288

Parahippocampal gyrus 68, 76
Perception 1, 6, 7, 35–37, 47, 61, 62, 68, 78, 83, 95, 136, 137, 194–196, 221, 236
perceptual
– criteria 222
– experience 221
– features 235, 240
– interactions 220
– motivations 223
pictorial
– metaphors 70
poetry 184, 203, 306
political
– communication 120
– speech 9, 119, 124
politics 3, 8, 12, 57, 120, 121, 209, 274, 277
prediction 83, 175
processing 7, 8, 62, 63, 66–70, 78, 82, 138, 203, 205, 212, 280, 291, 302

quanta 176, 178, 182, 183

RCTs 250, 251
Reaction/response time 66, 67, 69
reasoning 1, 12, 53, 85, 201, 202, 208, 210, 257
representations 46–48, 85, 86, 210, 220

representational actions 8, 82
responses 62, 64, 66, 70, 195, 227, 229, 231, 252, 253, 258–260
– associated with emotions 5–7, 31–39
RHD patients 62

Science 1, 3, 8, 2, 14, 18, 19, 30, 40, 48, 55, 112, 156, 158, 159, 171, 173, 179, 199–213, 217, 218, 232, 250, 261
– -fiction 112
– climate- 123
– behavioural- 193
– in medical texts 218
– -education 249
semantics 68, 174, 176, 187, 310
semantic
– feature 79
– incongruity 63
sentence/s 7, 52, 63–66, 78, 81, 82, 102, 174, 226–228, 236, 255, 257, 262, 270, 290
simile/s 46, 138, 184, 185, 226, 254, 257, 258, 260, 271, 306
sign 85
– - language 67, 80, 81, 85–87
– visual- 136, 138, 147
– verbal- 136, 138
– architectural- 139
source domains 4, 5, 32, 38, 76, 97, 101, 102, 105, 106, 121, 138, 141, 221–223, 232–234, 237, 240, 272
Source-Path-Goal (SPG) schema 45
space
– conceptual- 80
spatial 80, 85, 95, 110, 211, 289, 299
– imagery 7, 69
– processing 7, 63, 67, 69
– relationships 285, 307
spontaneous production 15, 221, 222, 225, 226, 229, 240
stimuli 7, 63–66, 68, 79, 191, 195, 223, 225–227, 235–237, 240, 246
stereotype 48
stereotypical 46–49, 53–55
– knowledge 54
– perspective 5, 44

– properties 46
– qualities 47
story-generator 52
subjects 62, 237, 273, 299
subjective 61, 280
– experience 36, 189
– perspective 106, 110
symbol/simbolicity 1, 79, 110, 136, 140, 174, 273, 274, 252
symbolic 95, 98, 109, 110, 137, 142, 174, 252
– representations 135, 142
– connotations 140
system 5–7, 14, 34, 53, 54, 61, 80, 85–87, 96,136, 139, 141, 142, 146, 147, 154, 161–171, 175, 189, 195–199, 210–212, 219, 221, 225, 227, 229, 231–236, 240, 253, 315, 316
– formal 1, 83
– living 2, 171
– sensory/motor 8, 78, 79, 82
– conceptual 11, 39, 40, 138, 147, 173
– semiotic 11, 80, 136, 139, 147
– nervous/neural 13, 83, 189, 190, 192, 193, 194, 197
– symbolic 142
– computer 46, 58
– generator/generative 46, 58
systematic metaphors like fighting 129
systematic reviews 251
specialized
– languages 222
– domains 135, 221

target 37, 43, 102, 130, 137, 141, 143, 197, 273, 280, 290
– audience 120, 270
– domain 78, 84, 96–98, 101, 107, 113, 114, 121, 126, 138, 151, 152, 157, 217, 237, 240
– language 16, 162, 163, 226, 240, 267, 269, 271
term
– creation 10, 11, 15, 135, 138–145, 147, 151, 152, 154, 156–165, 208, 209, 219, 220, 223, 226, 229, 232
time 84–86, 111, 124, 126, 195, 270, 289, 306

trainee translators 221, 240
translation tasks 221, 225, 226, 236, 237, 240

understanding 1–4, 8, 11, 14–16, 53, 62, 70, 78, 81, 83, 84, 86, 87, 95, 108, 123, 130, 138, 139, 145, 146, 154, 172, 185–187, 217–221, 267, 270–272, 291, 310–312, 316, 317
utterance 81, 291
usage-based paradigms 219, 222

validation 159
verbal 3, 6, 7, 12, 61–65, 67–70, 75, 76, 136, 138, 139, 146, 147, 152, 259

visual 3, 6, 7, 61–65, 67–70, 75, 76, 83, 95, 96, 101, 102, 106, 113, 136, 138, 139, 146, 147, 155, 196, 201, 221, 249
visualization 269, 270, 292
vocabulary 11, 13, 16, 17, 135, 140, 147, 155, 156, 160, 183, 208, 272, 273, 280

Western 85, 274
– culture/civilasation 113, 136
– society 232
– medicine 113, 232, 240